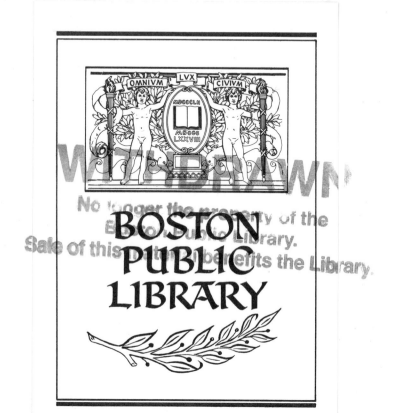

INVENTORS
OF THE
PROMISED LAND

INVENTORS
OF THE
PROMISED
LAND

LAWRENCE J. FRIEDMAN

Alfred A. Knopf
New York 1975

THIS IS A BORZOI BOOK
PUBLISHED BY ALFRED A. KNOPF, INC.

Copyright © 1975 by Lawrence J. Friedman
All rights reserved under International
and Pan-American Copyright Conventions.
Published in the United States
by Alfred A. Knopf, Inc., New York,
and simultaneously in Canada by Random House
of Canada Limited, Toronto.
Distributed by Random House, Inc., New York.

Library of Congress
Cataloging in Publication Data

Friedman, Lawrence Jacob, date
Inventors of the promised land.

Bibliography: p. 325
Includes index.
1. United States—Intellectual life—1783–1865.
2. Nationalism—United States.
I. Title.
E164.F88   1975   973   74–21305
ISBN 0–394–47263–2

Manufactured in the United States of America
First Edition

For Sharon
and Beth

*. . . the figure of the spread eagle is incorporated into the arms
of the United States. . . .
The Eagle is the chief of the feathered race,
at least on the old continent.
HE is to birds, what the lion is to quadrupeds;
fierce, rapacious, and holding a sort of empire over the whole race.*

—NOAH WEBSTER, 1812

It was a nation of white men,
*who formed and have administered our government,
and every American should indulge that* pride *and* honor,
*which is falsely called prejudice, and teach it to his children.
Nothing else will preserve the* American name,
or the American character.

—ANDREW T. JUDSON, 1833

*It is impossible to conceive of a more troublesome
or more garrulous patriotism;
it wearies even those who are disposed to
respect it.*

—ALEXIS DE TOCQUEVILLE, 1840

CONTENTS

PART *One*

OUTWARD HOPE
AND INNER TORMENT:
The Dilemmas of the Patriotic Crusader

PART *Two*

WOMAN'S ROLE
IN THE PROMISED LAND

ACKNOWLEDGMENTS

While this book was being researched, written, and rewritten, Donald B. Meyer and Robert A. Nisbet were constant inspirations. They furnished proof that intellectuality, scholarship, and commitment to social change are compatible phenomena. Librarians and archivists were indispensable, particularly in the Eastern states where my research centered. Above all, David O. White of the Connecticut Historical Commission and Frederick R. Goff and his staff at the Rare Book Division of the Library of Congress must be noted. Over the years, they kept me well supplied with unusual and invaluable materials. The National Endowment for the Humanities funded the crucial year of research that got this study under way, and the Bowling Green University Faculty Research Committee financed the summer that was necessary to put it into reasonably complete form. Three excellent History Department chairmen—Gary R. Hess, Paul Hubbard, and William R. Rock—helped through convenient class scheduling and by encouraging serious scholarly endeavor. Edmund J. Danziger, Jr., Lawrence J. Friedman, M.D., S. P. Fullinwider, Kirin Kim, Michael P. Rogin, Bernard Sternsher, Ronald G. Walters, and Joel Williamson detected and helped to remedy important conceptual problems. Words cannot properly acknowledge Richard H. King, Eliane and Sheldon Silverman, Arthur H. Shaffer, and Ronald T. Takaki for creatively criticizing several versions of this manuscript. Ashbel Green was everything one could want in an editor during the concluding stages of this project. His ability to detect remaining conceptual flaws in the manuscript was quite out of the ordinary.

Kathy Bachman, Nedra Bradley, and Phyllis Wulff kindly typed the final draft. Finally, my wife, Sharon Friedman, might well be cited as a co-author. She offered tough but balanced evaluations of *Inventors of the Promised Land* from genesis to completion.

The American Revolution was not a battle for national liberation so much as a struggle between Whigs and Tories in both
Great Britain and the thirteen colonies over the constitutional
rights of Englishmen. With the help of the absolute monarchies of
France and Spain, the Whigs triumphed and the American nation
came into being. Politically and militarily weak, the New Nation
labored under other serious disadvantages. It was made up of
diverse ethnic stocks, it lacked a common or official religion, and it
had neither a common ancestral soil nor a distinctive national
culture. In 1783 the United States was a victorious political state
but not a viable nation. Americans called that state a republic while
acknowledging that, according to eighteenth-century political theorists, republics were frail organisms with short life expectancies.
Unlike Old World monarchies, a republic was thought to lack the
administrative mechanisms to govern large territories; it did not
have the political cohesion afforded by the force of and personal
loyalty to a royal person.

With these generally unprecedented liabilities, the American
experiment in nation making was bound to be historically unique.
Because the republican state rested on no firm cultural base, and
because it could not exercise the coercion of Old World monarchies, it somehow had to cultivate the ideological loyalties of the
citizenry if viable nationhood were to come into being. A popular
identification with the nation-state similar to personal loyalty to a
king had to be developed for the United States to survive. Several
participants in the American Enlightenment tried to cultivate this
popular identification. As their efforts intensified, many began to
lose sight of the cosmopolitanism and tolerance of the Enlightenment and dogmatically advanced the New Nation's claim to pre-
eminence.

Carlton J. H. Hayes, Hans Kohn, and other students of comparative national development have characterized nationalism as a

people's conscious awareness of a common language, common historical traditions, a common geographic terrain, common governmental and social institutions, and a common art and literature. They have singled out patriotism as the most used and the most effective vehicle to cultivate or rekindle nationalism. At the end of the Revolution, the United States clearly lacked the basic ingredients of nationhood; efforts to cultivate loyalty to the state and society indicated that a patriotic crusade was indispensable. Men like David Ramsay, Noah Webster, Jedidiah Morse, and Mason Locke Weems tried to foster enthusiasm for the Federal Government, the "American language," "American geography," and a distinctive national history. They were engaged in patriotic efforts to cultivate and sustain nationalism.

Until the last three decades of the eighteenth century, patriotism had often been the subject of derision on both sides of the Atlantic. Jonathan Swift had regarded it with contempt, Bishop George Berkeley and Oliver Goldsmith had characterized it as a cloak for corrupt politicians and self-seeking adventurers, and Alexander Pope had charged that a patriot was a fool. However, Viscount Bolingbroke attempted to counter these attitudes by reviving the concept of the virtuous, principled, unsullied old Roman patriot as the exemplification of civic virtue. Desperately needing to draw the loyalties of their countrymen toward the New Nation, Ramsay, Webster, Morse, Weems, and others borrowed from Bolingbroke. The image of the virtuous and patriotic republican had to be cultivated. With national survival in the balance, these popularizers of doctrinaire (spread-eagle) patriotism could not tolerate the cynical mockings of Swift, Berkeley, Goldsmith, or Pope.

In the 1830's Alexis de Tocqueville attempted to assess their efforts. In *Democracy in America*, the brilliant French traveler noted that American nationalism had come into being and that it had been infused with a more substantial dose of *le patriotisme irritable* than he had encountered anywhere in the Old World. Common loyalties to national institutions had been the result of decades of uniquely harsh, crude exaltation of the Promised Land and concomitant degradation of other nations and peoples. American nationalism had been the product of years of anti-intellectual patriotic crusading. During this interval, few had voiced public opposition to the crusaders.

Inventors of the Promised Land is intended to analyze important features of this patriotic crusade from the end of the Revolutionary War through the 1830's, when Tocqueville made his observations. The topic is vast and I make no pretensions of covering every vital aspect. For one, the study focuses upon an influential but numerically small group of men and women who put their thoughts into print. Usually of the more prosperous classes, they were more deeply imbued with British culture than they cared to admit. They lived in all areas of the country, although a disproportionate number came from New England and Pennsylvania. Comparatively few came from a Southern society which, by the 1820's, was beginning to cultivate a uniquely regional nationalism. A second limitation of this book is that it concentrates upon patriotic ideas and attitudes. It is primarily intellectual history. However, it does not focus upon the most probing intellectuals of the period—men like Jefferson, Thoreau, Emerson, and Melville. Because the New Nation's patriotic crusade was antithetical to the life of the mind, second- and third-rate thinkers played the central roles. Most of them agreed that in a world of decadence and immorality, the United States merited very high marks. In public they rarely expressed doubts as to the potential of the Promised Land, and this near unanimity is one of the most striking features of early American patriotic thought (see Appendix A). Chronology imposes a third basic limitation upon this study. I have excluded extremely important Manifest Destiny theorists like John L. O'Sullivan and Moses Yale Beach. From the 1780's to the 1830's, patriots were preoccupied with the survival of the New Nation and the shape it would take. They wanted to know whether the American's long-standing dedication to his locality and to Britain could be replaced with a new attachment—a sense of dual citizenship in which the American's local community and his nation became inseparable. From the late 1830's on, however, patriots increasingly regarded the permanence and shape of the Promised Land as predetermined despite sectional tensions and Civil War. Accordingly, the meaning and worth of American society became increasingly central to patriotic thought. *Inventors of the Promised Land* focuses upon the first stage of the American patriotic crusade and leaves the second stage to capable scholars like Phillip S. Paludan and Harold M. Hyman.

Trying to fathom the thoughts and motives of spread-eagle patriots in the early national period, I was perturbed by their characteristically vague and ambiguous terminology. Two categories of terms needed to be clarified above all others, for they were crucial to those who used them: (1) Patriots repeatedly referred to the United States as the "Promised Land," "the Rising Glory of America," and "the chosen people." On the other hand, Old World inhabitants were characterized as "miserable" and victims of "tyranny" or "despotism." The animating impulse beneath all of this vague rhetoric was usually a simple one. It was the age-old vision of a flawless, utopian-like paradise emerging in a world of sin and discontent. At some point in the past, present, or future, America and its citizens had become or would become superior to all other nations and peoples. Nations were rated hierarchically and America had assumed or would assume top rank. (2) Patriots frequently characterized American heroes and spokesmen like George Washington and Benjamin Franklin as "friends of order," "steady," "calm," and "firm." But national enemies were "restless disorganizers," "rash," "imprudent," and "unsteady." Patriots gave voice, in this way, to their need for roots and a life of calm predictability. They wanted to feel securely anchored to a familiar home in a stable, orderly society. That which seemed to destroy their anchor—to uproot them—was castigated as "unsteady" and "chaotic." Patriots often identified their anchor or roots with a specific region, state, or local community. Sometimes they identified it with a specific group of people—often kinsfolk. Occasionally they sought roots in the nation itself. Perceptions of what constituted rooted stability varied greatly among patriots and often shifted within the individual patriot himself. Owing to their very vague language and the periodic changes in their perceptions of rootedness, we can often say no more than that a given patriot or group of patriots craved predictable security and stability. In many portions of this study, the concept of rootedness is necessarily vague. This is a reflection of the imprecision of patriotic writing and oratory.

The point, then, is that early American patriots were simultaneously concerned with national perfectibility and a personal sense of rootedness, although they usually expressed these concerns quite imprecisely. Their fundamental problem was that a quest for a perfect America had to be personally uprooting. Thomas Babington Macaulay once noted that American society was "all sail and no anchor," and this accurately summarized the dilemma of many spread-eagle patriots during the early national period. Concentrating their energies on discovering or sustaining flawless nationhood, many lost touch with the specific realities of daily existence; they became alienated with and uprooted from the tangible specifics of everyday life. Indeed, much of the frustration and discontent that Tocqueville perceived within *le patriotisme irritable* stemmed from this clash between the quest for perfection and the need for a sense of anchored stability.

Part One of this book focuses upon the precise dimensions of this clash and the extreme difficulty patriots had confronting it on realistic terms. Certain George Washington eulogists, for example, resorted to shoddy verbal gymnastics. They charged that the Founding Father was perfect *because* he was stable and well anchored. For the moment, irreconcilable conflict seemed to be reconciled. Part Two centers upon efforts to deploy sexual ideology to escape the clash. If the New Nation remained badly flawed or individual Americans felt uprooted, certain patriots maintained that this was owing to the deficiencies of True American Womanhood. Part Three concerns those patriots who sought relief in racial ideology. If troublesome blacks were removed from the white nation, they maintained, all would be well. Flawless nationhood and a sense of personal rootedness would eventuate. Indeed, patriots perceived anything that might conceivably reconcile perfectionist strivings with personal rootedness, or at least promote reconciliation, as a sort of safety valve or cure-all—something that might ease their increasingly troublesome dilemma. By the Jacksonian period many came to perceive patriotic schoolhouses as True American Womanhood and black removal had been perceived—as cure-alls or at least alleviants (Part Four). But because perfectionist striving and rootedness were inherently incompatible, all of these apparent safety valves or cure-alls merely compounded patriots' problems. Like the concept of flawless nationhood, apparent safety valves like True American Womanhood, black removal, and the patriotic schoolhouse were abstractions which drew patriots away from confrontation with specific daily realities—the rich and varied experiential possibilities of the real world. As such, these apparent safety valves added to their sense of rootlessness and had another dangerous effect. The safety valves promoted sexual and racial ideologies. Over time, these ideologies tended to coalesce. By the 1830's many were claiming that the patriotic schoolhouse would usher in the Promised Land, and that the Promised Land was the *white man's country*.

PART One

OUTWARD HOPE
AND INNER TORMENT
The Dilemmas of the
Patriotic Crusader

O happy people, ye of whom is giv'n,
A land enrich'd with sweetest dews of Heav'n!
Ye, who possess Columbia's virgin prime,
In harvests blest of ev'ry soil and clime!
Ye happy mortals, whom propitious fate,
Reserv'd for actors on a stage so great!
Sons, worthy sires of venerable name,
Heirs of their virtue and immortal fame;
Heirs of their rights, still better understood,
Declar'd in thunder, and confirm'd in blood!
Ye chosen race, your happiness I sing,
With all the joys the cherub peace can bring;
When your tall fleets shall lift their starry pride,
And sail triumphant o'er the bill'wy tide.
                                    —DAVID HUMPHREYS, 1786

I feel pain when I am reminded of my exertions in the cause of what
we called liberty, and sometimes wish I could erase my name from
the Declaration of Independence.
                                    —BENJAMIN RUSH, 1808

The language of early American patriots may have been more uneven than that of any other group in the nation's history. Their public enthusiasm for the Promised Land appeared to be unlimited. But their outward praise was often punctuated by the most foreboding private doubts. God's chosen people had not performed their mission; they seemed destined for eternal perdition.

Although these private apprehensions conflicted with patriots' public boastings, it is remarkable that the doubts never seemed to check the boastings. To the contrary, public exaltation of the New Nation expanded as self-doubts heightened. It was almost as if outward boastings compensated for inner apprehensions. Perhaps spread-eagle patriots needed to proclaim the supremacies of the New Nation all the louder to quiet the feeling that the United States was no better than the corrupt mother country from which it had broken.

For American patriots, then, the early national period was at once a time of intense hope and increasing worry, dogmatism and questioning, aggressive boastfulness and inner retrenchment. They were crusading not only for their nation but for themselves. They seemed intent on quelling chronic inner apprehensions—on making their outward proclamations of America's "Rising Glory" believable to themselves, the proclaimers. It was a time of troubles.

CHAPTER *1*

"THE RISING GLORY OF AMERICA"

Literature and Language
in Post-Revolutionary Society

Once the restraints of tyrannical government had been removed, culture and science would flower. Eighteenth-century republican theorists had pronounced this doctrine and it had no greater impact than in the United States. With independence won and a national government instituted, New World republicans anticipated great innovations—basic improvements over the "corrupt and decadent" ways of the mother country. But in the decades that followed the Revolution, these innovations did not materialize. There were few significant breakthroughs, and "corrupting" Old World culture continued to exert considerable influence. American Anglicans continued to look to British church leaders for standards and guidance. The "American" theater was no less populated by British actors and British plays. London and Edinburgh still trained a number of American physicians. British publications crowded the shelves of American bookstores and libraries, with Addison, Milton, and Shakespeare remaining mandatory reading for those who had any pretensions to culture and learning. British schoolbooks formed the basis of the educational curriculum even though they had been shaped by British customs, geography, and politics. Therefore, contrary to the expectations of American republican theorists, British cultural hegemony in the New World survived the surrender of Cornwallis. Although the

British cultural grip weakened during the 1780's and 1790's, its persistent hold was all too obvious.[1]

Benjamin Rush, Jeremy Belknap, Jedidiah Morse, David Ramsay, Noah Webster, and other leading American men of letters were disappointed because the anticipated cultural flowering had not come into being. Unless an indigenous national culture developed, the American experiment in nation making would remain tenuous. "The American war is over," Rush noted, "but this is far from being the case with the American revolution." He and numerous other cultural leaders wanted a second Declaration of Independence proclaiming the end of American servility to Old World ideas, fashions, and manners. They looked to magazines as important vehicles with which to destroy British cultural dominance before the passion for national independence cooled. Between 1775 and 1795 twenty-seven American magazines commenced publication—six more than had appeared during the entire colonial period. Most were dedicated to exalting the New Nation and freeing it of Old World cultural baggage. The May 1786 issue of the *New Haven Gazette and Connecticut Magazine*, for example, characterized American literature as the equal of British writing; John Trumbull reportedly possessed the poetical

---

[1] Students of early American culture disagree substantially over the degree to which Americans had departed from British cultural standards by the end of the Revolution. In *America at 1750: A Social Portrait* (New York: Alfred A. Knopf, Inc., 1971), for example, Richard Hofstadter claims that Americans were culturally distinctive from the mother country a full twenty-five years *before* the Revolution. On the other hand, Harry R. Warfel charges that British culture continued to dominate the New Nation in almost every essential despite political independence; see his *Noah Webster: Schoolmaster to America* (New York: The Macmillan Company, 1936), pp. 51–53. In *The Birth of the Republic, 1763–89* (Chicago: University of Chicago Press, 1956), p. 101, Edmund S. Morgan offers a sensible middle-ground position. Unlike Europeans, Asians, or Africans, Morgan contends, Americans lacked a *very strong* cultural identity before political independence: ". . . we struck for independence and were thereby stirred into nationality; our nation was the child, not the father of our revolution." Morgan acknowledges significant cultural departures from the mother country prior to the Revolution but contends that the basic task of forming a viable national culture came after the Revolution. For present purposes, we need probe no further into the intricacies of this debate within the scholarly community. Our pressing concern shall not be objective cultural conditions *per se* but subjective reality—cultural life as late-eighteenth- and early-nineteenth-century Americans perceived it.

genius of Swift. The *Royal American Magazine* boasted that, although it was printed with poor-quality ink, the ink was of "AMERICAN MANUFACTURE." In the decade that followed the Peace of Paris, similar statements appeared in most other American magazines—vital new vehicles for cultural emancipation and the validation of republican political theory.[2]

The *Columbian Magazine; or Monthly Miscellany* was the most prominent and successful of all of these immediate post-Revolutionary ventures in literary nationalism. It originated in the late summer of 1786 when five Philadelphians banded together and publicly proclaimed their intentions of establishing a literary and cultural publication in order to "embellish" America's newly won political independence—to promote cultural as well as political nationhood. At a time when the young country scarcely had a unique history of its own, much less a distinctive culture, the founders announced that they would emphasize America's "highly favoured" cultural traits.[3]

The *Columbian* survived for six years—a long life span by contemporary standards. During this interval some proprietors and editors left while others were added and there were only a few regular long-term contributors. Yet the list of promoters and occasional contributors included the names of some of the nation's foremost writers and thinkers—men like Benjamin Rush, John Trumbull, David Ramsay, Charles Brockden Brown, Francis Hopkinson, and Noah Webster. Perhaps a majority of America's intellectual and literary leaders—men of every political and philosophic disposition—had at least some connection with the magazine. In the main, however, the *Columbian* was produced by Philadelphia's more prosperous, moderately Federalist citizenry. And though it had the largest circulation of any eighteenth-

---

2 Rush is quoted in Bernard Bailyn, *The Ideological Origins of the American Revolution* (Cambridge, Mass.: The Belknap Press, 1967), p. 230. William J. Free, *The Columbian Magazine and American Literary Nationalism* (The Hague: Mouton & Co., 1968), pp. 11–13, comments intelligently on the development of post-Revolutionary patriotic magazines.

3 Free, *Columbian*, p. 15. The five Philadelphia founders were Mathew Carey, William Spotswood, Charles Cist, James Trenchard, and Thomas Seddon. Carey, Spotswood, and Cist had recently come to the Philadelphia area.

century American periodical, it had no grass-roots appeal. The $2.66 annual subscription was prohibitive for most Americans, even for the average Philadelphian, whose wage level was comparatively high. The *Columbian*'s 1,200 subscribers were therefore of the more prosperous classes.[4] They resided in every part of the country. When a federal postal act made it too costly to distribute copies beyond Philadelphia and this national readership was cut off, the journal ceased publication.[5]

That the *Columbian* could survive only as a national publication must have accounted, in part, for its patriotic tone. Mild Federalist loyalties aside, it had a financial stake in the political and cultural unity and growth of the New Nation. Provincialism was incompatible with expanding circulation and profits. Publishers made this clear to editors and editors pressed the point upon contributors, accounting for striking uniformity in the themes and subject matter that appeared in print. Thus, the New Nation's leading magazine was a dependable weather vane of the nationalist impulse that followed the Peace of Paris.[6]

The columns of the *Columbian* revealed a nationalist impulse that seemed to run at cross purposes. Publishers, editors, and contributors were committed to freeing the New Nation from the cultural sway of foreign powers, particularly from the influence of the mother country. But between 1786 and 1792 (especially by the early 1790's), contributors frequently penned a second theme— "the Rising Glory of America." The nation should and would perfect and humanize its institutions and then export those institutions to a world in misery. God had conferred this mission—this

[4] Frank Luther Mott, *A History of American Magazines, 1741–1850* (Cambridge, Mass.: Harvard University Press, 1939), pp. 33–34; Free, *Columbian*, p. 42.

[5] Free, *Columbian*, p. 26. There is chilling irony in the fact that the major journal for cultural nationalism in post-Revolutionary America was killed by a federal postal act.

[6] Free, *Columbian*, pp. 15–16. The editors of the *Columbian* regularly published a "To Correspondents" column, in which they indicated what contributions they were or were not accepting. They consistently refused to print materials that smacked of provincialism or lacked a tone of ardent cultural nationalism. For this reason, I am treating *Columbian* contributors as a collective totality throughout the first section of this chapter. In print, they appeared much the same.

breathtaking opportunity—upon Americans. "Who knows but it may be reserved for Americans to furnish the world, from her productions, with cures for some of those diseases which now elude the power of medicine," one contributor proclaimed.

> That voice, which by the western world was heard,
> By the whole world shall shortly be rever'd

another insisted. A third contributor predicted that "the muses, disgusted with the depravity both of taste and morals, which prevail in Europe, would soon take up their abode in these blissful seats of liberty and peace."[7] These sentiments appeared so frequently within the *Columbian* that allegiance to the concept of "the Rising Glory of America" could not have originated in the nineteenth century. The concept appeared alongside certain patently cosmopolitan expressions of the Founding Fathers generation. Decades before James K. Polk, John L. O'Sullivan, Moses Yale Beach, William Gilpin, and James Gordon Bennett proclaimed America's destiny to enlighten a benighted world, cultural leaders of the New Nation had articulated the concept in the *Columbian*. America would rise, perfect herself, and become the glory and model of the world. If the past and present offered little encouragement, future potentialities were limitless.

The two concerns of *Columbian* contributors—freeing America from foreign cultural influence and proclaiming the mission of "the Rising and Glorious Nation" to uplift foreign parts—seemed to call for conflicting roles. The first was a plea for cultural isolationism or withdrawal, while the second required involvement with and domination over foreign cultures. There was no effort to connect the two demands—no assertion that isolation would purify America so that she could uplift benighted regions. More than in any other decade in the early American experience, men of letters struggled during the 1780's to develop a national culture free of foreign ties. How could these same men separately endorse the cultural involvement in foreign parts that was inherent in the notion of America's "Rising Glory"? The fact of the matter is that

[7] *Columbian Magazine*, March 1789, p. 168; March 1791, p. 185; September 1787, p. 628.

though they embraced both cultural withdrawal from foreign influence and involvement abroad to fulfill the nation's glorious mission, and though they never noted connections between the two goals, expressions favoring withdrawal from and independence of British culture dominated the early years of the *Columbian* while articulations of America's "Rising Glory" were more noticeable in the final years. Thus, *Columbian* contributors were not involved in an intellectual contradiction so much as a change in emphasis. This change in emphasis from cultural isolation to a "Rising Glory" ideological posture must be accounted for. It is a key to the broad cultural crisis that post-Revolutionary society was experiencing.

The relationship of the Old World to the New was discussed in almost every issue of the *Columbian*. The way contributors perceived this relationship is crucial if we are to understand why they eventually came to embrace the concept of America's "Rising Glory" in the final years of the magazine's existence. Clinging to republican political theory and aiming to demonstrate the cultural flowering of a politically independent America, they persistently compared the Old World unfavorably to the New. European governments were characterized as barbaric tyrannies under which cruel despots neglected their subjects and allowed them to remain backward, hungry, and uneducated. In contrast, under republican government Americans enjoyed "perhaps the truest and fullest liberty, in the united states, that any political bodies ever did on earth."[8] With liberty and responsible government, Americans had become a virtuous, wholesome, and self-reliant people in comparison with vice-ridden, depraved European society.[9] *Columbian* contributors singled out Britain for special attack. They frequently condemned "unwholesome," "irregular" British vices and praised solid, regularized American virtues. The British stayed up half the night, wasted away their days in idle play, lacked respect for a viable and moral family life, supported a barbarous legal system, and delighted in the cruelties of their country's military. American life, on the other hand, was persistently characterized as

[8] *Columbian Magazine*, February 1787, pp. 263–64; February 1791, pp. 110–11; July 1792, p. 66.
[9] See, e.g., *Columbian Magazine*, June 1787, pp. 491, 497; September 1787, pp. 628, 644; October 1788, p. 561; May 1790, p. 290; October 1790, p. 254.

wholesome, humane, and responsible. The American "children" were more virtuous than their British "parents."[10]

But though the men of the *Columbian* tried to exalt the New World, debunk the Old, and thereby prove that the two regions were culturally as well as politically separate, they found themselves admiring and borrowing certain qualities of Old World life. In this journal dedicated to American cultural nationalism, the editors regularly printed excerpts from European publications, particularly from magazines, travel narratives, and the records of European cultural societies. They borrowed most heavily from Britain; the "child" truly needed the "parent." The *Columbian* modeled itself after *Cave's Gentleman's Magazine* and the *London Magazine*. Like most eighteenth-century British journals, it imitated the *Gentleman's Magazine* in format, with sixty-four octavo pages.[11] Vast quantities of material were excerpted from *Cave's* and from the *London Magazine*. Although the editors prided themselves on the many pieces that were written exclusively for the *Columbian*, about three-fourths of every issue consisted of items clipped from other sources, primarily from British newspapers, journals, and books. Sometimes *all* of the derivative materials came from British sources.[12] Even original materials revealed a heavy British influence. The editors openly lauded certain British grammarians and urged their contributors to emulate British literary styles.[13] The contributors frequently imitated materials in the *Spectator, Rambler, Tatler,* and lesser British magazines. Their fiction imitated Samuel Richardson's seduction stories, Laurence Sterne's sentimentality, or Samuel Johnson's and Oliver Goldsmith's Oriental tales. The writings of Alexander Pope, William

[10] See, e.g., *Columbian Magazine*, October 1787, pp. 701–02; April 1788, pp. 181–82; May 1788, p. 291; April 1790, pp. 215–16; May 1790, p. 289; August 1792, pp. 78–79.

[11] Albert H. Smyth, *The Philadelphia Magazines and Their Contributors, 1741–1850* (Philadelphia: Robert M. Lindsay, 1892), p. 61, comments on the use of the *Gentleman's Magazine* and the *London Magazine* as models. Mott, *American Magazines, 1741–1850,* p. 35, notes the *Gentleman's Magazine* page format. In the "Plan and Conditions for Publication" preceding the *Columbian* for July 1790, the editors noted that this was their format as well.

[12] Free, *Columbian*, pp. 48, 53–54.

[13] "To Correspondents" sections of the *Columbian* for April 1790, May and September 1791, January 1792. See also the issue for October 1791, p. 266, and Free, *Columbian*, p. 69.

Collins, and Thomas Gray were models for odes, lyrics, and elegies.[14] Literary historian William J. Free has quite properly noted that "the literature in the *Columbian* would have been as much at home in London as in Philadelphia." One can understand why. The growth and consolidation of an elite colonial upper class during the first half of the eighteenth century together with the imposition of an increasingly complex network of British official-dom had caused substantial imitation of British manners and cus-toms.[15] By the late eighteenth century, the literate, prosperous, and cultivated throughout the New Nation had thoroughly inter-nalized the values of British cultural life and expected those values to be reflected in America's leading literary periodical. Adolescent rebellion notwithstanding, those who edited, wrote for, and sub-scribed to the *Columbian* had been schooled for too many years in the culture of the mother country. It was predictable that a journal founded to prove the viability and uniqueness of American culture would resemble British publications.

Participants in post-Revolutionary America's leading literary venture were unable to escape their Old World heritage. In their efforts to satisfy the nation's cultivated and prosperous classes, they could not escape the fact that they were displaced Europeans and above all Britishers living in America. In June of 1790 the *Columbian* printed a letter allegedly written by a Chinese lady to a friend in Philadelphia: "We have been told that you [Americans] copy the British nation in your dress and manners. If so, we sup-pose the report we heard some years ago, that you had become a separate and independent empire, is wholly without foundation." A month later, an anonymous essay appeared in the *Columbian* noting that Old World customs, particularly British customs, "are insensibly stealing upon us. . . . As a nation, we ought to form some national customs, and not be eternally subservient to those *which prevail abroad.*"[16] Similar, generally anonymous essays appeared from time to time referring to the pervasive influence that the Old World, especially Britain, continued to exert upon

[14] See, e.g., Free, *Columbian*, pp. 77–78; *Columbian Magazine*, April 1788, pp. 202–06; December 1788, pp. 695–98; August 1792, p. 125; July 1792, p. 22.
[15] Free, *Columbian*, p. 78; Gordon S. Wood (ed.), *The Rising Glory of America, 1760–1820* (New York: George Braziller, 1971), pp. 2–3.
[16] *Columbian Magazine*, June 1790, p. 351; July 1790, p. 37.

American life despite the nation's political independence and republican government.[17] The frequency with which the editors
printed these commentaries suggested something of a crisis. The
Columbian proprietors had established, editors had organized, and
contributors had filled the pages of a journal that they hoped
would provide the cultural proof of American political independence and the validity of republican cultural theory. But as issue
after issue of the *Columbian* went into print, the weakness of the
proof and the problems inherent in republican theory were persistently demonstrated.

The patent influence of the Old World on the pages of the
Columbian made it difficult for her editors and contributors to
wave the patriotic banner and to point to the cultural outpourings
of American republican institutions. In some measure, they must
have been frustrated patriots. To suppress the patriotic banner—to
acknowledge openly the extreme dependence of the New World
upon the Old—would betray the *Columbian*'s patriotic mission.
But when they proclaimed American virtues, European corruptions, and the vast gulf between the two, many men of the
Columbian must have sensed that they were deceiving themselves,
disowning their British "parents," and repudiating their Old
World heritage. Otherwise, there would not have been the persistent and gloomy references to the extensive Old World influence
upon the Promised Land. Thus, the men of the *Columbian* were
caught within an irreconcilable dilemma. Whatever they wrote
about the relationship of the New World to the Old was bound to
leave them apprehensive and dissatisfied.[18]

[17] See, e.g., *Columbian Magazine*, February 1787, pp. 281–84; April 1787, p.
379; August 1787, p. 605; May 1790, p. 289.
[18] In *The First New Nation: The United States in Historical and Comparative Perspective* (New York: Basic Books, Inc., 1963), p. 62, Seymour
Martin Lipset accounts for the general phenomenon the men of the *Columbian* were experiencing: "All new nations must establish their own identities.
But along with a self-conscious effort to establish a separate identity, which
usually leads to a rejection of all things associated with the Mother Country,
there continues to exist a deep-rooted admiration for its culture and values. So
that on the one hand, the former colonial power is hated as an evil imperialist
exploiter or 'monarchical' conspirator, and on the other hand, it is emulated
and admired as the representative of a superior civilization." See also
Winthrop D. Jordan, *White over Black: American Attitudes toward the
Negro, 1550–1812* (Chapel Hill: University of North Carolina Press, 1968),

In their efforts to confirm republican theory—to prove that independent republican political institutions had promoted a unique and rich American culture—*Columbian* writers were distressed by more than the persistence of Old World influence. They also fretted over a spirit of localism that seemed to be intensifying during the post-Revolutionary decade. In contrast to the war years, there appeared to be no unified, cohesive American union but "languor and want of concert in the several states. . . ." There was no longer an external enemy—the major source of cohesion for the Revolutionary movement—and the spirit of localism seemed to be increasing. *Columbian* contributors noted, with great distress, that inhabitants of the various states knew little and cared less for each other's ideas and customs. There was "a less degree of confidence subsisting between the southern and eastern states, than is necessary to cement, and give sufficient stability to, the federal union." As "matters seem to be going now, we shall soon be at as great a loss to understand each other as were the builders of the tower of Babel."[19]

Desirous of bridging the isolation and dispelling the distrust between states and localities, *Columbian* editors frequently printed essays, poems, and news stories describing the positive qualities of life in various parts of the country, particularly in New England and the middle states.[20] At the end of every issue, they published a list of recent marriages and deaths throughout the nation—not just in Pennsylvania. Editorials and poems urged Americans to come together and form a genuine nation: "Union embrace and former feuds forget."[21] The persistence of these pleas and their increasingly grave tone (even after the Federal Constitution was ratified) made one thing clear. The men of the *Columbian* understood that, despite their efforts, the problem of localism remained unsolved. If vigorous nationhood required the triumph of national over local

---

pp. 335–36. Jordan offers an assessment much like Lipset's and applies it to the post-Revolutionary American context.

[19] *Columbian Magazine*, February 1787, p. 281; March 1787, pp. 313–14; September 1789, p. 531; November 1790, p. 326.

[20] Because most of the writers for and readers of the *Columbian* lived in Philadelphia, materials concerning Pennsylvania and bordering states appeared in every issue. For writings lauding the specifics of New England life, see, e.g., December 1787, p. 790; July 1789, pp. 443–44; October 1790, p. 258.

[21] *Columbian Magazine*, November 1790, p. 339.

loyalties, they knew too well that America did not fulfill the requirement. State and local loyalty seemed to have deepened. It replaced loyalty to the British Empire and to separate British colonies as the new focus of American allegiance. Thus, it appeared obvious why no distinctive republican culture had developed in post-Revolutionary America. The society lacked viable political nationhood. General loyalty to the nation and to the national government was required before republican culture could flourish.

As the years passed, it became increasingly evident that the efforts of the *Columbian* to promote an indigenous national culture were being thwarted. The process of implementing the desire to promote national culture—of publishing a national literary magazine—made it clear that the cultural life of the New Nation continued to be rooted in Britain, continental Europe, and local American communities. The contents of the *Columbian Magazine* attested to the shallow, flimsy state of national cultural development. Only this can explain the increasing sense of discouragement with post-Revolutionary American society that was evident in the *Columbian* by the late 1780's and early 1790's.

Because immediate post-Revolutionary national cultural developments amounted to so little, editors and contributors turned to future possibilities. Although the hard daily struggle to produce a national literary magazine belied the claim that the New Republic was the Promised Land, in time it *could* be. If republican institutions had not yet ushered in a cultural renaissance, there was hope for the future. A discouraged *Columbian* writer could always look ahead and envision "the Rising Glory of America"—a national culture so viable that it would invigorate the decadent Old World. Reacting against Alexander Pope's plea in his *Essay on Man* for the acceptance of conditions as they were, Philip Freneau and Hugh Henry Brackenridge wrote the poem *The Rising Glory of America* for Princeton's 1771 commencement exercises. John Trumbull had used that term and had elaborated the vision in his *Essay on the Uses and Advantages of the Fine Arts* (1770). Timothy Dwight had invoked the vision of "Rising Glory" in *America, or a Poem on the Settlement of the British Colonies* (178[?]), and Joel Barlow had also done so in his *Vision of*

Columbus (1787). Since there was no evidence to invalidate the vision of "the Rising Glory of America," and since it was compatible with the Enlightenment faith in progress, the men of the *Columbian* could proclaim it with some measure of hope. They quoted a July Fourth oration by Robert Porter: "The most brilliant imagination cannot form a point of human greatness which the united states may not attain." They charged that in science as well as in literature the United States "may reasonably expect to arrive at the highest degree of eminence. . . ." There was "room to hope that her [America's] literary will in time equal her military reputation."[22] In time, America would produce a shining illustration of free, perfected nationhood, "showing, by our example, to our fellow-citizens of the world, how FREE MEN ought to live." She would be "the country from whence all reformations must originally spring." As a perfected and glorious nation, the United States would go on to "civilize the world" and offer asylum to those who "groan in foreign lands." It would become an asylum where "every industrious man is likely to be opulent, every virtuous man beloved, and every ingenious man admired."[23]

In almost every issue of the *Columbian* there were at least some, and in some issues many, hopeful allusions to "the Rising Glory of America"—the eventual maturation and perfection of the New Nation. However, the number of these references markedly increased as the years passed and efforts to demonstrate a flourishing national culture seemed more and more futile. Paradoxically, a mood of dissatisfaction and doubt—not the buoyant optimism historically associated with the idea of progress—lay behind the concept of America's "Rising Glory" as it appeared in the pages of the *Columbian*. This distinguished the sources of the concept, in one important respect, from the psychology that later sustained it in the 1840's. To be sure, optimism and hope for the stimulation of

[22] *Columbian Magazine*, September 1791, p. 190; Free, *Columbian*, p. 167; Robert L. Brunhouse (ed.), "David Ramsay, 1749–1815: Selections from His Writings," *Transactions of the American Philosophical Society*, New Ser., LV, Pt. 4 (1965), 226.

[23] *Columbian Magazine*, October 1789, pp. 588–89; October 1790, p. 245; November 1790, pp. 317, 319; December 1790, p. 408; January 1791, pp. 51–52.

an indigenous national culture had initially drawn cultural patriots to the *Columbian* in 1786. Their initial venture in literary nationalism had been sparked by the belief that political independence would quickly be complemented by cultural independence. But by the end of the 1780's, that first venturous leap was almost certainly coming to be perceived as a disastrous plunge. Unable to promote an indigenous national culture very effectively, and unwilling to probe for uniquely American cultural strands in the colonial past as Irving and Hawthorne later learned to do, the men of the *Columbian* were soon forced to move in another direction—to modify their approach. But this second leap—for "the Rising Glory of America"—was accompanied by dejection and despair that was a far cry from the mood of the days of the *Columbian*'s founding. Only one factor united the hopeful venture of 1786 with the subsequent leap after "the Rising Glory." Both involved feelings of national cultural inferiority. Whether in hope or in despair, those who published, edited, and contributed to the New Nation's leading journal could never shed this cancerous feeling within.

As they promoted America's "Rising Glory," *Columbian* contributors proclaimed that the traditions of the Old World had no value; the lessons of history had no purpose. Contributors felt compelled to dismiss past and present realities as equally irrelevant. The past had been British and the present did not evidence significant departures from British cultural hegemony. Strive and strive again for a better future—this was what Americans had to do: "Whatever attainments are already reached," they charged, "attainments still higher should be pursued. Let us, therefore, strive with noble emulation. Let us suppose we have done *nothing*, while *any thing* yet remains to be done. Let us, with fervent zeal, press forward, and make *unceasing advances* in every thing that can SUPPORT, IMPROVE, REFINE, OR EMBELLISH society."[24] Similar words ran beneath the frontispiece of the January 1789 issue of the *Columbian:*

America! with Peace and Freedom blest,
Pant for true Fame, and scorn inglorious rest:

[24] *Columbian Magazine*, August 1788, p. 399.

> Service invites; urg'd by the Voice divine;
> Exert thy self, 'till every Art be thine.

By strenuous, honest, just, and sincere exertion, citizens will "advance in every step with her [America] to virtue and federalism, and ye will prosper as the flowers on the brooks of the valley." The eyes of the world were upon Americans, anxious to see whether citizens of the Promised Land would exert themselves sufficiently—whether "the Rising Glory of America" would eventuate.[25]

These pleas for "Rising Glory" were all quite vague. Indeed, they never indicated whether the striving citizen brought more "Glory" upon himself than upon his country. The general vagueness in this and other particulars may have been intentional. When the editors of the *Columbian* had initially tried in 1786 to transform their visceral impulse to exalt American national culture into a specific literary form, that impulse was thwarted by intellectual contradictions and hard facts. Attempts at precise, tangible commentary on the past and present of the Old World and local New World communities had frustrated and perverted their initial efforts. Expressed in an unspecific, vague, and amorphous way, the concept of persistent striving toward a "Glorious America" stood to free the men of the *Columbian* from the unpleasant facts and hard intellectual dilemmas arising from precise articulation. It stood to revive their flagging hopes in the cultural potential of the Promised Land.

At best, however, vague pleas to promote "the Rising Glory of America" afforded the men of the *Columbian* no more than a measure of relief. In the main, they were sophisticated men of letters imbued with the Enlightenment imperatives of rationality and clarity. Although contributors like Belknap, Ramsay, Rittenhouse, and Rush may have averted intellectual traps and unpleasant data through vague "Rising Glory" exhortations, the imprecise, ambiguous, and often illogical nature of their exhortations must have been at least mildly, if periodically, disturbing. Moreover, the vagueness and unreality of these pleas had the potential to draw

[25] *Columbian Magazine*, September 1788, p. 502; April 1789, p. 264; October 1789, p. 588.

the men of the *Columbian* away from the specific, complex, and diverse conditions of their everyday lives, particularly if they were somewhat alienated from those conditions beforehand. By taking their rhetoric too seriously, they ran the risk of drawing themselves away from the specific heritage of the past and the concrete realities of the present. Intellectually and psychologically, they could leave themselves dangling and detached from concrete concerns in their vague pursuit of a perfected and "Glorious" future. Although confrontation with the specifics of the past and present had led to intellectual dilemmas and disheartening facts regarding the New Nation, the avoidance of hard specifics—an avoidance that the concept of "the Rising Glory of America" encouraged— threatened to draw the men of the *Columbian* away from concrete daily realities.

Thus, whether *Columbian* editors and contributors attempted to satisfy their patriotic cultural longings through vague exhortations for America's "Rising Glory" or through precise, specific articulations, they encountered serious problems. Regardless of the approach, these cultural patriots of the immediate post-Revolutionary years had undertaken the task of saying much about comparatively little. Prompted by the assumption that republican institutions had to produce a cultural renaissance, they had attempted to demonstrate the wondrous past, present, and future traits of a nation that had not yet come into its own. Although America had become politically independent of the mother country, it remained a decentralized nation with strong local ties, and continued to depend upon its British cultural heritage. Unlike the nations that subsequently developed within Central Europe, America enjoyed political independence before the culture-inducing ingredients of soil, intermarriage, and common memories had been able to take deep root. The New Nation required these ingredients in order to alleviate the frustrations inherent in any venture in cultural nationalism.

II

Although the history of the *Columbian Magazine* as a literary enterprise reveals fundamental dilemmas that patriots of the post-

Revolutionary period confronted, it does not tell us how these dilemmas shaped specific human lives. Precious little is known about most *Columbian* publishers and editors, and it is virtually impossible to identify several of the contributors. Fortunately, we know a great deal about two of the most important contributors— David Ramsay and Noah Webster. Their careers reveal how visions of national glory could literally dominate the patriot's life.

David Ramsay was the most influential historian in the New Nation. His monumental *History of the American Revolution* ran serially in the *Columbian* between March 1789 and November 1792. Although the magazine was de-emphasizing the past and turning increasingly to "the Rising Glory of America" during those years, Ramsay's *History* was nevertheless featured in every issue. The *Columbian*'s reviewers praised it highly and lauded Ramsay's other writings.[26] Although Ramsay wrote political tracts, July Fourth orations, medical discourses, and seven separate multi-volume histories, his *History of the American Revolution* stood as a prototype for scholars of his generation. It was unrivaled in American historiography, before George Bancroft's *History of the United States* (1834–74), at drawing elements requisite for a national historical identity into a coherent whole.

Whether he contributed to the *Columbian* or to other enterprises, Ramsay was always intensely devoted to the historian's craft. Certain details of his personal life make this apparent. Several months after the death of his first wife, Sabina Ellis, in 1776, he wrote to Benjamin Rush "convinced that the soft blandishments of matrimonial happiness & et. are very inimical to literary pursuits." His historical research and writing had been thwarted by married life, for "love destroys ambition." Ramsay was married again, this time to John Witherspoon's daughter, but she died in childbirth fifteen months later.[27] In January of 1787 he married Martha Laurens, daughter of the prominent South Carolinian Henry Laurens. They had eleven children and eight lived beyond infancy. Ramsay characterized Martha Laurens as a perfect wife. She

---

[26] For reviews of Ramsay's writings, see the *Columbian Magazine*, September 1786, p. 23; June 1790, p. 374; September and October 1790, pp. 181–84; October 1790, p. 262; Brunhouse (ed.), *Transactions*, pp. 223, 226; Free, *Columbian*, pp. 73–74.

[27] Brunhouse (ed.), *Transactions*, pp. 23, 54.

managed his children and household so efficiently that he rarely had to spend time on family affairs and was able to concentrate upon literary pursuits. She doubled as a research assistant, copied Ramsay's manuscripts, and trained her daughters to do the same.[28] Consciously minimizing his leisure moments with friends and family, Ramsay devoted most of his time to his historical investigations.[29] Financial duress accounts, in part, for this single-minded devotion. Although he earned a substantial income as a Charleston physician, careless spending and bad investments cast him heavily into debt. Ramsay hoped that the sale of his scholarly writings would solve his financial problems and was disappointed at the poor revenues they yielded.[30] But even after he had discovered what the *Columbian* proprietors had also learned—that the New Nation would not support professional authorship—Ramsay continued to devote every hour that he could spare to historical writing.

The material that Ramsay wrote and published year after year, volume after volume, beginning before the *Columbian* commenced publication and concluding long after the magazine had collapsed, concerned the origins of American nationhood. He characterized the emergence of the Promised Land as the central event in his own life and much more; it was the most important occurrence in the experience of mankind:

How must the heart of every good man expand with joy in the prospect of so great an extension of human happiness? While the kingdoms of the old world are tottering to their foundations—oppressive taxes grinding their subjects—one war scarcely ended, when another is begun—it has pleased the Eternal to erect a representative system of government in the woods of America, founded on reason and equality, the only object of which is the happiness of the people.[31]

[28] David Ramsay, *Memoirs of the Life of Martha Laurens Ramsay* (Charleston: Samuel Etheridge, Jr., 1812), pp. 32, 35, 43–45.
[29] Brunhouse (ed.), *Transactions*, p. 23; Robert Y. Hayne, "Biographical Memoir of David Ramsay, M.D." *Analectic Magazine*, VI (September 1815), 213.
[30] Brunhouse (ed.), *Transactions*, pp. 25–27, 55, 221.
[31] David Ramsay, *An Oration on the Cession of Louisiana to the United*

America had developed "from a handful of people to a mighty multitude" where every "citizen is perfectly free of the will of every other citizen, while all are equally subject to the laws." Only in this New World republic were "the blessings of society . . . enjoyed with the least possible relinquishment of personal liberty. We have hit the happy medium between despotism and anarchy."[32] The rest of mankind would look to this Promised Land. The United States would serve as an asylum for the oppressed and as a standard by which to measure universal progress.[33] This was the message that consumed every hour that David Ramsay could set aside. It constituted the central theme of his historical writing— one that he had attached himself to personally as well as professionally. It was an exaltation of the current state of American life. But it also smacked of a theme that other *Columbian* contributors had enunciated—"the Rising Glory of America."

Within his message, Ramsay stressed that the single most important experience in his own life—the American Revolution—had been basic to the emergence of the Promised Land. Indeed, the Revolution was the central event in world history. As a South Carolina legislator, a member of the Privy Council, and a Charleston community leader who had been incarcerated for a time by the British, he proudly recalled how Americans of different localities and "prejudices" had cooperated to resist the mother country: "Local prejudices abated. By frequent collision asperities were worn off, and a foundation was laid for establishment of a nation

---

States, Delivered on the 12th May, 1804, in St. Michael's Church, Charleston (Charleston, 1804), p. 21.

[32] David Ramsay, *The History of South-Carolina, from Its First Settlement in 1670, to the Year 1808* (Charleston: David Longworth, 1809), I, vii; David Ramsay, *An Oration Delivered on the Anniversary of American Independence, July 4, 1794, in Saint Michael's Church to the Inhabitants of Charleston, South Carolina* (London, 1795), p. 7; Brunhouse (ed.), *Transactions*, p. 30.

[33] David Ramsay, *Universal History Americanized . . .* (Philadelphia: M. Carey & Son, 1819), III, p. 70; Brunhouse (ed.), *Transactions*, pp. 53–191; William Raymond Smith, *History as Argument: Three Patriot Historians of the American Revolution* (The Hague: Mouton & Co., 1966), p. 72. Indeed, Ramsay's twelve-volume world history, *Universal History Americanized*, praised or mocked other nations by the extent to which their values and practices paralleled or diverged from those of the United States.

out of discordant materials."[34] The outlook of every American was profoundly affected by the essential events of the Revolution. Somehow, Ramsay maintained, these events had fostered national unification while committing Americans to regularized, orderly processes. American revolutionaries were won over to responsible, ordered nationalism; there was no place for the hysteric mob psychology of the Old World in the liberation of the Promised Land. Since the orderly processes of the Revolution were crucial to the development of American nationality, those who had not been in the New Nation during that character-shaping event were not entitled to United States citizenship.[35]

Conceiving of the Revolution as both the highlight of his own life and the reason for the emergence of the Promised Land, Ramsay focused his investigations upon that event. His *History of the Revolution of South-Carolina* (1785), *History of the American Revolution* (1789), *Life of George Washington* (1807), *History of of South-Carolina* (1809), and *History of the United States* (1816–17) all dwelt upon the origin of the American Revolution. Alone in his study year after year, Ramsay wrote thousands of pages demonstrating that the essence of American history and the highlight of his personal history lay in the birth of the New Nation. This event was so momentous that the progress of civilization was doomed if it were ever reversed—if the Promised Land failed to perpetuate genuine independence from the mother country. Every American must, therefore, be on guard to remain clear of Britain's "cramped," "corrupting," "restraining" sway.[36] To teach contemporary and succeeding generations the significance of the great struggle in which he and other patriots had triumphed, Ramsay

[34] David Ramsay, *The History of the American Revolution* (London: John Stockdale, 1793), II, 316–17.

[35] David Ramsay, *History of the United States* . . . (Philadelphia: M. Carey, 1816–17), III, iii–iv; Ramsay, *History of South-Carolina*, I, 260; Ramsay, *History of the American Revolution*, I, 69, 145; II, 316; David Ramsay, *A Dissertation on the Manner of Acquiring the Character and Privileges of a Citizen of the United States* (Charleston [?], 1789), p. 8.

[36] See, e.g., David Ramsay, *An Oration on the Advantages of American Independence: Spoken before a Public Assembly of the Inhabitants of Charlestown in South-Carolina, on the Second Anniversary of the Glorious Era* (Charlestown, 1778), pp. 2, 4–5; Brunhouse (ed.), *Transactions*, p. 193.

devoted his life to the publication of a native *American* view of the past. Hopefully, this view would make Americans love and support their country.

Although Ramsay worked arduously to trace the development of an independent and glorious American nation, binding his personal and professional life to this task, he encountered the same dilemma that plagued most other *Columbian* contributors. He was not able to ignore the continued influence of the Old World upon the New. A fervent patriotic writer, Ramsay was forced by his historical research and writing to recognize the nation's continuing and substantial dependence upon Britain. He could not overlook the superior quality of British over American publishers and the greater appreciation of historical literature among the British reading public. British printers reproduced a writer's text more accurately and tastefully while their product cost far less, and there was a much larger British book market. America was "not the country to reward any literary publications." A devout patriot, Ramsay was forever torn between publishing his histories in America or in the country of "our late enemies."[37] The simple desire to exalt the contemporary merits of the New Nation was thwarted by the process of transforming that desire into printed pages—a dilemma that had been common to other *Columbian* contributors.

The conflict between Ramsay's patriotism and his recognition of the benefits of the mother country surfaced in another way. In the preface to his *History of the American Revolution*, Ramsay stated that he had relied entirely upon original American sources. Committed, like other Enlightenment intellectuals, to accurate documentation for all assertions, he noted that he had studied "the official papers of the United States"—the original correspondence and official documents of George Washington and other statesmen and military leaders. These were, he claimed, the sources upon which his narrative rested.[38] But the truth of the matter is that Ramsay rarely, if ever, consulted these original documents. Instead, he depended upon the British *Annual Register* for its summaries of the political and diplomatic events of the war. Edmund

[37] Brunhouse (ed.), *Transactions,* pp. 53, 63, 65, 81, 128, 130.
[38] Ramsay, *History of the American Revolution,* I, ix–x.

Burke had written most of the summaries and had included frequent references to original documents. Using the *Annual Register* as his basic source, Ramsay conducted his research along lines that contemporary scholarly opinion sanctioned—most other British and American historians had also centered their research upon the *Register*.[39] Unlike Ramsay, however, William Gordon, John Marshall, and most others admitted this. Ramsay's deceptive prefatory statement points, therefore, to a serious and unusual dilemma. To construct a properly documented history—to research and narrate the emergence of the Promised Land—he needed the *Register*. But it would have been painful for Ramsay, the patriot historian, to have characterized America as free, independent, and worthy of emulation while he visibly demonstrated America's dependence upon the mother country.

Within the main body of his histories, Ramsay demonstrated this same conflict between intense patriotism and substantial dependence upon Britain. Although his narratives firmly upheld the virtue and strength of the Promised Land, they were not the simplistic anti-British propaganda that had characterized the writings of several other *Columbian* contributors. Rather, Ramsay openly acknowledged that "the good resulting to the Colonies, from their connection with Great-Britain, infinitely outweighed the evil." The "wise policy of Great-Britain" had resulted in infinite benefits for the young American colonies; they increased "in number, in wealth and resources with a rapidity which surpassed all previous calculations." Most important, "the security of property and liberty derived from the English constitution, gave them [the American colonies] a consequence to which the colonies of other powers, though settled at an earlier day, have not yet attained."[40] America had derived her material well-being and her devotion to ordered liberty from the mother country. Because a

---

[39] Orin Grant Libby, "Ramsay as a Plagiarist," *American Historical Review*, VII, No. 4 (July 1902), 697–703; Brunhouse (ed.), *Transactions*, pp. 41, 219; Josephine Fitts, "David Ramsay: South Carolina Patriot, Physician, and Historian" (M.A. thesis, Columbia University, 1936), pp. 70–71; Smith, *History as Argument*, p. 33; Sidney G. Fisher, "The Legendary and Myth-Making Process in Histories of the American Revolution," *Proceedings of the American Philosophical Society*, LI, No. 204 (April–June 1912), 58.

[40] Ramsay, *History of the American Revolution*, I, 18–19, 43; Ramsay, *History of the United States*, I, 215–16.

few self-seeking elements within the British government illegally challenged America's traditional constitutional liberties, Ramsay and his countrymen had regretfully withdrawn from the British Empire. In both his *History of the Revolution of South-Carolina* and his *History of the American Revolution,* Ramsay accordingly depicted the movement for independence as an affirmation of those time-tested British values and traditions that the mother country had momentarily suspended. Americans were British through and through.

Because he acknowledged the British roots of American civilization, Ramsay's histories were more balanced and circumspect than the historical writing of most other *Columbian* contributors.[41] He even refused to dwell upon the traditional eighteenth-century New World arguments that Americans were Englishmen enriched by a new environment or that Americans had carried British ideas of liberty to their logical conclusion. Deeply committed to history as an account of truth, Ramsay would not proclaim the independence of the New World from the Old; he would not engage in the polemical combat of other post-Revolutionary cultural patriots.

This does not mean that Ramsay was unbiased or that he shared the cosmopolitan tolerance that is often attributed to the Founding Fathers generation. He had been an active participant in the Revolutionary War—a surgeon in the Continental Army, a witness to the siege of Savannah in 1779, a defender of Charleston against British invasion in 1780, and a prisoner of war in St. Augustine for the better part of a year. Like other eighteenth-century historians, he believed that his firsthand practical experience was indispensable for proper historical perspective. Historical writing was supposed to convey a quality of involvement—a direct link between the historian and the subject of his narrative. One merely has to read Ramsay's descriptions of British officers and loyalists (his major wartime opponents) and the profound biases of an activist become unmistakable. Moreover, David Ramsay operated on the

---

[41] In an exciting and thoughtful essay, "David Ramsay and the Causes of the American Revolution," *William and Mary Quarterly,* 3rd Ser., XVII, No. 1 (January 1960), 51–77, Page Smith argues that balanced, temperate writing characterized Ramsay's *History of the American Revolution* and made him an excellent historian.

commonplace eighteenth-century assumption that the historian's task was didactic—to propagate useful moral and political doctrines. He acknowledged that his own role was to create a body of patriotic literature that would "help mould us into a homogeneous people."[42]

Ramsay therefore wrote history with the commitment of a doctrinaire patriot. But unlike so many of his contemporaries, particularly fellow contributors to the *Columbian,* he did not treat Americans as God's chosen people or the British as agents of Satan. He held the commitment of a partisan revolutionary to national independence and the potential of the Promised Land, but he had the integrity and clarity to own up to American dependence upon the resources and heritage of "our late enemies." This split or duality almost certainly turned the partisan Ramsay against himself. A perusal of his private papers demonstrates that it caused him great personal irritation. His integrity was at war with his patriotism.

The *Columbian*'s most distinguished contributor was disturbed by yet another matter. It seemed even more serious than America's continued dependence upon Britain. Like many other cultural patriots who wrote for the *Columbian,* he was distressed by the strength and pervasiveness of local loyalties in the immediate post-Revolutionary decades. "We are one people in name," he told Jeremy Belknap in 1792, "but do not know half enough of each other to make our commerce reciprocally serviceable & to cement our friendship & intercourse."[43] "We are too widely disseminated over an extensive country," he noted, "and too much diversified by different customs and forms of government to feel as one people which we really are."[44] There seemed to be no united American nation—merely a collection of relatively isolated localities. Even if New World settlements became culturally independent of Britain, there would still be no unified and viable Promised Land.

To make matters worse, Ramsay sensed that he was totally rootless in a land of local loyalties. He was born in Lancaster County, Pennsylvania, the son of an Irish immigrant, attended the College

---

42 Brunhouse (ed.), *Transactions,* p. 133.
43 Brunhouse (ed.), *Transactions,* p. 133.
44 Brunhouse (ed.), *Transactions,* p. 74.

of New Jersey, and graduated from Philadelphia's new Medical School in 1773. Soon after, he arrived in Charleston as a practicing physician and remained there until his tragic assassination in 1815.

Spending four decades of his adult life in South Carolina, Ramsay found it difficult to conceive of himself as a Pennsylvanian. In all probability, he never returned to Lancaster County for even a day. In 1805, he wrote a revealing letter to a cousin who lived there:

> I long very much to revisit my native country, but am so entangled with business that I cannot leave Charleston. I often think of the friends of my youth & am particularly anxious to be informed of my relations. . . . Is the house standing in which I was born. What new buildings are there erected on it.[45]

Curiosity about "my native country" persisted. Yet lingering curiosity was not compelling enough for him to leave his Charleston medical and business activities to visit Lancaster County. Fond childhood memories, friendships with leading Philadelphia cultural figures like Benjamin Rush and the editors of the *Columbian*, and admiration for Pennsylvania's reform tradition constituted the extent of Ramsay's attachment to the state of his birth. This sharply distinguished him from most of the citizens of the New Nation. Even a cosmopolitan, widely traveled man like Thomas Jefferson retained paramount allegiance to Virginia—his birthplace and his "country."[46]

Nor could Ramsay find acceptance and a sense of belonging in South Carolina despite many decades of residency and political

[45] Brunhouse (ed.), *Transactions*, pp. 157–58. Also quoted in William U. Hensel, "Dr. David Ramsay," *Historical Papers and Addresses of the Lancaster County Historical Society*, X, No. 10 (November 2, 1906), 360–61.

[46] Hayne, *Analectic Magazine*, VI (September 1815), 204; David Ramsay, *An Eulogium upon Benjamin Rush, M.D. . . .* (Philadelphia: Bradford and Inskeep, 1813), pp. 9–13; Ramsay, *History of the American Revolution*, II, 322–23. Daniel J. Boorstin, *The Genius of American Politics* (Chicago: University of Chicago Press, 1953), pp. 73–74, comments on Jefferson. See also Merrill Jensen, *The Articles of Confederation: An Interpretation of the Social-Constitutional History of the American Revolution, 1774–1781* (Madison: University of Wisconsin Press, 1948), p. 163, and Max Savelle, "Nationalism and Other Loyalties in the American Revolution," *American Historical Review*, LXVII, No. 4 (July 1962), 916, for intelligent comments on the widespread localism of late-eighteenth-century America.

prominence. The second volume of his *History of South-Carolina* (1809) demonstrated remarkable knowledge of the social and economic life of the state—dress, manners, religion, literature, geography, and education in each of nine regions. But the longer he lived in South Carolina and the more he learned about the state, the more critical he became. It was backward, he charged, and lagged behind the North in agricultural methods, the fine arts, manufacturing, commerce, and even basic morals. South Carolina schools were deplorable, there was not a college worth the name, and schoolmasters were "deficient in that knowledge which republicans ought to possess."[47] Coupled with these adverse impressions, South Carolina's election in the fall of 1788 made it clear to Ramsay that his roots were not in the Palmetto State. He desperately wanted a seat in the new national House of Representatives but was defeated by William Longton Smith by a three-to-one voting ratio. Even the allegedly radical Commodore Gillon edged him out for second place. Humiliated, he wrote to his friend John Eliot:

> We have just finished our [South Carolina] election for representative to Congress. I was a candidate & lost my election on two grounds. One that I was a northward man & the other that I was represented as favoring the abolition of slavery.[48]

The last charge was patent political demagogy and Ramsay knew it. He had married into the Laurens family—prominent South Carolina slaveholders—the year before, and was not an abolitionist. But even though he had no roots in Pennsylvania, he could not deny the charge that he was a "northward man."

Detesting South Carolina, his permanent residence, Ramsay occasionally looked to New England—the only part of the New Nation where he had not resided. Historical investigations had impressed him with the region. In economic activities, education, and allegiance to republican theory, New England seemed to set the pattern for all other parts of the country. Ramsay sensed that it was the most energetic and cultivated region in the Promised

47 Brunhouse (ed.), *Transactions*, pp. 36, 37, 136, 141, 147, 173, 179.
48 Brunhouse (ed.), *Transactions*, p. 123. For additional data on this 1788 election, see *ibid.*, pp. 20, 36.

INVENTORS OF THE PROMISED LAND   2 8

Land. For this reason, he developed regular and friendly correspondence with scholarly New England ministers like Jedidiah Morse, John Eliot, and Jeremy Belknap, and openly acknowledged the supremacy of the region over South Carolina.[49] As he neared completion of his *History of the American Revolution* in the fall of 1786, Ramsay went to great lengths to persuade the New England delegates to the national Congress to read portions of the manuscript for "competent" criticism.[50] Intellectual exchanges with New Englanders may have been Ramsay's way of mentally leaving South Carolina while physically remaining.

But despite these and other attempts to build bridges with the New England states, Ramsay was not a New Englander. As he acknowledged in the preface of *The History of the Revolution of South-Carolina* and confessed to John Eliot: "My information of New England affairs is rather insufficient."[51] Ramsay was a Pennsylvanian who ceased to have roots in Lancaster County or in Philadelphia; he was also a Carolinian who despised South Carolina and was regarded by the inhabitants as a "northward man." The crux of the matter was that in a nation that he knew was dominated by local loyalties, Ramsay was rootless. He had only a sense of American nationality to fall back on.

Thus, one begins to understand why post-Revolutionary America's leading historian isolated himself in his study at every opportunity to prepare the historical case for the New Nation. Amidst the furor of the Revolution, he had proposed a national university and a uniform national system of criminal laws, hoping that both measures would unify the states and encourage national loyalties.[52] As early as 1778, he had insisted that the central government needed more powers than the Articles of Confederation provided, and he vigorously campaigned for ratification of the Federal Constitution in South Carolina.[53] Several other leading

[49] Ramsay, *History of the American Revolution*, I, 186; II, 322–23; Ramsay, *History of the United States*, I, 217–18; Brunhouse (ed.), *Transactions*, pp. 34, 166; Smith, *History as Argument*, pp. 48, 183.
[50] Brunhouse (ed.), *Transactions*, p. 40.
[51] Brunhouse (ed.), *Transactions*, p. 115. See also Fitts, "David Ramsay," p. 55.
[52] Brunhouse (ed.), *Transactions*, pp. 31–32.
[53] Robert L. Brunhouse (ed.), "David Ramsay on the Ratification of the Constitution of South Carolina, 1787–1788," *Journal of Southern History*, IX

men of the Revolution had promoted these same measures. But unlike most others, Ramsay never let up. In the years after the ratification of the Federal Constitution, he continued to plead with his countrymen that they must reduce their local loyalties in favor of unionist sentiment.[54] The reversion to local concerns that characterized so many other strong nationalists of the 1776–89 period appalled him. Ramsay's lack of local roots explains the persistence of his nationalism. His hope was to link his own destiny with that of the New Nation. If the American experiment in nation building failed, there was no Boston or Philadelphia or Charleston to which he could comfortably withdraw. Narrating the emergence of the Promised Land, Ramsay was describing nothing less than the construction of a national home—the one place on earth where he might feel rooted. If he did his job well— if his histories helped to supplant local loyalties with national loyalties—the reward would surpass any possible monetary compensation. But he died too soon. When he was assassinated by a deranged tailor in 1815, local loyalties among Americans had not been supplanted. He remained rootless to the end.

Ramsay's patriotism paralleled that of the *Columbian* editors and proprietors who had admired him so much. Several of them were new arrivals in Philadelphia; they may have felt as ill at ease there as Ramsay had felt in Charleston. Dependent upon a national readership for the survival of their enterprise and impressed with the importance of cultural nationalism to fortify American political independence, those who ran the *Columbian* hoped that a vigorous sense of American nationhood would supplant localism. They required this nationalist emphasis from all of their contributors. Publishing serialized versions of Ramsay's *History of the American Revolution* for three and a half years, they seemed to be holding him up as a model—the ideal contributor. For both the New Nation's leading magazine and that magazine's most distinguished writer, the strong spirit of localism that pervaded post-Revolutionary society was potentially disastrous. It had to be

---

(1943), 549–55; David Ramsay, *An Address to the Freemen of South-Carolina, on the Subject of the Federal Constitution, Proposed by the Convention which met in Philadelphia, May, 1787* (Charleston, 1788), pp. 11–12.

[54] See, e.g., Brunhouse (ed.), *Transactions*, p. 195; Ramsay, *Oration on Cession of Louisiana*, pp. 10–11.

negated to secure the future. If intense localism persisted, there would be no "Rising Glory of America."

III

Noah Webster was a second prominent *Columbian* contributor and used that journal as a model for his own short-lived *American Magazine*.[55] Despite his prominence in literary circles, Webster was widely disliked because he was arrogant and sarcastic. Indeed, literary figures would sometimes attack him in the *Columbian* for personal vulgarity as well as for factual errors.[56] But David Ramsay held Webster and his works in high esteem. The two men first met in New York late in 1785. Ramsay was representing South Carolina in Congress while Webster was trying to enlist congressional support behind his plan to simplify English spelling. Ramsay thought well of the plan and encouraged Webster in his efforts to reform American English— to purify the language of Old World "corruptions." Deep-seated patriotism was basic to this friendship. Ramsay sensed the urgency of fortifying America's newly won political independence with cultural nationalism and characterized Webster's linguistic efforts as a major cultural innovation. Support from the *Columbian*'s most prestigious contributor and the New Nation's leading historian deeply gratified Webster.[57]

Like Ramsay, Webster continually associated his personal career with the emergence of the Promised Land. In 1783, early in his scholarly career, he announced: "America must be as independent in *literature* as she is in politics . . . & it is not impossible but a person of my youth may have some influence in exciting a spirit of literary industry." Seven years later, Webster boasted to George Washington that he had "written much more than any other man

[55] Noah Webster to William Young, August 2, 1788, Dreer Collection of American Prose Writers, Vol. IX, Historical Society of Pennsylvania.
[56] *Columbian Magazine*, November 1790, p. 330; October 1791, p. 264; Free, *Columbian*, pp. 46–47.
[57] Brunhouse (ed.), *Transactions*, pp. 19, 115, 159, 272; Harry R. Warfel (ed.), *Letters of Noah Webster* (New York: Library Publishers, Inc., 1953), pp. 49, 290; Noah Webster, *A Letter to Dr. David Ramsay of Charleston, Respecting the Errors in Johnson's Dictionary and Other Lexicons* (New Haven, 1807), pp. 27–28; Ramsay, *History of the American Revolution*, II, 322.

of my age, in favor of the revolution & my country."[58] But he felt that the relationship between himself and his country had to be reciprocal. The more he served his country, the more the New Nation was obligated to respect him and to finance his literary ventures.[59] This was why Webster frequently accompanied boasts of his service to the nation with observations on his financial well-being or comments on the way Americans had received his contributions. But the balance sheet never seemed to tally and this was disturbing. Webster regularly noted that he had done more for America than Americans had done for him.[60]

Although few of his contemporaries honored Webster as they had honored Ramsay, he had local roots unavailable to Ramsay. Like Ramsay, he felt that New England had been instrumental in forging American national character:

> In this northern or commercial part of the United States [New England] are the *principal wealth, strength & resources* of the country. Inhabited by a hardy, industrious people, mostly freeholders who feel a personal interest in the safety & prosperity of the country, this section must supply the principal means of defense in war, as well as prosperity in peace.[61]

Unlike Ramsay, Webster had firm roots in New England. Born on the outskirts of Hartford, he traced his lineage to early-seventeenth-century Puritan settlers. He was the great-great-great-grandson of William Bradford of Plymouth Colony and the grand-

---

[58] Noah Webster to John Canfield, January 7, 1783; Noah Webster to George Washington, September 2, 1790 (both in the Noah Webster Papers, New York Public Library).

[59] Noah Webster to James Greenleaf, June 24, 1793, Frank M. Etting Papers (American Authors), Historical Society of Pennsylvania.

[60] See, e.g., Noah Webster to Jonas Platt, September 27, 1807, Noah Webster Collection, Library of Congress; Webster to Stephen Van Rensselaer, November 5, 1821, Simon Gratz Collection, Historical Society of Pennsylvania; Warfel (ed.), *Letters of Webster,* p. 292.

[61] Noah Webster, "To All American Patriots Who Value National Character," May 17, 1808, Noah Webster Papers, New York Public Library. Webster's *Ten Letters to Joseph Priestly* (New Haven, 1800) should also be consulted, for he consistently depicted New England in these letters as the basic agent in the formation of national character. See also Warfel (ed.), *Letters of Webster,* p. 214, and Kemp Malone, "A Linguistic Patriot," *American Speech,* I, No. 1 (October 1925), 30.

son of former Connecticut governor John Webster.[62] He took special pride in coming from Connecticut—the "heart" of New England: "I was born and educated in a state which is probably as republican as any on earth, a state where great *personal* independence united with *civil* subordination to law. My own principles are those which prevail generally in the state which gave me birth."[63] Unlike Ramsay, Webster spent most of his life in the region of his birth—Hartford, New Haven, and Amherst. He rarely expressed interest in moving elsewhere. On a visit to Washington, D.C., to lobby for a federal copyright law, he wrote to his wife: "I begin to be invited to parties, but shall avoid them as much as possible, except those which are given by New England people."[64]

If Noah Webster had geographic roots, he also had a problem. Writing to Timothy Pickering in 1785, he followed the precedent of a number of New Englanders since the days of John Winthrop and equated "America" with "New England." Personal correspondence demonstrates that he continued to make this equation for the next fifty years.[65] It gave rise to a dilemma that plagued Webster until his death. If, as he assumed, New England provided the essential ingredients of American national character, national problems became tests of the viability of the New England way. If these problems were not properly resolved and the American experiment in nation making failed, it followed that New England and he himself as a New Englander had failed. Thus, although Webster enjoyed the local roots that Ramsay lacked, he ran the risk of losing those roots and becoming estranged from his region if his patriotic crusade for national culture failed. Too many

[62] Ervin C. Shoemaker, *Noah Webster: Pioneer of Learning* (New York: Columbia University Press, 1936), p. 4; M. M. Mathews (ed.), *The Beginnings of American English* (Chicago: University of Chicago Press, 1963), p. 44; Charlton Laird, *Language in America* (Englewood Cliffs, N.J.: Prentice-Hall, Inc., 1970), p. 264.

[63] *The Herald* (New York) May 4, 1796. Also quoted in Warfel (ed.), *Letters of Webster*, pp. 134-35.

[64] Noah Webster to Rebecca Webster, January 7, 1831, Noah Webster Papers, New York Public Library.

[65] Warfel (ed.), *Letters of Webster*, p. 39, quotes the letter to Pickering. Subsequent letters in this volume demonstrate, again and again, the persistence with which Webster equated "America" with "New England." Indeed, he never ceased to do so.

reverses in Webster's campaign for the Promised Land would leave him as rootless as Ramsay.

Decade after decade Noah Webster pleaded with Americans to complete the Revolution by creating a New World culture:

> A fundamental mistake of the Americans has been that they consider the revolution completed when it was just begun. Having laid the pillars of the building, they ceased to exert themselves, and seemed to forget the whole superstructure was then to be erected. This country is independent in government but totally dependent in manners which are the basis of government.[66]

To gain genuine independence—to complete the Revolution—Webster urged his countrymen to take action on several fronts. They had to achieve economic self-sufficiency. Although foreign trade was vital, a truly independent country was capable of caring for its own internal economic needs.[67] Books and libraries were necessary if Americans were to engage in independent research and to teach their children properly. Above all, native publications were needed to teach Americans "the praises of liberty, and of those illustrious heroes and statesmen who have wrought a revolution in her favor."[68] Webster chastised his countrymen for displaying foreign flags: "We ought to unite under our *own flag* and learn to be a nation." More important, federal supremacy had to be firmly established. Until the central government prevailed over the states, "we can have no union, no respectability, no national character."[69] For this reason Webster joined Ramsay as one of the first to campaign for revision of the Articles of Confederation.

[66] Quoted in Noah Webster, *On Being American: Selected Writings, 1783–1828*, edited by Homer D. Babbidge, Jr. (New York: Frederick A. Praeger Publishers, 1967), p. 62, and Malone, *American Speech*, I, No. 1 (October 1925), 30.

[67] Noah Webster, *An Address, Delivered before the Hampshire, Franklin and Hampton Agricultural Society, at their Annual Meeting in Northampton, October 14, 1818* (Northampton, 1818), p. 20; Noah Webster, *A Rod for the Fool's Back* (n.p., 1800); Warfel (ed.), *Letters of Webster*, pp. 90–102.

[68] *American Magazine* (March 1788), pp. 215–216; Webster, *Ten Letters to Priestly*, p. 22; "Letters of Noah Webster, 1786–1840," *Proceedings of the Massachusetts Historical Society*, XLIII (November 1909), 147.

[69] *The Herald*, March 22, 1797, quotes Webster on foreign flags. The plea for federal supremacy is found in Noah Webster, *An Examination into the*

Like Ramsay, he continued to champion a strong Federal Government in the decades that followed ratification of the Constitution.[70]

Webster vented his patriotism most emphatically by urging his countrymen to adopt a uniquely American language: "A national language is a national tie, and what country wants it more than America?" A national language was an indispensable "band of *national union*." With this language, every American "would speak with some degree of precision and uniformity. Such uniformity in these states is very desirable; it would remove prejudice and conciliate mutual affection and respect."[71] A national language, moreover, would "extirpate the improprieties & vulgarisms which were successfully introduced by settlers from various parts of Europe." It would purify the American tongue of Old World corruptions.[72]

Attempting to tie nationality to language, Webster reflected the thinking of several Western scholars. Johann Gottfried von Herder, John Horne Tooke, Jeremy Bentham, Jacob Grimm, and Franz Bopp also stressed this interrelationship. But the importance Webster attached to language reform as a vehicle to achieve American cultural independence cannot be overemphasized. In 1807 he outlined his position to Joel Barlow:

> For more than twenty years, since I have looked into philology and considered the connection between language and

---

Leading Principles of the Federal Constitution . . . (Philadelphia: Prichard & Hull, 1787), p. 28.

[70] Warfel, *Noah Webster: Schoolmaster*, pp. 111–12; Webster, *On Being American*, p. 44; Ruth F. and Harry R. Warfel (eds.), *Poems by Noah Webster* (College Park, Md.: Harruth Lefraw, 1936), p. 10; Noah Webster, *A Collection of Papers on Political, Literary and Moral Subjects* (reprint. New York: Burt Franklin, 1968), p. 26; Noah Webster, *The Revolution in France, Considered in Respect to Its Progress and Effects* (New York: George Bunce, 1794), p. 46.

[71] *Proceedings of the Massachusetts Historical Society*, XLIII (November 1909), 129; Emily E. F. Skeel (comp.), *A Bibliography of the Writings of Noah Webster* (New York: New York Public Library and Arno Press, Inc., 1971), xvi; Noah Webster, "The Reforming of Spelling," *Old South Leaflets*, VIII, No. 196 (Boston: Directors of the Old South Work, 1902), 389–90; Noah Webster, *Dissertations on the English Language* (reprint. Menston, Eng.: The Scholar Press Limited, 1967), pp. 397–98.

[72] Noah Webster, "Memorial to the Legislature of New York," January 18, 1783, Noah Webster Papers, New York Public Library.

knowledge, and the influence of national language on national opinions, I have had it in view to detach the country as much as possible from its dependence on the parent country.

If he succeeded in freeing language in America from British encumbrances, Webster told Barlow, a whole new American mind, liberated from British values and opinions, would come into being. But if language reform failed, the entire American experiment in nation building would fail.[73] Sensing that he bore a tremendous burden—that the fate of the New Nation rested upon his shoulders—Webster launched a lifelong crusade to distinguish words, spellings, and pronunciations in the United States from those of the mother country. He frequently stressed the corruptions of British linguists. British "philology is in a very low condition; so low as to be a reproach to the nation." The British either had "no system in the regulation of sounds or accent, or they disregard them."[74] Samuel Johnson was chiefly responsible for these ills. His dictionary included words that did not belong to the English language: "Johnson's Dictionary therefore furnishes no standard of correct English: but in its present form, tends very much to corrupt and pervert the language." Therefore, Americans had "much over-rated British authorities in philology."[75] One issue remained: ". . . ought the Americans to retain these faults which produce innumerable inconveniences in the acquisition and use of the [English] language, or ought they at once to reform these abuses, and introduce order and regularity into the orthography of the AMERICAN TONGUE?"[76] The answer was obvious.

Webster delineated a simple theoretical procedure through which Americans could free themselves from the "corrupt English tongue" and replace it with a "pure American tongue." Ignoring erroneous British authorities like Samuel Johnson, Americans

[73] Noah Webster to Joel Barlow, November 12, 1807, as quoted in Gaillard Hunt, *Life in America One Hundred Years Ago* (New York: Harper & Brothers, 1914), pp. 141–42.

[74] "A Letter from Dr. N. Webster to a gentleman in this town," n.d., Noah Webster Collection, Library of Congress; Noah Webster, "Philology," *The Knickerbocker*, VII (February–March 1836), 246.

[75] Webster, *Letter to Dr. David Ramsay*, pp. 8–10; Noah Webster's draft of an advertisement for his *Practical Spelling Book*, November 25, 1840, Noah Webster Papers, New York Public Library.

[76] Webster, *Old South Leaflets*, VIII, No. 196, 387.

should simply use traditional English words to describe the new ideas and objects of the New World or they should invent words, spellings, and pronunciations of their own. New words and new uses for old words were entirely justifiable: "New circumstances, new modes of life, new laws, new ideas of various kinds give rise to new words, and have already made many material differences between the language of England and America." This trend should be encouraged to the point where there would be a separate "American language." As the "American language" developed through new words, new word usages, new spellings, and new pronunciations, this would stimulate a native American book industry. Finding it increasingly difficult to understand British books, Americans would write and publish more books of their own. With separate languages, literatures, and publishing industries, America and Britain would draw further and further apart. Communication between the two would become minimal. The Revolution would be completed.[77]

The message of the New Nation's leading crusader for language reform had a plausible if not a cosmopolitan ring; it was an argument for descriptive over prescriptive linguistics. Americans must cease to follow British authorities but should create an "American language" based upon common American usages. A proper word or accurate spelling should not be determined by Johnson or other British authorities. Propriety could be found through accurate descriptions of contemporary American usage.

There were problems with Webster's conceptual framework. No sharp distinction can be made between descriptive and prescriptive linguistics. Johnson and other British linguists had drawn upon common usage in the British Isles to modify earlier authorities. Webster, moreover, was playing the part of a prescriptive authority by asserting that Americans were duty-bound to follow the usages that he codified. Beneath his defense of common American usage, Webster was claiming that the real test of a word's validity in the New Nation was whether he—the supreme authority—had recognized the word as one of common American

[77] Warfel (ed.), *Letters of Webster*, p. 346; Warfel, *Noah Webster: Schoolmaster*, p. 289; Webster to the editor of the *Westminster Review*, April 11, 1831, Noah Webster Papers, New York Public Library (copy); Webster, *Old South Leaflets*, VIII, No. 196, 389.

usage. His sharp distinction between British authorities and American usages cloaked an enormous ego and an irrational patriotism that were the sources of his efforts at language reform.

Webster also seemed unaware that contemporary American usage was not uniform. In a nation marked by localism and regionalism, there was considerable linguistic variation. There was also a common British linguistic heritage. But Webster skimmed over these facts. His crusade for the Promised Land rested on the assumption that New England was the source of all American traits. Therefore, a description and codification of contemporary New England usage became his basis for a distinctive American national language. But as Kemp Malone notes, the New England way did not pervade the New Nation. Nor was it distinguishable in all important respects from the language of the mother country. On both counts, Webster had made unjustifiable assumptions.[78]

Although Webster's linguistic theory involved distortions in its application, there is no evidence that he was conscious of them. His theory seemed logical. Equating New England with America, he was oblivious to regional language variations. What caused him the most difficulty (and very nearly thwarted his language-reform efforts) was the sense that he was cheating—that he was violating his own linguistic theory. Although Webster was attentive to New England usage in formulating his spellers, dictionaries, and pronunciation guides for the "American language," he drew extensively upon the British authorities whom he had condemned. Although he defended descriptive over prescriptive linguistics, he knowingly followed British prescriptive authorities to an extreme. The American language reformer could not seem to operate without the linguistic authorities of the mother country. Severely chastising Samuel Johnson, Webster only occasionally deviated from Johnson in compiling his own dictionaries. His first *Speller*

[78] Malone, *American Speech*, I, No. 1 (October 1925), 30. See also Merle Curti, *The Social Ideas of American Educators* (Paterson, N.J.: Pageant Books, 1959), p. 48. On one occasion, in 1836, Webster admitted that the "New England Way" was a carry-over from England: ". . . now, educated men in New-England speak the language almost precisely as the same classes do in England. I have been several hours in company with gentlemen in Cambridge, England, without hearing any difference of pronunciation which would distinguish an Englishman from an American." Quoted in Webster, *The Knickerbocker*, VII (February–March 1836), 244.

was based on similar works by two prominent British linguists—
Thomas Dilworth and Daniel Fenning. Robert Lowth's compila-
tion formed the basis of his first grammar and he relied upon the
theories of John Horne Tooke for his second. Even his reader for
schoolchildren closely resembled readers that were used in the
academies and colleges of the mother country.[79]

Ebenezer Hazard, the wise and cultivated friend of many of the
men who published and wrote for the *Columbian Magazine*,
offered a short but profound analysis of the journal's most important linguistic contributor. In 1788 Hazard wrote to Jeremy
Belknap: "The Monarch [Webster] reigns supreme, and some of
his subjects (I am told) have only an English education. How they
will succeed in establishing a 'Federal Language' time must determine."[80] Like David Ramsay and most other *Columbian* contributors, Webster had learned his lessons in lexicography and in
other aspects of linguistics from the British. He privately acknowledged that he could not even complete his dictionary of the
"American language" without going to Great Britain for "books &
knowledge which I cannot obtain in this country [America]."[81]

When Webster completed the full edition of his dictionary, he
sent a copy to Queen Victoria. In an accompanying note, he wrote
that the book "may furnish evidence that the genuine descendants
of English ancestors, born on the west of the Atlantic, have not
forgotten either the land or the language of their fathers."[82]
Decade after decade, he remained sharply attuned to British com-

[79] Gerald A. Smith (ed.), "Noah Webster's Conservatism," *American
Speech*, XXV, No. 2 (May 1950), 101; Shoemaker, *Webster*, p. 302; Skeel,
Bibliography of Writings of Webster, p. 7; Laird, *Language*, pp. 281–82.

[80] Ebenezer Hazard to Jeremy Belknap, March 19, 1788, in "The Belknap
Papers," *Collections of the Massachusetts Historical Society*, Series 5, III,
59.

[81] Noah Webster to Samuel L. Mitchill, December 12, 1823, Noah Webster
Collection, Library of Congress.

[82] Noah Webster to Queen Victoria, June 22, 1841, Noah Webster Papers,
New York Public Library (copy). Writing to Englishman Andrew Steven-
son on June 22, 1841 (Webster Papers, New York Public Library), Webster
asked that the dictionary be delivered to the Queen. Then he added: "Our
common language is one of the ties that binds the two nations together; & I
hope the works I have executed will manifest to the British nation that the
Americans are not willing to suffer it to degenerate on this side of the
Atlantic."

mentary on his publications. Once, in 1807, he considered moving to England for a more stimulating scholarly climate; a student of linguistics could learn much more on the other side of the Atlantic.[83]

Noah Webster should not be condemned for drawing upon British linguists any more than David Ramsay should be criticized for relying upon the British *Annual Register* or the *Columbian* editors should be censured for reprinting British literary materials. But whereas Ramsay publicly and fully acknowledged the enormous influence of the British heritage upon the life and thought of the New Nation, Webster and the *Columbian* editors did not. Indeed, Webster bound his plea for American cultural nationalism to a simplistic theory of descriptive linguistics that belittled the British heritage. In practice this theory of descriptive linguistics proved so unworkable that Webster violated its essential tenets. The way Webster compiled his dictionaries, spellers, and other language guides was the most telling proof that there was no "American language"—that from the standpoint of the written and spoken word, the Promised Land remained quite dependent upon Britain.

Because Webster attached great importance to his crusade for an "American language," the flaws in that crusade posed potentially serious personal problems. The master of at least twenty languages and one of the most dedicated scholars in the New Nation, Webster had the intellectual capacity to understand how he exemplified the American dependence upon British authorities that he had so scathingly condemned. He acknowledged, in private correspondence, that he felt compelled to keep up with the most current British scholarship, and one senses that Webster was very nearly conscious of his linguistic dilemma. The strong possibility that he at least bordered on conscious awareness of his dilemma may account for the sense of inadequacy that Ebenezer Hazard saw in Webster, the scholar schooled so thoroughly in British ways, beneath Webster's dogmatic patriotism, his boastful, self-

[83] Noah Webster, "British Notices of Webster's Dictionary," n.d., Noah Webster Papers, New York Public Library; Webster to Samuel L. Mitchill, June 15, 1807, Noah Webster Collection, Library of Congress.

congratulatory public manner, and his defense of a pure American language.[84]

In later life, Webster realized that his language crusade had failed. Sometimes he openly acknowledged that erroneous British authorities remained dominant in the New Nation and that he had "nearly lost all hope of benefiting my country in correcting disorders of our language." "I have labored in vain and spent my strength for naught," he told a daughter.[85] Most often, Webster blamed his countrymen—not himself—for the failure of an "American language" to develop. "Perhaps this is the only country on the globe where men are determined not to have their errors disturbed," Webster charged, for Americans insisted upon following erroneous British standards. Americans had always looked down on him because he had properly criticized their "erroneous" opinions.[86]

Because Webster had assumed that his linguistic crusade would redeem the Promised Land, recognition of failure caused him to reflect upon the future of the New Nation. "We [Americans] are a degenerate and wicked people," he lamented seven years before his death.[87] The nation's founding principles had been buried. Moreover, in "real civility and courtesy, and in a due subordination of youth to age and superior station, our manners are far less correct than they were before the American revolution." In "no country is reputation held so cheap."[88] But for an aging Webster, the most telling proof that there would be no "Rising Glory of America" was in the quality of national political life. By the 1830's he was certain that—because of an extended franchise—ignorance,

[84] Ebenezer Hazard to Jeremy Belknap, March 5, 1788, *Collections of the Massachusetts Historical Society*, Series 5, III, 23.

[85] Noah Webster to Daniel Webster, March 30, 1837, as quoted in Skeel, *Bibliography of Writings of Webster*, pp. 379-80. Warfel, *Noah Webster: Schoolmaster*, p. 424, quotes Webster's remark to his daughter.

[86] Noah Webster to Samuel L. Mitchill, June 15, 1807, Noah Webster Collection, Library of Congress; Noah Webster to Stephen Twining, January 22, 1802, Noah Webster Papers, New York Public Library.

[87] Quoted in Warfel, *Noah Webster: Schoolmaster*, p. 425.

[88] *Connecticut Observer* (Hartford), April 2, 1836; *Connecticut Journal* (New Haven), December 22, 1829; *Connecticut Herald* (New Haven), October 18, 1836.

passion, and anarchy would always dominate the life of the New Nation.[89] This crisis of mass politics and concomitant social disintegration had infected New England—that basic source of American traits. Massachusetts was promulgating "illegal, or at least unjust" taxation policies and thereby forcing her best citizens out of the state. Even Webster's Connecticut, the "heart" of New England, had gone astray. "Violent" revivals "never known under the preaching of Christ and his apostles" were permitted.[90] In 1835 Webster pleaded to be "forever delivered from the democracy of *Connecticut*. This is now the *rankest despotism* which I have ever known; it goes far beyond the despotism of Jefferson's days. . . . I believe no state under heaven has ever experienced such determined efforts to *destroy* every thing good and *debase* every thing exalted and honorable, as we now experience." It was better to "become a troglodyte and live in a cave in winter, rather than be under the tyranny of our [Connecticut's] desperate rulers." With Connecticut and therefore New England subverted, the American experiment in nation making was doomed.[91]

It is not difficult to explain Webster's estrangements. He had commenced his patriotic crusade equating "American language" and national character with New England (particularly Connecticut). The equation of the nation with the region persisted as he encountered failures in his crusade. Because Americans at large were rejecting his "American language" reforms, New Englanders were as well. Therefore, the general decline in American life that his abortive crusade symbolized turned Webster against Americans in general and New Englanders in particular. His persistent but seemingly unfruitful efforts, decade after decade, to promote America's "Rising Glory" alienated Webster from his nation, his region, and his state. In the end, Webster's patriotic efforts left him rootless. During his final years, he was coming to experience the sense of unanchored instability that David Ramsay had felt for decades.

[89] Warfel (ed.), *Letters of Webster*, p. 449; Skeel, *Bibliography of Writings of Webster*, pp. 463, 472, 579; Shoemaker, *Webster*, p. 59.
[90] Warfel (ed.), *Letters of Webster*, pp. 409, 451–52.
[91] Warfel, *Noah Webster: Schoolmaster*, pp. 423–25.

IV

The history of the *Columbian Magazine* paralleled the experiences of its two leading contributors. Perceiving that Old World influences and local jealousies tarnished the past and present of the Promised Land, *Columbian* writers turned to the future. Americans should go all out, the *Columbian* urged, to promote a truly independent and flawless nation that would uplift mankind. Throughout his professional career, David Ramsay had voiced this concept—the need for constant striving to achieve "the Rising Glory of America." Although he saw more hope in the American past than many other *Columbian* contributors, Ramsay regularly concluded his histories with the vision of future glory. Although Noah Webster lost hope in the New Nation in later life, he spent decades urging his countrymen to adopt language reforms and thereby assure perfected nationhood.

Within the pages of the *Columbian*, the concept of America's flawless "Rising Glory" was articulated in such a vague, abstract, unreal manner that it had the potential to draw *Columbian* contributors away from the specific conditions of their everyday lives. The ill-defined quality of the concept created potentially hazardous conditions under which certain contributors might have felt uprooted from their past heritage and present realities—like men who were suspended or detached in strenuous pursuit of a perfected future. The nebulous pursuit upward toward "Rising Glory" threatened to make the specific, rooted ground of everyday existence seem tenuous and unstable, particularly if the patriot felt somewhat unanchored beforehand.

Ramsay and Webster both came to be plagued by feelings of rootless, unanchored existence. To be sure, Ramsay's rootlessness preceded his quest for a flawless America and was an important factor inducing him to take up that quest. It was of a type shared by cultural patriots like Mason Locke Weems, Hugh Williamson, John Daly Burk, and perhaps certain *Columbian* proprietors—men who never felt securely anchored to any one specific location or set of circumstances and sought self-identity and a homeland in the nation itself. Indeed, many authors of state histories in the early national period seemed to share Ramsay's precise sort of rootlessness. While portraying a particular state as a microcosm of the Promised Land, many of these early historians were neither born, raised, nor educated in the state whose "glorious American development" they had elected to narrate. Moreover, they did not feel particularly comfortable in any other state or locality. Unlike Ramsay and many state historians, Noah Webster had firm New England roots in the beginning but lost them in the course of decades of unsuccessful agitation for America's "Rising Glory." In this respect, he resembled certain New England intellectuals from Jedidiah Morse and Samuel Williams to Henry David Thoreau. Feeling securely rooted in the New England states, they perceived the region's ways as American ways and eventually became alienated from New England as a result of broader American failings.

Therefore, personal rootlessness drew Ramsay into a crusade for "the Rising Glory of America" while participation in that crusade left Webster rootless. Both of them wanted a sense of stable, anchored existence and both wanted to usher in a flawless Promised Land that would uplift benighted regions of the globe. The problem they confronted was that these two cravings were incompatible. Striving toward glorious national perfection required constant motion and a spirit of restless discontent with affairs as they were; it was antithetical to a sense of personal stability, place, and order. Thus, Ramsay was never able to feel securely anchored after decades of agitation for "Rising Glory," while Webster became uprooted in the course of his agitation.

CHAPTER 2

THE FLAWLESS AMERICAN
The Invention of George Washington

The careers of David Ramsay and Noah Webster pointed to a phenomenon that must have been common to several other *Columbian* contributors. Exalting "the Rising Glory of America," they were caught within a quest for perfected nationhood that could only provoke or intensify feelings of rootlessness. A pre-existing sense of rootlessness may have prompted a contributor like Ramsay to crusade for a flawless America, but the crusade could not furnish him with a sense of anchored stability.

The importance of this perfection-rootlessness dilemma that troubled Ramsay, Webster, and probably other men of the *Columbian* can be exaggerated. Neither the magazine, nor Ramsay's histories, nor most of Webster's linguistic essays were widely read. Although the experience of the *Columbian Magazine* and its two distinguished contributors may have typified a small group of cultivated, relatively prosperous men of letters from established Eastern communities, it was not necessarily representative of American society at large. To determine whether the specific sort of frustrations exhibited by Ramsay and Webster extended beyond a highly literate upper-class crust of post-Revolutionary society, it is necessary to explore an aspect of the patriotic crusade for the Promised Land that involved a significantly larger segment of the population.

This was the development of a George Washington mythology. Myth makers included the learned and the barely literate, men from the cities of the Atlantic coast and from the isolated frontier plots of Ohio and Tennessee, great planters and merchants along with subsistence farmers and petty clerks, Federalists and Republicans, deists and revivalists. If any single phenomenon was detectable among most classes, regions, parties, and denominations in post-Revolutionary America, it was the invention of the mythic Founding Father.

George Washington had not always been exalted. Before his death on December 14, 1799, he was sometimes the victim of biting criticism. In 1776, for example, a tutor in the Washington household claimed that he was awkward, clumsy, and dull.[1] Twenty years later Thomas Paine publicly ridiculed Washington as "pompous," "treacherous," and "a hypocrite." Some Virginians toasted "A speedy Death to General Washington," while a Pennsylvania Antifederalist tried to prove that the Founding Father was a common thief.[2] Following the Farewell Address, a group of congressmen refused to vote their thanks to the retiring President. The editor of the Philadelphia *Aurora* announced that Washington's retirement would end "political iniquity" and "corruption" in the land.[3] But for each critic there were many others who praised the man. During the American Revolution, babies and towns were named in his honor. Receptions, banquets, and balls were staged during the last quarter of the eighteenth century to pay Washington tribute, and he was hailed as "the Savior of His Country."[4] Contributors to the *Columbian Magazine* were among Washington's most enthusiastic boosters. In historical and belletristic writings, they compared him to the greats of classical

[1] William Spohn Baker (ed.), *Early Sketches of George Washington* (Philadelphia: J. B. Lippincott Company, 1893), pp. 26–27.
[2] Dixon Wecter, *The Hero in America: A Chronicle of Hero-Worship* (Ann Arbor: University of Michigan Press, 1963), p. 126; John R. Howe, Jr., "Republican Thought and the Political Violence of the 1790s," *American Quarterly*, XIX, No. 2 (Summer 1967), 149.
[3] Wecter, *Hero*, p. 127.
[4] Marcus Cunliffe, *George Washington: Man and Monument* (New York: New American Library, 1958), p. 15; Wecter, *Hero*, pp. 112, 136; Charles Warren, "How Politics Intruded into the Washington Centenary of 1832," *Proceedings of the Massachusetts Historical Society*, LXV (October 1932), 37.

antiquity and characterized him as "the American Fabius."[5] There can be no doubt that a Washington legend was in the making before the great man died.

After Washington's death, the praise became lavish. Simultaneously, public criticism almost totally ceased. John Adams, Thomas Jefferson, Thomas Paine, and others began to confine faultfinding to private correspondence. Between December 14, 1799, and February 22, 1800, memorial services were conducted in nearly 200 American towns, while 346 eulogies were delivered or written. Not a single eulogy contained derogatory or even neutral statements; all were overwhelmingly favorable. Of the approximately 2,200 titles printed by American presses in 1800, about 400 concerned Washington, and most were laudatory.[6] By 1815 a European traveler, Paul Svinin, reported that "every American considers it his sacred duty to have a likeness of Washington in his home, just as we have the images of God's saints."[7] By 1825 Mason Locke Weems's laudatory *Life of Washington* had gone into its fortieth edition—an unprecedented success for an American author. Textbooks were published to prompt schoolchildren to recite the great man's merits. Towns, villages, countries, colleges, lakes, streams, and mountains were named or renamed "Washington."[8] David Ramsay and Noah Webster were among the dead President's strongest champions. Ramsay delivered a funeral ora-

[5] See, e.g., *Columbian Magazine*, January 1787, pp. 227–28; November 1787, p. 781; February 1789, p. 128; August 1792, p. 140.

[6] Margaret B. Stillwell, "Checklist of Eulogies and Funeral Orations on the Death of George Washington, December, 1799–February, 1800," *Bulletin of the New York Public Library*, XX, No. 5 (May 1916), 403–50, lists most addresses which were subsequently printed. I have consulted all of these and have found only praiseworthy commentary. David Hackett Fischer, *The Revolution of American Conservatism: The Federalist Party in the Era of Jeffersonian Democracy* (New York: Harper & Row, 1965), p. 380, notes the American titles printed in 1800.

[7] Quoted in Marshall W. Fishwick, *American Heroes: Myth and Reality* (Washington, D.C.: Public Affairs Press, 1954), p. 42, and Wecter, *Hero*, p. 137. See also Bernard Mayo, *Myths and Men: Patrick Henry, George Washington, Thomas Jefferson* (New York: Harper Torchbooks, 1963), p. 43.

[8] William Alfred Bryan, *George Washington in American Literature, 1775–1865* (New York: Columbia University Press, 1952), p. 96, comments on the Weems biography. For eulogistic textbooks, see, e.g., William Grimshaw, *Questions Adapted to Ramsay's Life of Washington* (Baltimore: Joseph

tion in January 1800 and wrote a full-length biography; in both he eulogized Washington as a near God. Noah Webster also heaped praise on Washington and contemplated writing the definitive biography of the Founding Father.[9]

By the 1830's there was an enormous body of material to sustain a nostalgic vision of a demigod-like Founding Father. Western man had rarely declared so much with so little basis in fact. No printed collection of Washington's writings existed; few of those who praised him could therefore base their judgments on primary sources. Jared Sparks's edition of Washington's papers was not published until the late 1830's and it contained less than half of the extant manuscripts. In order to perpetuate the image of a demigod, Sparks corrected awkward expressions, grammatical flaws, spelling mistakes, and other errors without indicating that he had done so.[10] But even unlimited access to Washington's original letters and diaries might not have changed matters. They were specific, formal, cliché-ridden responses to specific, practical problems. Washington's deepest thoughts and values seldom surfaced.[11] This meant that even after the appearance of the Sparks edition, there was no substantial body of familiar, objective, and informative data to curtail or limit the myth-making process. Patriots could ascribe

Jewett, 1832); Samuel G. Goodrich, *The Life of George Washington* (Philadelphia: Desilver, Thomas & Co., 1837); Samuel George Arnold, *The Life of George Washington, First President of the United States* (New York: Carlton & Lanahan, 1840). For commentary on naming areas and institutions "Washington," see James Parton, *Life of Andrew Jackson* (Boston: Houghton Mifflin Company, 1887–88), I, 236; Cunliffe, *Washington*, p. 16.

9 David Ramsay, *An Oration on the Death of Lieutenant-General George Washington . . . Delivered in St. Michael's Church, January 5, 1800, at the Request of the Inhabitants of Charleston, South Carolina* (Charleston, 1800); Ramsay, *The Life of George Washington . . .* (London: T. Cadell and W. Davies, 1807); Noah Webster, "The History of the United States," *Old South Leaflets*, III, No. 198, p. 13; Harry R. Warfel (ed.), *Letters of Noah Webster* (New York: Library Publishers, Inc., 1953), pp. 215–16; Allen Walker Read, "Noah Webster's Project in 1801 for a History of American Newspapers," *Journalism Quarterly*, XI, No. 3 (September 1934), 260.

10 Herbert B. Adams (ed.), *The Life and Writings of Jared Sparks* (Boston: Houghton Mifflin Company, 1893), II, 269–74; Bryan, *Washington*, p. 240; Cunliffe, *Washington*, p. 22.

11 For a provocative discussion of this point, see John A. Krout, "The Washington Legend," *The New York Times Book Review* (July 1, 1945), p. 17.

almost any notion or ethic to George Washington without having to worry about contradictory evidence. The Mason Weemses and the John Kingstons could characterize America's first national hero as their imaginations dictated; it was unlikely that their portrayals could or would be invalidated.

Most characterizations of the Founding Father were thus self-serving—the products of patriots who used Washington to cope with disturbing ideological and emotional issues affecting *their own lives* and communities. The accumulation of Washingtonia was far more a reflection of the inner worlds of numerous spread-eagle patriots than a delineation of the actual life of a historical figure.[12] Impulses and apprehensions buried within the subconscious of early American patriots could surface and be articulated. The overwhelming similarity of their articulations pointed, therefore, to certain deep-seated ideological and psychological problems that were basic to a great many crusaders for the Promised Land.[13] Among these problems, the perfection-rootlessness dilemma was foremost. Acknowledging Washington as a heroic product of republican institutions, eulogists claimed that he was at once securely rooted and the essence of American perfection. Perhaps not quite believing that a securely anchored Founding Father could be flawless, they went to great length to establish his impeccable credentials. Eulogists also resorted to counterpointing, ascribing rooted qualities to Washington and carefully balancing these against his flawless features. Above all else, those who constructed the Washington myth seemed intent on proving the compatibility of rootedness and perfection. Many more patriots than Ramsay and Webster were therefore troubled by a clash of fundamentally irreconcilable forces.

[12] In his brilliant essay *Leonardo da Vinci: A Study in Psychosexuality* (reprint. New York: Random House, 1947), p. 109, Sigmund Freud comments cogently on the extreme importance of hero figures to articulate and salve inner emotional needs. The inner needs, he claims, create the hero; it is seldom the other way around.

[13] Unfortunately, most students of the Washington myth have concentrated upon Mason Locke Weems's efforts at constructing a flawless Founding Father and have either ignored or de-emphasized hundreds of other myth makers. As a consequence, they have failed to reveal important ideological and psychological forces common to Washington mythologists. Weems offers an interesting introduction, but only an introduction, to perhaps the most important development in early American popular culture.

II

In his novel *The Spy* (1821), James Fenimore Cooper described the feelings of the fictional Frances Wharton toward George Washington:

> Frances felt, as she walked by the side of this extraordinary man, that she was supported by one of no common stamp. The firmness of his step, and the composure of his manner, seemed to indicate a mind settled and resolved.[14]

This characterization epitomized early-nineteenth-century depictions of a man of solidity, steadiness, and dependability. Lacking the volatile or the impulsive, Washington was a leader who was securely anchored. Unlike David Ramsay and Noah Webster, however, mythic Washington's anchored roots were not explicitly geographic. He was anchored through personal characteristics much more than by association with a specific region or locality. This represented a very significant enlargement upon the concept of rootedness. Washington "stood like the rock which sometimes covered with waves and tempestuous storms seems to yield and depart from its place, but by and by the foaming surges recede and the rock remains firm and immovable." Although he had "a cool and dispassionate temper," he was invariably "firm in his country's cause."[15] In Stephen Simpson's popular 1833 study, *The Lives of George Washington and Thomas Jefferson*, Washington's firm, steady, well-anchored qualities contrasted sharply with Jefferson's erratic, unpredictable, flighty characteristics. The Founding Father's rootedness stood for highly subjective personal qualities that were more amorphous and less definable than the geographic

---

[14] James Fenimore Cooper, *The Spy* (New York: Charles Scribner's Sons, 1931), p. 449.
[15] John Kingston, *The Life of General George Washington* (Baltimore: J. Kingston, 1813), vii; Peter Whitney, *Weeping and Mourning at the Death of Eminent Persons a National Duty. A Sermon, Delivered at Northborough, February 22d, 1800* (Brookfield, Mass., 1800), p. 13.

rootedness that had meant so much to Ramsay and Webster. Eulogists were broadening a basic concept in early American patriotic thought.

Many patriots amplified upon the Founding Father's steady rootedness. Several associated his well-anchored life with his dedication to orderliness. In Samuel George Arnold's *Life of Washington* (1840), personal "order and regularity" somehow demonstrated the first President's steady and rooted quality. He attended to his affairs methodically and regularly. This gave him a clear sense of where he was and where he was going. John Marshall delineated this same quality in his five-volume biography; Washington kept his affairs orderly and regulated amidst the chaos of the Revolutionary War and the forging of a national government. This meant that his life remained stable and secure. The Reverend Eliab Stone made the same point; Washington was always orderly and systematic in his ways while opposing "the restless disorganizers of civil society."[16] Commentator after commentator noted how the Founding Father tried to imbue others with his orderly ways. Seeing chaotic conditions as inherently evil, he tried to convince his countrymen of the benefits of the organized, stabilized life. The organized and the stabilized became the anchored and the rooted.[17]

Eulogists also associated calm prudence and diligence with Washington's well-rooted existence. Because "his steady mind" had "persevered in resisting public clamour," he always achieved his goals. Washington never acted "until every circumstance, every consideration, was maturely weighed; refraining if he saw a doubt, but once decided, going through his purpose, whatever obstacles opposed." His behavior was never "marked with that

---

[16] Eliab Stone, *A Discourse, Delivered at Reading, February 22, 1800* . . . (Boston, 1800), p. 11.

[17] See, e.g., Samuel Tomb, *An Oration on the Auspicious Birth, Sublime Virtues, and Triumphant Death of General George Washington* . . . (Newburyport, 1800), p. 11; Richmond *Enquirer*, May 10, 1833 (essay by "Ned Hitter"); John Lathrop, *Patriotism and Religion, A Sermon Preached on the 25th of April, 1799* . . . (Boston, 1799); William Spohn Baker (ed.), *Character Portraits of Washington as Delineated by Historians, Orators and Divines* (Philadelphia: Robert M. Lindsay, 1887), p. 80; *Literary Magazine and American Register*, II, No. 10 (July 1804), 244.

inconsiderate rashness which often defeats its best-meant intentions." Benjamin Franklin could not have been more prudent.[18]

Extollers assumed that Washington had devoted his life to the New Nation. Because he had shaped America, they were certain that he had imprinted his orderly, prudent, persevering qualities upon the character of the nation. "[When] Columbus discovered a new world, a chaotic mass, dark were the dwellings of the forest," one admirer declared. "Like the eldest morn of time, feeble was the beam of light, till *Washington* kindled her sun, balanced her stars, established her hills, raised her barriers, diffused order and beauty." Washington's solid, persevering ways had "settled on a firm foundation the practical execution of the new system of government." "By his firmness, order soon took place" within the governmental councils of the nation.[19] This theme was stated and restated; the solid, stable, orderly qualities of the country's hero had become characteristic traits of the New Nation.[20] According to this logic, the tumult and uncertainties of post-Revolutionary society were either transitory or insignificant. The institutional dislocations inherent in any venture in nation making were to be ignored or minimized. Life was not as chaotic as it seemed.

Thus, there was great advantage in characterizing George Washington as the essence of Americanism: "His name and that of our country are inseparable." "The history of his life is the history of his country's glory."[21] It was predictable that the greatest of all

18 Anna C. Reed, *The Life of George Washington* (Philadelphia: American Sunday School Union, 1832), pp. 103-04; Thomas Jefferson to Walter Jones, January 2, 1814, as quoted in Bryan, *Washington*, p. 49; Tomb, *An Oration on . . . Death of General Washington*, p. 11.

19 Elijah Parish, *An Oration, Delivered at Byfield, February 22d, 1800, the Day of National Mourning for the Death of George Washington* (Newburyport, 1800), p. 17; Arnold, *Life of Washington*, p. 208; Ramsay, *Life of Washington*, p. 427.

20 See, e.g., John Bailey, *An Oration, In Celebration of American Independence, Pronounced at Natick, July 5, 1824* (Dedham, 1824), p. 7; Baker (ed.), *Character Portraits*, pp. 102, 165; Samuel West, *A Sermon Occasioned by the Death of George Washington . . .* (Boston, 1800), p. 16; Josiah Dunham, *A Funeral Oration on George Washington, Late General of the Armies of the United States* (Boston, 1800), p. 9.

21 Jeremiah Smith, *An Oration on the Death of George Washington; Delivered at Exeter, February 22, 1800* (Exeter, 1800), p. 9; John Horace Platt, *An Authentic Account of the Proceedings on the Fourth of July, 1815,*

men had come from the Promised Land. His "services and virtues" were distinctly American. To praise the man was to laud the New Nation.[22]

By equating Washington's solid, stable personal essence with American national character, eulogists were trying to cope with a problem that had plagued the men of the *Columbian*. For contributors like Ramsay and Webster, national characteristics seemed indeterminate. Political independence was a reality yet Americans remained excessively dependent upon the Old World, particularly upon Britain. Torn between dependence on the mother country and allegiance to the Promised Land, Ramsay, Webster, and other *Columbian* contributors were also distressed by the conflict between local and national loyalties. By characterizing Washington as a man of stable, clearheaded, rooted personal qualities and then linking these qualities with those of the New Nation, patriots were allowing themselves some measure of relief. Through their characterization of Washington, the American and the republican, they could assume that the Promised Land was coming into its own. Washington's well-integrated, sturdy, self-sufficient mind and body implied that the American Republic had been fully liberated from the mother country. His independence and self-sufficiency symbolized that of the New Nation. Most important, the firm, stable, harmonious aspect of the man indicated that the American patriot might also feel rooted. Like Washington, he might find stability in the New Nation. In reality a hot-tempered Virginia planter, Washington was transformed into the independent, well-rooted American. By identifying with his mythic qualities, patriots might gain a sense of personal stability and national pride.

---

with regard to *Laying the Corner Stone of the Washington Monument, Now Erecting in the City of Baltimore* (Baltimore, 1815), p. 44.

[22] Mason Weems, *A History of the Life and Death, Virtues and Exploits of General George Washington* (New York: Grosset & Dunlap, 1927), p. 15; Richmond *Enquirer*, July 13, 1819; Bryan, *Washington*, pp. 30, 234; Levi Frisbie, *An Eulogy on the Illustrious Character of the Late General George Washington* . . . (Newburyport, 1800), p. 8; Ramsay, *Oration on Death of Washington*, p. 29; Baker (ed.), *Character Portraits*, p. 243; Arnold, *Life of Washington*, p. 173; Charles L. Sanford, *The Quest for Paradise: Europe and the American Moral Imagination* (Urbana: University of Illinois Press, 1961), p. 156.

While they dwelled on characteristics associated with Washington's stable, rooted existence, laudators also stressed his flawless essence. In memorial services conducted between December 14, 1799, and February 22, 1800, they consistently asserted that the nation's savior was without blemish. *"Mark the perfect man,"* they declared. Critical of the living Washington, Thomas Paine proclaimed that the dead one had been "inaccessible to human weakness." "In him were combined the most excellent qualities of man," another eulogist asserted. "The picture of man in him was perfect, and there is no blot to tarnish its brightness."[23] Although John Marshall had pledged himself to erudition and balance in his multi-volume *Life of Washington* (1804–07), he perpetuated this appraisal: "No truth can be uttered with more confidence than that his ends were always upright, and his means always pure."[24] At July Fourth celebrations in the "Era of Good Feeling," Washington was toasted as "the greatest and most virtuous of great and virtuous men" and the "perfect Man."[25] In the 1830's patriots continued to refer to him as "a perfect hero, free from all excess," a man of "unparalleled perfection," and a leader of "great and perfect" attributes.[26] In Washington, "the perfect man seemed to have been created for the admiration of the world."[27]

History was cited to prove Washington's flawlessness. He was

23 John Mycall, *A Funeral Address on the Death of the Late General George Washington . . . Delivered in the Baptist Meeting-House in Harvard, February 22, 1800*, p. 25; Thomas Paine, *An Eulogy on the Life of General George Washington, who Died at Mount Vernon, December 14, 1799, in the 68th year of His Age* (Newburyport, 1800), p. 5; Aaron Bancroft, *An Eulogy on the Character of the Late Gen. George Washington. Delivered before the Inhabitants of the Town of Worcester, Commonwealth of Massachusetts, on Saturday the 22d of February, 1800* (Worcester, 1800), pp. 16–17.

24 John Marshall, *The Life of George Washington . . .* (Philadelphia: C. P. Wayne, 1804–07), V, 777.

25 Richmond *Enquirer*, July 18, 1817; July 15, 1825.

26 "Lines on the Statue of Washington in the Capitol," *Southern Literary Messenger*, II, No. 4 (March 1836), 253; *Speeches and Proceedings at the Public Dinner in Honor of the Centennial Anniversary of Washington* (Washington, D.C., 1832), p. 18; *The Early Life of Washington; Designed for the Instruction and Amusement of the Young. By a Friend of His Youth* (Providence: Knowles, Vose and Company, 1838), p. 78.

27 "An Oration delivered by John Tyler, at York Town, October 19, 1837," *Southern Literary Messenger*, III, No. 12 (December 1837), 749.

often compared to Moses.[28] But with the exception of the Hebrew deliverer, all great men of the ancient world and modern Europe dwarfed in comparison to the Founding Father. He represented the highest form of human existence: "Leonidas was patriotic; Aristides just; Hannibal was patient, Fabius prudent; Scipio was continent; Caesar merciful; Marcellus courageous, and Cato of inflexible integrity," but the "virtues which separately distinguished those mighty men of antiquity, were all united in the character of this singular great man, and raised him above the level of mankind."[29] Young Sarah Hale wrote a poem about Washington:

> Greece had her conq'rers—and her Warrior, Rome
> And some proud Column, or some sculptured dome
> Each nation hallowed to her heroes' fame—
> But Washington thy monument's thy Name!
> Their brightest names some sickly vapors shroud;
> Thine, the broad summer's sun without a cloud.[30]

Phillips Payson insisted that, in all of his historical investigations, he had never before encountered such perfection in human form. Others echoed the theme. They compared Washington to Caesar, Napoleon, and other foreign heroes, and concluded, illogically, that he was incomparable; he had all of their virtues, but none of their faults. Washington, the American, was perfect.[31]

Historical comparisons between Washington and foreign heroes were helpful to patriots who fretted over the American experiment in nation making. They posited that the Founding Father was synonymous with Americanism and then deduced that his

[28] Robert P. Hay, "George Washington: American Moses," *American Quarterly*, XXI, No. 4 (Winter 1969), 780–91, offers a very detailed survey of the Washington-Moses comparison.

[29] Quoted in Bryan, *Washington*, p. 68. This remark was subsequently quoted in a toast to Washington at a July Fourth celebration in Milton, North Carolina, in 1825 (Richmond *Enquirer*, July 19, 1825).

[30] Sarah J. Hale, *The Genius of Oblivion and Other Original Poems* (Jacob B. Moore, 1823), p. 87.

[31] Phillips Payson, *A Sermon, Delivered at Chelsea, January 14, 1800 . . .* (Charlestown, Mass., 1800), pp. 11–13; *Legacies of Washington: Being a Collection of the Most Approved Writings of the Late General Washington . . .* (Trenton, 1800), pp. 115–16; Joel Barlow, *Advice to the Privileged Orders in the Several States of Europe . . .* (London, 1793), I, 100; Daniel Dana, *A Discourse on the Character and Virtues of General George Washington . . .* (Newburyport, 1800), pp. 20–21.

superiority over all foreign heroes spoke well of the Promised
Land. A superior, united, independent New Nation followed from
Washington's personal perfection. Therefore, all Americans could
contemplate Washington's perfect character "with supreme de-
light: In it we view the dignity of our nature; and the glory of our
race. As an American character, we may exult in it, as the ornament of our nation and the honor of our age."[32] One eulogist
directly linked the perfect personal "character of our hero" with
the flawless essence of American nationhood:

> The God of Washington and of America, appears to have
> united in him those seemingly incompatible virtues and talents,
> which had been singly distributed among preceding warriors,
> because their combined efficiency and example were emi-
> nently required to form a lasting center of union for our na-
> tion.[33]

Washington's infallibility was the New Nation's hope. According
to late-eighteenth-century political theory, republics could not
endure over long periods because men were flawed creatures of
passion and self-interest whereas republican government required a
virtuous citizenry.[34] Since Washington was the epitome of virtue
and the essence of Americanism, the theory stood negated. Washington's strong, disinterested, errorless qualities assured that the
American Republic would survive.

III

Rootedness and perfection—the two vital concerns of *Columbian* contributors—became characteristic features of the emerging
Washington mythology. But whereas eulogists seemed fully convinced of Washington's rootedness, they took pains to justify his
flawlessness. A substantial portion of early-nineteenth-century
Washingtonia was argumentative—the attempt of patriots to re-

[32] Quoted in Baker (ed.), *Character Portraits*, p. 154.
[33] Quoted in Baker (ed.), *Character Portraits*, p. 105. See also the Richmond *Enquirer*, July 15, 1834, for a strikingly similar remark.
[34] Howe, *American Quarterly*, XIX, No. 2 (Summer 1967), 154–60, comments extensively on this theory. See also William Gribbin, "Republican
Religion and the American Churches in the Early National Period," *The
Historian*, XXXV, No. 1 (November 1972), 62.

move all doubts about the Founding Father's perfection. It was almost as if they were trying to convince themselves.

To establish Washington's flawlessness beyond all doubt, some laudators took up the Calvinist doctrine of human depravity. Although the influence of this doctrine was not as great as it had been at the time of Jonathan Edwards, it remained important at the end of the eighteenth century.[35] Influenced by the legacy of Calvinism, several patriots qualified their praise of the perfect Founding Father. Reverend Joshua Spalding of Salem issued the typical qualification: "There were doubtless, some imperfections in the character of WASHINGTON; but, like the spots in the sun's disk, they were lost in his excellences; they were comparatively small." Another Massachusetts cleric, Daniel Adams, concurred: "Altho perfection is not in man, yet like the sun whose dark spots are lost in the splendor of its own brightness, those little frailties inseparable from human nature, were unseen amidst the effulgence of his virtues."[36] Others perpetuated this characterization, acknowledging that Washington had faults but insisting that when the faults were compared to his virtues, they were inconspicuous.[37] David Tappan and James Kirke Paulding worded the proposition a bit differently. Although Washington was not divine and hence not flawless, he was much closer to the image of God than any other mortal.[38]

Through sophistic statements like these, the Calvinist doctrine of human depravity was accommodated. If America's savior was not entirely perfect, he was very nearly so. But if a fading Calvinist legacy could be circumvented without difficulty, Washington's mortality posed a more serious threat to the concept of a

[35] Donald Meyer, "The Dissolution of Calvinism," in *Paths of American Thought*, edited by Arthur M. Schlesinger, Jr., and Morton White (Boston: Houghton Mifflin Company, 1963), pp. 71–85.

[36] Joshua Spalding, *A Sermon, Preached at the Tabernacle in Salem, December 29, A.D. 1799, on the Death of General Washington* (Salem, 1800), p. 14; Daniel Adams, *An Oration, Sacred to the Memory of Gen. George Washington, Delivered at Leominster, February 22, 1800* (Leominster, Mass., 1800), p. 21.

[37] See, e.g., *Early Life of Washington*, p. 76; Stephen Simpson, *The Lives of George Washington and Thomas Jefferson: With a Parallel* (Philadelphia: Henry Young, 1833), p. 183.

[38] Bryan, *Washington*, p. 62, quotes David Tappan. James Kirke Paulding develops the same point in his *Life of Washington* (New York: Harper & Brothers, 1835), II, 230–31.

flawless Founding Father. How could Washington have been flawless if he died—if his body and mind had ceased to function? If
everything about him was perfect, how could his organs have
weakly succumbed to illness? To patriots who had labored to extol
Washington's strengths, these were serious and pressing questions.
If America's strongest and steadiest inhabitant could catch a chill
and die, how sturdy was he? How accurate were patriots in their
laudatory characterizations? More important, if Washington was
the essence of Americanism, what did his death portend for the
Promised Land? Had Providence ceased to bless the New Nation?
Was it true, as late-eighteenth-century political theorists had predicted, that republican institutions were necessarily of short dura-
tion?

Questions arising from Washington's mortality were absolutely
crucial to contemporaries. They regarded the issue with grave
seriousness. Almost every sermon, oration, essay, or biography
dwelt on the mortality issue. The deathbed scene was central to all
inquiry. A statement issued one week after Washington's death by
James Craik and Elisha C. Dick, his attending physicians, offered
important data for the eulogist. Craik and Dick told how, during
the afternoon and evening hours preceding Washington's death,
they had repeatedly bled him, required him to inhale vapors of
vinegar and water, and tried other remedies—all to no avail. During these last hours, the Founding Father arranged "such few concerns as required his attention, with the utmost serenity, and
anticipated his approaching dissolution with every demonstration
of that equanimity, for which his whole life had been so uniformly
and singularly conspicuous." At eleven-thirty in the evening, while
"retaining the full possession of his intellect, he expired without a
struggle."[39] Two days after this physicians' statement was released
and publicized, a select Senate committee reported an "official"
version of the death to President John Adams:

> Favored of heaven, he departed without exhibiting the weak-
> ness of humanity. Magnanimous in death, the darkness of the
> grave could not obscure his brightness. . . . Thanks to God!

[39] *Annals of the Congress of the United States*, 6th Congress, 1st Session
(1799), X, 206.

his glory is consummated; Washington yet lives—on earth in his spotless example—his spirit is in heaven.[40]

An addendum to the attending physicians' statement, the widely read Senate committee report indicated that Washington died precisely as he had lived—calm, noble, generous, solid, rooted, and without "the weakness of humanity." His organs may have stopped, but his spotless example survived. It was almost as if he had not died—as if Washington were immortal.

In the months and years that followed, commentators returned to this appraisal of the mortality issue whenever they described the deathbed scene. Washington's body remained strong and healthy to the end. He died "before he experienced the various infirmities of age; while his constitution was firm and unbroken." Unlike normal aging mortals, his sturdy body suffered from no "material decay." But he died with an alert mind, as well as a vigorous body. There were no signs of mental deterioration. "His [mental] faculties remained perfect to the last, that he might terminate his days with consistent greatness." "In full possession of his reason he breathed his last without a groan." While "retaining the full possession of his intellect, he expired without a struggle." Extollers repeated this theme with remarkable frequency.[41]

In death the Founding Father demonstrated more than a sturdy body and an active mind. He died as he had always lived—firm, solid, calm, and rooted. In the most acclaimed of all Washington funeral orations, Henry Lee asserted that "his last scene comported with the whole tenor of his life. Although in extreme pain, not a sigh, not a groan escaped him; and with undisturbed serenity he

[40] *Annals of the Congress of the United States,* 6th Congress, 1st Session (1799), X, 18; Baker (ed.), *Character Portraits,* p. 58.

[41] John V. Weylie, *A Funeral Sermon, in Commemoration of the Virtues of General Washington, Delivered by the Rev'd. John V. Weylie, on the Twenty-Second of February, at the Parish of Frederick, and County of Frederick* (Frederick, Md. [?], 1800), p. 17; William Linn, *A Funeral Eulogy, Occasioned by the Death of General Washington. Delivered February 22d, 1800, before the New-York State Society of the Cincinnati* (New York, 1800), p. 36; David Barnes, *Discourse Delivered at South Parish in Scituate, February 22, 1800* (Boston, 1800), pp. 3-4; George R. Burrill, *An Oration, Pronounced at the Baptist Meeting-House in Providence, on Tuesday the Seventh of January, 1800* . . . (Providence, 1800), p. 11; Kingston, *Life of Washington,* p. 78; Marshall, *Life of Washington,* V, 762; Aaron Bancroft, *Life of George Washington* (London, 1808), p. 523.

closed his well-spent life."[42] Washington's death was "a copy of his life," Parson Weems concurred: "In his last illness he behaved with the firmness of a soldier, and the resignation of a Christian."[43] Washington died as he had lived: with dignity, calmness, and confidence.[44]

Consistent with the attending physicians' statement and the Senate committee report, eulogists de-emphasized Washington's physical mortality. The Founding Father had not met with death in any traditional sense. Although laudators could not deny that he had died, they insisted that he never deteriorated in the face of death as other mortals do. If the one man who represented the promise of the New Nation could not live forever, he was one of the few mortals who had not deteriorated while he breathed. In this sense he remained infallible and very nearly immortal, and his death could not dash hopes for the Promised Land. There was no cause for discouragement; extollers had met the challenge of a Founding Father's passing from this world. They had discovered an immortal mortal—or so they hoped.

Because eulogists had linked Washington's life to that of the New Nation, his immortal mortality gave assurances that the Promised Land would survive. This was crucial, for according to the Revolutionary generation's view of history, nations, like individuals, experienced the cycle of birth, youth, maturity, and decay. British and American political theorists, moreover, had persistently noted that the frailty of republics accelerated their life cycles. Unlike monarchical societies, republics could not foster the administrative mechanisms necessary to govern large territories; they could not endure for long periods of time.[45] If America's

42 *Annals of the Congress of the United States*, 6th Congress, X (Appendix), p. 1311.

43 Weems, *Washington*, p. 274.

44 Jared Sparks, *The Life of George Washington* (Boston: Ferdinand Andrews, 1839), p. 487; Ramsay, *Life of Washington*, p. 405; Josiah Dunham, *A Funeral Oration on George Washington*, p. 15; Thomas Condie, *Biographical Memoirs of the Illustrious Gen. George Washington, Late President of the United States of America* (Brattleboro, 1811), pp. 194–95; *Ohio Observer* (Hudson), January 29, 1835; John Royer, *The Monument of Patriotism . . .* (Pottstown, Pa.: John Royer, 1825), p. 38; Arnold, *Life of Washington*, p. 218; Able Flint, *A Discourse Delivered in Hartford, Feb. 22, 1800* (Hartford, 1800), p. 12.

45 Howe, Jr., *American Quarterly*, XIX, No. 2 (Summer 1967), 147–65, clearly delineates both the cyclical view of history and the fear that republican government could not rule over large territories.

Founding Father had not perished, but had, instead, shaped the national character with his immortal qualities, then late-eighteenth-century republican political theory was flawed. It did not amply take progress into account—the capacity of the new American character to sustain republican institutions once they had been perfected. Civilizations progressed and the New Nation would endure.

To lend credibility to the vision of a flawless Founding Father, patriots therefore turned against a republican premise that had been central to the thinking of the Revolutionary generation, and implicitly embraced the more encouraging Enlightenment assumption of progress. But their vision of Washington as an immortal mortal offered directly personal benefits as well as assurances of national progress. It stood to soothe personal anxieties. Scholars like David Brion Davis and Leslie A. Fiedler have demonstrated how late-eighteenth- and early-nineteenth-century Americans were at once fascinated by yet fearful of death. As sentimental romanticism came into vogue, this ambivalence intensified. Calvinist visions of damnation continued to haunt Americans while clashing with new sentimental visions of ascendance to heaven. Death represented hopelessness, damnation, and despair, but it also symbolized a just and sweet remedy for life's ills.[46] By identifying the Founding Father with "Americanism," characterizing him as an immortal mortal, and then deploying him as a model, the patriot found some measure of relief from his own anxieties about death. Although death did occur—although every American citizen would die—death did not quite signify removal from this world and passage to heaven or to hell. As Washington demonstrated, the distinction between life and death was not hard and fast. Thus, the agonizing ambivalence that contemporaries felt concerning the nature and meaning of death stood to be reduced.

In addition to the Calvinist legacy and the mortality issue, there

[46] David Brion Davis, *Homicide in American Fiction, 1798–1860: A Study in Social Values* (Ithaca: Cornell University Press, 1968); Leslie A. Fiedler, *Love and Death in the American Novel* (Cleveland and New York: World Publishing Company, 1962). See also Carl Bode, *Antebellum Culture* (Carbondale: Southern Illinois University Press, 1970), pp. 273–74; Daniel Boorstin, *The Lost World of Thomas Jefferson* (New York: Henry Holt and Company, 1948), pp. 50, 206–08.

was a third problem eulogists wrestled with as they perpetuated a vision of Washington as infallible. They had argued that Washington's mind as well as his body had failed to deteriorate in the face of death. But how good a mind was it? In exalting the man's firm, plodding, well-anchored qualities, were patriots transforming a dull intellect who had lost more battles than he had won into America's first national hero? Had they chosen the wrong man for the vital post, thus subverting their crusade for national strength, independence, and unity? Would Benjamin Franklin have been a better choice? If patriots could exalt only a dullard as their Founding Father, their error might persuade a watching world that America was not the Promised Land. There would be no "Rising Glory of America."

Doubts about Washington's intellectual capabilities appeared in indirect and occasional expressions, but they were unmistakable. Jared Sparks was appalled that Washington could speak only English and had "never even commenced the study of the ancient classics." Thomas Jefferson acknowledged that Washington's mind was not "of the very first order. . . . his colloquial talents were not above mediocrity, possessing neither copiousness of ideas, nor fluency of words." Although he deplored Jefferson and characterized Washington as a demigod, Stephen Simpson agreed on this particular. There was something "deficient" in Washington's mental capability.[47] Others pointed to the man's apparent deficiencies in "wit" and "brilliancy."[48]

Most often, however, patriots took the offensive. They would not allow their hopes for America's "Rising Glory" to be thwarted and rushed to offer reassuring characterizations of Washington's mental qualities. David Ramsay and John Marshall contended that he was not quick-witted because he was cautious and methodical. Before he pronounced a judgment, he carefully accumulated all available evidence and meticulously examined all possible argu-

---

[47] Sparks, *Life of Washington*, p. 9. Jefferson is quoted in Baker (ed.), *Character Portraits*, pp. 168–69. Simpson, *Washington and Jefferson*, p. 1.

[48] See, e.g., Baker (ed.), *Character Portraits*, p. 132; Baker (ed.), *Early Sketches*, p. 77; Jonathan Clark, *Life of General Washington, Late President of the United States* (Albany, 1813), p. 95; *Washingtoniana: A Collection of Papers Relative to the Death and Character of General George Washington . . .* (Petersburg, Va.: The Bladford Press, 1800), xvi.

ments. This took time, but once a decision was made, it was invariably wise and was "steadily pursued."[49] Washington's cautious, steady mental habits were repeatedly cited to explain away the possibility of a dull and deficient national hero. "Neither wit nor vivacity brightened his features," for "it was a face of care, of thought, and of caution; all was calmness and deliberation." "He may have deliberated slowly," but "he decided surely; and when that decision was once formed, he seldom had occasion to reverse it." If the Founding Father's "genius, perhaps, was not of a quick and eccentric kind, his veracity, his integrity, and his judgment were solid."[50]

By confusing personality traits with intelligence, Washington's admirers were interpreting "solidity," "steadiness," "dependability," and "caution" as signs of mental proficiency. "Quickness," "genius," "polish," and erudition were quite secondary. Through these criteria, the patriot could characterize Washington as a more useful and practical thinker than the "visionary" Thomas Jefferson. Of the two, Washington had a mind that could build a nation.[51] Although he had no higher education and could speak neither Greek nor Latin, he had mastered everything that was required of a national leader: his mind was "directed to that which is practical and useful, and not to that which is shewy and specious." Washington had proven that a man "may become an able General without having read Cesar in the original, and a profound Politician without having studied either the Greek or Roman Authors."[52]

Clearly, eulogists were trying to erase doubts about Washington's mental ability by refusing to embrace learning and intellectuality as standards of mental capability. Quickness, brilliance, clarity, and classical education became the characteristics of visionaries who lacked the practical, methodical, steady qualities

[49] David Ramsay, *History of the United States* . . . (Philadelphia: M. Carey, 1816–17), II, 37; Marshall, *Life of Washington*, V, 776. See also E. C. M'Guire, *The Religious Opinions and Character of Washington* (New York: Harper & Brothers, 1836), p. 398.

[50] Baker (ed.), *Character Portraits*, p. 136; Arnold, *Life of Washington*, p. 223; Clark, *Life of Washington*, p. 8.

[51] Simpson, *Washington and Jefferson*, p. 356.

[52] Frisbie, *Eulogy on the Illustrious Character*, p. 9; Baker (ed.), *Character Portraits*, p. 110; *Washingtoniana*, p. x.

necessary to develop the Promised Land. The mind of an intelligent and useful patriot was worlds apart from the mind of an abstract philosopher. While winning the Revolutionary War and establishing the New Nation, Washington's mind had performed magnificently. It was irreproachable.

To rescue the first national hero—the perfect American—from doubts that they themselves had entertained, laudators had therefore resorted to anti-intellectualism. From the standpoint of patriotic contribution, the practical and the methodical were praiseworthy; abstract thought, Old World scholarship, and classical learning became quite useless. The Enlightenment stress on an international community of reason, scholarly dedication, and classical education was repudiated. If this was the cost of dispelling doubts about the Founding Father, it was a cost that most commentators seemed quite willing to bear. Late-eighteenth-century intellectuality and cosmopolitanism simply could not withstand the mounting pressures of *le patriotisme irritable*, particularly the requirement of a perfect national hero. Although Enlightenment assumptions had not always fared well within the pages of the *Columbian Magazine*, Washington eulogists had even less use for the life of the mind.

There was another issue that patriotic extollers confronted to prove that the Founding Father was perfect and that the New Nation's destinies were assured. Two weeks after Washington's death, Gouverneur Morris delivered a funeral oration in New York City:

Beloved, almost adored by the amiable partner of his toils and dangers, who shared with him the anxieties of public life, and sweetened the shade of retirement, no fruit was granted to their union. No child to catch with pious tenderness the falling tear, and smoothe the anguish of connubial affliction. No living image remains to her of his virtues, and she must seek them sorrowing in the grave. Who shall arraign, OH GOD! thy high decree? Was it in displeasure that to the father of his country thou hadst denied a son?[53]

53 Gouverneur Morris, *An Oration, Upon the Death of General Washington* (New York, 1800), p. 8.

What was wrong with Washington that accounted for death without issue? To a people who (as British subjects) had been accustomed to the legal and political stability assured by transitions in leadership within a royal family, the absence of an heir, particularly a male heir, was striking. Indeed, without children of his own, Washington had no family at all. This was a very ominous sign in a society where cherished family ties seemed to be declining—where children seemed increasingly defiant of their parents and where sons left their fathers' farms for cities or opportunities in the West at an increasingly tender age.[54] There were also fears that Washington had done something to bring on God's retribution—that this was why he was left childless. Because Washington was the chief architect of American national character, this possibility pointed to a bleak future for the Promised Land. With obvious apprehensions, eulogist after eulogist noted that the nation's savior had died without issue. The significance of the deficiency had to be discovered.[55]

Washington married Martha Custis in 1759 at the age of twenty-seven and became the legal father of her children from an earlier marriage. The wedlock continued for forty years. Because no effective contraception existed and because Martha Custis had conceived four children in rapid succession during her first marriage, the possibility that Washington was sterile or impotent cannot be dismissed.[56] Dixon Wecter suspects that a youthful attack of mumps rendered the Founding Father sterile. Certain data suggest that Washington had a serious case of smallpox when he was nineteen and a major bout with dysentery six years later. Given the relatively ineffective medical cures of the period, either

[54] Edwin A. Burrows and Michael Wallace, "The American Revolution: The Ideology and Psychology of National Liberation," *Perspectives in American History*, VI (1972), 264–67.

[55] See, e.g., Alexander Garden, *Anecdotes of the Revolutionary War in America* . . . (Charleston: A. E. Miller, 1822), p. 395; Charles W. Upham, *The Life of Washington* . . . (Boston: Marsh, Capen, Lyon, and Webb, 1840), II, 302; *Entertaining Anecdotes of Washington* (Boston: Carter, Hendee, and Company, 1833), pp. 123–24; Weems, *Washington*, p. 374; Bancroft, *Washington*, pp. 532–33.

[56] In *George Washington: Anguish and Farewell, 1793–1799* (Boston: Little, Brown and Company, 1972), p. 492, biographer James Thomas Flexner concludes: "There are strong indications that, despite his known denial, Washington was sterile."

illness could have affected his reproductive capabilities.[57] But the correspondence between Washington and his wife—a potential source of information on sexual deficiencies—has been tampered with. When Jared Sparks compiled the Washington papers, he discovered that Martha Washington had destroyed all but one letter from her husband.[58] We may never know why.

Unrestricted by evidence, patriots offered explanations for Washington's childlessness to fit their needs. None advanced explanations pointing to sterility or impotence, for the Founding Father was necessarily perfect. Patriots had posited too many claims on this assumption to challenge it. Instead, they resorted to heavy-handed polemics to deny Washington's childlessness and to characterize him as a traditional family man. Since Washington took excellent care of Martha Custis' two surviving children, some claimed that this made him their father.[59] Others charged that because the Marquis de Lafayette had served in Washington's army and had learned from the great man, he was Washington's "adopted son."[60] Still other laudators maintained that Washington's "actual family consists of eight persons," directly implying that he had children of his own.[61]

There were other patriots who shunned verbal gymnastics and admitted that Washington fathered no children. But they insisted that this fact was insignificant, for Washington had fathered a nation: "AMERICANS! he had no child—BUT YOU—and HE WAS ALL

---

[57] Wecter, *Hero*, pp. 119, 121; *Early Life of Washington*, p. 31; Baker (ed.), *Early Sketches*, p. 77.

[58] *Connecticut Journal* (New Haven), April 15, 1834.

[59] See, e.g., Arnold, *Life of Washington*, p. 61; Samuel G. Goodrich, *Lives of Celebrated Women* (Boston: Bradbury, Soden & Co., 1844), p. 80; Sparks, *Life of Washington*, pp. 98–99, 344; M'Guire, *Religious Opinions of Washington*, p. 209; Upham, *Washington*, I, 89.

[60] Edgar E. Brandon (ed.), *A Pilgrimage of Liberty: A Contemporary Account of the Triumphal Tour of General Lafayette* (Athens, Ohio: The Lawhead Press, 1944), p. 84; Gilbert J. Hunt, *The Tour of General Lafayette, Through the U. States* . . . (New York, 1825), p. 5; Fred Somkin, *Unquiet Eagle: Memory and Desire in the Idea of American Freedom, 1815–1860* (Ithaca: Cornell University Press, 1967), p. 150.

[61] Jedidiah Morse, *A True and Authentic History of His Excellency George Washington* (Philadelphia, 1790), p. 9; Baker (ed.), *Early Sketches*, p. 142; Jedidiah Morse, *The American Geography* (reprint. New York: Arno Press, Inc., 1970), p. 132. In actuality the eight in the Washington "family" were George and Martha, a nephew and his wife, Martha's two surviving children, Washington's private secretary, and Colonel Humphreys.

YOUR OWN." "WASHINGTON was our *Father*. For his country he felt *more* than the affection, the tenderness, the care and solicitude of a parent."[62] In *The Spy*, James Fenimore Cooper had Mr. Harper, the fictional Washington, wish that his marriage "should not have been childless" and proclaim that "all who dwell in this broad land are my children, and my care."[63] The great man was sometimes toasted: "The Father of his country; his ghost now hovers with parental fondness over the destinies of his child."[64] Others reiterated that Washington's public career made him the greatest parent of all, the father of every American. He was the head of a viable national family.[65] To clinch this argument, patriots contended that childlessness had allowed Washington to channel his energies into national duties. He had been able to devote far more of himself than other mortals to the development of the Promised Land—to supervising the national family. Indeed, he was the most important and fatherly of all Americans because he had produced no children.[66] Theoretically, this claim clashed with the pervasive assumption that population growth was basic to viable nationhood. Washington, the epitome of Americanism and the head of the national family, was being exalted because he did not contribute to the population and because he had no family of his own. Clearly, eulogists were willing to venture far into fantasy to sustain the vision of an impeccable Founding Father. Once again, the Enlightenment imperatives of reason and logic did not weigh in the balance.

Washington's childlessness became a positive asset—a partial explanation for his flawless character. This was precisely the way

[62] Gouverneur Morris, *An Oration*, p. 8; Daniel Dana, *A Discourse on the Character and Virtues of General George Washington . . .* (Newburyport, 1800), p. 7.
[63] Cooper, *The Spy*, p. 450.
[64] Quoted in Richmond *Enquirer*, July 20, 1827.
[65] See, e.g., Benjamin Wadsworth, *An Eulogy on the Excellent Character of George Washington . . . Pronounced February 22, MDCCC* (Salem, 1800), p. 23; *Legacies of Washington: Being a Collection of the Most Approved Writings of the Late General Washington . . .* (Trenton, 1800), iii; Charleston *Courier*, February 22, 1833. In this vein, it is instructive to note that throughout the hundreds of Washington eulogies delivered between December 14, 1799, and February 22, 1800, the famous Farewell Address was persistently referred to as the "parental address."
[66] *Washingtoniana*, xii (footnote); Baker (ed.), *Character Portraits*, p. 216; *The Life and Memorable Actions of George Washington, General and Commander of the Armies of America* (Frederick-Town, 1801), pp. 27–28.

extollers had manipulated other issues that threatened to undermine the concept of the perfect Founding Father. True to Calvinist precepts, he had faults, but they were so insignificant that he was distinguishable from other mortals. Like other humans, he died; yet he remained alert and strong to the end and his spirit survived. His mind seemed dull, but this was because he was extraordinarily thorough and meticulous. There was a consistent pattern of converting potential liabilities into assets. Through reinterpretation, deficiencies became strengths and fortified the image of the infallible Founding Father. There was too great a stake in the image to allow it to be tarnished by hard facts or even by the inner doubts of the spread-eagle patriot. If Washington was flawed and had not conferred durable, meritorious qualities upon the New Nation, there could be no "Rising Glory of America." Local jealousies and persistent Old World influence had cast the American experiment in doubt. The notion of a perfect Founding Father might negate these nagging realities and kindle hopes in America's "Glorious" future. If republican theory did not sanction a demigod—if the head of state was supposed to represent the full range of traits of his constituency—an exception had to be made in the case of the Founding Father. In order to assure national glory, Washington could embody only perfect American characteristics.

There was one final threat to the notion of an infallible Washington. Between 1799 and 1815 the Virginian stood unchallenged as *the* American national hero and the sole embodiment of national perfection. Although Franklin, Jefferson, Paine, and other Revolutionaries were praised, only Washington was persistently characterized as the embodiment of American perfection. By 1815 Americans had another national hero and the Founding Father had a rival. After the American victory in the Battle of New Orleans, the commanding officer, Andrew Jackson, captivated the patriotic imagination. Toasts, songs, sermons, and daily rhetoric frequently characterized Jackson as the "second Washington." "Talk of him as the second Washington!" New York arch-conservative Philip Hone protested. "It won't do now. Washington was only the first Jackson."[67] Nobody was denying the flawless essence of the

[67] Quoted in Carl N. Degler, *Out of Our Past: The Forces That Shaped Modern America* (New York: Harper Colophon, 1962), p. 147.

Founding Father. But as eyes turned to heroic Old Hickory, something worse threatened "the Rising Glory of America." The dead Washington stood to be surpassed in hero worship by his living rival from the West.

Certain obvious facts promoted the characterization of Jackson as the "second Washington." As military heroes against "the mighty British," both men could be characterized as "generals of the best Roman breed." Neither man had children of his own; consequently, Jackson benefited from polemics equating Washington's childlessness with fatherly devotion to the national family. Finally, both men were controversial Chief Executives at crucial intervals in the nation's history. Nonetheless, Washington and Jackson were men of separate generations and had conducted themselves so differently that the myths surrounding each were bound to differ in important respects. In his definitive study of the mythic Old Hickory, John William Ward has concluded that Jackson (in the popular view) lacked Washington's august, steady, methodical, superhuman qualities. Contemporaries perceived Jackson as a man with a shock of unruly hair, sloppy attire, rough manners, and a hot and impulsive temper. Whereas the "first Washington" was characterized as moral and discreet in all particulars, the "second" was depicted as a swearing, card-playing, hard-drinking Westerner who might occasionally become implicated in brawls and sexual indiscretions. The faults of the "second Washington" were openly acknowledged. Followers, as well as opponents, voiced certain doubts about Jackson's assault on the Bank of the United States, his handling of the South Carolina nullification crisis, and even his genocidal Indian policy. According to Professor Ward, this vision of a national hero with personal and public faults indicated that early American patriots were creating an image to mirror their own fallibilities. In developing the mythic Jackson, they were partially exalting their own homespun weaknesses and incompetencies.[68]

Thus, the mythic Jackson differed from the mythic Washington in important respects. But the contrast did not undermine the

---

[68] This is a basic theme within John William Ward, *Andrew Jackson: Symbol for an Age* (New York: Oxford University Press, 1955). Dixon Wecter develops much the same theme in *Hero*, pp. 199–221.

vision of an impeccable Founding Father. Jackson was characterized as a fallible, mortal hero—an earthbound eagle. Within popular mythology, he was easily distinguishable from Washington; he
was not a human deity or even a near deity, and he did not
symbolize the perfection of the New Nation. But though Washington's flawless image survived intact, Philip Hone's observation
remained at issue. Was Washington being eclipsed in the patriotic
imagination by the fallible hero from the West—the "second
Washington"? If he was, the concept of a perfect Founding Father
was being undermined (if only by inattention). Although Louis
Hartz never compares the mythic Jackson directly to the mythic
Washington in his probing essay *The Liberal Tradition in America,* he does note that within two or three decades of Washington's
death it was becoming exceedingly difficult to sustain the myth of
a faultless hero. According to Hartz, the nervous, status-oriented,
profit-seeking life style that Alexis de Tocqueville delineated so
perceptively in *Democracy in America* was accelerating. American
patriots were becoming so deeply embroiled in the quest for
money and reputation by besting their competitors that they
found it hard to believe in a perfect and disinterested warrior-
statesman. For Tocqueville's nervous man on the make, an image
of a fallible Jackson was more credible than the image of an
impeccable Founding Father.[69]

Although this Hartz-Tocqueville hypothesis seems quite plausible, it overlooks the durability of the Washington mythology
with its warrior legend. As a Jackson mythology developed after
1815, it competed with the Washington mythology. Many patriots
who might otherwise have delivered sermons and July Fourth
orations or written biographies on the flawless Washington turned
instead to the flawed Jackson. Nonetheless, the volume of Washingtonia remained very substantial throughout the Age of Jackson.
Influential men like James Kirke Paulding, Samuel Goodrich,
Samuel Arnold, John Tyler, James Fenimore Cooper, and Daniel
Webster crusaded to perpetuate the image of the perfect national

---

[69] Louis Hartz, *The Liberal Tradition in America* (New York: Harcourt,
Brace & World, Inc., 1955), p. 118. The American democrat, Hartz claims,
was "too thoroughly torn by inner doubt, too constantly in danger of selling
out to his opponents, for a warrior legend ever successfully to be built
around him."

hero. Although many patriots of the Jacksonian decades may have needed a fallible Old Hickory, they continued to require a perfect Washington. The concept of a faultless Founding Father continued to be viable and Jackson never supplanted Washington in the patriotic imagination.

The simultaneous existence of a flawless "first Washington" and a fallible "second Washington" requires explanation. In a brilliant pioneering essay, Michael Fellman sees the two contrasting hero images as integrally related: "In order to secure Washington in heaven, Jackson was shaped to exist on earth, to take upon himself any of Washington's possibly dangerous features." Patriots projected many of their personal fears and self-doubts upon the character of the fallible Jackson, Fellman argues. Through the use of the Jacksonian escape valve, the character of the perfect Founding Father could become all the more credible and durable. Mythic Old Hickory reinvigorated mythic Washington and assured that the latter would survive for generations to come.[70] The Fellman thesis explains why contemporaries could perceive of Jackson as the "second Washington"; Old Hickory made the impeccable image of the "first Washington" more believable. If Fellman is correct, the development of a Jackson mythology stemmed from ideological and psychological needs similar to those that had prompted patriots to cultivate a mythic Washington. Indeed, two mythologies, not one, seem to have been required to make the concept of a godlike mortal believable.

IV

Before Jared Sparks published the Washington papers, various arguments and tactics were therefore constructed to perpetuate the vision of a flawless Founding Father who embodied the hope of America. This perfectionist quality of the Washington myth represented a personalized if nostalgic and past-directed focus for the concept of "the Rising Glory of America" that *Columbian* contributors like Ramsay and Webster had articulated. During most of their lives, Ramsay and Webster perceived that the New Nation

[70] Michael Fellman, "The Earthbound Eagle: Andrew Jackson and the American Pantheon," *American Studies*, XII (Fall 1971), 68–71.

was far from perfect—"the Rising Glory of America" was still a hope—but the constant striving of an enlightened citizenry could transform the hope into a reality. According to Washington eulogists, the proof that there would be "Rising Glory" derived from the faultless personage of the Founding Father. His perfection epitomized the potential of the New Nation. He had set the proper precedents for national development. Succeeding generations had to strive to emulate these impeccable precedents for "the Rising Glory" to materialize. He was the beacon light for a "Glorious" future. James Kirke Paulding put the proposition well:

> He [Washington] becomes the great landmark of his country; the pillar on which is recorded her claim to an equality with the illustrious nations of the world; the example to all succeeding generations: and there is no trait which so strongly marks a degenerate race as an indifference to his fame and his virtues.

If Americans failed to emulate Washington's virtues, the New Nation was doomed.[71] The vague patriotic exhortations of *Columbian* contributors for America's "Rising Glory" became more specific and personalized with the Washington mythology.

Pleas like Paulding's were reiterated by others who urged Americans to judge their progress by comparing it with Washington's: "His character is the scale by which the people will graduate the measures and conduct of his successors." Washington's virtues formed standards for proper patriotic behavior.[72] In his 1825 essay, "Pulaski Vindicated," Jared Sparks portrayed Washington as the embodiment of perfection against which all mortal conduct had to be measured.[73] Because Washington was the nation's "brightest ornament" and errorless in every way, he was "the statesman's polar star; the hero's destiny; the boast of age; the companion of maturity, and the goal of youth."[74]

[71] James K. Paulding, *A Life of Washington* (New York: Harper & Brothers, 1835), I, 14.
[72] Richmond *Enquirer*, July 23, 1822; Benjamin Whitman, *An Oration, Pronounced at Hanover, Massachusetts, on the Anniversary of American Independence, July 4, 1803* . . . (Boston, 1803), p. 24.
[73] Jared Sparks, "Pulaski Vindicated from an Unsupported Charge . . . ," *North American Review*, XX (April 1825), 392.
[74] Kingston, *Life of Washington*, p. 147.

More graphically, the rungs of a ladder ran between Washington and the American citizenry. He was perfect and sat upon the top of the ladder while the flawed masses were closer to the bottom. As they imitated his virtues, they became less fallible and ascended the ladder toward perfection. Late-eighteenth-century republican political theory aside, Americans were not necessarily restricted to lives of passion and self-seeking. Washington's flawless qualities proved that they could shed their evil ways. It was particularly incumbent upon the nation's young—the future citizens of the Promised Land—to emulate Washington and strive to ascend the ladder of perfection.[75] But Americans of all ages had to strive to follow Washington's example in both public and private capacities. The effort was the truest test of American patriotism.[76]

If citizens were to ascend the ladder of perfection by emulating Washington's qualities, these qualities had to be defined. Eulogists pointed them out at length. A typical commentator mentioned a general quality that purportedly characterized Washington; then he went on to cite a second and strikingly opposite quality. Washington's infallible features were, therefore, described as counterpointed opposites. Erik Erikson maintains that such counterpointing characterizes the way countries seek out unique identities,[77] and this was precisely what was occurring. Whereas the men of the *Columbian* had concentrated on distinguishing America from Britain in their effort to forge a unique national identity, Washington laudators had focused upon counterpointed descriptions of America's greatest claim to fame.

[75] See, e.g., Ramsay, *Life of Washington*, p. 429; James Madison, *A Discourse on the Death of General Washington . . . Delivered on the 22d of February, 1800, in the Church in Williamsburg* (New York, 1800), p. 3; Thomas W. Gilmer, "An Address delivered before the Virginia Historical and Philosophical Society . . . ," *Southern Literary Messenger*, III, No. 2 (February 1837), 99.

[76] Ramsay, *Life of Washington*, p. 430; Upham, *Washington*, II, 291–92; Whitney, *Weeping and Mourning*, p. 24. Indeed, nearly all funeral orations delivered during the nine weeks following his death carried this plea.

[77] Erik H. Erikson, *Childhood and Society* (New York: W. W. Norton & Company, 1950), p. 244. See also Michael Kammen, *People of Paradox: An Inquiry Concerning the Origins of American Civilization* (New York: Alfred A. Knopf, Inc., 1972), and Michael Kammen (ed.), *The Contrapuntal Civilization* (New York: Thomas Y. Crowell Company, 1971), for excellent materials on counterpointing in American history.

Counterpointing occurred in descriptions of Washington the military man. He was both a fierce, hard, daring warrior and a soft, gentle, prudent commander. He "united the courage of a soldier, the intrepidity of a hero, and the humanity of a Christian." An American soldier emulated Washington when he was bold but prudent, harsh but humane. "Like the Hero of Ossian, he was terrible in the battles of steel. His sword was like the lightning in the field; his voice like thunder on the distant hills. Many fell by his arm; they were consumed in the flames of wrath." But this fierce warrior had a "face like the SUN after the rain; like the Moon in the silence of night; calm as the breast of the lake, when the loud wind is laid!" Washington exemplified both the hard, stern warrior-statesman and the gentle, meek Christian.[78]

The counterpointed description of Washington's military qualities frequently extended to his temperament. In *all* that he did— not only military activities—he was allegedly blessed with a strong, heated, impulsive temper as well as remarkable restraint, discipline, and calmness. "His temper was naturally irritable and high-toned," patriots noted, but he was a firm and well-disciplined man. "His passions were strong, and when really roused, the exhibition was withering," but he was also firmly in control of his impulses. Washington was a man of "clear intellect" and discipline on the one hand, and "passion pure" on the other. With regularity, patriots perpetuated this conflicting characterization.[79]

Americans were usually urged to emulate the social qualities of Washington the civilian. These qualities were also presented within a counterpointed framework. Washington's manners were both "resolute and martial" and "gentle and obliging." He was "modest

[78] Samuel Berrian, *An Oration, Delivered before the Tammany Society, or, Columbian Order . . . in the City of New York, on the Fourth of July, 1811* (New York, 1811), p. 9; Horace Pratt, *An Authentic Account of all the Proceedings on the Fourth of July, 1815, with regard to Laying the Corner Stone of the Washington Monument, Now Erecting in the City of Baltimore* (Baltimore, 1815), p. 12; Dunham, *A Funeral Oration on George Washington*, pp. 12–13; Baker (ed.), *Character Portraits*, pp. 216–17.

[79] Baker (ed.), *Character Portraits*, p. 169; Arnold, *Life of Washington*, p. 225; Oliver Holden, *Sacred Dirges, Hymns, and Anthems, Commemorative of the Death of General George Washington, The Guardian of His Country, and the Friend of Man* (Boston, 1800), p. 18; Clark, *Life of Washington*, p. 95; Simpson, *Washington and Jefferson*, p. 181; Marshall, *Life of Washington*, I, vii.

and unassuming, yet dignified in his manners—accessible and communicative; yet superior to familiarity." "In his manners, he was inclined to be reserved and dry," yet this haughty aspect invariably "relaxed to cheerfulness and sociability." Washington had an exceedingly serious and formal manner but "relished a pleasant story, an unaffected sally or wit, or a burlesque description." More generally, those who praised Washington characterized a man who was formal and haughty yet loose, easygoing, and eminently sociable.[80]

The qualities of the perfect Founding Father were almost invariably articulated through such contrasts. Since Washington was infallible and his qualities were the basis of American character, true patriots were obligated to emulate him. As they succeeded in emulating one counterpointed set of qualities after another, they ascended rungs up the ladder of perfection. Becoming more and more like the Founding Father, they were helping to assure the success of the American experiment—"the Rising Glory of America." In this way, personal achievement was united to national achievement.

To understand why extollers elected to characterize Washington in counterpointed descriptions, one simply has to note the qualities that they emphasized in those descriptions. Washington was perfect, and patriots had to emulate his faultless qualities. But a portion of his perfection consisted of solidity, steadiness, and a sense of place. *Columbian* contributors like Ramsay and Webster had not been able to reconcile perfectionist strivings with their cravings for steadiness and rooted stability. The vagueness and unreality of the concept of perfected nationhood—"the Rising Glory of America"—had threatened to pull the ground from under them—to draw them away from the specific conditions of their everyday lives as they strove for better days. Perfectionist striving could uproot them from their past heritage and contem-

[80] *Early Life of Washington*, p. 20; Kingston, *Life of Washington*, p. 146; Simpson, *Washington and Jefferson*, p. 181; Baker (ed.), *Early Sketches*, p. 142; Uzal Ogden, *Two Discourses, Occasioned by the Death of General Washington, at Mount-Vernon, December 14, 1799* (Newark, 1800), p. 43; Bancroft, *Life of Washington*, p. 535; Marshall, *Life of Washington*, V, 773; Jedidiah Morse, *A True and Authentic History of His Excellency George Washington* (Philadelphia, 1790), p. 9.

porary realities or it could aggravate a pre-existing uprooted condition. By implanting the element of rootedness *within* the concept of a flawless Founding Father, Washington eulogists seemed to have reduced the conflict between perfectionist strivings on the one hand and the need for stability and roots on the other.

Put more explicitly, the counterpointed structure for perceiving and characterizing the mythic Washington gave patriots the language with which to reconcile their quest for perfection with their urge for roots. Rhetorically, the structure was able to accommodate a model of calm stability and a sense of place with a model of aggressive striving toward infallibility. Washington was perfect, and Americans must work to emulate his qualities. In large measure he was impeccable because he had contributed his stable, rooted qualities to the New Nation to make it a secure homeland. The temperamental, mobile qualities of the Founding Father went alongside the rooted qualities, precluding any apparent conceptual clash or contradiction.

Thus, Washington laudators had fused the notion of a rooted homeland to the concept of national perfection—something that *Columbian* contributors had not done—by counterpointing their descriptive language. But though counterpointing could rhetorically fuse conflicting qualities, it could also have psychologically disruptive effects. By drawing together conflicting qualities, the language of counterpointing could expose a conflict that the patriot might otherwise have been able (at least momentarily) to ignore. When the mobile, temperamental war hero was paired with the stable, calm statesman, certain patriots may have sensed that the Founding Father's life ran at cross purposes. As they were urged to attempt to change their ways in order to emulate a solid, unchanging, eminently stable Washington, some may even have feared that they were being required to do the impossible.

Because counterpointing could merge the concept of perfection and the notion of rootedness, it could therefore hold in tension the basic variables of early American patriotic thought. What mattered was the way the patriot perceived the mythic image of the Founding Father. He could perceive a rooted sense of past and present as part of Washington's perfection along with the man's striving, mobile qualities. Both could be smoothly united in the

Washington image. James Fenimore Cooper's popular novel *The Spy* (1821) exemplified this unification. As he led the Continentals to victory in the final months of the Revolution, Washington's thoughts, plans, efforts, and above all his noble mission conveyed the unmistakable image of perfection in motion. Through his errorless, dynamic, moving leadership, national victory was close at hand. But Washington's perfection also comprised calm, stable, methodical, well-rooted qualities. He was never flustered by events, always remaining orderly, methodical, and securely anchored. On a secret mission in unsafe Westchester County, New York, during the war, Washington never panicked. He retained his inner calm and anchored stability while taking shelter with a prominent loyalist family in the vicinity and helping a son in that family who had been accused of espionage for the British. He remained the faultless but eminently stable American patriot, passing one trying test after another. Solid, rooted qualities and bold strivings blended beautifully. While mythologists like Cooper could unify perfectionist endeavor and rootedness, others like Mason Locke Weems could not. In Weems's popular characterization of Washington (*The Life of George Washington*), certain attributes of a stable, well-rooted gentleman were noted. The Founding Father enjoyed religious calm, unruffled loyalty to the nation, steady devotion to friends, self-control, regular habits, and no disturbing "gusts of passion." But Weems's Washington was primarily a man of mobile, striving qualities—military, political, and personal missions to right wrongs and build the Promised Land. Washington was almost always characterized as flawlessness in motion—so much so that the calm, rooted qualities Weems also attributed to him seemed out of place. The Founding Father's perfectionist strivings were ummistakably at odds with his rooted features.

As a Washington mythology developed in the early decades of the nineteenth century, it therefore revealed a dialectic in the thoughts and emotions of a variety of patriots—a Cooper as well as a Weems. Propelled to action by patriotic visions and by diverse other motives, they felt the need for constant striving to effect "the Rising Glory of America" and to commit themselves personally to the ideals that Washington represented. But while they struggled to make the New Nation an honorable land and themselves honorable, Washington-like citizens, they also carved roots and stability. By creating an image of a Founding Father along counterpointed lines, certain patriots must have at least somewhat reconciled their dual aims of perfection and rootedness. But in other cases, counterpointing probably made the underlying clash between perfectionist endeavor and rooted stability even more troublesome.

This is all to say that the Washington mythology offered different theoretical possibilities for different patriots. The counterpointing organizational structure through which that mythology was articulated provided language that must have put many people at ease. Otherwise it would not have been invoked so frequently. But it probably tormented others. In all likelihood, counterpointing had a far-ranging and uneven impact upon patriotic psychology in the New Nation. This is not to say that it had a "liberating" impact in any quarter. The underlying conflict or potential conflict between rooted stability and perfectionist striving persisted. It remained whether one chose, like Cooper, to see a mythic Washington conciliating the conflict or whether one shared Weems's sense of an intensifying clash of opposites. After all, the patriot's image of the Founding Father was only a myth. The words that contoured the myth could cloak or expose the underlying conflict, but however words were arranged, they could not quell the conflict. The relief that counterpointing offered to some patriots could therefore have been neither long-lasting nor curative. In essence, counterpointing was no more than a popular word game. Sometimes the words could convey a temporary and false sense of coping with a perfection-rootedness conflict that could never be resolved in the real world.

The most fundamental problem with the Washington myth was, then, that it created a heroic abstraction for patriots to emulate which, like "the Rising Glory of America," was quite distant from the complex realities of daily existence. It discouraged patriots from dealing on realistic terms with the variously imperfect people and the periodically unstable social conditions that necessarily surrounded their daily lives. The Washington myth made patriots less tolerant of human frailties and diversities (even in themselves), and more reluctant to tolerate personal and social disruptions. The Founding Father that they were to emulate was antithetical to fallibility and instability—he transcended both and the patriot should as well. Consequently, the Washington myth tended to draw patriots away from the tolerance, empathy, and flexibility upon which rich and diversified interpersonal relationships are based. Charles Brockden Brown, the most gifted literary artist of the early national period, successfully analyzed this basic problem that was inherent in Washington mythology. But, as we shall see, sophisticated understanding of the problem did not lead Brown to happiness.

CHAPTER 3

DISSIDENCE

The Case
of Charles Brockden Brown

Charles Brockden Brown was the first American novelist who tried to support himself through his writings. He completed six major novels by the age of thirty, published three literary magazines, edited *The American Register*, and may have been one of several anonymous publishers of the *Columbian Magazine*.[1] However, spread-eagle patriots usually ignored him. Few of his writings generated widespread discussion or controversy. *Alcuin* (1796–97), a fictional dialogue and the first systematic plea for women's rights in the New Nation, went almost unread. Although Brown spent his entire life in Philadelphia and New York, newspapers in both cities overlooked his death. So did David Ramsay, Noah Webster, and almost all Washington eulogists.[2]

Yet Brown's career represented an important episode in the history of early American patriotic thought. He was isolated,

[1] Brown's literary magazines were the *Monthly Magazine and American Review* (1799–1800), the *American Review and Literary Journal* (1801–02), and the *Literary Magazine and American Register* (1803–07). In her essay "A Speculation Concerning Charles Brockden Brown," *Pennsylvania Magazine of History and Biography*, LIX, No. 2 (April 1935), 101, Bertha Monica Stearns argues that he probably belonged to the "Society of Gentlemen" which published the *Columbian* between 1790 and 1792.

[2] Harry R. Warfel, *Charles Brockden Brown: American Gothic Novelist* (Gainesville: University of Florida, 1949), p. 85; Annie Russell Marble, *Heralds of American Literature* (Chicago: University of Chicago Press, 1907), p. 315.

intensely introspective, and attentive to the intricacies of private life and personal emotion. He was not an active patriot until the last seven years of his life. Brown read patriotic materials in the *Columbian,* he was familiar with many Washington eulogies, and he studied works by doctrinaire patriots like David Ramsay and Noah Webster. But he rarely debated with these men and they were not influenced by anything he wrote or said. Sometime around 1803, Brown abandoned his literary career and became a political pamphleteer who championed "the Rising Glory of America" and the flawless Washington. Preoccupied with his literary achievements, scholars have not systematically examined the reasons for this change. Yet these reasons suggest much about the impact of *le patriotisme irritable* upon private, relatively apolitical citizens. Brown's conversion came at a time when George Washington was worshipped with increasing fervor, when Webster's linguistic crusade was at its peak, and when Ramsay was acclaimed by men of letters as America's leading historian. To study Brown before, during, and after his conversion is to get some measure of the strength and influence of avid patriotism in the early national period. The changes that occurred in Brown's life suggest much about the *effects*—the converting power—of the doctrinaire patriots and patriotic writings that we have been considering.

II

Information on Brown's earliest years is thin. Born into a family of Philadelphia Quakers in 1771, he attended the Friends' Latin School in the New Nation's most cosmopolitan city until he was sixteen. With a frail, sickly body, he never experienced the rough and tumble of boyhood but gave himself over to books, maps, prints, and architectural design.[3] Brown's early reading encompassed the liberal and radical political and social thought of the eighteenth century. He was familiar with the works of Locke,

[3] William Dunlap, *The Life of Charles Brockden Brown* (Philadelphia: James P. Parke, 1815), I, 12–13, 49; Donald A. Ringe, *Charles Brockden Brown* (New York: Twayne Publishers, Inc., 1966), p. 18.

Rousseau, Voltaire, and Condorcet, and he frequently visited with Benjamin Franklin. But he was most fascinated with such exponents of radical political and social change as Mary Astell, Thomas Holcroft, William Godwin, and Mary Wollstonecraft.[4] Privately, Brown noted that he was not excessively concerned with their specific proposals for change. Rather, he was mainly attracted to radical theorists for personal reasons. Like many of them, he felt estranged from the accepted ideas and life styles of his society.[5] He first broke into print in the *Columbian Magazine* at the age of eighteen. In a series of four essays entitled "The Rhapsodist," Brown wrote in delicate, retreating prose and shunned the hard, aggressive, calculating ways that he felt pervaded contemporary Western culture.[6] This same gentle, subdued quality pervaded his Common Place Book. For young Brown, maturity involved the "accession of wisdom" through the "diminutions of our sensibilities." To adjust to the dominant culture of the society was to become "cold, sapless, and inanimate."[7] He could therefore sympathize with the soul searchings of contemporary Old World radical intellectuals.

Although Brown was quite alienated, it appeared for a time that he would have to deal with the dominant society through the seemingly fierce competition of the legal profession. His parents and older brothers recognized the young man's intellectual gifts and urged him to enter one of the New Nation's most honored callings. Sixteen years old in 1787, he went to read law with Alexander Wilcocks, a prestigious Philadelphia attorney.[8] Brown detested his

[4] David Lee Clark, *Charles Brockden Brown: Pioneer Voice of America* (Durham: Duke University Press, 1952), pp. 110–11; William Dunlap, *Memoirs of Charles Brockden Brown, the American Novelist* (London: Henry Colburn and Co., 1822), p. 96; Janet Wilson James, "Changing Ideas about Women in the United States, 1776–1825" (Ph.D. dissertation, Harvard University, 1954), p. 114. See also the extensive passages from Wollstonecraft and Godwin that Brown copied into his Common Place Book for 1795–97 (Charles Brockden Brown Papers, Vol. IX, Historical Society of Pennsylvania).

[5] Common Place Book, Charles Brockden Brown Papers, Vol. IX, Historical Society of Pennsylvania.

[6] Brown's "The Rhapsodist" was serialized in the *Columbian Magazine* from August through November 1789.

[7] David Lee Clark (ed.), "Unpublished Letters of Charles Brockden Brown and W. W. Wilkins," *Studies in English*, XXVII, No. 1 (June 1948), 104.

[8] Clark, *Brown*, p. 22; Dunlap, *Life of Brown*, I, 41.

INVENTORS OF THE PROMISED LAND 8 2

apprenticeship and left Wilcocks' offices in 1793, determined never to return. He saw the legal profession as a mirror of the ills of society. It was characterized by a dishonest, mind-warping, money-grubbing spirit: "Our intellectual ore is apparently of no value but as it is capable of being transmuted into gold, and learning and eloquence are desirable only as the means of more expeditiously filling our coffers."[9] Brown's family and friends strongly disapproved of his decision to abandon the law. But they were more distressed when he announced his new choice of a profession—fictional literature. Their opposition was consistent with the widespread distaste for fiction throughout the New Nation—it implanted false ideas about life. *Columbian* editors and contributors and many Washington eulogists had, for example, vigorously censured the reading of novels. But Quakers were even more opposed to fiction. The Society of Friends regarded the novel as a degraded amusement. Brown was therefore set against his immediate family and Philadelphia Quaker culture.[10]

The selection of professional writing as a calling was consistent with Brown's general abhorrence of the anti-intellectualism and self-seeking ways of the society about him. Above all, this choice represented a rejection of accepted sexual roles, for fictional literature was regarded as an unmanly occupation. Sarah Wentworth Morton or Susanna Haswell Rowson might write novels for a female readership, but a man's work had to involve agriculture, law, commerce, manufacturing, or the ministry. Brown accepted this occupational dichotomy. He characterized law as a coarse, sordid, masculine activity and fictional literature as refined and feminine.[11] Thus, in leaving the law for literature, he must, to some extent, have been trying to withdraw from a crude and self-

[9] Clark (ed.), *Studies in English*, XXVII, No. 1 (June 1948), 94. Many other Brown letters that Clark publishes here for the 1787–93 period confirm Brown's contempt for the legal profession.

[10] Herbert Ross Brown, *The Sentimental Novel in America, 1789–1860* (Durham: Duke University Press, 1940), Ch. 1; William J. Free, *The Columbian Magazine and American Literary Nationalism* (The Hague: Mouton & Co., 1968), pp. 60–64; Harry R. Warfel (ed.), *The Rhapsodist and Other Uncollected Writing by Charles Brockden Brown* (New York: Scholars' Facsimiles & Reprints, 1943), p. vi.

[11] Charles Brockden Brown, *Alcuin: A Dialogue* (reprint. New York: Grossman Publishers, 1970), p. 18; Warfel (ed.), *Rhapsodist*, p. 108; Clark, *Brown*, pp. 103–04.

seeking masculine culture in order to embrace a vaguely conceived feminine culture that seemed to be free from these ills.

Brown's published works during his half-dozen years as a professional novelist confirm this hypothesis. Between 1795 and 1802 one novel followed another in rapid succession. A woman was usually the most laudable character; Brown fully identified with her and wanted his readers to do so as well. She was Elizabeth Carter in *Alcuin*, Sophia Westwyn in *Ormond*, Clara Wieland in *Wieland*, Achsa Fielding in *Arthur Mervyn*, Louisa Calvert in *Stephen Calvert*, and Clara in *Clara Howard*. Through these characters, Brown pleaded for expanded female options. In a society dominated by crude, expedient males, it was important to widen the influence of women. Brown made his most forceful plea for the enhancement of feminine influence in *Alcuin*, his first novel. The narrative featured a dialogue between a widowed Philadelphia bluestocking, Elizabeth Carter, and Alcuin, a poor and confused schoolmaster. Carter quickly emerged as the more sophisticated of the two and Brown endorsed her perspective. From the start, she condemned society's retriction of sexual roles:

> Nothing has been more injurious than the separation of the sexes. They associate in childhood without restraint; but the period quickly arrives when they are obliged to take different paths. Ideas, maxims, and pursuits, wholly opposite, engross their attention. . . . All intercourse between them is fettered and embarrassed.[12]

This separation of the sexes was unjustified, Carter charged, for women were fully the equals of men in everything except morality; in that they were superior. For this reason, women had to be granted political equality, full property rights, and the same competent, solid education that men received: ". . . of all forms of injustice, that is the most egregious which makes the circumstances of sex a reason for excluding one half of mankind from all those paths which lead to usefulness and honour."[13] Although

---

[12] Brown, *Alcuin*, p. 24.
[13] Brown, *Alcuin*, p. 14. It is noteworthy that by the end of the nineteenth century, the notion of female moral superiority had become basic to the anti-suffragette position. Women were too refined and delicate for crude electoral politics.

woman was unjustly restricted in many areas, Carter added, traditional marital life posed the grossest limitation of all. It "renders
the female a slave to the man. It enjoins and enforces submission on
her part to the will of her husband . . . it leaves the woman
destitute of property. Whatever she previously possesses, belongs
absolutely to the man." The solution—the way to widen female
options—was to drastically modify married life. Man and wife
should retain their personal property and should dwell in separate
quarters. Their relationship should consist of "occasional interviews
and personal fidelity" where they could meet one another as good
friends. If this meeting ever became strained—if it ceased to be
"found on free and mutual consent"—either party was entitled to
a divorce.[14] Thus, marital bonds had to be loosened for greater
individuality. But to promote woman's freedom, Mrs. Carter
would not go so far as to overthrow the institution of marriage.

In subsequent novels, Brown continued to demand new opportunities for women. However, he did not argue as systematically as he had in *Alcuin*. In *Arthur Mervyn*, for example, a
neighbor boy asked Arthur if it was not "whimsical" and foolish
for a young man to knit stockings. "Just as whimsical a business
for a young active woman," Arthur replied. "Pray, did you ever
knit a stocking?"[15] In *Ormond*, Constantia Dudley argued against
female intellectual inferiority: "Her reasonings might be fallacious
or valid, but they were so composed, arranged, and delivered, were
drawn from such sources, and accompanied with such illustrations,
as plainly testified a manlike energy in the reasoner."[16] In *Wieland*, Clara Wieland was similarly characterized. She had a better
mind than any of the men whom she encountered.

As a novelist, Brown became more than a special pleader for the
expansion of women's rights. He fretted over increasing cruelty
and callousness in the entire society. Arthur Mervyn was disturbed
because he was able to bury his beloved Susan Hadwin without
deep emotions: "I heaped earth upon her limbs and covered them

14 Brown, *Alcuin*, pp. 71, 78, 84, 88.
15 Charles Brockden Brown, *Arthur Mervyn; or, Memoirs of the Year 1793*
(Philadelphia: M. Polock, 1857), II, 62.
16 Charles Brockden Brown, *Ormond; or The Secret Witness* (reprint,
New York: American Book Company, 1937), p. 131.

from human observation, without fluctuations or tremors."[17] In *Ormond*, the hard and callous woman emerged as a threat. Martinette de Beauvais had been so active in the battles and intrigues of the American and the French revolutions that she became a coarse, insensitive beast. On the other hand, totally soft, sexual, feminine women like Helena Cleaves of *Ormond* or Mary Waldegrave of *Edgar Huntly* could not respond constructively to the hardening of society, for they were malleable, dependent, undeveloped creatures. Sophia Westwyn (*Ormond*) represented an alternative to these extremes. Westwyn embodied a wholesome integration of coarse "masculinity" and soft, passionate "femininity." She was sentimental, cultivated, and thoroughly schooled in the ways of female propriety. But Westwyn was also tough and shrewd. She was willing to leave her husband in Europe, to search throughout the New Nation for her friend Constantia Dudley, to manage Constantia's property, and to take her protectively back to Europe in "masculine" fashion. Clara Wieland, heroine of *Wieland*, resembled Sophia Westwyn. She had her full share of feminine delicacy and propriety and was even the victim of that traditional female weakness—fainting spells. Clara could also endure severe emotional stress; leading men in the novel could not. Above all, she had a tough, shrewd mind with striking powers of analysis. Achsa Fielding of *Arthur Mervyn* shared this mixture of the hard and the soft—the masculine and the feminine—and could also cope with the ways of the world without self-seeking or degrading others. Well educated and familiar with the bitterness of life, Fielding was able to protect and stabilize the confused, indecisive Arthur Mervyn. At the same time, she could practice female "gentility" and sensitivity; she was no brute. In *Clara Howard*, the heroine was soft, emotional and sensuous but also cautious, tough, and self-reliant. Whereas Philip Stanley, her lover, was overrun by the "Enthusiasm of Love," Clara Howard's commanding, prudent ways allowed her to guide Philip away from rash, impulsive acts. Even Elizabeth Carter of *Alcuin* balanced hard and soft qualities. She demanded radical social innovations while her solid, steady persuasive powers dominated the unstable, flighty Alcuin. At the

[17] Brown, *Arthur Mervyn*, II, 62.

same time, Carter was kind and well-mannered and displayed the proper measure of female reserve.

In rejecting the coarse masculine culture of the dominant society, Brown, then, did not entirely embrace soft, emotional, sensuous womanhood. Helena Cleaves was to be pitied, not emulated. The ideal human being possessed softness and hardness, dependence and self-sufficiency, restraint and aggressiveness. Indeed, the ideal qualities of Sophia Westwyn, Clara Wieland, Achsa Fielding, Clara Howard, and Elizabeth Carter resembled the counterpointed descriptions of George Washington; these women were characterized by opposite traits. But whereas Washington laudators had delineated counterpointed traits to move patriots up a ladder of perfection, Brown had no such intention. He was irritated by a shallow, transitory quality in Washington eulogies. They represented "intellectual drivelings" of "simpletons" and reflected poorly on American taste.[18] Differing from Washington eulogists, Brown did not urge people to strive toward perfection—to emulate Washington's flawlessness or to bring on "the Rising Glory of America." Like the extollers, he counterpointed his descriptions of desirable qualities, but he placed these descriptions within a flexible, open-ended, hard-soft framework that stood to broaden human options. The crude coarseness of the dominant male culture seemed confining, but so did the soft, sensuous world of Helena Cleaves. For Brown the novelist, people should not struggle to perfect themselves; they should experience and act out all of life's possibilities—the crude and the harsh as well as the refined and the sentimental. There should be no climbing or perfecting—simply experiencing life's diversities.

Through the self-perfecting strivings of a noble citizenry, *Columbian* contributors and Washington boosters had predicted that a flawless nation would arise. But Brown rejected the concept of perfectibility. At the age of fifteen, he had written an applicable verse:

> The human mind in various shape is made,
> Our godlike virtue, foibles cast a shade,

[18] *Monthly Magazine and American Review*, I (December 1799), 447; II (February 1800), 102–05; Warfel, *Brown*, p. 172.

Tho' chief she reigns, tho' sage discretion guide:
Perfection to a Mortal—is denied.[19]

Later, as a full-time novelist, Brown explained why he rejected the concept of human perfectibility. Human beings were error-prone and always would be. "I reflected with amazement on the slightness of that thread by which human passions are led from their true direction," Arthur Mervyn proclaimed.[20] In *Wieland*, Henry Pleyel qualified a summary of a conversation that he had overheard: "Considering the limitedness of human facilities, some error may possibly lurk in those appearances which I have witnessed." Theodore Wieland criticized a jury that had found him guilty of murdering his wife and children. The jurors had failed to recognize their human judgmental limitations; they had offered their "bounded views and halting reason, as the measure of truth."[21] Young Edgar Huntly echoed this theme: "How little cognizance have men over the actions and motives of each other! How total is our blindness with regard to our performances!"[22] Charges such as these—demands for the recognition of perpetual human fallibility—appeared so frequently in Brown's fiction that he must have rejected the perfectionist premises of *Columbian* contributors and Washington eulogists. His characterization of Carwin, the ventriloquist in *Wieland*, makes this unmistakably clear. Carwin was brilliant, rational, calculating, and exceedingly cautious; yet his ventriloquism unintentionally led to Theodore Wieland's suicide and to the death of Wieland's wife and children. Even the most exceptional of men could not act flawlessly; because Carwin was human he could not control life's course. Brown insisted that chronic weakness, limitations, and proneness to err were natural elements within the human personality whereas *Columbian* contributors and Washington extollers did not. Brown saw no point in man struggling after a target he could never even approach,

---

19 Elijah Brown copied this verse, a portion of Brockden Brown's first poem, into his Common Place Book (Charles Brockden Brown Papers, Historical Society of Pennsylvania).

20 Brown, *Arthur Mervyn*, I, 38.

21 Charles Brockden Brown, *Wieland; or, The Transformation* (New York: Hafner Publishing Co., 1958), pp. 137, 199.

22 Charles Brockden Brown, *Edgar Huntly; or, Memoirs of a Sleep-Walker* (reprint. Port Washington, N.Y.: Kennikat Press, Inc., 1963), p. 267.

whether it was an impeccable Founding Father or "the Rising Glory of America."[23]

Therefore, Brown totally rejected the premise that man's purpose in life was to struggle upward upon the rungs of a ladder of perfection. Because man was easily confused and perpetually error-prone, it was foolish to urge him on in this way. Arthur Mervyn, for example, could not comprehend the true dimensions of a yellow-fever epidemic in Philadelphia; reasoning failed him. To gain perspective on the causes and consequences of the epidemic, he would foster a mythic conceptual structure in his own mind. This mythic structure would lead him to disastrous conduct and would cause him to foster a second mythic structure with even more horrendous consequences. There were random qualities in life that man could neither accurately conceive nor properly respond to. Brown hammered home this point again in *Wieland*. Clara Wieland's attempt to explain why her brother had destroyed his wife, his children, and himself constituted the heart of her narrative. In the end Clara concluded that she could not explain her brother's conduct. She saw that her senses, like those of all other humans, were imperfect—that they were persistently absorbing erroneous information. This invalidated her reasoning: "If the senses be depraved it is impossible to calculate the evils that may flow from the consequent deductions of the understanding." Yet people constantly ingested faulty data through "depraved" senses, and they acted upon this data. This is what happened to Henry Pleyel; he broke with Clara after he thought he had heard her express love for Carwin—in reality he heard only Carwin's imitation of Clara's voice. "Ideas exist in our minds that can be accounted for by no established laws," Clara Wieland concluded. Since man was a fallible creature who frequently perceived

[23] Kenneth Bernard points toward this general appraisal of Brown's thoughts as a novelist in his provocative essay "Charles Brockden Brown," in *Minor American Novelists*, edited by Charles Alva Hoyt (Carbondale: Southern Illinois University Press, 1970), pp. 3–4. Bernard suggests that Brown's close friend Elihu Hubbard Smith (a pioneer researcher in abnormal psychology) may have impressed upon Brown the fallible essence of human personality. See also Robert Hemenway, "Fiction in the Age of Jefferson: The Early American Novel as Intellectual Document," *Midcontinent American Studies Journal*, IX, No. 1 (Spring 1968), 97.

erroneous data and acted upon it, life was necessarily random and unpredictable.[24]

Brown's plea for a life combining hard and soft qualities—refined feminine sentimentality and rough masculine aggression—was in logical conflict with his notion of human fallibility and a random, contingent universe. How could a fallible person in a random universe consciously attempt to open his life to both the hard and the soft? Were not human direction and planning useless? Brown never discussed this conflict in his thought, perhaps because he did not feel that it was of overriding importance. Urging readers to combine hard and soft qualities, he was pleading with them not to block off any vital aspect of human experience. Expounding the fallibility of man and the randomness of man's world, Brown was warning readers to avoid self-complacency—to recognize that there was much to life that went beyond their usual experiences and understandings. On the most fundamental level, Brown was pleading for the mind and the body to be kept open to all varieties of experiential possibilities. Rigid dogmas and set directions, so easy to come by, were the bane of human existence. By combining hard and soft qualities as Sophia Westwyn had, one could lead a more open-ended existence. There was no flawless Founding Father or Glorious Nation as the goal of her pursuits. Life's diversities were to be experienced here and now; they were not abstract and distant goals to be sought after.

Opposed to the perfectionist quest that was basic to early American patriotic thought, Brown detested the whole dogmatic spirit of *le patriotisme irritable*. He praised benevolent European (particularly British) characters who crossed the ocean to rescue American friends in peril, and he even resolved the dilemmas of certain American characters by having them move to Europe. Brown also opposed Noah Webster's plan for a distinctive "American language" because it would foster an unnecessary separation and tension between Britain and America. Webster suffered from excessive "*amor patriae*, the national spirit."[25] Brown analyzed several Washington eulogies and found them equally extreme and

24 Brown, *Wieland*, pp. 39, 99.
25 Clark, *Brown*, pp. 145–46.

dogmatic.[26] Spread-eagle patriotism was cliché-ridden and obscured the many problems that the New Nation would have to confront. These problems were substantial. For example: "Even the government which is said to be the freest in the world, passes over women as if they were not." It was totally unjustifiable for propertied white males to continue to dominate the New Nation.[27] America's cultural backwardness constituted another blemish that the doctrinaire patriot obscured. Owing to the "unpolished habits" of the citizenry, skilled and proficient artists were usually denied patronage to sustain themselves.[28] Rather than support their artists, Americans were busy fighting duels, and this put them "at least upon a level with the corruptest of them [nations]."[29] Obscuring the country's many faults, avid patriots were urging the expansion of her territorial boundaries. Brown adamantly opposed territorial aggrandizement.[30]

Thus, during his years as a professional novelist (1795–1802), Brown was decisively at odds with *Columbian* contributors like David Ramsay and Noah Webster and with Washington eulogists as well. Although he opposed doctrinaire patriotism, Brown did not develop a simplistic or dogmatic anti-American posture. Rather than attack or exalt the New Nation, he chose to describe and to analyze. Through the words of Sophia Westwyn, Brown compared America to Europe along lines Alexis de Tocqueville would advance three decades later:

> I found that the difference between Europe and America lay chiefly in this: that, in the former, all things tended to extremes, whereas, in the latter, all things tended to the same level. Genius and virtue, and happiness, on these shores, were distinguished by a sort of mediocrity. Conditions were less unequal, and men were strangers to the heights of enjoyment and the depths of misery to which the inhabitants of Europe are accustomed.[31]

[26] *Monthly Magazine and American Review*, II (February 1800), 102–05, 131.
[27] Brown, *Alcuin*, pp. 29–32.
[28] Brown, *Ormond*, pp. 194–95.
[29] *Monthly Magazine and American Review*, III (December 1800), 408–09.
[30] *Monthly Magazine and American Review*, III (August 1800), 131–37.
[31] Brown, *Ormond*, pp. 195–96.

The New Nation was neither superior nor inferior to the Old World; it was simply different. In *Wieland*, Brown made it clear that the United States had no European castles or dungeons; life went on in simple, ordinary houses constructed upon a unique American landscape. Nonetheless, America was no less exempt from terror and horrors than the Old World. The tragedies of the Wieland family proved that sin could triumph in the Promised Land.[32] Brown made the same point in *Edgar Huntly*. He consciously shunned the "Gothic castles and chimeras" that typified Europe and focused upon the "incidents of Indian hostility, and the perils of the Western wilderness" which were uniquely American.[33] The "puerile superstition and exploded manners" of the Old World setting were no worse than the American frontier wilds, where both Clithero and Edgar Huntly went insane. Brown's was not the romanticized frontier that would soon characterize the nineteenth-century Western novel. Finally, although Brown carefully distinguished life in the New World from the Old, he did not use polemics to try to deny the past. Unlike many *Columbian* contributors and Washington eulogists, he would not explain away the English origins of American civilization:

> We are united by language, manners, and taste, by the bonds of peace and commercial intercourse, with an enlightened nation, the centre of whose arts and population may be considered as much *our* centre, as much the fountain whence *we* draw light and knowledge, through books, as that of the inhabitants of Wales and Cumberland.[34]

During his years as the New Nation's first professional novelist, therefore, Brown dissented from the basic elements of American patriotic thought in *all* important respects. Unlike avid patriots, he offered a message of gloom and despair. Life was dismal in the Old World but it was also dismal in the Promised Land. Brown refused to recite the characteristic July Fourth dogmas, but he also rejected the rabid anti-Americanism that characterized numerous

[32] Larzer Ziff, "A Reading of *Wieland*," *PMLA*, LXXVII, No. 1 (March 1962), 55–56, provides a useful discussion of this point. See also Warfel, *Brown*, p. 5.

[33] Brown, *Edgar Huntly*, p. 4.

[34] *American Review and Literary Journal*, I (1801), iv.

European travelers. Most important, he did not evidence certain psychological qualities of the doctrinaire patriot. Unlike *Columbian* contributors or Washington eulogists, there is no indication that he sought either geographic roots or a more amorphous psychological sense of rootedness and stability in the emergence of the Promised Land. Brown, moreover, explicitly rejected the perfectionist psychology designed to inspire patriots to promote national grandeur. Thus, unlike David Ramsay, Noah Webster, and other active patriots, he was not plagued by the uprooting consequences of perfectionist strivings.

III

Although Brown's novels contained fresh and significant ideas, they did not support him financially. He could not afford to continue as the New Nation's first professional novelist. His brothers pleaded with him to abandon literature and thereby re-establish rapport with the Society of Friends. They also urged him to become a partner in their Philadelphia importing firm and to share equally in the management and the profits; great risks were involved but the potential monetary rewards were substantial. Poor and discouraged, Brown joined the firm in 1801 and remained until it dissolved in 1806. Then he began his own pot-and-pan retail business and pursued this trade until his death in 1810.[35] As he turned to business activities, Brown disengaged from most of his literary projects. He wrote only two fictional pieces during the last seven years of his life—"Sketches of a History of Carsol" and "Sketches of a History of the Carrils and Ormes." Although he continued as a literary editor, he seemed apologetic for the achievements of his novel-writing years. In October of 1803, Brown introduced the first issue of his *Literary Magazine and American Register* on a striking note:

> I am far from wishing, however, that my readers should judge of my exertions by my former ones. I have written much, but take much blame to myself for something which I have written, and take no praise for any thing. I should enjoy a larger

[35] Clark, *Brown*, pp. 194, 197, 216; Warfel, *Brown*, pp. 9, 189–90.

share of my own respect, at the present moment, if nothing had ever flowed from my pen, the production of which could be traced to me.[36]

Brown's change involved more than a repudiation of his novels and a vigorous involvement in commercial affairs. As the Napoleonic Wars hampered the shipping ventures of his import firm and cut into the profits of other Philadelphia merchants, he became a pamphleteer. Brown took up his pen again, this time in the interests of local Federalists and their mercantile activities. He earned much more money and praise from his anti-Jeffersonian political pamphlets for merchant rights than he had ever earned from fiction. His 1803 pamphlet, *An Address to the Government of the United States, on the Cession of Louisiana to the French,* created a national sensation. For the first time in his life, Brockden Brown had achieved widespread recognition.[37] He became more than a merchant-pamphleteer. Between 1806 and 1809 Brown completed the first five volumes of *The American Register.* The volumes detailed contemporary international diplomacy, summarized federal laws, listed currently published books, and provided specialized economic data. Brown's focus was upon the minute details of public affairs; he never commented about the philosophic roots of private experience. Brown's Common Place Book also illustrated his new orientation; it contained very specific information on international trade and diplomacy. Abstract philosophic issues no longer concerned him.[38]

Brown's sexual attitudes also changed. He ceased to favor a Sophia Westwyn or an Elizabeth Carter—a woman who combined soft sentimentalism with hard, domineering aggression. A woman should possess "all the soft and winning graces, the sweet smiles of winning beauty, the obedient blush of modesty, the charming fears of dependent weakness, and the tender apprehensions of the feeling heart." "The principal destination of all women is to be mothers," Brown proclaimed. Their qualities differed markedly from those of men. It was regrettable that occasionally, through

---

[36] *Literary Magazine and American Register,* I, No. 1 (October 1, 1803), 4–5.
[37] Warfel, *Brown,* pp. 10, 206–07.
[38] Common Place Book for 1808–09, Charles Brockden Brown Papers, Vol. X, Historical Society of Pennsylvania.

"some gross accident, as happens in the production of monsters, the external *male form* has been superinduced upon a *female stock.*" Women were soft creatures designed for male consolation; men were hard and aggressive breadwinners. Brown had reversed himself, accepting the rigid hard-soft dichotomy he had once worked to discredit.[39]

As a novelist, Brown had not only resisted the coarse masculinity of the dominant society; he consistently opposed war, American territorial expansion, and the accompanying jingoistic sloganeering. But in his later years there was the Brown brothers' importing firm to consider. James and Armitt Brown denounced President Jefferson for leaving American merchant ships unprotected and at the mercy of British and French war vessels. They demanded an American fleet to guard merchant ships.[40] Responding to his brothers' appeals, Brockden Brown penned one attack after another against Jefferson (and later Madison) with the crude patriotic clichés he had deplored during his literary years. The President was duty-bound to defend American shipping and commerce against foreign interference, Brown proclaimed, even at the risk of war:

> Things may be brought to the alternative of submitting to insult or going to war. In that case, not pretending to conceal the misfortune which must attend hostility, we think everything is to be done and suffered to vindicate the national honour. . . . If any gentlemen suppose the war will be feeble and harmless, they are deceived. It must be severe and bloody. But it must be sustained manfully.[41]

Brown persistently reiterated this theme during his last seven years. American honor had to be upheld; the Old World had to be forced to respect the rights of the New Nation.[42] Patriotic fervor

[39] *Literary Magazine and American Register*, III, No. 16 (January 1805), 15; III, No. 21 (June 1805), 417; V, No. 33 (June 1806), 407; VI, No. 34 (July 1806), 71.

[40] Warfel, *Brown*, p. 204.

[41] Charles Brockden Brown, *The British Treaty of Commerce and Navigation, Concluded Dec. 31, 1806* (Philadelphia[?], 1807[?]), p. 8.

[42] Brown, *British Treaty*, pp. 51, 54, 70–72; Charles Brockden Brown, *Monroe's Embassy, or, The Conduct of the Government, in Relation to Our Claims to the Navigation of the Mississippi* . . . (Philadelphia: John Conrad, 1803), pp. 27–28, 34.

would sustain America's sons at war: "The patriotic passion or principle of doing all we can for the glory and power of our country, is sufficient to sustain us."[43] But armed defense of American maritime rights was not enough. Brown also demanded vindication of the nation's honor through aggressive territorial expansion. The "present limits of our territory are not immutable," he declared. "They must stretch with our wants. The South sea only can bound us on one side; the Mexican gulph on the other; the polar ices on the third."[44] Combat with European powers would be necessary to extend the national boundaries, but no true patriot could retreat: "Yet no wise man will think a renewal of all the devastation of our last war, too great a price to give for the expulsion of foreigners from this land; for securing to our posterity, the possession of this continent."[45] Forceful action was required to seize new land, to exclude dangerous enemies, to provide space for future generations, and to establish the visible greatness of the New Nation.[46] If Brown was not espousing the doctrine of Manifest Destiny thirty years before John L. O'Sullivan coined the term, the differences between him and the editor of the *Democratic Review* were slight.

From 1803 until his death, therefore, Brown exemplified the doctrinaire patriotism he had once abhorred. He articulated most of the dogmas regarding national grandeur and virtue that *Columbian* contributors and Washington eulogists had voiced. More important, beneath the rhetoric, Brown seemed to demonstrate the psychological qualities of devout patriots like David Ramsay and Noah Webster. His only fictional works during this period, "Sketches of a History of Carsol" and "Sketches of a History of the Carrils and Ormes," represented a thoroughgoing search for rootedness—for a stable place in a chaotic world. Tradition, cultural uniformity, established religion, and firm, stable government

43 Charles Brockden Brown, *An Address to the Congress of the United States, on the Utility and Justice of Restrictions upon Foreign Commerce* . . . (Philadelphia: C. & A. Conrad & Co., 1809), p. 43.

44 Brown, *An Address to the Congress*, pp. 89–90.

45 Charles Brockden Brown, *An Address to the Government of the United States, on the Cession of Louisiana to the French* . . . (Philadelphia: John Conrad, 1803), p. 80. Also quoted in Dunlap, *Life of Brown*, II, 66.

46 Brown, *An Address* . . . *on Cession of Louisiana*, pp. 86, 92. This is also the essential theme in Brown's pamphlet *Monroe's Embassy*.

were necessary to give a citizen a secure sense of place—a home-land.[47] "I observe a turbulent and factious spirit is just beginning to manifest itself, in some parts of this still unsettled country, which would tear up the ancient land marks of government, and eradicate every principle of a really free constitution," Brown wrote in 1805. "Innovations are always dangerous, and innovators have always been feared." Change and conflict would tear at the roots of the New Nation; preservation of a stable social fabric was essential. For this reason, Northern agitation against the Southern slave system had to cease. Slavery was evil but abolition would tear at the roots—the very fabric—of American civilization. Emancipation would uproot the homeland.[48] Coupled with his craving for this rather vague, amorphous sense of rooted stability, Brown embraced the notion of perfecting the Promised Land—the other essential within early American patriotic thought. This was most evident in his characterization of the Founding Father. Although he had mocked Washington boosters in earlier years as myth makers, Brown now joined them and characterized the man as a leader who had placed the New Nation on a wise, firm, and stable foundation. Washington was great as a warrior and as a man of peace, as a proponent of individual liberties and as a defender of governmental power. In Washington's person the various conflicting interests of the country were united. By emulating his diverse (and counterpointed) qualities, Brown asserted, Americans would assure the success of their experiment in nation making. Indeed, the perfecting spirit of Washington already seemed to be guiding the Promised Land: "The evils of internal dissension and rebellion, instead of approaching nearer, are every day removed to a greater distance," Brown noted. "The gulf which divides the master and the slave is becoming gradually narrower, and the ties which bind together the members of the nation multiply and strengthen by time." The citizenry was striving for perfection, and the nation

---

[47] The two sketches are published in Dunlap, *Life of Brown*, I, 170–258, 262–396. W. B. Berthoff, "Charles Brockden Brown's Historical 'Sketches': A Consideration," *American Literature*, XXVIII, No. 2 (May 1956), 147–54, offers an excellent analysis of the sketches, noting Brown's conservatism and his quest for rooted stability.

[48] *Literary Magazine and American Register*, III, No. 18 (March 1805), 175; Brown, *British Treaty*, p. 69.

was reaping the benefits. "The Rising Glory of America" would eventuate.[49]

IV

Charles Brockden Brown had obviously changed his orientation. As the country's first professional novelist, he had written with sophistication, articulating theories on the fallibility of human behavior, the hard and soft qualities of the full life, and the dangers of dogma. He had constructed a rich and complex fictional world of randomness and diversity, terror and joy, loneliness and community. But during the first decade of the nineteenth century, he all but terminated his literary activities, entered business, and became a dogmatic patriotic pamphleteer with simplistic solutions for complex problems. He had retreated from a frighteningly complex intellectual world to an orderly and tidy one.

Certain scholars propose an economic and status explanation for Brown's change. As a novelist propounding a self-styled philosophic radicalism, they argue, he was generally unknown and constantly pressed for money. But as a Philadelphia shipper and patriotic pamphleteer, he made a good living and won recognition. Therefore, there were strong incentives to become a doctrinaire patriot who defended the interests of Philadelphia's merchant class.[50] This interpretation is supported by Brown's complaints of insufficient remuneration and recognition for his fiction.[51] However, it can be only a partial explanation for Brown's transformation. Early in the 1790's he had broken from a legal career precisely because money, status, and coarse manipulation were all that the law seemed to offer. Until 1802 he wrote novels that attacked the hard, dogmatic essence of the dominant society. He could not have made such a strong commitment in the 1790's

[49] *The American Register*, II (July–December 1807), 175; Brown, *British Treaty*, p. 41; *The American Register*, I (1806–07), 66.

[50] Warfel, *Brown*, p. 207; Charles C. Cole, Jr., "Brockden Brown and the Jefferson Administration," *Pennsylvania Magazine of History and Biography*, LXXII, No. 3 (July 1948), 255, 260.

[51] Dunlap, *Life of Brown*, II, 100; *Monthly Magazine and American Review*, I (April 1799), 18; I (August 1799), 339.

against the financial and social ways of society, holding to that commitment until 1802, suddenly to abandon it for money and status. There must have been accompanying inducements.

Brown's participation in the New York City Friendly Club during the late 1790's has been cited as one of these accompanying inducements.[52] Conservative, doctrinaire, staunchly Federalist patriots like James Kent and William Johnson were active in the club and focused discussions on the political, commercial, and diplomatic topics Brown was attracted to during his last seven years. After attending seventeen meetings of the Friendly Club, Brown penned a Washington eulogy. It was indistinguishable from the hundreds of others that dogmatically exalted the flawless Founding Father for laying the foundation for America's "Rising Glory."[53] In 1801 *Jane Talbot*, the last of Brown's novels, was published. Character Henry Colden, a philosophic radical with the unorthodox social ideas of William Godwin and Mary Wollstonecraft, was pledged to positions Brown had defended in his earlier novels. But Colden recanted, adopted more traditional ideas, won the love of Jane Talbot, and gained happiness. Inasmuch as the Washington eulogy and *Jane Talbot* both reflected ideas and values that characterized Brown during his last seven years, and the Friendly Club was a vital source of those ideas and values, it seems evident that the club moved him toward the right. However, certain facts reduce the strength of this thesis. For one, although Brown had attended seventeen meetings of the club, they had all been crowded into a single winter. He not only restricted his contact with the Friendly Club to a few months, but was never referred to as a member. Either he never cared to join or he was refused admission by the regular membership. Whichever was the case, his contacts with the club could not have been excessively cordial. Moreover, although the Friendly Club was dominated by conservative Federalists, it was a sophisticated society of intellectuals committed to examining *all* current new ideas. Philosophic radicals like Godwin and Wollstonecraft were discussed at length,

[52] Clark, *Brown*, pp. 130–31, 151; Cole, Jr., *Pennsylvania Magazine of History and Biography*, LXXII, No. 3 (July 1948), 254–55.
[53] New York *Commercial Advertiser*, January 2, 1800.

as were Burke and Hamilton. Therefore, the club may actually have deepened Brown's exposure to philosophic radicalism.[54]

Physical illness may have been more important in Brown's move toward doctrinaire patriotism. Most of his adult life he suffered from incipient tuberculosis and gastric abnormalities.[55] "When have I known that lightness and vivacity of mind which the divine flow of health, even in calamity, produces in some men?" Brown asked in 1809. "Never; scarcely ever; not longer than half an hour at a time, since I have called myself a man."[56] Certain scholars argue that worsening health emptied Brown of the energy and determination to continue his literary crusade for philosophic radicalism. Poor health inclined him toward the path of least resistance—shipping and patriotic pamphleteering.[57] This argument has a plausible ring. Facing serious illness and death, people often try to concentrate their energies—physical and psychic—on the task of surviving. Demanding, self-consuming causes that are extraneous to this task are often de-emphasized or abandoned. But illness can only be a partial explanation for Brown's change. After all, commercial ventures and patriotic pamphleteering hardly represented the easy life for a sick man. Moreover, in November of 1804 he married Elizabeth Linn of New York, had children, and during the five remaining years of his life there was every indication that, despite poor health, he was exceedingly happy. He was not totally preoccupied with illness and death.[58] Thus, poor health

---

[54] James E. Cronin, "Elihu Hubbard Smith and the New York Friendly Club, 1795–1798," *PMLA*, LXIV, No. 3 (June 1949), 471–79, provides detailed information on Brown's attendance and membership status with the club. Jane Townsend Flanders, "Charles Brockden Brown and William Godwin: Parallels and Diversities" (Ph.D. dissertation, University of Wisconsin, 1965), p. 36, comments on the club's discussions of philosophic radicalism.

[55] Warfel, *Brown*, p. 8.

[56] Dunlap, *Life of Brown*, II, 86. Also quoted in William H. Prescott, *Bibliographical and Critical Miscellanies* (New York: Harper & Brothers, 1845), p. 47.

[57] Frank Luther Mott, *A History of American Magazines, 1741–1850* (Cambridge: Harvard University Press, 1939), p. 222; Cole, Jr., *Pennsylvania Magazine of History and Biography*, LXXII, No. 3 (July 1948), 255.

[58] See, e.g., Charles Brockden Brown to William Linn, December 8, 1804, Simon Gratz Collection, Historical Society of Pennsylvania; Dunlap, *Life of Brown*, II, 113, 114, 117; Warfel, *Brown*, p. 230; Dunlap, *Memoirs of Brown*, p. 181.

may have been a significant influence, but it alone cannot explain the change that came over Brown.

The fact that Brown enjoyed a happy marriage while suffering from exceedingly poor health points to another reason for his change in philosophic orientation and his full embrace of patriotic dogmas. The period before the marriage had been tense. Brown had met Elizabeth Linn, daughter of a New York Presbyterian minister, in November of 1800—a time when he was still writing unorthodox novels and still at odds with the Society of Friends. He courted her for nearly four years. Their correspondence during this period indicates that marriage was delayed for two reasons: Brown did not have much money and Linn was reluctant to wed him. Her reluctance stemmed, in part, from strong objections to a Quaker-Presbyterian marriage from family and friends. (Indeed, three months after the wedding, Brown was formally and completely read out of the Philadelphia Society of Friends.) More important, Linn was not avidly in love with Brown. In marked contrast to his own letters, hers carried tones of coolness, detachment, indifference, and sometimes contempt. The contrast between Brown's enthusiasm for the marriage and Linn's reluctance demonstrates that more than conventional social proprieties were involved. He was trying to *convince* her to become his wife.[59]

Brown had been unhappy as an unmarried novelist writing philosophically probing materials. Early in 1798 he remarked to his close friend William Dunlap: "I am sometimes to think that few human beings have drunk so deeply of the cup of self-abhorrence as I have. There is no misery equal to that which flows from this source. I have been for some years in full fruition of it. Whether it will end but with my life I know not."[60] A year later, he wrote to his brother Armitt telling of his extensive unhappiness and adding: "I have neither wife nor children, who look up to me for food:

[59] Clark, *Brown*, pp. 198–212, reproduces a great many of the letters between Brown and Linn in the years before their marriage. Others are found within collections at the Historical Society of Pennsylvania. For other relevant data on the background of the marriage, see Clark, *Brown*, pp. 187, 202–03, 212–13; Warfel, *Brown*, pp. 227–29.

[60] Charles Brockden Brown to William Dunlap, January 1, 1798, Letters of American Prose Writers, Historical Society of Pennsylvania. Also quoted in Lulu Rumsey Wiley, *The Sources and Influence of the Novels of Charles Brockden Brown* (New York: Vantage Press, Inc., 1950), p. 98.

and, in spite of all refinements, conjugal and paternal cares can never be fully transferred to one who has neither offspring nor spouse."[61] In the late summer of 1799, Brown published a short fictional piece, "Walstein's School of History." His fictional narrator stressed a significant theme: "On the circumstances which produce, and the principles which regulate the union between the sexes, happiness greatly depends."[62] Throughout the 1790's Brown had regularly told friends about to marry that he hoped to follow their example. "My conceptions of the delights and benefits connected with love and marriage are exquisite," he had written. "They have swayed most of my thoughts and many of my actions, since I arrived at an age of reflection and maturity."[63] In Brown's introduction to *Clara Howard* (1801), he told of a "simple lad" unhappily apprenticed to a watchmaker. But the lad soon found happiness through "that most exquisite of all blessings,—a wife, endowed with youth, grace, discretion." It is clear, then, that Brown had a substantial incentive to convince Elizabeth Linn to marry. Wedlock seemed to be the path to happiness and Brown was deeply in love with her. Linn was apolitical but eager for money, status, and social recognition; she was no Elizabeth Carter. To convince her to marry, Brown had to improve his finances. But, like Henry Colden of *Jane Talbot*, he may also have felt compelled to improve professionally and ideologically. The occupations of a Philadelphia importer and a prominent patriotic pamphleteer represented obvious improvements. During the year before their marriage, Linn's letters became warmer and less reluctant; one suspects that Brown's increasing prosperity and popularity influenced her change of heart. Moreover, Linn's willingness to become a bride after Brown drew away from fiction and philosophic radicalism must have encouraged him to deepen the break from his past.

The marriage that followed probably moved Brown even further in his new direction. Three weeks after the wedding, Brown wrote to his father-in-law that he and his new wife "have nothing to wish for but the continuance of our present tranquility

61 Dunlap, *Memoirs of Brown*, p. 202.
62 Quoted in Warfel (ed.), *Rhapsodist*, p. 152.
63 Dunlap, *Memoirs of Brown*, pp. 156–57, 223, 226.

& happiness."[64] "I cannot be happier than I am," he told William
Dunlap the following year. "Every change therefore must be for
the worse. My business, if I may so call it, is altogether pleasur-
able. . . . My companion is all that an husband can wish for, and
in short as to my own personal situation, I have nothing to wish
but that it may last."[65] Children were born in 1806 and this made
Brown happier. Despite his own illness, life was an enormous
joy.[66] Dunlap, his companion and biographer, noted that Brown
was "enjoying in an uncommon degree that domestic happiness
which had always appeared to him as the consummation of human
felicity, and for which he was so eminently formed."[67] The good
life had come—first for Henry Colden and then for Brockden
Brown.

This is not to say that Brown abandoned his subtle fictional
probings and became a doctrinaire patriot solely because of his
relationship with Elizabeth Linn. Many factors simultaneously
converged at the turn of the century and pushed him in that
direction. The enticements of wealth and status and the attractions
of marriage and family to an impoverished, alienated Quaker all
overlapped. The acquaintances that he cultivated with conservative patriots at the Friendly Club made the prospect of becoming a
pro-Federalist pamphleteer more attractive. In this sense, the
Friendly Club experience made it easier to do what was necessary
to persuade Elizabeth Linn. Physical illness must have interacted
with these other factors; it gave Brown something to ponder that
was more pressing and immediate than philosophic radicalism.
Moreover, the prospect of a wife and a stable home was bound to
appeal to a man who was seriously ill and required care. Finally,
the certitude of patriotic dogmas may have been more comforting
to a man who sought conventional happiness and companionship
than the themes of randomness, terror, and instability that had
characterized many of his novels.

[64] Charles Brockden Brown to William Linn, December 8, 1804, Simon
Gratz Collection, Historical Society of Pennsylvania.
[65] Dunlap, *Life of Brown*, II, 113. Also quoted in Warfel, *Brown*, p. 230.
[66] See, e.g., Charles Brockden Brown to Elizabeth Linn Brown, June 17,
1806, Letters of American Prose Writers, Historical Society of Pennsylvania;
Dunlap, *Life of Brown*, II, 114, 117.
[67] Dunlap, *Memoirs of Brown*, p. 181.

Evidently, then, Brown was miserable during his years as a probing, obscure novelist who attacked patriotic thought in the New
Nation. The contrast between Brown's private letters before he
abandoned fiction and his letters after he married Elizabeth Linn
makes this apparent.[68] Money, status, family life and happiness
came not simply because he abandoned fiction—a field that Americans were unwilling to patronize. The good life came after he
deployed his rich talents in orthodox commercial pursuits and in
embellishing the patriotic dogmas of *Columbian* contributors and
Washington eulogists. Following the lead of Philadelphia's Federalist merchants and American society generally, both the fictional Jane Talbot and the real Elizabeth Linn rewarded the
respectable and prosperous spread-eagle patriot over the cosmopolitan, intellectually probing dissenter. An interrelated array of
social, economic, and psychological pressures made it very hard
for Brown to remain an outsider.

V

In Charles Brockden Brown's conversion from radical dissidence
to spread-eagle patriotism, we may therefore perceive certain basic
undercurrents in the emerging crusade for "the Rising Glory of
America." As a novelist writing in the Godwin-Wollstonecraft
tradition, he was able to articulate some of the fundamental problems of that crusade, particularly the insistence upon human strivings for perfection. Perceiving that man was naturally fallible and
error-prone, Brown understood that pressures to perfect the
nation and to emulate a flawless Founding Father had to result in
serious discontent. He understood one of the basic sources of
much of the irritability and desperation that plagued men like
David Ramsay and Noah Webster. Besides noting where patriots
had gone astray, Brown outlined an alternative. Rather than strive
for flawlessness, human beings should leave themselves open to the
rich diversities of life—diversities and living possibilities that many

[68] The Historical Society of Pennsylvania houses most surviving Brown
letters. Contrasting the letters for the 1795–1802 period with those from
December 1804 until his death in February 1810, the researcher senses, almost,
that he is dealing with two different people.

Americans were blinded to through the rigid, dogmatic imperatives of *le patriotisme irritable*.

But for all of his sensitivity, Brown as novelist was never fully aware of the limitations of abstract intellectual analysis. Like the patriotic concepts of "the Rising Glory of America" and the flawless Founding Father, his alternative plea for an open and diversified human existence was a theoretical construct—a product of abstract mental activity. There is no evidence that Brown was able to feel or to experience the diversities that he endorsed. In his years as a novelist, Brown never realized that it was necessary to go beyond abstract intellectual constructs if he was to live the diversified life that he had prescribed. Brown also needed to move beyond drawing-board criticisms and solutions in order to effectively derail the experientially narrowing crusade for the Promised Land. Intellectual analysis of the failings of spread-eagle patriotism in obscure novels was insufficient. *Columbian* contributors, Washington eulogists, and other doctrinaire patriots paid Brown no heed. They did not have to, for the brilliant young novelist never threatened to win away their following or to subject their ideas to public ridicule.

Alexis de Tocqueville and Émile Durkheim, the two great sociologists of the nineteenth century, would have understood the problem underlying Brockden Brown's life and his ultimate conversion from the drawing-board radicalism of his early career to social orthodoxy and dogmatic patriotism. Tocqueville and Durkheim recognized that the dominant ways of a society could produce insecurity and discontent among those who conformed. But unless the dominant ways were changed—unless penetrating solutions were effectively implemented through social action—failure to conform could produce even greater inner discontent and personal distress. Brown's inability to implement solutions reduced his options to two. He could continue as a brilliant but obscure and miserable social critic; he could remain isolated, ignored, and left to wallow in his sorrows. On the other hand, he could join the crusade for the Promised Land with knowledge of its shortcomings, repress consciousness of those shortcomings, and eventually become a respectable and materially prosperous Philadelphia Federalist. Brown exercised this latter option and was glad

that he had. The doctrinaire patriot was burdened by serious problems. But they seemed less burdensome to Brown than the problems of the isolated dissenter. This was why *le patriotisme irritable*
could crush intellectuality and turn a probing critic into a narrow,
dogmatic conformist. The dogmatic patriot was at least a vigorous
social animal—much more so than the isolated dissident.

PART Two

WOMAN'S ROLE IN THE PROMISED LAND

Columbian Fair,
Generous disposers of our happiness, and amiable protectors of our
felicity!—To you it belongs to rule the milder empire of virtue. Long
continue, as at present, the watchful guardians of our morals; and by the
mildness of your persuasive conversation, and the sovereign influence of
your example, teach us the pure principles of virtuous liberty, and
crown all our blessings with your smiles! Remember that no heart can
resist the voice of patriotism, when urged by the lips of beauty and
innocence.

—ELIAS GLOVER, 1806

While woman's intellect is confined, her morals crushed, her health
ruined, her weaknesses encouraged, and her strength punished, she is told
that her lot is cast in the paradise of women: and there is no country in
the world where there is so much boasting of the "chivalrous" treatment
she enjoys.

—HARRIET MARTINEAU, 1837

Although the ideological and psychological dilemmas of *Columbian* contributors, Washington eulogists, and other spread-eagle patriots were severe, the quest for "the Rising Glory of America" had such a profound impact upon popular culture in the New Nation that it seemed to leave few viable alternatives. Like Charles Brockden Brown, one could recognize impending disaster in the quest for flawless selfhood and nationhood; one could detect that the quest was bound to become personally uprooting or to intensify a pre-existing sense of rootlessness. But patriots ignored Brown and left him in his misery until he had repudiated his analysis and had joined them in their crusade.

Determined to perpetuate the crusade for "Rising Glory," patriots were therefore weaving chronic insecurities and discontent into the fabric of their daily lives. Failure to strive to promote personal and national flawlessness made them feel that they were not fulfilling their patriotic obligation. But constant striving toward abstract flawlessness had to remove much of the floor or stability from their everyday existence. A sense of rooted stability was simply incompatible with strivings toward "the Rising Glory of America." Through rhetorical counterpointing, a mythic George Washington arose who seemed to combine these two incompatibles, but the mythology could not remedy the everyday problems of living patriots.

During the early decades of the nineteenth century, several male crusaders for "Rising Glory" came to seek relief through sexual ideology—to seek cures or alleviants for their discontent in the behavior of the "Fair Daughters of Columbia." They perceived some mysterious quality in women that would ease their insecurities and refresh them as they pursued patriotic selfhood and perfected nationhood. The search for this mysterious female quality continued for decades and had a telling effect upon women as well as upon men.

In 1851 the popular New York magazine *Ladies' Wreath* sponsored an essay contest on the question: "How may an American Woman best show her Patriotism?" A panel of three men, E. W. Chester, S. D. Burchard, and Asa D. Smith, judged the essays and awarded the fifty-dollar prize to Elizabeth Witherell. Her essay maintained that the American woman was obligated to encourage her sons, her brothers, and her husband "to be patriots." She should encourage them to perfect their personal qualities and the qualities of their country. At the same time, woman should try to provide restful stability and a firm foundation for the domestic life of the "dominant sex." Chester, Burchard, Smith, and Witherell were obviously perpetuating the old perfection-rootedness dilemma but were characterizing it as a mysterious patriotic female cure-all. Three men and one woman had been drawn so far into fantasy that they had mistaken a problem for a solution.

In a sense, this *Ladies' Wreath* contest represented the culmination of a quest that had pervaded the early decades of the nineteenth century—a search for a safety valve, for something that could ease the discontent inherent in the crusade for the Promised Land. If men could not reconcile perfectionist strivings with the craving for rooted stability, patriotic women's efforts might effect that reconciliation. Within the patriotic literature of the early national period, this supposed capacity of women to do what men could not do—to reconcile the irreconcilable—came to be characterized as the achievement of True American Womanhood.

CHAPTER 4

TRUE AMERICAN
WOMANHOOD

In *Alcuin* and other novels, Charles Brockden Brown disapproved of both *le patriotisme irritable* and the restrictive roles assigned to American women. He usually characterized these twin ills as interrelated. Society's ways were rigid and restrictive. They repressed the varieties of potential human experience. Doctrinaire patriotism typified these ways and women suffered the most from them. Brown seemed particularly anxious to drive these points home through bluestocking Elizabeth Carter, his shrewd women's-rights theorist. Sophia Westwyn of *Ormond* implemented some of Carter's ideas. Sophisticated and humanitarian, Westwyn realized that she would have to remove Constantia Dudley from America for relief and for fresh opportunities. Both Carter and Westwyn understood that independent, aggressive roles outside of the domestic sphere were a necessary part of human development. But both women also realized that females who acted out these roles violated a certain vague ideal in the life of the New Nation. To escape this ideal, Carter championed the case for women's rights and Westwyn returned to Europe.

It is exceedingly difficult to delineate the ideal that Brown attacked through figures like Carter and Westwyn. Patriots often referred to it as True American Womanhood. Unlike characterizations of the flawless Washington, however, no specific body of

literature centered on the proper role of True American Womanhood. Some doctrinaire patriots made regular yet hasty allusions to
this ideal, most made occasional, random references, and a few
totally ignored it. Unlike David Ramsay and Noah Webster, who
were somewhat representative of *Columbian* contributors, and
unlike Mason Locke Weems and James Fenimore Cooper, who
typified basic approaches to the Washington myth, no single male
patriot of the early national period can be singled out as a representative spokesman for True American Womanhood.

Most often articulated within spread-eagle patriotic rhetoric, the
ideal of True American Womanhood had to be relevant to many
early American patriots. The frequency of patriotic references to
the ideal indicated that aspects of early American sexual ideology
meshed with aspects of a developing crusade for the Promised
Land. To be sure, scholars like Ronald W. Hogeland, Gerda
Lerner, and Glenda L. Riley have demonstrated that early sexual
ideology can be explored as a phenomenon in its own right. They
have made credible insights about sexual orientations without linking those orientations to patriotic goals. But it is also important to
take a broader view and to place sexual allusions into the context in
which they were very often found—in a crusade for America.

As a radical novelist, Brockden Brown usually took the broader
view. He fretted over True American Womanhood and he construed it as the most dangerous and limiting ingredient within
American patriotism. The problem was that he did not know who
or what was primarily responsible for the ideal. He could never
single out a villain, a group of villains, or even a specific body of
reproachable literature. Half a century later, Nathaniel Hawthorne
was battling the same elusive enemy. Like Brown, he struck out at
random rhetoric and events that seemed so important and yet so
disconnected and intangible. In *The Scarlet Letter*, for example, he
could not clearly identify the constrictive ideal of True American
Womanhood through the words or deeds of Governor Bellingham,
Reverend Wilson, Roger Chillingworth, Arthur Dimmesdale, or
Hester Prynne.

From Brown's day to Hawthorne's, references to the responsibilities of True American Womanhood were persistent, widespread, yet elusive. Most often disseminated by men, these

references stressed woman's domestic, family-centered duties. In random passages, certain *Columbian* essayists noted that patriotic women's responsibilities were soft, sentimental, and in the area of the hearth.[1] Noah Webster proclaimed that American women had a single duty—to fill their homes and their children's minds with "such sentiments of virtue, propriety and dignity, as were suited to the freedom of our government."[2] In 1811 David Ramsay memorialized Martha Laurens, his late wife. She had properly cultivated patriotism, soft sentimentality, morality, and virtue in her children and had diligently copied her husband's histories.[3] In undeveloped passages, several Washington eulogists had also equated woman's refined, sentimental duties about the hearth with patriotism.[4] James Kirke Paulding dedicated his *Life of Washington* (1835) to the "pious, retired domestic Mothers" of America. At certain July Fourth celebrations, "The Fair Daughters of Columbia" were toasted for the soft, sentimental morality that they inculcated at home to assure the welfare of the Promised Land.[5] William Butler's popular early-nineteenth-century arithmetic textbook presented a short problem in "FEMALE PATRIOTISM." Students were to calculate how the soft, retiring ladies of the American Revolution had sat by the hearth measuring fabric to make shirts for the great cause—how they had gone about accomplishing "their patriotic purpose."[6]

Many of these male patriots who pointed to the soft, sentimental domesticity of True American Womanhood were disturbed by

[1] See, e.g., *Columbian Magazine*, June 1787, pp. 473–74; September 1787, p. 644; Supplement III, 1789, p. 759.

[2] Quoted in Peter Gregg Slater, "Views of Children and Child Rearing during the Early National Period: A Study in the New England Intellect" (Ph.D. dissertation, University of California, Berkeley, 1970), pp. 223–24.

[3] Ramsay constantly repeated this theme in his *Memoirs of the Life of Martha Laurens Ramsay* (Charleston: Samuel Etheridge, Jr., 1812).

[4] See, e.g., Aaron Bancroft, *An Eulogy on the Character of the Late Gen. George Washington* . . . (Worcester, 1800), pp. 18–19; Ezekiel Savage, *An Eulogy on Gen. George Washington, Who Died Dec. 14, 1799* . . . (Salem, 1800), p. 22; William Linn, *A Funeral Eulogy, Occasioned by the Death of General Washington* . . . (New York, 1800), p. 43.

[5] See the Richmond *Enquirer*, July 10, 17, 1818, and numerous July Fourth toasts quoted in Robert Pettus Hay, "Freedom's Jubilee: One Hundred Years of the Fourth of July, 1776–1876" (Ph.D. dissertation, University of Kentucky, 1967).

[6] Quoted in Albert Bushnell Hart, "Imagination in History," *American Historical Review*, XV, No. 2 (January 1910), 243–44.

the potential growth of effeminacy in a nation run by and for the so-called dominant sex. According to David Ramsay, the same softness and effeminacy which had characterized America under British rule could very easily revive in the New Nation.[7] Other *Columbian* contributors warned of this potential danger to the men of the Promised Land.[8] July Fourth orators who prescribed women's patriotic domestic duties frequently cautioned against a nation whose leaders were becoming gentle, weak, cowardly, and "sunk into effeminacy."[9] Numerous others echoed this theme.[10]

Proponents of True American Womanhood seemed, therefore, to be encouraging women to serve the country by displaying their soft sentimentality in the home and with their families. At the same time, these proponents feared effeminacy's growth among the "dominant sex" which ran the country. They almost seemed to be contradicting themselves: (1) National character was hard and masculine. (2) Women contributed to national character by caring for the menfolk of their families with soft, effeminate, retiring domestic qualities. Hence, women were required to deal softly with men who were too soft to begin with. As they came near to advancing this absurd proposition, proponents of patriotic womanhood were motivated by a vague persuasion that pervaded male culture in the New Nation. To determine the qualities of this persuasion—to grasp what neither Brown nor Hawthorne could quite comprehend—it is necessary to subject the proposition to closer scrutiny.

[7] David Ramsay, *An Oration on the Advantages of American Independence: Spoken before a Public Assembly of the Inhabitants of Charlestown in South-Carolina, on the Second Anniversary of the Glorious Era* (Charlestown, 1778), p. 4; Ramsay, *The History of the American Revolution* (London: John Stockdale, 1793), II, 355; Ramsay, *History of the United States . . .* (Philadelphia: M. Carey, 1816-17), III, 35.

[8] *Columbian Magazine*, June 1787, pp. 473-74; September 1791, pp. 190-91.

[9] See, e.g., M. M. Noah, *Oration, Delivered by Appointment, Before Tammany Society of Columbian Order, Hibernian Provident Society . . . United to Celebrate the 41st Anniversary of American Independence* (New York, 1817), p. 12; Samuel Swett, *An Address, Delivered at Salem, July 4, 1806 . . .* (Boston, 1806), p. 15; David Humphreys, *A Valedictory Discourse, Delivered before the Cincinnati of Connecticut, in Hartford, July 4, 1804* (Boston, 1804), p. 21.

[10] See, e.g., *The Philanthropist* (Cincinnati), June 24, 1836; Dwight L. Dumond (ed.), *Letters of James Gillespie Birney* (New York: D. Appleton-Century Company, 1938), I, 179; Sylvester Graham, *A Lecture to Young Men, on Chastity* (Boston: Charles H. Pierce, 1848), p. 60.

II

In their random remarks on soft, retiring domestic True American Womanhood, male patriots added bits of information that hinted at the qualities of this persuasion. A patriotic woman was to provide decorative ornament. She was required to embellish the victories and successes of American men. "Thy blooming Fair, in innocence attir'd, shall deck thy glories with unnumber'd charms," Noah Webster asserted. Joseph Gleason singled out women attending a July Fourth celebration in Boston: "on this day, to behold the smiles complacently seated on their countenances, adds brilliancy to our efforts and lustre to the occasion."[11] "The fair daughters of *Columbia*," another orator proclaimed, "the ornament of virtue, as virtue is the ornament of them."[12] But patriotic women had to be more than decorative ornaments. They were required to supervise morality in the Promised Land: "The Fair— the Guardians of morality and virtue—may they duly appreciate the responsibility which attaches to such a character." The "Columbian Fair" should "long continue, as at present, the watchful guardians of our morals."[13] Lecturing on the ills of male masturbation, Sylvester Graham hoped that American women would prompt men, through their example, to abandon this immoral and unpatriotic habit: "Forever may the females of our blessed country remain pure in themselves, and exert a purifying and exalting influence on the other sex."[14] Others echoed this broad theme; despite men's sins, patriotic women were to preserve

[11] Ruth F. and Harry R. Warfel (eds.), *Poems by Noah Webster* (College Park, Md.: Harruth Lefraw, 1936), p. 5; Joseph Gleason, *An Oration Pronounced on the Thirtieth Anniversary of American Independence, Before The Young Democratic Republicans of the Town of Boston, At the Second Baptist Meeting House, July 4, 1806* (Boston, 1806), p. 20.

[12] Quoted in *An Historical View of the Public Celebrations of the Washington Society, and Those of the Young Republicans. From 1805, to 1822* (Boston: True and Greene, 1823), p. 15.

[13] Richmond *Enquirer*, July 12, 1811; Elias Glover, *An Oration, Delivered at the Court-House in Cincinnati, on the Fourth of July, 1806* (Cincinnati, 1806), pp. 23–24.

[14] Sylvester Graham, *A Lecture to Young Men*, p. 25.

national morality.[15] Finally, along with demonstrations of decora-
tiveness and morality, patriotic women were obligated to exhibit
sweet sentimentality and soft emotion whenever the occasion
demanded it: "The American Fair—As Sweet as when fond lovers
meet, Soft as the parting tear."[16] Between December 14, 1799, and
February 22, 1800, Washington eulogists regularly pleaded with
women in the audience to demonstrate American softness, emotion, and sentimentality by crying for their departed Father.[17]

The male patriot's vision of True American Womanhood was,
therefore, a creature who could exhibit decorative, moral, or
sentimental qualities at a moment's notice. Yet she was not to
invoke these qualities at her own discretion—only when men
called upon her or needed her to compensate for their coarse,
masculine qualities. "Without it we [American men] should degenerate into brutes." The patriotic obligation of American
women was "to soften the harder hearts of men."[18] A July Fourth
celebrant toasted *"The American Fair . . .* without whose civilizing powers, man would be a savage and the earth a desert."
Woman's civilizing powers were enormous: "The graces of her
mind refine our manners, the virtues of her heart correct our
morals."[19] Man's needs determined woman's behavior. When he

[15] See, e.g., Richmond *Enquirer,* July 10, 1827; *American Ladies' Magazine,*
IX, No. 12 (December 1836), 691; Ethan Smith, *Daughters of Zion Excelling:
A Sermon Preached to the Ladies of the Cent Institution, in Hopkinton, New-
Hampshire, August 18, 1814* (Concord, 1814), p. 10.

[16] Richmond *Enquirer,* August 3, 1824.

[17] See, e.g., Abiel Abbot, *An Eulogy on the Illustrious Life and Character
of George Washington . . .* (Haverhill, 1800), p. 24; Walter King, *A Discourse, Delivered in Chelsea, in the City of Norwich, Jan. 5, 1800, As a
Token of Humiliation before God, on Account of the Death of Gen. George
Washington . . .* (Norwich, 1800), p. 13; Daniel Sewall, *An Eulogy, Occa-
sioned by the Death of General Washington* (Portsmouth, 1800), p. 17;
Samuel Bishop, *An Eulogium on the Death of Gen. George Washington,
Commander in Chief of the Armies of America* (Gilmanton, N.H., 1800),
p. 15; Abiel Holmes, *A Sermon, Preached at Cambridge, on the Lord's Day,
December 29, 1799, Occasioned by the Death of George Washington . . .*
(Boston, 1800), p. 19.

[18] *The Liberator,* June 14, 1834; Thomas Barnard, *A Sermon Preached
before the Salem Female Charitable Society, in the First Church in Salem,
July 6th, 1803* (Salem, 1803), p. 17.

[19] Richmond *Enquirer,* July 9, 1811; Edgar E. Brandon (ed.), *A Pilgrimage
of Liberty: A Contemporary Account of the Triumphal Tour of General
Lafayette* (Athens, Ohio: The Lawhead Press, 1944), p. 100. For similar
expressions, see Frederick Rudolph (ed.), *Essays on Education in the Early*

was overly crude, hard, and aggressive, she was obligated to become decorative, morally refined, soft, and sentimental.

Duty-bound to moderate men of all ages, the True American Woman operated within the structure of a family and was required to focus upon her sons. Her primary purpose was to rear children, particularly young boys. John Abbott, the influential Congregational minister, put the proposition well: "When our land is filled with virtuous and patriotic mothers, then will it be filled with virtuous and patriotic men. The world's redeeming influence must come from a mother's lips."[20] "We know, that virtuous, enlightened, and patriotick Mothers, give us a virtuous, enlightened, and patriotick community," proclaimed the principal of Lexington, Kentucky's Female Academy.[21] An American mother's teachings would determine whether her son would rise "from the obscurity of a cottage home to the highest station her country can bestow. No other nation allows the humble mother to assert so much." "*The Matrons of our land*" had a crucial role. "The intelligence and morals of the rising generation will tell how they have discharged their duty."[22] Because America's "Rising Glory"—the nation's future—was in their hands, mothers had to willingly subordinate their own desires to their patriotic responsibilities. They were not to veer from the task to indulge in those strange romantic dreams and fancies so common to the softer sex. Fearing that certain American mothers might prove too frail or fanciful to be trusted with the nation's future leaders—that they might transplant their unsteady qualities to their sons—some proponents of patriotic womanhood detailed the mothers' teaching duties. They should "teach their infant tongues to lisp the praises of patriots and heroes, and long live the republic." To assure the

---

Republic (Cambridge, Mass.: The Belknap Press, 1965), p. 69, and Samuel Rockwell, *An Oration, Delivered at the Celebration of American Independence, at Salisbury, Fourth July, Ninety-Seven* (Litchfield, 1797), p. 13.

[20] John S. C. Abbott, *The Mother at Home, or Principles of Maternal Duty* (Boston, 1835), p. 148.

[21] Brandon (ed.), *Pilgrimage of Liberty*, p. 303.

[22] *American Ladies' Magazine*, V, No. 1 (January 1832), 11; *Connecticut Courant* (Hartford), July 8, 1833. According to Anne L. Kuhn, *The Mother's Role in Childhood Education: New England Concepts, 1830–1860* (New Haven: Yale University Press, 1947), p. 72, comments of this sort were quite prevalent in antebellum New England.

survival of the Promised Land, mothers must "try instilling into your children such principles as may render them the WARRENS, the GREENS, and the WASHINGTONS of future time." If they inculcated "the future warriors and statesmen of the nation" with sound patriotic doctrines as they nurtured them, American women would be honored as "nursing mothers of the republic."[23]

Although the "nursing mother of the republic" did not vote or hold office, and although her tasks were often prescribed by males for males within a family context, patriots insisted that she had an important political role. The principles she taught her sons were registered on the political institutions of the New Nation. A properly indoctrinated family insured "the Rising Glory of America." "Cherish, then, my countrywomen, in the bosoms of your children, patriotic and moral sentiments, a love of their country and its institutions," Joseph Sprague proclaimed. "You can give an effectual currency to your opinions. Whatever fashions you adopt, we readily imitate."[24] The American mother held "a power of greater bearing than that of earthly monarchs." It did not matter that women never voted or did much else at their own discretion. They played a major role by molding "the hearts of those whom their instruction and example may make our future rulers."[25]

Clearly, proponents of True American Womanhood were characterizing a viable national character as hard, aggressive, and masculine while requiring women to contribute indispensable qualities to the nation by being soft and retiring. But what they never made explicit was that they conceived of a soft and retiring female

[23] N. B. Boileau, *An Oration Delivered on the Fourth of July 1814 . . .*, as quoted in Robert P. Hay, "Freedom's Jubilee," p. 248; John V. Weylie, *A Funeral Sermon, in Commemoration of the Virtues of General Washington, Delivered by the Rev'd. John V. Weylie, on the Twenty-Second of February, at the Parish of Frederick . . .* (Frederick, Md.[?], 1800), p. 16; "Female Education," *Southern Literary Messenger*, VI, No. 6 (June 1840), 455.

[24] Joseph E. Sprague, *An Address Delivered before the Salem Charitable Mechanic Association, on Their Fourth Anniversary, July 4, 1821, in the North Meeting House* (Salem, 1821), pp. 20–21.

[25] Charles A. Goodrich, *The Influence of Mothers on the Character, Welfare and Destiny of Individuals, Families and Communities* (Boston: Crocker and Brewster, 1835), p. 8; James Humphrey Wilder, *An Oration Delivered at the Request of the Young Men of Hingham, on the Fourth of July, 1832* (Hingham, 1832), pp. 32–33.

patriot in two distinct ways. She had, quite literally, to be a delicate, ornamental, sentimental reservoir of morality and domesticity. She had to embody those frail qualities that Professor Barbara Welter delineates in her well-known pioneering essay "The Cult of True Womanhood."[26] This literal construction produced a contradiction—soft women purportedly contributed to hard nationhood. But Professor Welter overlooks a second and broader construction that male patriots frequently placed upon female frailty. Soft and retiring behavior was also construed as *malleable* behavior. The soft, retiring, family-centered woman complemented the strong, aggressive man. She had the flexibility to serve man in any variety of ways that man might require, thereby complementing man's actions as man promoted hardy nationhood. Because patriotic woman deployed delicacy, sentimentality, and morality only *at man's behest,* her soft, retiring nature stood for a flexible, pliable quality through which she could be molded and remolded to meet man's needs. This equation of soft womanhood with flexible, malleable womanhood widened the scope of permissible female behavior. On occasions, the patriotic woman could legitimately be called upon to display hard and assertive qualities. On those occasions, woman's softness stood entirely for her ability to transform herself—to be malleable enough to meet changing male needs. Though she was usually withdrawn and ornamental, woman's fundamental malleability made it possible for men to demand assertive daring when national or personal exigencies required. The retiring goddess of the hearth could become tough and hardheaded; she could rear a Spartan family to promote an assertive and masculine nation. She might even step beyond the hearth.

Therefore, there was a narrow, literal way of perceiving True American Woman's essential softness and a broader way that at once encompassed and transcended literal interpretation. Under the broader interpretive framework, patriotic women were malleable women; they sometimes served men by decorating the hearth and sometimes by leaving the hearth in men's behalf. This distinction between narrow and broad interpretations of True American

[26] Barbara Welter, "The Cult of True Womanhood: 1820–1860," *American Quarterly,* XVIII, No. 2, Pt. 1 (Summer 1966), 151–74.

Woman's softness becomes clearer in the context of a specific phenomenon—the reaction of male patriots to what they came to call the Wollstonecraft tradition. Indeed, the distinction becomes most obvious in the way that they perceived this Wollstonecraft tradition during the New Jersey woman's suffrage debate and the subsequent controversy surrounding female abolitionism.

III

At a July Fourth celebration in 1815, Reverend Asa Packard of the West Church in Marlborough, Massachusetts, spoke at length on the duties of True American Womanhood:

> Tho' exempted from the perils and hardships of the tented field, they [American women] may display their patriotism, by guiding the inquiries, enriching the minds, and forming the childish and youthful habits of future Citizens, future Legislators, Magistrates, Judges and Generals, now dependent on their mothers' care and instruction. . . . But, Ladies, when you, like ardent politicians, assume a part in political disputes, on points, where great and good men cannot meet; or when you declaim political subjects for the improvement of female circles; you will permit statesmen to smile, and pleasantly to enquire, whether your husbands are wielding the distaff, plying the needle, or crimping muslin?

[handwritten marginal note: Is your husband a real man?]

Packard insisted that women properly displayed their patriotism by guiding young boys at the hearth. To transcend the domestic sphere—to mix with men in the rough and tumble of political life—was to confuse the distinct and separate function of each sex. If women could survive in a patently masculine sphere, might not men be relegated to the domestic, feminine sphere? The chaos inherent in such a situation was unthinkable.[27]

There were other devout patriots who shared Packard's allegiance to retiring True American Womanhood and who feared that woman might enter and subvert man's traditional sphere. During the first decades of the nineteenth century, these men came

[27] Asa Packard, *An Oration, on the Means of Perpetuating Independence. Delivered at East-Sudbury, July 4th, 1815* (Boston, 1815), pp. 14–15.

increasingly to equate the threat of female aggression with the rise of a hard, seductive, scheming Wollstonecraft tradition. After two premarital affairs, Mary Wollstonecraft published her *Vindication of the Rights of Woman* in England in 1791. It was republished in Philadelphia and Boston in 1792 and became the subject of considerable controversy. Pleading for new political, social, and economic opportunities for women beyond the confines of home and family, Wollstonecraft's *Vindication* represented a milder feminist plea than Brockden Brown's *Alcuin*. But whereas *Alcuin* was either ignored or construed as the fanciful play of a naïve young man, the woman who wrote the *Vindication* was widely regarded as a threat to man's traditional political and economic hegemony. The genders of the authors may have caused these different reactions to two similar books. Because Wollstonecraft was a woman, the *Vindication* may have had to be taken as more than fanciful literary play—as a genuine sign of female impropriety. David Ramsay felt relieved because his wife, Martha Laurens, remained devoted to child rearing and to copying his patriotic histories after reading the "dangerous" *Vindication*. William Alcott, the moral crusader, charged that any woman who followed Wollstonecraft's advice and mounted the public rostrum was an unpatriotic wretch who "departs widely from the providence which God in nature seems to have allotted her."[28] Wollstonecraft was a foreign "female lunatic"—a woman who sought to strip her sex "of everything feminine, and to assimilate them [women], as fast as possible, to the masculine character." This was why patriotic duty compelled American women to renounce Wollstonecraft and to stay well outside the masculine sphere. The True American Woman embraced "the quiet of domestic peace" while disavowing Wollstonecraft's "Amazon legions."[29]

Expressions along these lines were not uncommon well into the nineteenth century. Almost any sign of female independence was

[28] Ramsay, *Memoirs of . . . Martha Laurens Ramsay*, pp. 43–45; William A. Alcott, *The Young Woman's Guide to Excellence* (Boston: George W. Light, 1840), p. 97.
[29] Samuel Lorenzo Knapp, *Letters of Shahcoolen, a Hindu Philosopher* (Boston, 1802), pp. 23–24; Benjamin Silliman, *An Oration, Delivered at Hartford on the 6th of July, A.D. 1802 . . . to Celebrate the Anniversary of American Independence* (Hartford, 1802), pp. 22–23.

characterized as "Wollstonecraft-like."[30] Clearly, male patriots perceived the woman and her *Vindication* as the literal antithesis of True Womanhood. But they were objecting to her for more than her disregard of retiring domesticity. By characterizing Wollstonecraft as a crude "Amazon," a wild "lunatic," a scheming "seductress," and even a masturbator, they were describing a woman who was too self-centered, self-reliant, and independently assertive to be malleable. A woman with these qualities had neither the pliancy nor the inspiration to mold her conduct around changing male needs. She was a self-interested and self-sufficient human entity. Indeed, by encouraging women to become bold and hard and to aggressively invade man's traditional domain for their own interests, Wollstonecraft and her *Vindication* were contradicting the most fundamental construction of True American Womanhood. Aggressive women who asserted themselves independently and by force or scheming seduction could not possibly be made to fill men's needs; they could not perform their most essential function. By operating free of male directives, they were harming their country.

Between 1790 and 1807 certain men from New Jersey sensed that they were witnessing the bleakest repercussions of the Wollstonecraft tradition; it was being actualized in their own local communities. According to the 1776 state constitution, "every person of full age and one year's residence and worth fifty pounds" was entitled to vote. In 1790 the New Jersey legislature passed a law that perpetuated these residency and property requirements and retained voting power for "all free Inhabitants of this State." There is no evidence that legislators had used the phrases "every person" and "all free Inhabitants" in order to give women voting rights. However, between 1790 and 1807 some New Jersey women read them this way and went to the polls. In October of 1797 a number of Elizabethtown women voted against Republican John Condict in a close Essex County contest for a state legislative seat and Condict barely escaped defeat. A powerful and persuasive politician, Condict never forgot the incident. Ten

[30] Janet Wilson James, "Changing Ideas about Women in the United States, 1776–1825" (Ph.D. dissertation, Harvard University, 1954), pp. 84, 99.

years later, in the wake of supposed election irregularities caused by women voting in another Essex County contest, he introduced a bill to disfranchise all women. The suffrage was to be restricted to "free, white, male citizens." The Condict bill passed both houses of the New Jersey legislature without debate or partisan divisions.[31]

Two students of New Jersey politics, Sophie H. Drinker and J. R. Pole, interpret this suffrage controversy as an inconsequential matter. They note that most women did not vote between 1790 and 1807; some were simply called upon to tip the balance in certain close local elections. Moreover, because a significant property requirement was retained throughout the period, state legislators probably did not feel that they were engaged in an egalitarian experiment.[32] This interpretation misses a larger point. Although ten of the thirteen British North American colonies had not explicitly banned female voting, they had not assented to general woman's suffrage any more than New Jersey had between 1790 and 1807.[33] What matters is that, as did not happen in the ten colonies or in any other state in the early national period, women voted in New Jersey and their conduct provoked a significant male

31 For the facts of the New Jersey woman's suffrage controversy, see Edward Raymond Turner, "Women's Suffrage in New Jersey: 1790-1807," *Smith College Studies in History*, I, No. 4 (July 1916), 165-77; Richard P. McCormick, *The History of Voting in New Jersey* (New Brunswick: Rutgers University Press, 1953), pp. 99-101; Mary Philbrook, "Woman's Suffrage in New Jersey Prior to 1807," *Proceedings of the New Jersey Historical Society*, 4th Ser., LVII, No. 2 (April 1939), 88-89; Nancy Graham Hassler, "Early Sexism in the United States: A Study of Women in New Jersey, 1790-1807" (unpublished ms., University of California, Berkeley, 1970), pp. 3-4, 6; William A. Whitehead, "A Brief Statement of the Facts Connected with the Origin, Practice and Prohibition of Female Suffrage in New Jersey," *Proceedings of the New Jersey Historical Society*, 1st Ser., VIII (1856), 103; Walter Fee, *The Transition from Aristocracy to Democracy in New Jersey, 1789-1829* (Somerville: Somerville Press, Inc., 1933), pp. 93, 96-97.

32 Sophie H. Drinker, "Votes for Women in 18th-Century New Jersey," *Proceedings of the New Jersey Historical Society*, 4th Ser., LXXX, No. 1 (January 1962), 44-45; J. R. Pole, "The Suffrage in New Jersey, 1790-1807," *Proceedings of the New Jersey Historical Society*, 4th Ser., LXXI, No. 1 (January 1953), 59.

33 According to Chilton Williamson, *American Suffrage: From Property to Democracy, 1760-1860* (Princeton: Princeton University Press, 1960), p. 15, only Pennsylvania, Delaware, and South Carolina explicitly restricted the vote to males during the colonial period.

backlash. The few incidents of woman's suffrage were construed as dangerous Wollstonecraft-like trespasses upon man's traditional prerogatives and threats to the national well-being. A "Friend to the Ladies" charged that since "female reserve and delicacy are incompatible with the duties of a free elector," it was woman's patriotic duty to abstain from voting. Balloting undermined the *"timid and pliant"* essence of True American Womanhood.[34] The Trenton *True American* maintained that woman's aggressive, seductive, unpatriotic incursion upon the masculine political sphere would undermine the nation. The *True American* went on to endorse Condict's disfranchisement bill:

> Election bill met better fate,
> On every hand defended,
> To check confusion through the State,
> The female's voting ended.[35]

William Griffith, one of the most influential and devoutly patriotic attorneys in the state, concurred. Since voting was a male responsibility, woman's suffrage subverted representative government in the New Nation: "It is perfectly disgusting to witness the manner in which women are polled at our elections. Nothing can be a greater mockery of this invaluable and sacred right, than to suffer it [to] be exercised by persons, who do not even pretend to any judgment on the subject."[36] But Condict was the most adamant opponent of woman's suffrage and set the tone for the opposition. The female vote promoted political chaos, it had "a direct tendency to the subversion of a free government," and it could cause the New Nation "to fall an easy prey to some ambitious individual —some second Bonaparte—who might invade it or start up against us." Women's sly but aggressive entry into electoral politics had to be halted to head off foreign invasion and save the Promised Land. The suffrage had to be restricted "to *free, white, male, citizens*—to those who had property and interest in the country."[37]

---

[34] Trenton *True American*, October 18, 1802 (emphasis added).

[35] Trenton *True American*, November 20, 1807.

[36] William Griffith, *Eumenes* (Trenton, 1799), p. 33, as quoted in J. R. Pole, *Proceedings of the New Jersey Historical Society*, 4th Ser., LXXI, No. 1 (January 1953), 54.

[37] Trenton *True American*, November 23, 1807; Philbrook, *Proceedings of the New Jersey Historical Society*, 4th Ser., LVII, No. 2 (April 1939), 97.

Condict, Griffith, and other New Jersey opponents of woman's suffrage were equating female entry into electoral politics with an invasion of the New Nation by a foreign power. Both were unjustifiable acts of aggression and both threatened to subvert national life. This equation followed logically from late-eighteenth-century republican political theory. Because a republic depended upon the popular consent of the electorate, it was thought to be quite vulnerable to outside influence upon that electorate.[38] Inexperienced and unsuited for political life, women voters were particularly susceptible to outside influence. Secret agents from abroad or domestic traitors could easily turn them against their country and facilitate America's demise. But Condict and his followers were also implicitly pointing to a second evil. If "timid and pliant" women cunningly forced themselves into public life, they would cease to be deferent to the dominant sex. They would become men's coarse competitors. With sexual distinctions gone, the electoral process could become chaotic; the natural leaders of society (like Condict) could be defeated.

The two theoretical objections of New Jersey anti-suffragettes ran at cross purposes. If voting women became aggressive and masculine, then they could not be innocent, tractable novices who were easily subverted by foreign agents. Surface objections therefore obscured the more basic fears of Condict and his followers. On a deeper level, they were more concerned with winning elections than with women's theoretical hardening or softening. They primarily wanted women to satisfy their political needs at a given point in time. Between 1797 and 1807 those needs happened to encompass non-voting women. The woman who stayed home election day and did not endanger the political careers of men like Condict were characterized as soft, retiring True American Women. Malleability or adjustability to variant male needs was more fundamental in this situation than soft, ornamental True American Womanhood literally construed. If women of Elizabethtown had not voted against him in 1797, as they had not on previous occasions, there is no reason to believe that Condict would have opposed them, as he had not on prior occasions.

38 John R. Howe, Jr., "Republican Thought and the Political Violence of the 1790s," *American Quarterly*, XIX, No. 2, Pt. 1 (Summer 1967), 154–55.

Federalist William Crane won Elizabethtown's female vote that year; he did not apologize for it and he did not charge that suffrage hardened the softer sex. Thus, there had to be a double meaning in the anti-suffragette plea for soft, withdrawn womanhood. Because women were voting his way, Crane did not feel compelled to issue this ambiguous plea. Because those women who exercised the suffrage were doing what he wanted, he had no need to demand female malleability through pleas for soft, retiring True American Womanhood. For Crane, the malleable patriotic woman was the voting woman while for Condict she was the hearth-centered figure. Had the female vote gone to Condict instead of Crane, it is likely that their constructions of the role of True American Womanhood would have been reversed.

During New Jersey's suffrage controversy, Condict and his followers had often claimed that women voters were under the seductive, pernicious Wollstonecraft influence. Two decades later the stereotypes survived in the context of a heated debate as to whether the abolition movement helped or hindered the Promised Land. However, the issue was not woman's suffrage so much as whether newly recruited female abolitionists were True American Women or Wollstonecrafts in disguise. Anti-abolitionists took the latter posture; slavery was a public issue and therefore one for men to decide. Not yet President, John Tyler charged that by entering into the slavery debate, the female abolitionist became "the instrument of destroying our political paradise, the Union of these States; she is to be made the presiding genius over the councils of insurrection and discord; she is to be converted into a fiend, to rejoice over the conflagration of our dwellings and the murder of our people."[39] James Kirke Paulding concurred. Abolitionism made woman tough, aggressive, and unpatriotic. It caused her to repudiate "those sacred [domestic] duties, the performance of which makes her guardian angel of the happiness of man" and the keeper of national morals.[40] From Portland, Maine, Reverend Jason Whitman attacked female abolitionism with much the same

---

[39] Quoted in Leonard L. Richards, *"Gentlemen of Property and Standing": Anti-Abolition Mobs in Jacksonian America* (New York: Oxford University Press, 1970), p. 57.

[40] James Kirke Paulding, *Slavery in the United States* (reprint. New York: Negro Universities Press, 1968), pp. 311–12.

argument. The patriotic way "of exerting female influence is, by the cheerful and faithful discharge of appropriate [domestic] duties, rather than by direct efforts in public movements, aimed to produce visible and striking results" (the undermining of the Republic). Albert A. Folsom, another prominent anti-abolitionist of the cloth, articulated identical sentiments.[41] In his *Letters Against the Immediate Abolitionists* (1835), Thomas Russell Sullivan contended that the domesticated woman served her country by conducting herself "regularly and calmly . . . as lovely as the evening star." However, abolitionists drew woman into public life and "dis-orbed" her. The dangerous consequence of this role confusion was greater than "the disastrous shock of comets, striking our trembling globe."[42] These arguments against women in the antislavery movement pervaded anti-abolitionist literature and contained frequent patriotic allusions. They were restatements of the many popular characterizations of True American Womanhood. Retiring, moral, delicate, and ornamental, the domestic family-centered patriot was to balance or modify male crudity. When she transcended her sphere—when she mounted an abolitionist platform—woman was subverting the national well-being, for she left society unbalanced. She was no longer serving men's needs.

Chapter 7 emphasizes the profoundly patriotic commitment of nineteenth-century abolitionists. For present purposes, however, it is important to note that several of them encouraged female participation in public phases of the antislavery crusade while articulating concepts of True American Womanhood strikingly similar to anti-abolitionists.

William Lloyd Garrison was the most significant proponent of female abolitionism and took an active part in the debate that divided the movement during the late 1830's and early 1840's. He wanted women to be regular, full-time participants in antislavery activities, and he encouraged them to mount the forbidden lecture platform and to speak before mixed audiences. But Garrison firmly

---

[41] Jason Whitman, *The Young Lady's Aid, To Usefulness and Happiness* (Portland, Me.: S. H. Colesworthy, 1838), pp. 214–15. *The Liberator*, September 22, 1837, quotes Folsom.

[42] Quoted in Richards, "*Gentlemen of Property and Standing*," pp. 59–60.

believed that "Nature has provided opposite spheres for the two sexes, and neither can pass over the limits of the other, without equally deviating from the beauty and decorum of their respective characters." Woman owed it to her country to administer "ease, comfort,—nay, almost life itself, to the husband, the son, the brother, or the friend." When she worked with men against slavery, woman served as "an important auxiliary" by conducting herself with modesty and refinement. Like certain reformers who sought female involvement in temperance and moral reform, Garrison felt that women could add supportive grace and humane sentiment to organized abolitionism. In this way, they could aid the cause which would redeem the Promised Land. American women had administered delicate feminine qualities to enhance the family circle and should administer these same qualities to the patriotic antislavery crusade. The abolitionist movement was no more than an extended family circle.[43] Garrison's friend New England Unitarian minister Samuel J. May concurred. One of the strongest champions of female involvement in abolitionism, May felt that this role was compatible with the domesticated nature of a female patriot: "The wise, virtuous, gentle mothers of a state or nation might contribute as much to the good order, the peace, the thrift of the body politic, as they severally do to the well being of their families, which, for the most part, all know is more than the fathers do." Because women were soft and moral mothers, they could aid men and country in a public sphere.[44] Benjamin Lundy had drawn Garrison into organized abolitionism during the late 1820's. He had also enlisted Elizabeth Margaret Chandler—perhaps the first significant female abolitionist of the nineteenth century. Like Garrison and May, Lundy felt that women's private family duties and their public antislavery activities were integrally related. Precisely because "the virtuous matrons of our country" were soft, retiring domestics, they could acquaint "the rising

[43] *The Liberator,* March 12, April 9, 1831; September 6, 1834; Bennington (Vt.) *Journal of the Times,* December 12, 1828; Keith E. Melder, "The Beginnings of the Women's Rights Movement in the United States, 1800–1840" (Ph.D. dissertation, Yale University, 1963), p. 145.

[44] Samuel J. May, *The Rights and Condition of Women: A Sermon Preached in Syracuse, Nov., 1845* (Washington, D.C., 1845), p. 4.

generation" with the evils of slavery and thereby help to save the nation.[45]

There were other abolitionists (Garrisonians and anti-Garrisonians) who would not allow True American Womanhood to function outside the home. A woman might help redeem the Promised Land by knitting shirts for fugitive slaves or by attending antislavery bazaars, but these were the limits of her public role. Like anti-abolitionists, they felt that any extensive involvement in the public sphere tarnished woman's retiring sentimentality. Away from the hearth, she would not soften the hard masculine nation; she would become a crude Wollstonecraft-like Amazon. This was the posture of such diverse antislavery activists as Elizur Wright, Jr., Amos A. Phelps, James Gillespie Birney, John Greenleaf Whittier, James H. Fairchild, and Henry Grew. Female abolitionism represented a nationally suicidal program of "sexless democracy" conducted by *"male women."*[46] In 1837 the General (Congregational) Association of Massachusetts issued a "Pastoral Letter" to which most antifeminist antislavery men could subscribe: "When the mild, dependent, softening influence of women upon the sternness of man's opinions is fully exercised, society feels the effects of it in a thousand forms." Thus, when women transcended their dependent family sphere, they ceased to contribute to men or to a viable national character.[47]

Antifeminist abolitionists had nearly echoed the argument of anti-abolitionists, and men like Garrison, May, and Lundy had not quite departed from this consensus. Even these three agreed that whether women spoke out against slavery or stayed silent, they

[45] *Genius of Universal Emancipation*, I, No. 1 (July 1821), 14–15.

[46] See, e.g., *The Liberator*, January 14, 1832; May 3, 24, 1839; June 5, November 27, 1840; February 26, 1841; Aileen S. Kraditor, *Means and Ends in American Abolitionism: Garrison and His Critics in Strategy and Tactics, 1834–1850* (New York: Vintage Books, 1970), pp. 43, 51, 52, 61, 70n., 75, 76n.; James H. Fairchild, *Woman's Rights and Duties* (Oberlin, Ohio, 1849), p. 18; Dwight Lowell Dumond, *Antislavery: The Crusade for Freedom in America* (New York: W. W. Norton & Company, 1966), p. 269; Gilbert Hobbs Barnes, *The Antislavery Impulse, 1830–1844* (New York: Harcourt, Brace & World, Inc., 1964), p. 160; Wendell Phillips Garrison and Francis Jackson Garrison, *William Lloyd Garrison, 1805–1879* (reprint. New York: Arno Press, Inc., 1969), I, 156–57.

[47] Quoted in *The Liberator*, August 11, 1837.

were to remain soft, virtuous, domestic, and ornamental. Garrison, May, and Lundy thought that women could retain these qualities on the antislavery platform while other abolitionists and most anti-abolitionists disagreed. To be sure, there were abolitionists totally outside this True American Womanhood consensus—men like Stephen Symonds Foster and Henry C. Wright. However, they did not shape the debate on "the woman question." It was a standard assumption of that debate that a woman served her country by retaining her soft domesticity whether she was restricted to the hearth or allowed to mount the antislavery podium. All participants in the debate construed soft, retiring domesticity in a literal sense; True Woman served her country by retaining her ornamental, moral, hearth-centered attributes. Unlike anti-abolitionists, men like Birney, Phelps, and Fairchild would allow them to knit clothing or bake pies and sell them at antislavery bazaars. Although they also professed allegiance to the ideal of True American Womanhood, Garrison, May, and Lundy went further; women should mount the lecture platform and participate actively against slavery in order to promote an abolitionist crusade that was humane and moral. From their perspective, True Woman's softness was interpreted literally but it also stood for her capacity to change roles—to go beyond her immediate family circle into the antislavery family and to obey the men at its head.

Thus, the debate over the female abolitionist's contribution to the national well-being centered on variant constructions of soft, retiring, ornamental, family-centered True American Womanhood. Men with different needs invoked different constructions. Anti-abolitionists, seeking to minimize antislavery agitation, naturally invoked the narrowest, most literal construction; True Womanhood must do nothing against slavery. Seeking to broaden the scope of abolitionist activity and to turn the movement into a moral crusade to redeem a nation from shame, William Lloyd Garrison used a far broader construction of domesticity; he justified active public roles for women like the Grimké sisters and Abby Kelley. James Gillespie Birney, the political abolitionist who feared that "the woman question" might discredit the movement, invoked a middle-ground construction of True American Womanhood; patriotic woman remained by the hearth nurturing the young, though she might also sew or bake for antislavery bazaars and thus help to fund organized abolitionism.

Whether they attacked Wollstonecraft's *Vindication* or the extension of a supposed Wollstonecraft tradition into New Jersey electoral politics and organized abolitionism, proponents of True Woman's patriotic role had remarkably similar thoughts. They insisted that True American Women had to retain their delicate, domestic, ornamental features. But though soft, retiring domesticity was often interpreted literally, it also stood for pliant, putty-like qualities. Under this second construction, public, nondomestic activities that benefited certain men could be characterized as retiring True American Womanhood; these activities were supportive of the dominant sex. John Condict invoked a literal construction of woman's place because he was damaged by women voters in New Jersey; benefiting by women at the polls, William Crane preferred the broader interpretation of woman's domesticity. The constructions of anti-abolitionists and profeminist and antifeminist abolitionists also corresponded with diverse male interests. Sometimes the same man invoked both narrow and broad constructions of patriotic woman's retiring essence. For example, John C. Calhoun often used patriotic rhetoric to proclaim that True American Woman was a delicate domestic who remained by the hearth and out of public life. Yet he did not object to the coterie of Washington society women who worked for his election to the Presidency in 1824 and he never opposed his wife when she stood up to President Jackson in the Peggy Eaton affair. In these more assertive areas that benefited him, True American Women allegedly retained their soft, retiring features.[48]

Thus there was a viable if unclearly articulated sexual ideology in the New Nation. Barbara Welter is right when she delineates a far-reaching cult of True American Womanhood. Men like Condict, Garrison, Birney, and Calhoun were not defining patriotic woman's place solely to sustain specific economic or political self-interests. The evidence is overwhelming that these men were also committed to the idea that soft, ornamental, family-centered

---

[48] Some data on this point is found in Gaillard Hunt, *Life in America One Hundred Years Ago* (New York: Harper & Brothers, 1914), p. 74, and Douglas T. Miller, *The Birth of Modern America, 1820–1850* (New York: Western Publishing Company, Inc., 1970), p. 130.

woman was necessary to balance male crudity and thereby save the Republic. But True American Womanhood was susceptible to diverse applications to serve a variety of male interests. If they imputed malleable qualities to patriotic womanhood, men could call upon women to be retreating or aggressive as their interests required. As they demanded these diverse behavioral patterns, men could think all the while that they were adhering to the ideal of True American Womanhood. More than soft, ornamental womanhood, they were therefore propounding a cult of *pliant* womanhood; pliancy allowed for diverse and contradictory uses of patriotic woman's essential softness. The anonymous male author of *The Female Friend* (1809) put the proposition well:

> Man, by nature, is unequal and uneven; he cannot say that he will be tomorrow what he is to-day, and therefore the business of a wife is to conform herself to the present disposition of mind her husband is in, and apply her act to reform what is amiss, or at least to prevent an ill effect from the change of his temper.[49]

Woman altered herself to meet and balance man's changing moods and interests. Patriotic woman's "virtuous affections are the best relief to the heart agitated by the waywardness of life." When American men triumphed, she reinforced them "with smiles of congratulations and triumph." When they suffered defeat or depression, "she reanimated their decaying patriotism and sent them forth again to conquer and to die." And when they were ill or dying, she would "comfort and console, with tender mercies and offices of kindness and love."[50] Her softness was actually a pliancy that enabled her to adjust herself to meet changing male needs under the guise of serving the nation. She was to ornament and

[49] *The Female Friend; or The Duties of Christian Virgins* . . . (Baltimore, 1809), p. 212.
[50] *Historical View of Public Celebrations of Washington Society*, p. 123; John Jersey Mauger, *An Oration, Delivered in the French Calvinist Church, on the Fifth of July, 1819* . . . (Charleston, 1819), p. 7; Ivers James Austin, *An Oration Delivered by Request of the City Authorities, before the Citizens of Boston* . . . *July 4, 1839* (Boston, 1839), p. 15; Benjamin Gleason, *An Oration Pronounced before the Associated Citizens of Lechmere Point, Cambridge, Mass. on the Memorable Fiftieth Anniversary of American Independence* (Boston, 1826), p. 31.

moralize family life, but she was also expected to abandon her family for other callings when male needs required. Immediate male interests dictated the nature and scope of female experience.

IV

It is clear, then, that diverse male proponents of the ideal of True American Womanhood sought to satisfy various specific needs by requiring female malleability. Given the paucity of information about most of the proponents and their generally vague rhetoric, it is exceedingly difficult to tie their articulations to specific self-interests. More can be gained by noting broad social-cultural developments in the New Nation and suggesting how these developments promoted the ideal of pliant True American Womanhood.

In *Democracy in America*, Alexis de Tocqueville pointed to one development that had become widespread by the early Jacksonian period. He brilliantly characterized the devoutly patriotic "nervous American" of the period as a man who desperately sought wealth, power, and popularity but feared that they would elude him. In the public mind, there were few who had great fortunes and few who were hopelessly impoverished. Most seemed to share a relative equality of wealth and status. Great risks were involved in climbing above the masses, for one could easily fall below in the process. Hence, Tocqueville's patriotic "nervous American" was plagued by acute anxiety and by constantly changing moods— moods that were dependent upon temporary economic victories or defeats. A construct that equated woman's patriotism with her pliancy in support of male needs was precisely what the "nervous American" required. When he was suffering economic decline and needed capital to reverse his fortunes, the patriotic woman was one who molded herself to the ideals of thrift and domestic economy. In some cases, she might justifiably take a job; she might become a teacher, a nurse, or even a factory worker. But when business was good and the "nervous American" rose above the masses, the patriotic woman became an ornamental, idle luxury of the hearth. At a time when wealth was ceasing to take the form of sweeping fields and flocks and herds—when profits were increasingly chan-

neled into stocks, bonds, and commercial or industrial ventures—
the vision of idle woman by the hearth furnished proof of man's
success. If she adapted to the role of soft pliancy literally construed, a decorative wife or daughter who ornamented the hearth
proved that the head of the household could afford objects for
waste as well as necessities for use.[51] Therefore, the ideal of pliant
True American Womanhood would seem to have emerged, in
part, to meet the shifting economic and status needs of the "nervous American"—the man on the make whose devout patriotism
caused him to articulate personal preferences as national benefits.

To climb and succeed, the "nervous American" could not afford
to be seduced by a lecherous woman—an Eve, a Hester Prynne, or
a follower of Mary Wollstonecraft. He had to be able to closely
order and reorder his economic behavior within an increasingly
complex level of social organization. When his passions were
aroused, the "nervous American" lost the capacity to properly
order his economic life—to plan and to organize. Since the colonial
period, American men had fretted over seductive, passion-arousing
women. These women had been stereotyped as defiant, independent, self-centered, and therefore semi-masculine. The Anne
Hutchinson episode was perhaps the most notable example. As Professor Ben Barker-Benfield convincingly demonstrates, the divines
of the Bay Colony had perceived Hutchinson as a wretched
seductress who was generating a host of independent, self-centered
Eves throughout Massachusetts. Social and theological disorder
was the consequence.[52] However, by the end of the eighteenth
century and the beginning of the nineteenth, one encounters
images of woman as an independent, self-centered seductress much
more frequently. These images were particularly conspicuous in
patriotic literature. In large part, they were responsive to changing
male sexual habits. By this time, it was not uncommon for men of

[51] In a brilliant article, "The Lady and the Mill Girl: Changes in the Status
of Women in the Age of Jackson," *Midcontinent American Studies Journal*,
X, No. 1 (Spring 1969), 5–15, Gerda Lerner notes the increasing preference
for the idle woman by the hearth but detects a parallel acceptance of low-
skill industrial jobs, teaching, and nursing as properly "woman's work."
[52] Ben Barker-Benfield, "Anne Hutchinson and the Puritan Attitude Toward Women," *Feminist Studies*, I, No. 2 (Fall 1972), 78–80. See also Helen
Waite Papashvily, *All the Happy Endings* (New York: Harper & Brothers,
1956), pp. 103–04.

means to have mistresses and for men of lesser income to take up with prostitutes.[53] It was easiest to impute this new and economically disordering pattern of male sexual existence to lecherous women—to the seductive ways of Mary Wollstonecraft's following. The tradition of female seduction "began with poor Eve," Landon Carter noted, and "ever since then has been so much of the devil in women."[54] David Ramsay agreed and maintained that women were damned "as part of the curse denounced on Eve, as being 'the first in the transgression.' "[55] A Massachusetts minister, Jonathan Stearns, and Charles Knowlton, a physician from the same state, were apprehensive that the devil in women would cause them to "lay aside delicacy" and entrap men.[56] By the 1830's, the stereotype of woman as potential seductress had reached the point where a man of nineteen could beat a New York prostitute to death and break no law. Violent attacks on whores were increasingly persuasive.[57] In the opinion of some, at any rate, to kill an Eve-like temptress seemed more of a public service than an act of murder. The sources of disorientation in male lives had to be eradicated. The temptress diverted men's attentions and energies from central business pursuits. How could a man succeed under the intensely competitive conditions of the New Nation if Eve-like figures constantly drew him away from his economic affairs? They represented images of strength and were independent of men's conscious goals; the notion of female malleability may have emerged, in part, as a necessary corrective. Pliant True American

[53] Page Smith, *Daughters of the Promised Land: Women in American History* (Boston: Little, Brown and Company, 1970), p. 68.

[54] Quoted in Robert E. and B. Katherine Brown, *Virginia 1705–1786: Democracy or Aristocracy?* (East Lansing: Michigan State University Press, 1964), p. 55.

[55] David Ramsay, *Memoirs of the Life of Martha Laurens Ramsay* (London: T. Bayley, 1815), pp. 33–34.

[56] Jonathan F. Stearns, *Female Influence: And the True Christian Mode of Its Exercise; A Discourse Delivered in the First Presbyterian Church in Newburyport, July 30, 1837* (Newburyport, 1837), p. 18; Charles Knowlton, *Fruits of Philosophy or the Private Companion of Adult People* (reprint. Mount Vernon, N.Y.: Peter Pauper Press, 1937), p. 12.

[57] Robert E. Riegel, *Young America, 1830–1840* (Norman: University of Oklahoma Press, 1949), pp. 222–23, cites the New York incident. David J. Pivar, *Purity Crusade: Sexual Morality and Social Control, 1868–1900* (Westport, Conn.: Greenwood Press, Inc., 1973), p. 27, cites the general pattern of violence.

Women assured nervous, ambitious men that they would not be lured off the road to success. By positing that the temptation to take up with mistresses and prostitutes came from self-directing women, and by asserting that tractable True American Women were not temptresses, it followed that the latter were the cure for the increasing and debilitating sexual forces that were drawing men away from their proper callings.

Without temptresses, the male patriot stood to live a more wholesome family life. The True American Woman promoted viable family life by substituting for the temptress, but she also aided the family in another important way. During the early nineteenth century, there were profound fears that the traditional patriarchal family was deteriorating. The man of the house often had to work great distances from his wife and children and was seeing less and less of them. Children seemed increasingly insolent and disorderly. Older sons were departing, lured by the apparent opportunities in new urban centers and frontier societies. By the Jacksonian decades, some elder daughters were even going to work in the factory and the schoolhouse if wedding bells did not chime beforehand.[58] Under these disruptive conditions, hopes for restoration of family stability rested more and more upon the wife and mother. As the only family member whose role did not seem to be changing, she had to make a number of adjustments to hold the seemingly disintegrating household together. She had to assert the authority over the home that her husband had once exercised, to check the younger children's insolence, and to curb or regulate the migratory patterns of the older children. The concept of True American Womanhood encouraged the woman of the house to undertake these widely diverse tasks. According to that concept, she was the central member of the family circle. Her pliant essence gave her the flexibility to do whatever was necessary to hold the circle together. As the keeper of man's home, she was to do whatever had to be done to retain its viability. But if male patriots felt that a concept of submissive patriotic womanhood might promote stable family and home life, that concept could also justify social

[58] William E. Bridges, "Family Patterns and Social Values in America, 1825–1875," *American Quarterly*, XVII, No. 1 (Spring 1965), 3–11; Lerner, *Midcontinent American Studies Journal*, X, No. 1 (Spring 1969), 5–15.

disruption. Whenever men required, even the True American Woman could be drawn from the household to labor in the countinghouse, in the factory, or possibly on the lecture circuit. Men's varying needs dictated women's activities. Thus, although a sense of family disintegration may have made the True Woman the keeper of the idealized hearth, her underlying elasticity might sometimes require her withdrawal from that hearth. Even patriotic woman could not always be counted on to hold the family together.

Tractable patriotic woman also became necessary as nature yielded less. Between 1786 and 1792, *Columbian* contributors frequently characterized America's vast natural terrain as a source of her "Rising Glory." At the same time, they contended that the loyal American must conquer the natural terrain. During the decades that followed, Americans sought fresh land, steam power, and factories, and destroyed an enormous portion of the physical landscape. In the process they were, of course, eliminating the purported source of national grandeur. Two scholars, Perry Miller and Douglas T. Miller, have detected a set response to this dilemma by a number of early-nineteenth-century American writers. Often within patriotic rhetoric but often without, these writers equated nature with femininity. While a man's world was tainted by crude competitiveness and artificiality, woman embodied the lovely naturalness of the untouched physical landscape. Nature, in the guise of woman, survived as a source of national greatness even as the landscape perished with the march of civilization.[59] This interpretation draws support from the typical toast to the "American Fair" at July Fourth celebrations during the early nineteenth century:

O Woman, Nature's loveliest child,
Breathed into life in happy hour,
The World without thee, were a wild,
A waste without a flower.[60]

[59] Perry Miller, "The Romantic Dilemma in American Nationalism and the Concept of Nature," *Harvard Theological Review*, XLVIII, No. 4 (October 1955), 239–55; Douglas T. Miller, *Birth of Modern America*, p. 63.
[60] Richmond *Enquirer*, July 27, 1827.

The patriotic American woman was characterized as "the green spots on the desert of life," "the Sublimest of nature's works," "*Nature's* perfect part," the essence of "artless nature," and "the fairest link in nature's chain."[61] By this logic, Washington's mother became the direct "voice of nature."[62]

A corollary of the belief that femininity could substitute for a disappearing landscape was that women had to be manageable. Physical nature was being shaped and reshaped before men's eyes—its malleable qualities were visible for all to see. Only if women were also patently malleable could men hold to the conviction that the "American Fair" were manifestations of nature. It was therefore woman's patriotic duty to be pliant. In Washington eulogies, July Fourth orations, and a variety of written materials, patriots frequently boasted of the superiority of the American landscape over the crowded Old World. If that landscape was obliterated with no apparent substitute, the future of the Promised Land was bleak. Therefore, a great burden rested on the shoulders of the "Fair Daughters of Columbia."

In hoping that the True American Woman would sustain man's economic ventures, hold together his family, and perpetuate his physical landscape, patriots were basically looking to her as a guarantor of stability and security. They were very nearly claiming that she could promote the rooted or anchored existence that *Columbian* contributors, Washington eulogists, and other proponents of "the Rising Glory of America" had so desperately required. The words and phrases that they used to characterize True Womanhood bear this out. According to the typical July Fourth orator, American women dedicated to their country were like "the Corinthian pillar, which adorns while it supports the temple of liberty." "On you, ladies, depends, in most important degree," the future stability of the nation. Others toasted "Our Fair Country-men to whom the Republic looks with pride for its moral and physical strength and for its perpetuation."[63] Male patriots per-

---

[61] Richmond *Enquirer*, July 8, 1823; July 11, 14, 21, 1826; July 14, 1829.

[62] Jonathan Clark, *Life of General George Washington, Late President of the United States* (Albany, 1813), p. 16.

[63] Richmond *Enquirer*, July 14, 1829; Clifton Joseph Furness (ed.), *The Genteel Female* (New York: Alfred A. Knopf, Inc., 1931), p. 215; Richmond *Enquirer*, July 14, 1826.

sistently reiterated this theme; they contended that soft, tractable women proved their dedication to the country by offering "a safe port" and by serving as "the bosom of HOME," "the stewards and guardians" of the nation, and the "pillars of the Republic."[64] Expressions such as these call to mind Erich Fromm's contention that both the nation and the mother confer a sense of rootedness and collective identity, and that there is an inherent tendency to link the one with the other.[65] The pillar of national existence, True American Womanhood promoted an anchored and secure life for its citizenry. Like the Washington myth, True Womanhood promised a sense of rootedness that transcended geographic bounds. It was a sense of rootedness keyed to a vague and personalized need for order and stability.

Pliant patriotic woman not only offered rooted stability. By striving to sustain man's economic ventures and his family life, and by helping to perpetuate his glorious physical terrain, she exemplified the quest for personal and national perfection. But the True Woman needed emulatable models to sustain her in this quest. George Washington would not do; he was a model of perfection for boys and men. Instead, True Woman had to look to the impeccable women of the American Revolution: "The traditions of our Revolution abound in the most affecting instances of female courage and patriotism, such as posterity will do well to imitate." Revolutionary women gave money and supplies to American forces, and suffered insults and injuries from British soldiers rather than betray their countrymen. It was this perfect and "affecting patriotism by which they were so highly distinguished."[66] Benjamin Gleason held up Revolutionary womanhood for emulation: "as the ancients honoured their household gods; so should we respect and bless the memory of the fair ones of that remarkable period, designated as the 'honourable Matrons of the Revolution.' "[67]

[64] See, e.g., "Female Education," *Southern Literary Messenger*, VI, No. 6 (June 1840), 456; Paulding, *Slavery in the United States*, p. 312; *Columbian Magazine*, April 1790, p. 209; Richmond *Enquirer*, July 13, 1832.

[65] Erich Fromm, *The Sane Society* (New York: Holt, Rinehart & Winston, 1955), pp. 38–60.

[66] James Kirke Paulding, *A Life of Washington* (New York: Harper & Brothers, 1835), II, 41–42.

[67] Benjamin Gleason, *An Oration . . . on the Memorable Fiftieth Anniversary of American Independence*, pp. 31–32.

The "Fair daughters of Columbia" were urged to "lend a retrospective sympathy" to Revolutionary women and to follow their errorless example.[68]

Even though Mary Ball Washington, mother of the Founding Father, had favored the British during the Revolutionary War, proponents of True American Womanhood singled her out for special praise. She was the model of a perfect mother. David Ramsay admitted that Washington's mother "frequently regretted the side her son had taken in the contest between her king and her country." Notwithstanding, Ramsay concluded that Mary Washington was a model female patriot and should be emulated. She excelled in child rearing and brought her son up to be a flawless American.[69] "Here we see one secret of his [Washington's] greatness," Worcester minister John Abbott proclaimed. "George Washington had a mother who made him a good boy, and instilled into his heart those principles which raised him to be the benefactor of his country, and one of the brightest ornaments of the world."[70]

Whereas Mary Ball Washington was the impeccable mother for True American Women to emulate, Martha Custis Washington was the perfect wife. "Few women have figured in the great drama of life, amid scenes so varied and imposing, with so few faults, and so many virtues, as Martha Washington." Because of Martha's amiable and dignified excellence of character, patriotic women were to "copy her example, imitate her virtues." Above all, Martha Washington was a domestic patriot. Her most excellent qualities centered on her family: "she loved the scenes of domestic peace

---

[68] Frederick Frelinghuysen, *An Oration, Delivered July Fourth, 1812. Before the New-Jersey Washington Benevolent Society, in the City of New-Brunswick* (New Brunswick, 1812), p. 10.

[69] David Ramsay, *The Life of George Washington* . . . (London: T. Cadell and W. Davies, 1807), p. 2.

[70] John Abbott, *Mother at Home*, pp. 10–11. For similar remarks by doctrinaire patriots, see, e.g., *Columbian Register* (New Haven), June 29, 1833; John Quincy Adams, *The Jubilee of the Constitution. A Discourse Delivered at the Request of the New York Historical Society, in the City of New York, on Tuesday, the 30th of April, 1839* . . . (New York, 1839), p. 6; Samuel Lorenzo Knapp, *Female Biography* (Philadelphia: Thomas Wardle, 1842), p. 501; *The Early Life of Washington* (Providence: Knowles, Vose and Company, 1838), p. 27; William Jackson, *Eulogium, on the Character of General Washington, Late President of the United States* . . . (Philadelphia, 1800), p. 9.

and quiet, more than the gayeties of the fashionable, or the splendors of the great world." She "adorned by her domestic virtues the sphere of private life." Within the home, she was of inestimable value to the Founding Father. During troubled times, "her cheerfulness soothed his anxieties, her firmness inspired confidence." Through Martha's "tender participation in the anxieties of a husband," she "relieved his cares, and protracted the invaluable life" of the national savior.[71] Like Mary Ball Washington, Martha Washington's perfection consisted of her outstanding assistance to the Founding Father. Only Washington, the man, founded a nation. Woman's perfection consisted of striving to feed, clothe, and comfort him as he created a country.[72]

On the most fundamental level, then, the patriotic woman possessed and conferred a sense of anchored stability as she exemplified the quest for American perfection. This meant that True Womanhood embraced qualities that many male patriots were not able to draw together in their everyday lives. As *Columbian* con-

[71] Samuel G. Goodrich, *Lives of Celebrated Women* (Boston: Bradbury, Soden & Co., 1844), pp. 88-89; David Appleton White, *A Eulogy on George Washington, Who Died at Mount Vernon, December 14, 1799* . . . (Haverhill, 1800), p. 17; Charles W. Upham, *The Life of Washington* . . . (Boston: Marsh, Capen, Lyon, and Webb, 1840), II 302n.; Jared Sparks, *The Life of George Washington* (Boston: Ferdinand Andrews, 1839), p. 99; George W. P. Custis, "Mrs. Martha Washington," *American Ladies' Magazine*, IX, No. 8 (August 1836), 478; George Richard Minot, *An Eulogy on George Washington, Late Commander in Chief of the Armies of the United States of America, Who Died December 14, 1799* (Boston, 1800), p. 20.

[72] These characterizations of Mary Ball Washington and Martha Custis Washington were implicit disavowals of woman's independent creative powers; man invariably set the conditions of her conduct. This may explain why male patriots gave only cursory notice to any patently independent acts of Washington's mother and his wife—even the birth act. In his controversial pioneering essay "Masculine and Feminine: Some Biological and Cultural Aspects," *Psychiatry*, VII, No. 3 (August 1944), 257-96, Gregory Zilboorg maintains that this birth act has made men perpetually jealous of woman's ability to create life and to win most of the infant's love. According to Zilboorg, this male jealousy is more fundamental than female envy of the penis. Labor and delivery has challenged man's sense of mastery and has caused him to persistently seek out remedies. See also Lawrence J. Friedman, "Art Versus Violence," *Arts in Society*, VIII, No. 1 (1971), 328. If Zilboorg is correct—if males envy women for bearing children—the concept of malleable patriotic womanhood might have helped to remedy matters. With putty-like women, men clearly emerged as the molders of human events; woman could create nothing. The fact that Washington's mother and wife gave birth was dwarfed by the Founding Father's creative act of giving birth to a nation.

tributors and Washington eulogists struggled for personal and national perfection, they necessarily provoked or intensified an inner sense of unanchored insecurity. In the reality of daily existence, the abstract pursuit upward toward "Rising Glory" necessarily weakened or destroyed the male patriot's sense of roots and stability. But the True American Woman purportedly had the flexibility to stabilize economic life, family life, and the physical landscape as she strived to emulate the impeccable women of the American Revolution. If she was behaving as she should—if she was sufficiently pliant—the female patriot embraced both rootedness and the quest for flawlessness. Her pliancy was therefore crucial if male hopes for the compatibility of incompatibles were to survive. Her seeming ability to embrace both rooted security and a striving toward perfection may explain why male patriots singled out the notion of pliant True Womanhood more frequently than they spoke of the solid, infallible George Washington.[73]

By counterpointing the Founding Father's solid rootedness against his perfection, Washington eulogists like Mason Locke Weems and James Fenimore Cooper had also tried to draw together incompatible elements. Indeed, the process of blending rootedness with perfection in True American Womanhood was similar to counterpointing Washington's opposite qualities. The concept of a rooted but flawless Founding Father had been based upon mythic images that were foreign to human experience. Opposite qualities that were not, in fact, true, came together in exaltations of a perfect Washington who had never existed. The Washington mythology was therefore a popular word game that afforded troubled patriots no more than a temporary sense of relief from the daily realities that they could not repeal. By striving to emulate a Founding Father whose qualities could never have existed, they were not coming to grips with the actual possibilities and varieties of experience within the human realm. Similarly, the notion of pliant True American Womanhood had little relationship to daily realities. It was a model for what women should

[73] Whereas many references to pliant patriotic womanhood were not accompanied by references to the Founding Father, most Washington eulogies included pleas for women to fulfill their varied patriotic obligations.

be—not a description of what they were or necessarily could be. Unlike the rooted, perfect Washington, however, men's personal failings did not take on the same significance in a sexual context as they did when men sought to emulate the Founding Father. The fault lay in women; the "Fair Daughters of Columbia" were insufficiently tractable and supportive of male needs—they did not sustain men with the flawless or rooted features that were possessed by truly patriotic women. Male inadequacies could always be projected onto women.

More explicitly, the concept of pliant True American Womanhood might help male patriots to retain faith in the compatibility of rootedness and perfectionist strivings. When vague feelings of rootless discontent set in or when perfection continued to elude men, the stable and flawless "Fair Daughters of Columbia" could be blamed for failing to invoke their soft, supportive graces. A man like John Condict might blame politicized women while William Lloyd Garrison might blame women who were not politicized. By conceiving of True Womanhood as manageable supportive womanhood and the embodiment of well-rooted perfection, male patriots had a ready scapegoat for the failures that were inherent in the crusade for "Rising Glory." This must at least partially explain why so many male patriots of diverse regions, classes, and political allegiances dwelt upon the duties of True American Womanhood.

In some measure, then, the vaguely articulated ideal of female malleability became basic to patriotic thought in the New Nation because it was linked with the patriot's most fundamental problem—reconciling perfectionist aspirations with a rather ill-defined and amorphous sense of rooted stability. To ease the long-range anxieties of one part of the population—to give male crusaders for the Promised Land a sense that their ideals were right and that their everyday lives could conform to those ideals—True American Womanhood came to be conceived as a kind of cure-all. Since everyday problems and particularly the uprooting anxieties of perfectionist strivings could be attributed to the deficiencies of the "American Fair," male patriots might avoid agonizing introspection. Unlike young Charles Brockden Brown, they might cast off apprehensions that life had no rules or structure, that randomness reigned supreme. By insisting that American women were obligated to restrict their activities and their experiences to conform to specific male needs, that they abdicate will, and that they become less than human, men could retain a sense of order and control. Male patriots could continue to hope to progress upward on a relatively stable ladder of perfection—one that would not uproot them. Women had to volunteer to be nothing more than the stabilizing rungs upon which men could climb toward perfection, for that was woman's patriotic obligation.

Like the mythic Washington, the ideal of True American Womanhood was therefore an abstraction that had little grounding in the daily realities of living patriots. Thus, it obviously tended to blind men to the diverse possibilities inherent in daily existence—to simplify if not obscure life's complex and varied potentialities. Much more than the mythic Washington, however, True Womanhood limited the richness and diversity of female existence in the Promised Land. To function independently of male needs, women often had to play "a little game."

CHAPTER 5

"A LITTLE GAME"
Mercy Warren, Elizabeth Chandler, and Sarah Hale

In her pioneering study of early-nineteenth-century sexual ideology, Barbara Welter makes no distinction between male and female proponents of the ideal of True American Womanhood. Welter assumes that the ideal dominated the thought of both sexes. Certain evidence justifies this assumption; several women joined men and argued that the True American Woman was soft, ornamental, and pliant. Female participants in July Fourth celebrations often made this assertion.[1] Anna C. Reed, the first female biographer of the Founding Father, urged women to emulate Martha Washington, Mary Ball Washington, and other Revolutionaries of their sex by ornamenting the hearth while remaining responsive to the changing needs of their menfolk.[2] Lydia Sigourney, the very prominent New England author-journalist, repeated Reed's theme. Sigourney insisted that men must monopolize public life but that women must support them in any way possible in "the recesses of domestic privacy."[3] Essays by Catharine Beecher, a leader in the

[1] See, e.g., Robert Pettus Hay, "Freedom's Jubilee: One Hundred Years of the Fourth of July, 1776–1876" (Ph.D. dissertation, University of Kentucky, 1967), p. 102, and the Richmond *Enquirer*, July 11, 1828.

[2] Anna C. Reed, *The Life of George Washington* (Philadelphia: American Sunday School Union, 1832), especially pp. 44, 108–09, 135–36, 241, 255. This biography was initially published in 1829.

[3] Lydia H. Sigourney, *The Boy's Reading-Book; In Prose and Poetry, for Schools* (New York: J. Orville Taylor, 1839), pp. 19, 80–86; Lydia H.

female seminary movement, also sustained the ideal of True American Womanhood. According to Beecher, a pliable wife and mother gave solidity and excellence to the Republic. Proper female education would develop patriotic woman's supportive qualities.[4]

Citing statements by women like Reed, Sigourney, and Beecher, Professor Welter's refusal to distinguish male from female patriots seems sensible. But can such statements be taken at face value? Moreover, what are we to do with women who explicitly disagreed with the notion of pliant True American Womanhood? Abigail Adams claimed that American women had the capacity to fight in the Revolutionary War. She explicitly noted that women "possess a spirit that will not be conquered. If our men are all drawn off and we should be attacked you would find a race of Amazons in America."[5] Must this statement be written off as a jest? In her popular novel *The Coquette*, Hannah Webster Foster urged American women to "meddle with politics" because this would benefit the nation. "Why should the love of country be a masculine passion only?" the fictional Mrs. Richmond inquired.[6] Was her question irrelevant to female sexual and patriotic ideology? By the 1830's the Grimké sisters were crusading throughout the North against slavery and for women's rights. Sarah Grimké's

Sigourney, "The Mother of Washington" and "Washington's Birthday," in Sarah Hale (ed.), *The Ladies' Wreath* (Boston: Marsh, Capen and Lyon, 1837), pp. 242, 245; Lydia H. Sigourney, *Poems* (Boston: S. G. Goodrich, 1827), pp. 138–39; Lydia H. Sigourney, *Letters to Young Ladies* (New York: Harper & Brothers, 1837), pp. 14, 15, 244.

[4] Catharine E. Beecher, *The Duty of American Women to Their Country* (New York: Harper & Brothers, 1845), especially p. 65; Catharine E. Beecher, *A Treatise on Domestic Economy, for the Use of Young Ladies at Home and at School* (New York: Harper & Brothers, 1845), pp. 27, 33–34; Catharine E. Beecher, *An Essay on Slavery and Abolitionism, with Reference to the Duty of American Females* (Philadelphia: Henry Perkins, 1837), pp. 101–02, 104–05; Anne L. Kuhn, *The Mother's Role in Childhood Education: New England Concepts, 1830–1860* (New Haven: Yale University Press, 1947), pp. 181–82; Jill K. Conway, "Evangelical Protestantism and Its Influence on Women in North America, 1790–1860" (American Historical Association, Annual Meeting, 1972), p. 5.

[5] Charles Francis Adams (ed.), *Familiar Letters of John Adams and His Wife Abigail Adams, During the Revolution* (New York: Hurd and Houghton, 1876), p. 169; Katharine Anthony, *First Lady of the Revolution: The Life of Mercy Otis Warren* (Garden City, N.Y.: Doubleday & Company, Inc., 1958), p. 99

[6] Quoted in Elizabeth Anthony Dexter, *Career Women of America, 1776–1840* (Francetown, N.H.: Marshall Jones Company, 1950), pp. 99–100.

Letters on the Equality of the Sexes (1838) stressed that woman was man's equal. The potential of the Promised Land could never be achieved until all of men's rights were enjoyed by women. Angelina Grimké concurred: "Are we aliens because we are women? . . . Have *women* no country—no interest staked in public weal—no liabilities in common peril—no partnership in a nation's guilt and shame?"[7] Were the issues that the Grimkés raised insignificant in the lives of most women? Must we ignore a Virginia Whig politician like Lucy Kenney who attacked Martin Van Buren and the Democrats in strong, earthy, super-patriotic language?[8]

Professor Welter can portray the "Cult of True Womanhood" as the pervasive ideology of women as well as men only by taking certain remarks by specific women at face value and ignoring obvious signs of female dissidence. Gross oversimplification of the psychologies and ideologies of women in the early national period is the unfortunate result. In a sophisticated analysis of Lydia Sigourney, Ann Douglas Wood has shown that this influential writer only half believed her pleas for retiring womanhood. Sigourney's thoughts and motives were complex, often contradictory; she was not simply another proponent of True American Womanhood.[9] Gerda Lerner has detected the same pattern of complexity and ambivalence in a book-length study of the Grimké sisters; they cannot be written off as uncompromising opponents of True American Womanhood.[10]

For some notion of women's sexual and patriotic ideologies in the New Nation, this more fruitful Wood-Lerner biographical framework is required. Unlike male patriots, there were several devoutly patriotic women who centered their intellectual efforts on

[7] Angelina Grimké, *An Appeal to the Women of the Nominally Free States* . . . (New York, 1837), pp. 5–6. See also Angelina Grimké, *Letters to Catharine E. Beecher* (reprint. New York: Arno Press, Inc., 1969), p. 112, and Gerda Lerner, *The Grimké Sisters from South Carolina: Rebels against Slavery* (Boston: Houghton Mifflin Company, 1967), p. 7.

[8] Lucy Kenney, *A Pamphlet, Showing how easily the Wand of a Magician may be broken* . . . (Washington, D.C., 1838), pp. 8, 12, 16. See also Lucy Kenney, *A Refutation of the Principles of Abolition; by a Lady of Fredericksburg, Va.* (Washington, D.C.[?], 1836[?]).

[9] Ann Douglas Wood, "Mrs. Sigourney and the Sensibility of the Inner Space," *New England Quarterly*, XLV, No. 2 (June 1972), 163–81.

[10] Gerda Lerner, *The Grimké Sisters*.

defining the "woman's sphere" in America. The topic seemed to preoccupy women more than men. Our focus shall be upon three such spread-eagle patriots—Mercy Otis Warren, Elizabeth Margaret Chandler, and Sarah Josepha Hale. Warren was one of the most powerful women of the Revolutionary era and the very early national period. Chandler, "Female Editor" of Benjamin Lundy's *Genius of Universal Emancipation*, wrote during the late 1820's and early 1830's and was the first prominent female abolitionist. Hale became active in literary journalism at this time. By 1840 she exerted unprecedented influence in prescribing "American" manners and morals for middle-class homes. Because Warren was a leading patriot and theorist on the "female sphere" at the close of the eighteenth century, Chandler in the late 1820's and early 1830's, and Hale from the 1830's to the Civil War, comparison of their careers points to changing problems female patriots had to confront during the first half of the nineteenth century.

II

Mercy Warren's patriotic qualifications were impeccable. During the American Revolution, she wrote popular pamphlets cast as plays that urged on rebellious Americans and denounced the British and the loyalists as cruel, immoral "blockheads."[11] Her 1788 pamphlet *Observations on the New Constitution* vehemently attacked the proposed Federal Constitution; it would subvert the libertarian precepts of the Promised Land. Her *History of the Rise, Progress, and Termination of the American Revolution* (1805) characterized a New Nation propelling the world toward a final completion of God's plan for man. As she constructed this historical tribute to the "greatest nation," Warren differed from David Ramsay and most other early American historians in one particular: she refused to borrow wholesale from the British

[11] Warren's Revolutionary plays were "The Adulateur, a Tragedy (1773)," *The Magazine of History,* Extra Number 63 (1918), pp. 225–59; *The Blockheads* (Boston, 1776); *The Group* (Boston, 1775); and *The Retreat* (n.d.). For commentary on these plays, see Maud Macdonald Hutcheson, "Mercy Warren, 1728–1814," *William and Mary Quarterly,* 3rd Ser., X, No. 3 (July 1953), 384, 387–88; Annie Russel Marble, "Mistress Mercy Warren: Real Daughter of the American Revolution," *New England Magazine,* XXVIII, No. 2 (April 1903), 175.

Annual Register.[12] James Otis' famous sister was patriotically derelict in only one essential. A zealous Jeffersonian Republican, she could not characterize Washington as infallible—the essence of perfected nationhood. On the contrary, she scorned Federalist Washington for "his coldness in the cause of France—his love of adulation—his favouriteism—and in many instances his injudicious appointments."[13]

Mercy Warren was more than an outspoken woman of letters. She was an active and influential politician. Massachusetts rebel leaders often visited the Warren house in Plymouth during the Revolution and requested Mrs. Warren's political opinions more frequently than those of her husband, James, a prominent merchant-farmer.[14] As President, Thomas Jefferson referred to Mercy Warren's "high station in the ranks of genius" and ordered copies of her *History* for all federal department heads.[15] John Adams was even more laudatory: "I have a feeling of inferiority whenever I approach or address you. I feel that your attainments dwarf those of most men." Adams regularly consulted Warren on public issues and credited her with far-reaching impact upon national policies.[16]

Although she was influential and outspoken in public affairs, Warren sometimes seemed to support the concept of pliable

[12] William Raymond Smith, *History as Argument: Three Patriot Historians of the American Revolution* (The Hague: Mouton & Co., 1966), p. 38. Smith notes that this refusal to copy large portions of the *Annual Register* marked Warren out as the only early American historian not subject to the charge of plagiarism. See also Jean Fritz, *Cast for a Revolution: Some American Friends and Enemies, 1728–1814* (Boston: Houghton Mifflin Company, 1972), p. 295.

[13] Mercy Warren, "To a Respectable Gentleman at Congress," 1795, Mercy Warren Papers, Massachusetts Historical Society.

[14] Augusta Genevieve Violette, "Economic Feminism in American Literature prior to 1848," *The Maine Bulletin*, XXVII, No. 7 (February 1925), 31; Smith, *History as Argument*, p. 36.

[15] Hutcheson, *William and Mary Quarterly*, 3rd Ser., X, No. 3 (July 1953), 378; Maud Macdonald Hutcheson, "Mercy Warren: A Study of Her Life and Works" (Ph.D. dissertation, The American University, 1951), pp. 250–51.

[16] Violette, *The Maine Bulletin*, XXVII, No. 7 (February 1925), 31; Janet Wilson James, "Changing Ideas about Women in the United States, 1776–1825" (Ph.D. dissertation, Harvard University, 1954), pp. 263–64, 266. Because Warren later characterized Adams in unflattering terms in her *History*, he turned on her: "History is not the Province of the Ladies." (Quoted in Anthony, *First Lady of the Revolution*, p. 225.)

patriotic womanhood. She paid no attention to Mary Wollstone-craft—the most striking feminist of the day.[17] Instead, Warren praised tractable womanhood: "Our weak and timid sex is gen-erally but the echo of the other and like some pliant piece of clock-work the springs of our souls move slow or more rapid just as hope, fear, or fortitude give motion to the conducting wires, that govern all our actions." A True American Woman should serve the needs of her husband, Warren told her new daughter-in-law. "Prudence, alacrity, mildness, and condescension must at all times be the counterpart to the hurry of spirits and the ruffle of dis-appointment to which most men of business are liable in the common avocations of life, or in the feuds of politics, private animosities and public disputes."[18] Despite her low opinion of George Washington for his support of the Federalist party, Warren approved of Martha Washington. Mrs. Washington regu-lated her disposition so as to give her husband "domestic felicity." The great First Lady had also disciplined herself to "engage the partiality of the stranger," to soothe "the sorrows of the afflicted," and to aid impoverished manhood.[19] In 1778 Warren scolded Abigail Adams. Although her husband was often abroad negotiat-ing in behalf of the Promised Land, Mrs. Adams had no right to complain of his absence; the patriotic woman "will Throw no Impediment in his way."[20] Throughout her life, Warren warned American women that they must concentrate upon the delicate duties of the hearth; these and not political matters were the patriotic obligations of "our febler sex."[21]

Mercy Warren's advice contradicted her conduct. Active, influ-

[17] Anthony, *First Lady of the Revolution*, p. 189.

[18] Mercy Warren to Abigail Adams, December 29, 1774; Mercy Warren to Mrs. Henry Warren, November 1791—both in Mercy Warren Letterbook 1770–1800, Mercy Warren Papers, Massachusetts Historical Society.

[19] Mercy Warren, *History of the Rise, Progress, and Termination of the American Revolution* (reprint. New York: AMS Press, Inc., 1970), III, 321; Mercy Warren to Madam Hancock, April[?] 13, 1776, Mercy Warren Letterbook 1770–1800, Mercy Warren Papers, Massachusetts Historical Society.

[20] *Warren-Adams Letters* (Boston: The Massachusetts Historical Society, 1925), II, 1.

[21] See, e.g., Mercy Warren to Mrs. Robert Temple, June 2, 1775; Warren to Sally Sevier, June 20, 1784; Warren to Mrs. Henry Warren, November 1791—all in Mercy Warren Letterbook 1770–1800, Mercy Warren Papers, Massachusetts Historical Society.

ential, and outspoken in public affairs, she urged other women to serve as tractable domestic servants of their husbands and their sons. Warren recognized this disparity between her doctrine and her practice. She apologized for writing about public issues. Her book of poetry was purportedly "written as the amusement of solitude, at a period when every active member of society was engaged, either in the field, or the cabinet, to resist the strong hand of foreign domination." A woman could properly pen the volume because "every active member of society" had to participate in the battles and diplomacy of the American Revolution.[22] In her history of the Revolution, Warren's apology was more elaborate. She acknowledged that a narrative of the Revolution was "the more peculiar province of masculine strength" and noted that her "trembling heart has recoiled at the magnitude of the undertaking." Nevertheless, because "every manly arm was occupied" in political and military affairs, her duty was to record "the new and unexperienced events exhibited in a land previously blessed with peace, liberty, simplicity, and virtue."[23] Because her poems were not published until 1790 and her *History* until 1805, Warren could conceivably have given her wartime notes to a man—one whose "peculiar province" it was to write about such matters. Instead, she published both works under her own name and they contained unorthodox opinions about George Washington's fallibilities, American tendencies to emulate European "corruptions," excessive anti-French feeling in the land, and other controversial matters. Warren's correspondence evidenced this same general approach. She would apologize for going "so much out of the road of female attention" or into an area "not altogether consonant to Female Genius." Then she would comment at length on the specifics of current national questions.[24] Like Warren's defense of tractable womanhood, these apologies seemed designed to disarm any who might criticize her frequent trespass upon the male sphere. She did

---

[22] Mercy Warren, *Poems, Dramatic and Miscellaneous* (Boston, 1790), p. iii.

[23] Warren, *History*, I, iii–iv.

[24] See, e.g., Mercy Warren to Hannah Lincoln, June 12, 1774, and Warren to Hannah Winthrop, ——, 1774–both in the Mercy Warren Letterbook 1770–1800, Mercy Warren Papers, Massachusetts Historical Society; *Warren-Adams Letters*, II, 285–86.

not make herself malleable to male needs, but by defending the very theory that she violated, the violation became less conspicuous.

In essence, Mercy Warren practiced sexual politics. Writing her play "The Sack of Rome," she was apprehensive about her own literary abilities and about American disdain for that art form. If the play was distasteful, Warren asked her readers to forgive her, for "there have been instances of men of the best abilities who have fallen into the same error." Her status as a woman exempted her from fault if Americans disliked the play; yet sex was no barrier to favorable recognition.[25] For years, Warren had advised John Adams on a variety of public issues. In her *History*, however, abhorrence of the Federalist party caused her to portray him as a man with corrupt "monarchical tendencies." Adams disavowed the characterization and told Warren to document her charge. As the letters passed between the two, Warren made greater and greater use of patriotic dogma; Adams had no right to question the accuracy of the solidly American Warren family. At the same time, Warren raised the sex issue; she accused Adams of indecently attacking retiring womanhood. He ought not "continue to reproach and affront a writer whose sex alone ought to have protected her from the grossness of your invectives."[26] Put more directly, Warren insisted upon being active in the "masculine sphere" but drew upon the notion of retiring, pliant womanhood to obscure the fact and to ward off attacks.

Beneath the level of sexual politics, Warren had a distinct feminist philosophy and sharply departed from the ideal of True American Womanhood. Sometimes she hinted at her philosophy in published writings, as when she dedicated her *Poems, Dramatic and Miscellaneous* (1790) to Elizabeth Montagu, the English writer:

A Sister's hand may wrest a female pen,
From the bold outrage of imperious men.

[25] "The Sack of Rome," in Warren, *Poems*, pp. 10–11.
[26] "Correspondence between John Adams and Mercy Warren relating to her 'History of the American Revolution,' July–August, 1807," *Collections of the Massachusetts Historical Society*, 5th Ser., IV (1878), 315–511. The quote on Adams affronting retiring womanhood is on p. 455.

In random, guarded comments found almost exclusively within Warren's private correspondence, one discovers a woman who rejected the very notion of malleable patriotic femininity that she herself had espoused. "I ever considered human nature as the same in both sexes, nor perhaps is the soul very differently modified by the vehicle in which it is placed," she confided to her son Winslow.[27] Men seemed more proficient than women because they were educated and experienced while women were "confined to the Narrow Circle of Domestic Care."[28] Warren felt that Catharine Macaulay, the prominent English Whig historian-politician, was a living refutation of the charge "that women make but indifferent politicians." She defended Macaulay's right to marry a man thirty years her junior on the ground that older men were never censored for marrying young girls.[29] Warren was convinced that proper marital life should not confine a woman to the domestic sphere and that a "minute similarity of sentiment" between man and wife was not required for "a friendly union of hearts." Woman did not have to mold herself to meet man's changing needs; she had an independent life of her own.[30]

Although American women were fully men's equals, Warren felt that they had to play "a little game." Traditionally men wanted subordinate and manageable women. For the sake of social stability, American women ought to offer the appearance of subordination and malleability but never the substance: "While we own the appointed Subordination (perhaps for the sake of order in families) let us by no means acknowledge such an inferiority as would check the ardour of our endeavours to equal in all mental

[27] This undated letter was printed in the *Independent Chronicle and Advertiser* (Boston), January 18, 1781 (Mercy Warren Papers, Massachusetts Historical Society).

[28] Mercy Warren "to a Very Young Lady," n.d., Mercy Warren Letterbook 1770–1800, Mercy Warren Papers, Massachusetts Historical Society; Alice Brown, *Mercy Warren* (New York: Charles Scribner's Sons, 1896), pp. 241, 243; Warren, *Poems*, p. 114.

[29] Mercy Warren to Catharine Macaulay, December 29, 1774, Mercy Warren Letterbook 1770–1800, Mercy Warren Papers, Massachusetts Historical Society. For information on the Warren-Macaulay friendship, see Anthony, *First Lady of the Revolution*, p. 123. Warren's defense of Macaulay's marriage is noted in Fritz, *Cast for a Revolution*, p. 225.

[30] Mercy Warren to Mrs. Henry Warren, November 1791, Mercy Warren Letterbook 1770–1800, Mercy Warren Papers, Massachusetts Historical Society.

accomplishments the most masculine heights."[31] "My dear, it may be necessary for you to *seem* inferior," Warren told a young female admirer, "but you need not be so. Let them have their little game, since it may have been so willed. It won't hurt you; it will amuse them."[32] She gave the same advice to a favorite niece. Women should appear uninformed on public questions; they should appear to excel only in "the toilet, the tea table or the card table."[33]

Telling all but her most confidential acquaintances that patriotic womanhood was retiring and domestic, Warren carried on as an active partisan. Offering the appearance of traditional patriotic womanhood, she tried to deny the substance and to live a more varied and fulfilling existence. By all counts, she succeeded, and John Adams knew it. On the eve of the Revolution, he wrote to James Warren regarding their wives, Mercy (Marcia) and Abigail (Portia):

> But if I were of opinion that the fair should be excused from the arduous cares of War and State, I should certainly think that Marcia and Portia ought to be exceptions, because I have ever ascribed to those Ladies a Share and no small one neither, —in the Conduct of our American affairs.[34]

Like the more directly combative Abigail Adams, Mercy Warren needed no man to allow her to be an exception. James Warren and John Adams had no choice in the matter; they had married remarkable women.

Mercy Warren was a remarkable woman by any standards. In a definitive study of relations between the sexes at the end of the eighteenth century, historian Janet Wilson James notes that only a few women from prominent patriot families were important in the nation's political counsels and that Warren was among them.[35]

[31] Mercy Warren "to a Very Young Lady," n.d., Mercy Warren Letterbook 1770–1800, Mercy Warren Papers, Massachusetts Historical Society. Also quoted in James, "Changing Ideas about Women," p. 72.

[32] Quoted in Brown, *Warren*, p. 242.

[33] Mercy Warren to Sally Sevier, January 5, 1780, Mercy Warren Letterbook 1770–1800, Mercy Warren Papers, Massachusetts Historical Society. Also quoted in Hutcheson, "Mercy Warren: A Study," p. 48.

[34] Quoted in Brown, *Warren*, p. 240.

[35] James, "Changing Ideas about Women," p. 67.

Thus, she did not really threaten male political hegemony. But Warren still felt compelled to play "a little game" in order to exercise her privilege. An astute politician, she did not feel that she could carry on as a partisan historian and public figure without covering her tracks by stressing the notion of manipulatable, retiring patriotic womanhood and by avoiding direct, honest debate over woman's proper sphere. In this sense, the Warren example indicated that although significant options were open to a few select women at the end of the eighteenth century, "woman's sphere" was defined rather rigidly. There was no place for Mary Wollstonecraft, much less for a candid Mercy Warren. Successful departure from the ideal of True American Womanhood required a certain measure of calculated deception.

III

Born of Quaker parents near Wilmington, Delaware, in 1807, Elizabeth Margaret Chandler spent her youth and early adult years in Philadelphia, where she received a Quaker common-school education and participated in local Quaker social and philanthropic groups. In 1826 Chandler began to submit occasional poems and essays to Benjamin Lundy's abolitionist newspaper, the *Genius of Universal Emancipation*. Three years later Lundy appointed her editor of the publication's "Ladies' Repository" column. Other newspapers reprinted her writings and Chandler attracted wide attention. Some of her poems were set to music and became part of the ritual of antislavery meetings. In her earliest writings, Chandler had discussed several topics in strongly patriotic language—the crudity of dueling, the horrors of war, exploitation of Indians, and cruelty to the deaf and dumb. By early 1829, she characterized Negro slavery as a cause of these and other national ills, and she consistently urged abolition. By the time she left Philadelphia for the Michigan Territory in the summer of 1830, Chandler had become the most important female abolitionist in the nation. Lamenting her death in 1834, William Lloyd Garrison noted that "there is not a female in the United States who has labored so assiduously, or written so copiously, in the cause of the oppressed." According to Benjamin Lundy: "She was the first American female author that ever made this subject [abolition] the principal theme of her active exertions. . . . no one of her sex, in America, has hitherto contributed as much to the enlightenment of the public mind, relative to this momentous question, as she had done."[36]

The Philadelphia Quaker circles within which Chandler lived had permitted women to exercise more opportunities than most other communities in early America. By the end of the eighteenth century, Quaker women in that city participated with men in certain public events; they were taught to view themselves as men's equals at the Quaker Meeting and before God.[37] Yet despite her Philadelphia Quaker background and her career as a pioneer female abolitionist, Chandler spoke and wrote as a spread-eagle patriot and a proponent of True American Womanhood. Drawing upon standard patriotic clichés, she persistently contended that an American woman must serve men's needs as a retiring domestic. In the New Nation, woman's "timid, shrinking soul" was designed "To share his [man's] fate—whate'er he feels, to feel—to breathe in his fond arms her latest breath and murmur out the loved one's name in death."[38] Patriotic women must not "aspire to emulate the conduct and capacity of men" but rather to be the domestic "helpers, the companions, of educated and independent men." The True American Woman was, above all, a mother. She was obligated "to wipe the starting tear" of her son, to "soothe his little woes," to "guard his morals," and to teach him "to serve the land that smiled upon his birth." Chandler never noted the duties of a patriotic mother to her daughters; males were the important figures in the Promised Land. It was far more important for an American woman to prepare her sons for adult responsibilities than

[36] The basic facts regarding Chandler's life are noted in Elizabeth M. Chandler, *The Poetical Works of Elizabeth Margaret Chandler with a Memoir of Her Life and Character by Benjamin Lundy* (Philadelphia: Lemuel Howell, 1836), pp. 7–12, 38–39, and in Merton L. Dillon, "Elizabeth Chandler and the Spread of Antislavery Sentiment to Michigan," *Michigan History*, XXXIX (December 1955), 481–94. Garrison commented on Chandler's death in *The Liberator*, November 29, 1834. Lundy's remark is found in Chandler, *Poetical Works*, pp. 12–13.
[37] Thelma M. Smith, "Feminism in Philadelphia, 1790–1850," *Pennsylvania Magazine of History and Biography*, LXVIII, No. 3 (July 1944), 244.
[38] Chandler, *Poetical Works*, p. 178.

"To sit with men in legislative hall, To govern realms, or mark their rise and fall; These things are not for her."[39]

Chandler seemed to extend this notion of retiring patriotic womanhood into her abolitionist activities. Out of deference to men, American women were not to meddle in antislavery politics: "The question of *how* abolition will be accomplished, must be the province of other and wiser heads than ours to determine." The formulation and implementation of abolition measures were political acts and therefore belonged to the dominant sex: "that portion of the good work, women will very freely resign into the hands of her brethren."[40] But though the patriotic woman was unsuited for these public duties, "it would also be unnatural for her to see her sister plunged into a gulf of darkness and misery, and not spring forward to her succour. . . . Such conduct as this would, indeed, be unwomanly." White women had to extend the privileges of the fair sex to their black sisters in bondage—the freedom to be soft, sweet, and tractable: "It is because we highly prize, and we hope, feel properly grateful for the domestic privileges of our sex, that we would have them extended to those who are less fortunate than ourselves."[41]

Unlike the Grimké sisters, Elizabeth Chandler had never witnessed Negro slavery. Her knowledge derived from publications, hearsay, and imagination.[42] Chandler assumed that black slave women were members of the "softer sex" and had to be rescued from harsh treatment by reforming and by ultimately abolishing slavery. Yet she was never able to feel or to summon visions of the overseer's whip, the anxiety-ridden auction block, or the planter's sexual assaults on his bondswomen. Beneath a surface commitment to abolition, Lundy's "Female Editor," like Warren before her, was fundamentally concerned with white women like herself.

[39] Thelma Smith, *Pennsylvania Magazine of History and Biography*, LXVIII, No. 3 (July 1944), 249–50. *Genius of Universal Emancipation*, December 11, 1829, p. 108; January 1831, p. 153; February 1831, pp. 170–71; Chandler, *Poetical Works*, pp. 177–78.

[40] *Genius of Universal Emancipation*, January 15, 1830, p. 145; June 1831, p. 28.

[41] *Genius of Universal Emancipation*, June 1831, p. 28; Chandler, *Poetical Works*, p. 24. See also *Genius of Universal Emancipation*, January 1832, p. 131; November 1832, p. 12.

[42] Dillon, *Michigan History*, XXXIX (December 1955), 486.

Writing at a time when there was no feminist movement to sustain her, Chandler had to draw support for her sexual ideas from the emerging antislavery crusade. She frankly acknowledged that "if we [white women] confine our views to the female slaves, *it is* a restitution of *our own* rights for which we ask:—their cause is our cause—they are one with us in sex and nature—a portion of ourselves." In "their degradation, we are degraded." If black bondswomen continued to be degraded, white women would ultimately be shamed.[43] More important, if they ignored the plight of their black sisters, white women would demonstrate hard, unsentimental qualities that contradicted their nature; they would violate the requirements of delicate, emotional True American Womanhood. This was why the majority of white women who remained indifferent to black bondswomen were in jeopardy: "Have their hearts become hard—have they lost the compassionateness of their natures, that the cry of the miserable is so strangely unattended to—or responded only by the voice of inactive lamentation?"[44] White women at large must join with Chandler and other American reformers who "have already flung off the unwanted callousness that so long benumbed their hearts." The apathetic white female majority must strive to restore their sensitivities and to retain respect for a soft, sentimental femininity in America. It "is well to be engaged in a good cause, even if all the energies devoted to its service should be ineffectual to advance its interests one step." Even if white female abolitionists did not have the power to end slavery or to improve the lot of black bondswomen, concerted activism preserved their delicate, sentimental qualities. This was what really mattered![45]

Shulamith Firestone notes that "to champion the cause of a more conspicuous underdog is a euphemistic way of saying you yourself are the underdog."[46] This properly summarized Elizabeth Chan-

[43] Chandler, *Poetical Works*, p. 23 (emphasis Chandler's); *Genius of Universal Emancipation*, May 1831, p. 9.

[44] *Genius of Universal Emancipation*, November 27, 1829, p. 92.

[45] *The Liberator*, January 7, 1832; *Genius of Universal Emancipation*, January 1, 1830, p. 132. See also Chandler, *Poetical Works*, pp. 106–08; Elizabeth M. Chandler, *Essays, Philanthropic and Moral* (Philadelphia: Lemuel Howell, 1836), pp. 64–65.

[46] Shulamith Firestone, *The Dialectic of Sex: The Case for Feminist Revolution* (New York: William Morrow & Co., Inc., 1970), p. 33.

dler's abolitionist ideology. Crusading for black bondswomen, she was out to preserve the soft sensitivities of free white women like herself. Because Benjamin Lundy explicitly hired her to campaign against slavery, not for white female sensitivity, she was playing a variation of Mercy Warren's "little game." To some extent, she was deceiving her male sponsor.

The parallel between Chandler and Warren carries further. Both women propounded the ideal of True American Womanhood while retaining active and independent careers. Idolizing the wife and mother by the hearth, Chandler was an unmarried and out-spoken poet-journalist who urged American women to become active in defense of retiring, sensitized femininity. Drawing upon John Wollman's journal, eighteenth-century Quaker tradition, and Benjamin Lundy's early writings, Chandler became deeply at-tracted to the free-produce movement—the boycott of all produce of slave labor. In strong, commanding language, she often de-manded organized female boycotts of all "slave-tainted" goods as "a service which they [American women] owe to their country . . ." She wanted the free-produce movement to be run by women independent of the direction or even the wishes of the "dominant sex."[47] More generally, Chandler urged white women to "rise up and *demand* for our miserable sisters a restitution of the rights and privileges of her sex." They should "let men be *forced* into the necessity of acting" against slavery. If "men refused to abide by the laws of God" by destroying slavery, women should continue to press men even if they had to transcend the proper sphere of the True American Woman and to enter public life. The crusade against hardening, callous white womanhood and in behalf of oppressed bondswomen was worth the price.[48]

Active in antislavery journalism, Chandler was asking True Women to put down their domestic chores for a while and to join her in antislavery agitation even if "morally warped" men ob-

[47] See, e.g., *Genius of Universal Emancipation*, July 1830, p. 57; November 1832, pp. 14–15; Chandler, *Essays*, p. 38. Dillon, *Michigan History*, XXXIX (December 1955), 487, notes the early Quaker origins of the free-produce movement.
[48] *Genius of Universal Emancipation*, November 27, 1829, p. 92; October 30, 1829, p. 60; December 11, 1829, p. 108; June 1831, p. 28; Chandler, *Poetical Works*, p. 24.

jected. But though her feminist plea was stronger than Benjamin Lundy had counted on, her "little game" did not go beyond using an abolitionist periodical for a feminist message. Whereas Mercy Warren had consciously propounded True American Womanhood to decoy men and to lead a life that encompassed independence and assertiveness, Chandler propounded that notion without realizing that she violated its essential tenets. Combing Chandler's private papers and published writings, there is not even a hint of the need to profess soft malleability in order to function independently and vigorously in public life. Rather, Chandler saw no conflict between the tractable patriotic woman sensitive to men's needs and her own career and ventures. The slave system was the major threat to white women's capacities to serve men. Whatever white women did to resist slavery helped them to ward off callousness; antislavery agitation preserved their soft pliancy so that they could continue to be good wives and mothers.

Chandler, then, represented a blend of opposite ingredients. Urging women to combat the wretched institution of slavery, she was forging a mildly feminist program. She was telling white women to take charge of the free-produce movement and to force men to act against slavery. It did not matter whether men wanted white women to assume this assertive role. At the same time, Chandler genuinely believed that women served their country as retiring, pliant, sentimental servants of the "dominant sex." Unlike Mercy Warren, Chandler assumed that pliancy was consistent with active assertiveness. She saw no need to pretend to be tractable in order to mask female independence. Lacking Warren's analytic clarity, Chandler did not have to play Warren's "little game" at the level that Warren played it. She did not subordinate woman's needs to abolitionism as Lundy would have preferred, but this constituted the limits of her deception of the "dominant sex."

In the summer of 1830 Elizabeth Chandler astonished Eastern reformers by joining her brother and her aunt in their move from Philadelphia to the Michigan Territory. The three settled and cultivated a farm in Lenawee County on the Raisin River—a rugged frontier area southwest of Detroit. Chandler continued to edit the "Ladies' Repository" of the *Genius of Universal Emancipation*. At Benjamin Lundy's prompting, she also convened a

Quaker meeting to found the first antislavery society in the Michigan Territory. Through this society and through her distribution of the *Genius of Universal Emancipation* and *The Liberator*, Lundy and Garrison influenced abolitionist thought in southern Michigan before Theodore Weld and Charles Finney invaded from Ohio.[49] During the early 1830's, however, the Atlantic seaboard remained the center of significant abolitionist activity. Moving from the East Coast, Chandler was reducing her contacts with organized abolitionism.

It seems likely that Chandler agreed to accompany her brother and her aunt to an isolated frontier farm community in order to slow the pace of her antislavery activities. In the correspondence covering her years on the Michigan frontier, there are strikingly few references to the abolitionist crusade even though Eastern abolitionists were vitally concerned over Michigan statehood. If the Territory gained admission as a free state, Southern slaveholding power in Congress stood to be reduced. "Folks begin to talk of having our Territory converted into a state," Chandler remarked. "To me as an individual it is a matter of very little consequence."[50] The family farm seemed more important than a major abolitionist issue that affected her community. After her first winter in Michigan, Chandler noted how she "felt pleased with the country at first; but I think it still better now; at any rate I feel *much* more at home." For the first time in her life, Chandler declared, she felt rooted and at one with herself.[51] From time to time she described how busy and elated she was helping her brother with spring planting, attending to her mulberry trees, and harvesting the fruits of her labors.[52]

As Carl N. Degler notes, relatively primitive subsistence-

[49] Dillon, *Michigan History*, XXXIX (December 1955), 482, 494; Merton L. Dillon, *Benjamin Lundy and the Struggle for Negro Freedom* (Urbana: University of Illinois Press, 1966), p. 174.

[50] Elizabeth Chandler to Jane Howell, 8th . . . 1831 [no month designated], Elizabeth M. Chandler Papers, Michigan Historical Collections, University of Michigan.

[51] Elizabeth Chandler to Jane Howell, July 7, 1831, Elizabeth M. Chandler Papers, Michigan Historical Collections, University of Michigan.

[52] Elizabeth Chandler to Jane Howell, October 10, 1830; April 15, 1831; March 27, June 20, 1832; April 24, 1833—Elizabeth M. Chandler Papers, Michigan Historical Collections, University of Michigan.

farming societies have often minimized the sexual division of labor. When the chores of home and child rearing permitted, women worked in the fields alongside the men.[53] Without children, and with her aunt, Ruth Evans, attending to many of the household chores, Elizabeth Chandler had plenty of time to work alongside her brother in the fields, to plant, and to harvest. She was farmer Chandler now, not simply the "Female Editor" of Lundy's *Genius of Universal Emancipation* and not limited to pleas for female sensitivity through an antislavery movement that was never her primary concern. The sexual division of labor was much less conspicuous on the Michigan frontier, and this probably contributed to Chandler's happiness. It is certain that she found this arrangement more rewarding than writing in her house in Philadelphia and sending off the copy to Lundy's offices.

Chandler's abandonment of the cosmopolitanism and companionship of Philadelphia's progressive Quaker reform community for the isolation of a rugged frontier existence has important implications. For such a woman, life in the storm center of racial and sexual reform was not altogether liberating. Unlike Charles Brockden Brown, Chandler was never at odds with Philadelphia's Quaker community. But under the guise of abolitionism, she voiced apprehensions over the lives of the women about her— about their seeming indifference and callousness despite the reformist agitation of the times. Perhaps Chandler saw her own sensitivities blunted as "Female Editor" of the *Genius of Universal Emancipation.* An unmarried writer whose life was hardly a model for True American Womanhood, she may have sensed that abstract pleadings for female sensitivity in a movement concerned with black bondage was simply too limiting—limiting to both herself and her cause. Perhaps Chandler also decided to leave Philadelphia owing to a belief in the potential of the American West. In her Michigan letters, she characterized the West as a land of opportunity where a woman could roam freely and regain lost options. This may have been the vision that drew her from the

[53] Carl N. Degler, "Revolution Without Ideology: The Changing Place of Women in America," *Daedalus,* XCIII; Pt. 1 (Winter–Spring, 1964), 654. For an interesting departure from Degler, see Fred R. Mabbutt, "The Myth of the American Woman," *Colorado Quarterly,* XXI, No. 3 (Winter 1973), 295–96.

metropolis to the frontier. Although there is no hard evidence indicating precisely why Chandler left a successful career for the isolation of the Michigan Territory, it is certain that the move worked out well. Out of the mainstream of American life, she felt she was living the sort of life that she never even conceptualized in the most tolerant and cosmopolitan of cities. There seemed to be time for a woman to leave the hearth behind so that she could enjoy mulberry trees, spring planting, fall harvesting, summer sun, and winter snow. In the early 1830's, the experientially narrowing, perfection-oriented culture that *Columbian* contributors, Washington eulogists, and proponents of pliant True American Womanhood were inculcating throughout the settled regions of the New Nation had not yet entered Lenawee County in full force. There seemed to be time to take in life's diverse experiences and emotions—to live the sort of existence Brockden Brown had prescribed in the abstract but had been unable to enjoy.

IV

Elizabeth Chandler respected Sarah Hale as a woman who "has added largely to the reputation of her sex, and who is exerting a beneficial influence, far and wide, through the medium of her very popular *Magazine* [the *Ladies' Magazine*]."[54] But Hale's career differed significantly from Chandler's. Whereas Benjamin Lundy's "Female Editor" abandoned her public career in the nation's social and cultural center and headed for the provinces, Hale felt compelled to move toward the center of action—from rural New Hampshire to Boston and then to Philadelphia.

Hale was born in isolated Newport, New Hampshire, in 1788, the daughter of Gordon Buell, a soldier of the Revolutionary War. Her mother and sister died in 1811 and her father's tavern failed the following year. Economic necessity required her to teach school in Newport from 1806 until 1813, when she married a young New Hampshire lawyer, David Hale. Continuing to reside in Newport, she gave birth to five children during the next decade. David Hale died suddenly in 1822, leaving his wife with no income and a household of children. Desperate for money, she began to

---

[54] *Genius of Universal Emancipation*, November 27, 1829, p. 92.

write poetry and fiction. Impressed by *Northwood*, her first novel, John Lauris Blake, the principal of Boston's Cornhill School for Young Ladies, offered her the editorship of the *Ladies' Magazine*, a publication he intended to commence in 1828. Gladly accepting the offer, Sarah Hale moved to Boston to begin one of the most successful careers in literary journalism in the nineteenth century. Her *Ladies' Magazine* was a popular if not a profitable journal, and appealed to middle-class women with increased leisure on their hands. The perfection of the kitchen stove, the availability of textiles, and the supply of domestic help from new immigrant groups had released a number of women from the tedium of the hearth. Sentimental novels and romantic-domestic journalism allowed them to fill their idle hours. Reading women also constituted visible proof that the man of the house was economically successful and could afford to have leisured, cultivated females around. Hale retained this middle-class female audience for the balance of her career. In financial trouble after nine years in Boston, she decided to merge the *Ladies' Magazine* with Louis Godey's Philadelphia-based *Lady's Book*. Becoming Godey's chief editor, Hale moved to Philadelphia and remained on the job for thirty-eight years. The *Lady's Book* soon became the most popular women's magazine in the country and Hale won recognition as one of Philadelphia's leading citizens. In addition to fulfilling her demanding editorial duties and social responsibilities in Philadelphia, she wrote two dozen books and hundreds of poems and became the most influential woman in mid-nineteenth-century America.[55]

Throughout her long life, Hale was always an active patriot. She raised funds to complete the Bunker Hill Monument, she established Mount Vernon as a national shrine, and she successfully

[55] Data on Hale's life may be garnered from two relatively poor biographies—Isabelle Webb Entrikin, *Sarah Josepha Hale and Godey's Lady's Book* (Philadelphia: Isabelle Webb Entrikin, 1946), and Ruth E. Finley, *The Lady of Godey's: Sarah Josepha Hale* (Philadelphia: J. B. Lippincott Company, 1931). See also Paul S. Boyer, "Sarah Josepha Buell Hale," *Notable American Women, 1607–1950* (Cambridge, Mass.: The Belknap Press, 1971), II, 110–11; Sarah Josepha Hale, *Northwood; or, Life North and South* (New York: H. Long & Brother, 1852), iii; Sarah J. Hale to Mathew Carey, June 19, 1834, Edward Carey Gardiner Collection, Historical Society of Pennsylvania.

campaigned for the recognition of Thanksgiving Day as a national holiday. Unlike Mercy Warren, however, she had no memories of the Revolution or conversations with Washington, Adams, and Otis to substantiate her exaltation of American tradition. She had only hopes and dreams. "The wish to promote the reputation of my own sex and my country, were among the earliest mental emotions I can recollect," Hale noted in her forty-eighth year.[56] Vague, emotional references to the Promised Land characterized her literary career. Much affected by the passing of both Thomas Jefferson and John Adams fifty years to the day from the Declaration of Independence, Hale proclaimed:

We [Americans] should seriously reflect on this event, sealing as it were, the sacredness of our freedom, and resolve to act worthy of the destinies of a great nation, selected, as we may confidently trust, to teach the world the oracles of true liberty, and show an example of men who, by governing themselves, will render kings unnecessary.[57]

She averred that the New Nation would lead the world in advancing "freedom's glorious dower"; it would "show the nations as they gaze in awe That wisdom dwells with Liberty and Law!"[58] She justified exclusion of European authors in her anthology of the world's best poetry: "I have preferred, exclusively, extracts from American poets. I think it is time our people should express their own feelings in the sentiments and idioms of America." Promotion of American cultural nationalism was more important than accurate representation of the finest universal poetry.[59]

Like many other patriots, Hale linked the New Nation's glory with George Washington, his mother, and his wife. She recalled her soldier father's frequent references to the infallible Founding Father, she looked to Washington as the symbol of Americanism, and she conceived of him as the standard of perfection for all true

[56] Sarah J. Hale, *The Ladies' Wreath* (Boston: Marsh, Capen and Lyon, 1837), p. 385.
[57] *American Ladies' Magazine*, IV, No. 7 (July 1831), 328.
[58] Quoted in *The Liberator*, February 5, 1831.
[59] Sarah J. Hale, *Flora's Interpreter* (Boston: Marsh, Capen and Lyon, 1832), iv.

patriots. His marriage was a model for Americans: "The marriage union, as it subsisted between George and Martha Washington, is shown to be the happiest, as well as the holiest, relation in which human beings can be united to each other."[60] But for Hale, who had never remarried after the premature death of her husband, a patriotic woman was above all a mother. She characterized Mary Ball Washington as the exemplar of American motherhood: "She shares, with her illustrious son, the admiration of the world—with his *name* comes her *remembrance;* and what loftier praise could any woman covet, than to be like her?" Through "maternal solicitude and judgment" she formed Washington's character and thereby laid the foundation for his fortune and his fame. The Founding Father was her own creation. For this reason, it was unthinkable, even disloyal, to accuse Mary Ball Washington of favoring the British during the American Revolution. She epitomized female perfection, Hale claimed, and American women should emulate her as they struggled to improve themselves. This "desire for perfection" was the most meritorious of all human qualities: "We must exert ourselves, in order that we do not descend, and this can be done only by endeavoring to rise." By struggling to emulate Mary Ball Washington, American women could continue to bless the nation with flawless male leadership.[61]

Much more of a proponent of perfectionist striving than either Mercy Warren or Elizabeth Chandler, Hale also espoused the concept of malleable patriotic womanhood with greater vigor. The True American Woman was man's "helpmate" and should support him. Woman provided a home base or anchor for man's life and she organized her domestic chores around his changing needs: "She sits at home and thinks of him the live long day. All her arrangements are made in reference to his return; and she feels that without him the world and her history would be blank." She attends to his bed when he is ill, she sheds "the tear of sympathy"

---

[60] Finley, *Lady of Godey's,* p. 174; Sarah J. Hale, *The Genius of Oblivion and other Original Poems* (Concord, Mass.: Jacob B. Moore, 1823), p. 87; Sarah J. Hale, *Woman's Record; or, Sketches of all Distinguished Women* . . . (New York: Harper & Brothers, 1860), p. 550.

[61] *American Ladies' Magazine,* IV, No. 9 (September 1831), 386–89, 391, 394; VI, No. 6 (June 1833), 268–69; VII, No. 9 (September 1834), 385; IX, No. 1 (January 1836), 24.

when he becomes discouraged, and she applauds his every success.[62] In *The Lecturess* (1839), Hale emphasized this theme. Her character Marian Gaylord Forrester had lost sight of the duties of True American Womanhood. She had become active in the anti-slavery crusade as a public lecturer and neglected her husband's personal needs. Mr. Forrester quite properly left her and the balance of her life was filled with guilt and misery. On her deathbed, Marian Forrester confessed her sin; she had not struggled to satisfy her husband:

> . . . True independence in a woman, is to fill the place which God assigns her; to make her husband's happiness her own; and to yield her will to his in all things, conformable to her duty to a higher power. By such conduct will a woman attain her *rights,* the affection of her husband, the respect of her children and the world, and the approval of heaven. These are the *rights* of woman.[63]

Although Hale perceived several male needs that American women should strive to meet, one was paramount. Men in the New Nation were captivated by the pursuit of wealth and needed women to check their acquisitive propensities—to balance their materialism with culture and morality. Woman's ability to perform this task would "decide the destiny of our Republic."[64] "This is a speculating and selfish age," Hale charged, "and to think 'money will answer all things' is too much the characteristic" of American men. "Honour, patriotism, religion, even delicacy and affection, are sacrificed on the altar of avarice. God of my country! Is there no word or power [that] can exorcise this demon among us!" Patriotic woman was duty-bound to check the male's acquisitive propensity by cultivating "moral sentiments," "the better, holier emotions of his [man's] heart," kindness and delicacy. Only when man "feels that companionship with her refines

---

[62] Sarah J. Hale, *Northwood: A Tale of New England* (Boston: Bowles & Dearborn, 1827), II, 197; Sarah J. Hale, *Sketches of American Character* (Boston: Freeman Hunt, 1831), p. 104; *American Ladies' Magazine*, VIII, No. 8 (August 1835), 440–41; Sarah J. Hale, *The Lecturess: or Woman's Sphere* (Boston: Whipple and Damrell, 1839), pp. 39–40.

[63] Hale, *Lecturess*, p. 120.

[64] *American Ladies' Magazine*, VII, No. 5 (May 1834), 216.

and exalts his nature" would America's crass materialism be arrested and the nation saved.[65]

Although Sarah Hale argued for patriotic woman's higher morality with frequency and fervor, the facts of her career demonstrated that she was no True American Woman; her career did not conform to her doctrines. She began by teaching school in Newport, New Hampshire, for seven years, something of an innovation for the time and place. Moving on to Boston to become America's first female magazine editor in 1828, she left four of her five children behind so that they could be raised and educated by others. She alternated between boardinghouses and residing in the homes of her daughters for the next half century and retained a servant, Hannah Murray, to attend to all domestic needs. Without child-rearing responsibilities and with no husband to serve, Hale editorialized on a variety of public issues from abolition and African colonization to prohibition, war, and electoral politics.

Exalting True Womanhood by the hearth while divorcing herself from domestic responsibilities and commenting on public issues, Hale characterized herself as a moral crusader from the fireside. "I disdain all intention of writing politically," she contended in 1828. "But still considerations allied with the prosperity, the fame, indeed the very existence of our Republic will press on the mind" of a woman genuinely concerned with the moral reform of her country.[66] Two years later, she reprinted a portion of Benjamin Lundy's *Genius of Universal Emancipation* in her *Ladies' Magazine* but denied any intention of favoring female intervention in "so momentous and appalling a subject" as slavery. Rather, she simply wanted to peruse the debate over slavery from a moral perspective with a "womanly delicacy in an unobtrusive manner."[67] In 1835 Hale contended that her role as one of the most influential and outspoken editors in the land constituted no violation of man's traditional prerogatives. Neither she nor her staff ever "advance or advocate any theories of the 'rights of

[65] Sarah J. Hale, *Traits of American Life* (Philadelphia: E. L. Carey & A. Hart, 1835), p. 239; *Godey's Lady's Book*, XIV (January 1837), 1–3; XX (April 1840), 154; Hale, *Northwood* (1852 edition), p. 407.
[66] *American Ladies' Magazine*, I, No. 8 (August 1828), 337–38.
[67] Quoted in Entrikin, *Hale*, p. 28.

women,' based on the natural equality of the sexes—our aim is to inculcate all womanly virtues, and found the influence of the sex on moral elevation of feeling, and a deep sense of religious duty." Her opinionated remarks on questions that men debated merely represented female moralism and decorum to sustain men. She was simply trying to balance male materialism with female morality— the proper duty of a female patriot supportive of her countrymen. Her career was therefore totally consistent with True American Womanhood.[68]

Whenever she came under attack for her activities and comments on public issues, Hale maintained this defense. In the 1830's she had led New England women in a fund-raising venture to complete the Bunker Hill Monument. Newspapers charged her with impropriety. Hale retorted that women of New England were not trying to take charge of fund raising independent of male direction. "We come and offer our assistance only in the character of *helpers*—an office with which the Creator invested woman." Women were simply acting as moral agents to stimulate their menfolk in this vital economic and patriotic activity.[69] When Boston women formed a Ladies' Peace Society in 1835, Hale rebutted its critics and defended all organized female pacifist activities. Patriotic woman's moral obligation was to achieve peace in the home. Consistent with this obligation, she must lend her pure principles to effect honorable international accords.[70] This same argument justified improved female education and job opportunities. Through better mental training and through employment in female seminaries, in public schools, and in medicine, women became more moral and patriotic. They also learned how to transmit morality and patriotism to their menfolk.[71] Consistent with her own career, Hale wanted women to develop in areas outside the

[68] *American Ladies' Magazine*, VIII, No. 1 (January 1835), 54.
[69] Finley, *Lady of Godey's*, pp. 67–73; *American Ladies' Magazine*, III, No. 3 (March 1830), 135–36; III, No. 4 (April 1830), 180; VI, No. 6 (June 1833), 280.
[70] *Godey's Lady's Book*, XXI (August 1840), 88–89.
[71] See, e.g., *American Ladies' Magazine*, I, No. 1 (January 1828), 1–2; VII, No. 4 (April 1834), 162; *Godey's Lady's Book*, XIV (January 1837), 4–5; XIV (April 1837), 185–86; Hale, *Sketches of American Character*, p. 106; Hale, *Woman's Record*, p. 900.

home. But she always stressed that her recommendations strengthened woman's role as moral guardian of the Republic and
supporter of patriotic masculinity. Unlike Mercy Warren or Elizabeth Chandler, Hale never implied, even in private correspondence, that the "rights of women" were legitimate ends in
themselves. To the contrary, she constantly opposed extension of
those "rights" in areas like the suffrage and liberalized property
law, where new options might discourage women from serving
men.[72] If Hale was a feminist, she had a perspective significantly
different from her two predecessors.

Although Hale consistently defended herself and certain other
activist women as champions of True American Womanhood
while publicly attacking the concept of "women's rights," she
propounded a broader view of True Womanhood than many of its
male proponents. Although supportive domestic duties remained
women's primary responsibility, females also had important moral
and patriotic duties beyond the hearth. They raised funds to
construct national monuments. Female pacifist leagues were encouraged. Facilities had to be developed to train women for
medicine, teaching, and other significant callings. Hale always
claimed that these activities were consistent with patriotic womanhood. She publicly departed from the sexual ideology of male
patriots in a second respect as well. Her praise of Mary Ball
Washington differed from theirs in one essential. Washington's
mother was more than an inspiring sidelight in the Founding
Father's life. She, as woman, preceded Washington and formed his
features; the female played a primary role in contouring the New
Nation. Hale's contention that only woman could perpetuate the
Promised Land as the Founding Father had left it distinguished her
from male patriots in still a third respect. Woman alone could
check the increasing greed and materialism of the "primary sex."
Increasingly distant from the sources of wealth and power in an
industrializing, urbanizing, commercialized nation, woman was the
lone repository of pure morality. Woman's morality and selfless-
ness in a society of money grubbers was the key to the future;
"the Rising Glory of America" was in her hands.

[72] See, e.g., *Godey's Lady's Book*, XX (January 1840), 4; XXII (February
1841), 95.

Sarah Josepha Hale was, therefore, no mere echo of male proponents of True American Womanhood, but she differed from Mercy Warren and Elizabeth Chandler as well. Exalting marriage, child rearing, and the hearth, she departed from all three early in her life, dwelt in the boardinghouses she criticized as dens of immorality, and became one of the most influential writers in the nation. Hale led a more unorthodox life style than Warren, the diligent wife and mother, or even Chandler, the spinster who lived with her brother. At the same time, Hale was a stronger proponent of malleable patriotic womanhood than her two predecessors. Unlike Warren or Chandler, she opposed the "rights of women" and any philosophy or measure designed to benefit women at the expense of traditional male prerogatives. In the great body of Hale's correspondence, short stories, poems, novels, and essays, there is not the vaguest hint that she championed the ideal of True American Womanhood to cloak her unusual living habits. She was not playing "a little game" to reconcile the gross disparity between her ideology and her life style. Sincerely believing that patriotic woman should center her life on the hearth and should act as man's moral agent, Hale saw herself doing just that. She never perceived the highly unorthodox nature of the career and the habits that had become her daily routine. Conceiving of herself as a moral agent from the hearth in all that she said and did, Hale felt no need to reconcile her preachings with her practice.

Failing to perceive the conflict between her allegiance to True Womanhood and her unorthodox life style, Hale represented no isolated example. Scholars have recently discovered that Lydia Sigourney, Grace Greenwood, and other important sentimental-romantic "Scribbling Women" of the mid-nineteenth century shared this failure of perception. Like Hale's, for example, Sigourney's life style was more irregular than Mercy Warren's or even Elizabeth Chandler's, her doctrines were more orthodox than either of the two, and (like Hale) she was not able to see the disparity between her doctrines and her daily life. The examples of "Scribbling Women" like Hale and Sigourney point to a crucial social phenomenon. More than at any other period in early American history, the opinions and life styles of certain very influential women ran at cross purposes and there seemed to have been very little conscious realization of the disparity.[73]

Of the many characters in Hale's novels and short stories, her planter gentlemen were the most important. William R. Taylor thoroughly documents the way Hale's Southern planter, through his abundant leisure, moral decency, and human understanding, balanced the more aggressive, materialistic Northern male.[74] Like the True American Woman, the Southern planter checked the masculine Yankee quest for profit. North Carolinian Henry Sinclair of the short story "The Springs" typified Hale's planter. Like his lover, Emily Woodworth of Connecticut, Sinclair was kind, soft, sincere, and amiable, but powerful and brave as well.[75] South Carolinian Horace Brainard of *Northwood* was also a cultivated, tender but commanding planter who understood that slavery was immoral and looked to the day when it would cease. Another planter in *Northwood*, Georgian Charles Stuart, shared Brainard's revulsion for slavery and was also a man of cultured yet patently assertive and dignified carriage. But Hale's attempt to portray a refined, moralistic yet powerful Southern planter was best exemplified by Sidney Romelee, the hero of *Northwood* and her most important fictional character. Born in New Hampshire, Romelee moved to a Charleston plantation at an early age. It "was in Charleston [where] his habits had been formed, opinions imbibed and friends selected."[76] Like his lover, Susan Redington of New Hampshire, he had acquired sensitive, moralistic qualities, but he was also a figure of strength.

Reviewing the facts of Hale's life, there is a clear resemblance between Sidney Romelee and the lady of *Godey's*. Like Romelee, she left New Hampshire and family behind for the city (Boston

[73] Ann Douglas Wood comments at length on this pattern that was shared by several mid-nineteenth-century sentimental writers in two outstanding articles: "The 'Scribbling Women' and Fanny Fern: Why Women Wrote," *American Quarterly*, XXIII, No. 1 (Spring 1971), 3–24; "Mrs. Sigourney and the Sensibility of the Inner Space," *New England Quarterly*, XLV, No. 2 (June 1972), 163–81. See also Helen Waite Papashvily, *All the Happy Endings* (New York: Harper & Brothers, 1956).

[74] William R. Taylor, *Cavalier and Yankee: The Old South and American National Character* (Garden City, N.Y.: Doubleday-Anchor, 1963), pp. 101–19.

[75] Hale, *Sketches of American Character*, pp. 179–98.

[76] Hale, *Northwood* (1827 edition), II, 211.

and Philadelphia—not Charleston) where her "habits had been formed, opinions imbibed and friends selected." Breaking away from a hearth-centered family existence in New Hampshire, Hale became permanently single, a boardinghouse dweller, and a familiar face among Philadelphia's social elite. A powerful and influential writer and editor who felt free to speak out on public controversies, she had much of Romelee's strength and command. Yet she filled most of her printed pages with sentimental delicacies and moral preachings; like Romelee, she had a conspicuous soft side. Although Sinclair, Brainard, and Stuart did not resemble Hale as closely as Romelee did, they too shared this balance between masculine strength and command on the one hand and gentle delicacy and morality on the other. Like Romelee, these virtuous planters embodied both elements in Hale's fragmented existence.

Hale never used female characters to draw together her diverse qualities into an integrated and admirable whole. There was no female equivalent of Sidney Romelee—no heroic "Lady Editor" who abandoned home and family in the provinces for the excitement and profits of Boston and Philadelphia literary circles. There was not even a Southern plantation belle who merged strength and independence with delicacy and softness. One might argue that Hale limited literary projections of herself to Southern men in order to obscure her fictional efforts at self-integration—that this was her "little game." If it was "a little game," there is no evidence that Hale was conscious of what she was doing—of building a smoke screen to mask a struggle for self-integration. This is because the lady from *Godey's* could never perceive the role conflict that was central to her entire career. She could never quite say to herself, "I wish I were Sidney Romelee"—a viable integration of retiring femininity and assertive masculinity. A full awareness of what one was and where one was going was necessary to play "a little game." We know that Mercy Warren had this awareness. There is nothing to indicate that Sarah Hale had it—that she could consciously see the disparity between her doctrines and her career.[77]

[77] For the most systematic effort to determine whether Hale could in any way perceive the disparity between her doctrines and her life style, see Karol Gyman, "The 'Woman's Sphere': A Study of the Life and Work of Sarah

V

In 1852 Sarah Hale published her *Woman's Record*—a massive study of "all Distinguished Women" in world history. Most women received brief thumbnail sketches. Neither Elizabeth Chandler nor Mercy Warren was treated extensively. But Hale was impressed by and even envious of Warren because men of the Revolutionary generation had sought her advice on public issues.[78] Although the editor of *Godey's* was the most prominent woman in the land, national leaders like Daniel Webster, Henry Clay, and John Calhoun had not consulted her.

As Sarah Hale looked nostalgically to the American past, Nathaniel Hawthorne was also looking back into time:

> Morally, as well as materially, there was a coarser fibre in those wives and maidens of old England birth and breeding than in their fair descendants, separated from them by a series of six or seven generations; for, throughout that chain of ancestory, every successive mother has transmitted to her child a fainter bloom, a more delicate and briefer beauty, and a slighter physical frame, if not a character of less force and solidity, than her own.[79]

Hawthorne believed that American women had taken on "less force and solidity" with each succeeding generation; "faint," "delicate," and "slight" qualities had become increasingly conspicuous. Looking to Warren, Chandler, and Hale for changes in feminine ideology and psychology over three generations, Hawthorne's contention stands up well. Warren was a tough and forceful woman who insisted on playing a significant part in public affairs; she was even willing to debate former President John

---

Josepha Hale" (M.A. thesis, Bowling Green State University, 1973). Gyman concludes that Hale was never able to perceive the disparity, especially by the late 1830's, when she was captivated by the myth of True Womanhood.

[78] Hale, *Woman's Record*, p. 546.

[79] Nathaniel Hawthorne, *The Scarlet Letter, A Romance* (Boston: Ticknor, Reed, and Fields, 1850), pp. 59–60.

Adams on the character of his administration. To be sure, Warren felt that she had to play "a little game" to give men a sense of ascendance, but the "game" could not compromise women's rights. By the late 1820's and early 1830's, Elizabeth Chandler was engaged in a somewhat different "game." Like Warren, she was wielding influence in public affairs (on the increasingly controversial issue of chattel slavery). But unlike Warren, Chandler never urged women to deceive men. Rather, she frequently espoused the notion of tractable patriotic womanhood and seemed convinced that the female abolitionist retained and preserved her malleable qualities. Notwithstanding, Chandler was not totally captivated by the tendency Hawthorne noted toward the "faint" and the "delicate." She had the strength to go against Benjamin Lundy's wishes by structuring a plea for women's rights in her defense of black bondswomen and she had the "coarser fibre" to leave Philadelphia's cultivated reform circles for a rugged, more sexually egalitarian farming life on the Michigan frontier. Spokeswoman for middle-class womanhood of the mid-nineteenth century, Sarah Hale reversed Chandler's tracks, moving from the rural farming area to Boston and Philadelphia. She publicly opposed Warren's habit of advising men on public affairs and her 1839 novel, *The Lecturess,* was probably the most powerful emotional assault on female abolitionism ever written. A more adamant publicist of the notion of pliant patriotic womanhood than Warren or Chandler, Hale refused to deceive men or to deny their wishes in any particular. On a conscious level, she could not bring herself to play "a little game" against the "superior sex."

True American Womanhood was the message that the lady from *Godey's* propounded and sincerely believed. But although both Hale and her many male and female admirers conceived of her as a prime agent in the crusade for retiring patriotic femininity, her conduct was not entirely distinct from Warren's or Chandler's. She was never, in fact, a malleable woman who existed to serve men's changing needs. Like her predecessors, she remained active in public affairs, she exerted more influence than most men, and she did not allow her life to be consumed by the duties of the hearth. Therefore, the process that Hawthorne was tracing from strong, forceful women to the slight and delicate seems to have represented more of an alteration of subjective perceptions than of objective conditions. To be sure, travelers noted that women were becoming sicklier as they moved from eighteenth-century farms and plantations to nineteenth-century towns and cities. Moreover, John Adams and James Otis of 1776 did in fact consult with Warren, whereas Henry Clay and Daniel Webster of 1850 did not consult with Hale. Yet Hale, like Warren, remained quite influential in public affairs and experienced many of life's diversities. The major distinction between Warren's world and Hale's was that Warren and her admirers knew that she was no soft, delicate domestic, whereas the lady from Godey's and her following did not have the same perception. None seemed to see Hale's role for what it was, not even Hale herself. The intervening decades from Warren's day to Hale's witnessed the spread of the ideal of pliant patriotic womanhood in diverse segments of American society, and this certainly contributed to the change in subjective perceptions. But Sarah Hale's influential career testified to the fact that the ideal of True American Womanhood had not totally altered sexual realities—that it was still possible for a woman to resist pliancy and to take the initiative on matters distant from the hearth.

In 1848 many male proponents of True American Womanhood lamented the "misguided" woman suffragettes who were meeting at Seneca Falls and who seemed intent on behaving like Mary Wollstonecraft and her cohorts. But these men were relieved to find "Scribbling Women" like Sarah Hale opposing woman's suffrage and denouncing the alleged "rights of women." Men opposed to the historic Seneca Falls meeting proclaimed that the duty of American women was to serve their husbands and sons within the home. They never dreamed that the editor of Godey's Lady's Book and others like her were exerting more influence outside the home and within the "male sphere" than many voting women ever would. The tragedy was that women like Hale and Sigourney seemed to have little idea of the extent of their power and the heretical nature of their careers. There appeared to have been a significant decline in the accuracy of female perceptions—a flight from realism—between Mercy Warren's day and Sarah Hale's. If influential women of the nineteenth century like Hale and Sigourney had retained Warren's realistic perception of the power that they wielded and the "little game" that was played to retain this power, the degrading pressures of doctrinaire patriotism might have been less intense. A basic element in patriotic thought —the ideal of True American Womanhood—might have been less damaging to female self-images. Hale and other "Scribbling Women" might have tipped off their female audience as Warren had done decades earlier: a woman may need to convey appearances of delicacy and pliancy, but she should not abdicate her rights and cut off exposure to life's diverse feelings and experiences. By the middle decades of the nineteenth century, however, it may have been impossible for a woman like Hale to have remained conscious of Warren's "little game" and to have tipped off her readers. After all, the pressures of *le patriotisme irritable,* particularly the constrictive ideological pressures for True American Womanhood, were more intense by then than they had been in Warren's America. The fact that the editor of *Godey's* did not lead the life of retiring domesticity that she prescribed and thought she lived may have approached the limits of effective female dissent.

This continuing capacity of very influential women to dissent— if not through their rhetoric at least through their life styles— underlined the limitations of the ideal of pliant True American Womanhood. The ideal had been devised by men to serve diverse male needs at women's expense—particularly the need to reconcile perfectionist strivings with a sense of rooted stability. Neither Warren, Chandler, nor Hale would actually live lives of pliancy in anticipation of men's needs. The most emotional patriotic appeals did not change them in this particular. Thus, together with a general ideological consensus among many early American patriots on the way women were to serve their country, there was a subtle but significant conflict. Influential women like Warren, Chandler, and Hale who joined men and espoused the imperatives of tractable True American Womanhood would not lead malleable lives. Because True Womanhood was an ideal which widened male options and hopes at women's expense, it resulted in a covert, subtle, and often unconscious conflict in certain quarters. Occasionally this conflict became visible for all to see, as when Mercy Warren attacked John Adams in her *History* or when Sarah Hale took over fund raising for the Bunker Hill Monument. Most often, however, the conflict took place behind the shared verbiage of True American Womanhood.

PART Three

TOWARD
WHITE NATIONHOOD

*My heart is fully set on discharging the patriotic duty of contributing
to relieve our country of its black population.*
—GERRIT SMITH, 1827

*Of all the achievements of this age, this [Negro repatriation to Africa]
will be the greatest; for it will arise out of calm conviction, a feeling
of patriotism not yet pressed with a fear of immediate danger.*
—JESSE BURTON HARRISON, 1828

*Who would not rejoice to see our country liberated from her black
population? . . . Who that has reflection, does not tremble for the
political and moral well-being of a country, that has within its bosom, a
growing population, bound to its institutions by no common sympathies,
and ready to fall in with any faction that may threaten its liberties?*
—African Repository and Colonial Journal, 1829

As they struggled to reconcile a quest for personal and national perfection with a sense of rooted stability, male patriots were often prompted to invoke the notion of a pliable True American Woman. Woman's national obligation was to mold herself to satisfy men's changing needs. Certain prestigious and influential women resisted this imperative, but they became less and less conscious of their resistance between Mercy Warren's day and Sarah Hale's. On the conscious level, patriots of both sexes were therefore increasingly committed to the assumption that the gender of the New Nation was male. As Mary Ball Washington and Martha Custis Washington had devoted their lives to the Founding Father who had forged the Promised Land, patriotic women were to support the men who perpetuated the Founding Father's nation. A man—George Washington—had forged the national character, and men would see to it that the national character remained intact to bring on "the Rising Glory of America."

The notion of a True American Woman who sustained men's efforts was, then, an affirmation of the male gender of the Promised Land as well as a potential safety valve against the uprooting results of perfectionist strivings. But the nation's color also had to be defined and affirmed. Indeed, "Rising Glory" and rooted security could not eventuate unless the American people were of God's chosen race. Only a white America could be a flawless America where citizens felt a sense of place and belonging. Like sexual ideology, racial ideology was often viewed as a remedy to reconcile the irreconcilable—perfection and rootedness.

Before the American Revolution, Benjamin Franklin had voiced his color preference for the Promised Land: "Why increase the Sons of Africa, by Planting them in America?" he asked. The "Number of purely white People in the World is proportionably very small." Yet white must become the "Complexion of my Country." Patrick Henry echoed Franklin: "Our country will be peopled. The question is, shall it be with Europeans or with Africans?"[1] The preference for a white America was institutionalized soon after the Constitutional Convention. Naturalization was limited to whites, the federal militia was restricted to white male citizens, only whites could deliver the United States mails, city officials for the District of Columbia had to be white, and the District's Capitol Square was restricted to whites. Only whites could donate funds for the erection of the Washington Monument.[2] Chronicling the development of American nationhood, David Ramsay, Jeremy Belknap, John Daly Burk, Samuel Williams, and other historians of the early national period characterized the American Republic as the exclusive achievement of white men. Blacks, like women, played no formative role. By the Jacksonian period, allegiances to the concept of white nationhood were detectable in the everyday life of the Republic. White boys drove blacks from Philadelphia's Independence Square with stones and clubs, chanting,

[1] Winthrop D. Jordan, *White over Black: American Attitudes Toward the Negro, 1550–1812* (Chapel Hill: University of North Carolina Press, 1968), pp. 143, 544.
[2] Leon F. Litwack, *North of Slavery: The Negro in the Free States, 1790–1860* (Chicago: Phoenix Books, 1965), p. 31; Jordan, *White over Black*, p. 412; Henry S. Robinson, "Some Aspects of the Free Negro Population of Washington, D.C., 1800–1862," *Maryland Historical Magazine*, LXIV, No. 1 (Spring 1969), 47; *The Philanthropist* (New Richmond, Ohio), January 15, 1836.

"Niggers had nothing to do with the fourth of July." The Founding Father's grandson George Washington Parke Custis proclaimed that America was properly "the white man's country."[3]

Although the vision of a white nation was pervasive in early America, the notion of racial colonization—of removing free blacks (and sometimes slaves) from white society—was almost as widespread. As early as 1691 Virginia required emancipated bondsmen to be transported "beyond the limits of the colony within six months from the date of manumission." From 1713 until the end of the eighteenth century, Pennsylvania Quakers devised plans to emancipate blacks and to remove them from North America.[4] Two days after the Declaration of Independence, the prominent Virginia planter Landon Carter warned: "If you free the slaves, you must send them out of the country." During the Revolution, the Reverend Samuel Hopkins of Newport, Rhode Island, commenced a crusade for voluntary African colonization. In time, he began negotiations with English reformers to send American blacks to their newly founded Sierra Leone colony.[5] The editors of the *Columbian Magazine* had also supported racial colonization and frequently printed

[3] Edward R. Turner, *The Negro in Pennsylvania: Slavery—Servitude—Freedom, 1639–1861* (Washington, D.C.: American Historical Association, 1911), p. 146, quotes the Philadelphia chanters. Custis is quoted in the *Fourteenth Annual Report of the American Society for Colonizing the Free People of Colour of the United States* (Washington, D.C., 1831), p. xxi.

[4] Brainerd Dyer, "The Persistence of the Idea of Negro Colonization," *Pacific Historical Review*, XII, No. 1 (March 1943), 53, quotes the 1691 Virginia requirement. The plans of Pennsylvania Quakers are noted in Stanley K. Schultz, "The Making of a Reformer: The Reverend Samuel Hopkins as an Eighteenth-Century Abolitionist," *Proceedings of the American Philosophical Society*, CXV, No. 5 (October 15, 1971), 362, n. 58, and in Thomas E. Drake, *Quakers and Slavery in America* (New Haven: Yale University Press, 1950), p. 121.

[5] Jack P. Greene (ed.), *The Diary of Colonel Landon Carter of Sabine Hall, 1752–1778* (Charlottesville: University of Virginia Press, 1965), II, 1055. Schultz, *Proceedings of the American Philosophical Society*, CXV, No. 5 (October 15, 1971), 362–64, and Jordan, *White over Black*, pp. 550–51, note Hopkins.

materials favorable to that policy. Although Thomas Jefferson's racial thoughts were complex and often contradictory, he consistently favored colonization "on the coast of Africa." David Ramsay also condemned "the folly of accumulating negroes" and asserted that the reduction of America's black population "will render us [whites] more free."[6]

The vision of a white nation did not always prompt thoughts of racial colonization. Yet the two concepts were very compatible; colonization was a potentially viable procedure for achieving white nationhood. It is therefore somewhat strange that although the two concepts had coexisted for generations, no national organization dedicated to a white America through black resettlement came into being until the end of the War of 1812.[7]

In December of 1816 the American Colonization Society was organized to promote white nationhood by resettling Afro-Americans in Liberia. A devoutly patriotic organization from the beginning, it quickly became the most powerful racial or-

---

[6] *Columbian Magazine*, September 1786, p. 6; March 1788, p. 144; June 1788, p. 306. For Jefferson on colonization, see "Thomas Jefferson's Thoughts on the Negro," *Journal of Negro History*, III, No. 1 (January 1918), 82, 84–86; Thomas Jefferson, *Notes on the State of Virginia* (New York: Harper Torchbooks, 1964), pp. 132–33; Philip Slaughter, *The Virginia History of African Colonization* (Richmond: Macfarlane & Fergusson, 1855), p. 7; Henry Noble Sherwood, "The Formation of the American Colonization Society," *Journal of Negro History*, II, No. 3 (July 1917), 210; Frederick Bancroft, "The Early Antislavery Movement and African Colonization," in Jacob E. Cooke, *Frederick Bancroft, Historian* (Norman: University of Oklahoma Press, 1957), p. 171. Ramsay is quoted in Robert L. Brunhouse (ed.), "David Ramsay, 1749–1815: Selections from His Writings," *Transactions of the American Philosophical Society*, New Ser., LV, Pt. 4 (1965), 60.

[7] The absence of a viable colonization organization before 1816 is striking in view of popular support of the program. Historian Walter L. Fleming insists that most Americans of the late eighteenth and early nineteenth centuries who were opposed to slavery had favored colonization; see his "Deportation and Colonization: An Attempted Solution of the Race Problem," in *Studies in Southern History and Politics* (New York: Columbia University Press, 1914), p. 3. Thomas E. Drake agrees (*Quakers and Slavery*, p. 121).

ganization in the country. Although the Colonization Society reached the height of its influence in the 1820's and had begun to lose membership in the 1830's, its racial ideas and tactics remained central to the lives of a large number of influential patriots. A colonization legacy survived the effective years of the A.C.S. and greatly influenced both the shape of American race relations and the crusade for the Promised Land. By the middle decades of the nineteenth century, the goal of white nationhood through black removal had become a basic element of American patriotic thought. The Colonization Society and its legacy had drawn many of the most influential patriots of the New Nation over to the assumptions that black expulsion facilitated white nationhood and that white nationhood would promote "the Rising Glory of America."

CHAPTER 6

THE AMERICAN
COLONIZATION SOCIETY

One of the most crucial yet most frequently ignored facts about the American Colonization Society was that it originated with a multi-interest constituency. By the end of the War of 1812, three groups within the New Nation were particularly interested in a systematic program to expatriate American blacks to Africa. One faction consisted of Chesapeake slaveholders who fretted over the freedmen's role in the slave revolts of Toussaint L'Ouverture in Haiti and Gabriel Prosser in Virginia and who feared that their biracial society could disintegrate unless all free Negroes were quickly removed. African colonization also appealed to Noah Webster and to other primarily Northern Federalists who had formulated rigid political and social philosophies in the 1790's and never parted from them. Like Webster, several of these Old School Federalists favored colonization out of an irrational hope that it might help to arrest the "dangerous, disorderly egalitarianism" of Jeffersonian America. Designating blacks as forces of disorder and efforts to emancipate them as disruptive egalitarianism, they counted on organized colonization to repeal the "mob spirit" of the time and to restore the hierarchical society and deferential politics of an earlier day. Once a cause of egalitarian disorder was removed, these Old School Federalists hoped for the return of a presumed Old Republic stability. Finally, racial colonization found favor among Protestant clergymen of the major evangelical denominations who were worried about the apparent anarchy and moral laxity ascendant in American culture in the aftermath of the Revolution. Several attributed this decline to the erosion of specific church-state partnerships; most turned to moral-reform groups like the American Bible Society, the American Tract Society, and the American Sunday Union to try to restore structure and order to society. Like Old School Federalists and Chesapeake planters, they reasoned that an organized colonization movement might help to restore the order that had allegedly existed at the nation's founding by removing troublesome, anarchistic blacks.[1]

The three groups that went to form the Colonization Society looked back nostalgically, then, to Revolutionary America. They characterized it as a society of hierarchically organized classes, races, and institutions. It was a society whose citizens felt a sense of place and regarded their lives as ordered and secure. Decline had set in and the task at hand was to remove causes of disorder—to restore a purportedly pristine status quo of 1776. Since the America of 1776 had a substantial black population, colonizationists of every group were articulating an illogical position. Negro removal could not restore the allegedly structured and hierarchical status quo of 1776. Indeed, the very existence of a significant black population in the era of the American Revolution had promoted racial hierarchy and class-based social organization—particularly in the South. Ignoring this obvious fact, colonizationists proceeded with their crusade.

In December of 1816 African colonizationists throughout the nation traveled to Washington, D.C., for the first formal meeting of the American Colonization Society. The gathering had been organized by the Reverend Robert Finley of Basking Ridge, New

[1] The increase in Southern (particularly Chesapeake) planter advocacy of colonization is discussed in Jacob E. Cooke, *Frederick Bancroft, Historian* (Norman: University of Oklahoma Press, 1957), pp. 156–57; Alice Dana Adams, *The Neglected Period of Anti-Slavery in America* (Gloucester, Mass.: Peter Smith, 1964), p. 104; Charles S. Sydnor, *The Development of Southern Sectionalism, 1819–1848* (Baton Rouge: Louisiana State University Press, 1948), pp. 96–97. Old School Federalist and Protestant clergy support for the idea is thoroughly analyzed in George M. Fredrickson, *The Black Image in the White Mind: The Debate on Afro-American Character and Destiny, 1817–1914* (New York: Harper & Row, 1971), pp. 6–30.

Jersey. Convinced that an ignorant, "wretched" black population was growing throughout the country, Finley had called upon Old School Federalists and clergymen in New Jersey, New York, and Pennsylvania. He had also corresponded with Chesapeake planters. Finley urged all of these people to join him in a benevolent society to colonize free Afro-Americans in Africa much as the British were doing with their blacks through their Sierra Leone colony. Francis Scott Key, an influential Georgetown attorney and the composer of the national anthem, helped Finley to promote the first formal gathering of the A.C.S. Key was particularly successful in attracting influential Southern planters like Bushrod Washington and Henry Clay.[2]

Historian David J. Rothman demonstrates that the birth of the A.C.S. coincided with the organization of new penitentiaries for the criminal, asylums for the insane, almshouses for the poor, orphanages for the homeless, and reformatories for the delinquent. Like the Colonization Society's proposed African colony, these institutions were established to draw disorderly elements out of the mainstream of American society. Like the founders of the A.C.S., organizers of these early asylums for the control of deviant behavior were trying to restore the purported community cohesion and social balance of the eighteenth century that seemed to be rapidly disintegrating. In this sense, the Colonization Society was part of a larger impulse that followed the War of 1812 to ferret out, institutionalize, and thereby eliminate sources of irregular behavior. Free blacks were to be incarcerated in an African asylum while poor, insane, or delinquent whites were to be taken to asylums on American shores.[3]

[2] P. J. Staudenraus, *The African Colonization Movement, 1816–1865* (New York: Columbia University Press, 1961), pp. 15, 24; William Lloyd Garrison, *Thoughts on African Colonization* (reprint. New York: Arno Press, Inc., 1968), p. v; Robert Finley, *Thoughts on the Colonization of Free Blacks* (Washington, D.C., 1816), pp. 4–5; Archibald Alexander, *A History of Colonization on the Western Coast of Africa* (Philadelphia: William S. Martien, 1846), p. 78; Isaac V. Brown, *Biography of the Rev. Robert Finley, D.D., of Basking Ridge, N.J.* (Philadelphia: John W. Moore, 1857), pp. 99–100; Bruce Rosen, "Abolition and Colonization, the Years of Conflict: 1829–1834," *Phylon*, XXXIII, No. 2 (Second Quarter 1972), 177.

[3] David J. Rothman, *The Discovery of the Asylum: Social Order and Disorder in the New Republic* (Boston: Little, Brown and Company, 1971), particularly pp. 69–71, brilliantly analyzes this quest to restore stability by establishing institutions to incarcerate deviants.

During the lifetime of the Colonization Society, activities centered in Washington and issues were perceived more from a national than a local perspective. At the outset, the founders recognized that federal subsidies would be needed in order to remove a significant number of blacks. In 1819 they believed that they were beginning to tap the resources of the national treasury. Congress had authorized President Monroe to appoint and subsidize an agent to organize an African colony for repatriation of American Negroes. By selecting Samuel Bacon, the nominee of the Colonization Society, Monroe opened a formal cooperation between the organization and the Federal Government that lasted for decades.[4] Notwithstanding, federal funding was never substantial and private contributions became the lifeblood of the organization. The Society staged July Fourth celebrations throughout the country to promote private contributions. A.C.S. officials urged clergymen to demonstrate their patriotism through Independence Day sermons—sermons designed to persuade a nation of churchgoing patriots to empty their pockets in behalf of a whiter America. These patriotic appeals were basic to the operation and survival of the Colonization Society.[5]

To some extent, then, financial considerations explain why colonizationists turned July 4 into the most important day in their working calendar. For decades, the Independence Day collection funded many of the most essential A.C.S. activities. However, more than monetary expediency accounted for the merger of patriotic appeals with Colonization Society operations. Private correspondence between the A.C.S. national office and its local agents in the field was replete with the standard patriotic clichés of the early national period—exaltations of the flawless Founding Father, True American Womanhood, "the Rising Glory of America," and the like. Hopes for funding could not have

[4] Cooke, *Frederick Bancroft*, p. 164; Donald L. Robinson, *Slavery in the Structure of American Politics, 1765–1820* (New York: Harcourt Brace Jovanovich, Inc., 1971), p. 343; Willis D. Boyd, "The American Colonization Society and the Slave Recaptives of 1860–1861," *Journal of Negro History*, XLVII, No. 2 (April 1962), 109; Staudenraus, *African Colonization*, p. 56.

[5] *African Repository*, IX, No. 5 (July 1833), 159; XI, No. 6 (June 1835), 192: XIII, No. 6 (June 1837), 200; Staudenraus, *African Colonization*, pp. 119, 122; Fredrickson, *Black Image*, p. 7.

prompted these private exhortations; devout patriots were express-
ing honest convictions. Both the patriotic rhetoric found in pro-
colonization July Fourth orations and the patriotic rhetoric in
private A.C.S. correspondence resembled expressions used in the
African Repository. As the official journal of the A.C.S., the
Repository directed its appeal to members of the Society; the
editors openly admitted that they published what they thought
committed African colonizationists wanted to hear. Thus the
Colonization Society was an organization run by and for spread-
eagle patriots. Indeed, it was probably the nation's most influential
patriotic organization in the two decades that followed the War of
1812. The crusade for Negro removal and the crusade for "the
Rising Glory of America" went hand in hand.[6]

Although the A.C.S. never collected enough money to remove
many free Negroes, it received a number of impressive endorsements. Between 1816 and 1820 legislatures in Virginia, Georgia,
Maryland, Tennessee, and Vermont officially endorsed the organization. State auxiliary societies were formed in Louisiana, Mississippi, Kentucky, Virginia, Maryland, Pennsylvania, New Jersey,
New York, Massachusetts, Connecticut, Vermont, and Ohio.
Local and county organizations came into being in nearly every
state. There was verbal support from a remarkable number of
prominent figures—James Madison, Andrew Jackson, Noah
Webster, Daniel Webster, John Taylor, John Randolph, William
Crawford, John Marshall, Abbot Lawrence, Stephen Douglas,
Sarah Hale, and Roger Taney, to name a few.[7] By 1829 the opposi-

[6] Although spread-eagle patriotic rhetoric is detectable throughout the
Papers of the American Colonization Society, it is particularly apparent in
letters between national secretary R. R. Gurley and local Society agents
between 1827 and 1833 (A.C.S. Papers, Series IA, Library of Congress). For
typical patriotic expressions in the *African Repository*, see III, No. 11
(January 1828), 336; V, No. 3 (May 1829), 88–89; XIV, No. 12 (December
1838), 352–53. See also Staudenraus, *African Colonization*, pp. 102, 150–68; R.
R. Gurley, *Life of Jehudi Ashman* (New York: Robinson & Franklin, 1839),
p. 277; Lewis Perry, *Radical Abolitionism: Anarchy and the Government of
God in Antislavery Thought* (Ithaca: Cornell University Press, 1973), p. 9.

[7] Herman V. Ames (ed.), *State Documents on Federal Relations: The
States and the United States* (Philadelphia: University of Pennsylvania, 1906),
p. 195; Brainerd Dyer, "The Persistence of the Idea of Negro Colonization,"
Pacific Historical Review, XII, No. 1 (March 1943), 56; Leon F. Litwack,
North of Slavery: The Negro in the Free States, 1790–1860 (Chicago:
Phoenix Books, 1965), p. 24; Cooke, *Frederick Bancroft*, pp. 163–64.

tion American Convention of Abolition Societies acknowledged that most Americans supported both the Colonization Society and the ideal of African colonization. According to William Lloyd Garrison, this was particularly true of Northerners: ". . . wherever I turned my eye in the free states, I saw nothing but unanimity; wherever my ear caught a sound, I heard nothing but excessive panegyric. No individual had ventured to counteract the influence of the scheme."[8]

As it retained and enlarged its diverse following, the Colonization Society became a major national pressure group. Pledging to cleanse America and restore the assumed purity and rooted stability of her Revolutionary beginnings by removing free Negroes, the Society attracted Southern slaveholders beyond the Chesapeake as well as numerous Northern opponents of slavery. Many Southern planters came to laud colonization as a way to eliminate a free black population that gave their bondsmen hopes for emancipation. Their ideal was a lightened but biracial America—a viable slave order cleansed by the removal of troublesome free blacks. Other Southerners, along with an increasing number of Northern Old School Federalists and clergymen of a philanthropic bent, calculated that planters would be encouraged to emancipate more of their bondsmen if free Negroes were eliminated; this would gradually undermine slavery. Still others, North and South, supported the A.C.S. simply because they did not want Negroes around, free or slave. Finally, certain ambitious political and cultural leaders backed the organization because of its large and diverse following; advocacy might win them the support of whites of diverse racial ideologies. This mixed following of adamant slaveholders throughout the South, Old School Federalists, antislavery philanthropists, extreme negrophobes, and expedient leaders was united by the notion of cleansing America, promoting her "Rising Glory," and restoring the supposed virtue and rooted stability of the Revolutionary period.[9]

[8] Litwack, *North of Slavery*, p. 24; Garrison, *Thoughts on African Colonization*, Part I, p. 4.

[9] *The Abolitionist*, I, No. 3 (March 1833), 44; Adams, *Neglected Period*, pp. 205–06; Penelope Campbell, *Maryland in Africa: The Maryland State Colonization Society, 1831–1857* (Urbana: University of Illinois Press, 1971), pp. 9–10; James Hotchkin to R. R. Gurley, June 9, 1829, Papers of the

To avoid alienating any single segment of its heterogeneous and growing constituency, the high command of the Colonization Society shunned the controversial issues of slavery and emancipation. With slaveholders and antislavery interests supporting the same organization, A.C.S. leaders were loath to speculate about the effects that deportation of free blacks might have upon the slave system. Instead, they issued patriotic appeals for sectional reconciliation: Americans North and South could properly unite behind the ideal of establishing a white man's country. Proslavery interests could perceive this as a program to remove troublesome free Negroes. Antislavery and negrophobe elements could assume that white nationhood would require the eventual removal of all Negroes. Ralph Randolph Gurley, the Society's active and influential national secretary, characterized this ambiguous posture as a *"common and unexceptional ground"* that would "soften down all prejudices between the south and the north." It "invites a powerful nation of Christians to offer up minor differences and contrarieties of interest on the altar of an undivided patriotism and philanthropy." If these "minor differences" could not be reconciled, if the Society's program could not command widespread allegiance "on the subject of our colored population, . . . we may indeed tremble for our country."[10] Gurley's position was endorsed by the *African Repository:* as an approach to the race problem, the ambiguous plea for white nationhood and sectional reconciliation was "better adapted than all others to destroy sectional prejudice, and to produce a unanimity of sentiment throughout the nation." Sectional animosities could be erased and the Promised Land united as it never had been since the Revolution.[11] Other leaders of the Society reiterated Gurley's message. They noted how the colonization ideal of white nationood pre-

American Colonization Society, Library of Congress; Charles S. Sydnor, *Slavery in Mississippi* (New York: D. Appleton-Century Company, 1933), pp. 204–05.

[10] Franklin L. Riley (ed.), "A Contribution to the History of the Colonization Movement in Mississippi," *Publications of the Mississippi Historical Society,* IX (1906), 364; Gurley, *Life of Jehudi Ashman,* p. 277; *African Repository,* X, No. 3 (May 1834), 72; XIII, No. 12 (December 1837), 364.

[11] *African Repository,* I, No. 6 (August 1825), 1; I, No. 8 (October 1825), 225; VI, No. 7 (September 1830), 207; XII, No. 3 (March 1836), 80–81.

served "fraternal feeling throughout the Union," built "a feeling of patriotism," was in the tradition of George Washington, and was consonant with the purportedly high spirit of 1776.[12]

Rhetoric merging sectional reconciliation, white nationhood, and spread-eagle patriotism soon came to characterize the public pronouncements of Colonization Society officials and supporters in state and local affiliates. It allowed colonizationists to vent their visceral patriotism, to cloud the divisive issue of emancipation, to retain their multi-interest constituency, and to make a relatively uncontroversial appeal to white Americans of widely diverse ideologies. Moreover, the rhetoric of reconciliation, white nationhood, and patriotism gave leading colonizationists language with which to build a complex argumentative smoke screen that obscured their innermost intentions and motivations. Activists like Gurley, Key, and Clay constructed this smoke screen so skillfully that it has often deceived historians as well as contemporaries.

II

To fathom the intentions and the underlying psychic drives of African colonizationists, it is necessary to expose and disassemble this argumentative smoke screen. One argument that leading colonizationists stressed in building their smoke screen was that free men of both races could never live together in peace and as equals. "Nature has made the distinction of color, and in it, had laid the foundation of the partialities which bind us to our own likeness, and of the repugnance which turn us from those who do not resemble ourselves," a Kentucky colonizationist proclaimed. "Endless jealousies and strife would be the natural fruits" of any egalitarian biracial society. "The black and white population are in a state of war" in America, John Latrobe explained to Alexis de Tocqueville. "Never will they mingle. One of them will have to yield place to the other." Virginia colonizationist Charles L. Mosby charged that although egalitarian precepts were appealing in the abstract, the Negro's color provoked "a principle of repul-

[12] African Repository, III, No. 11 (January 1828), 336; V, No. 3 (May 1829), 88–89; IX, No. 3 (May 1833), 85; William W. Sleigh, Abolitionism Exposed! (Philadelphia: D. Schenck, 1838), pp. 22–24.

sion, so strong as to forbid the idea of a communion either of interest or of feeling, as utterly abhorrent."[13] Because whites detested blacks, discriminations that ran against the egalitarian grain of the Declaration of Independence were inevitable. Amalgamation of the races was no solution to this dilemma, for it produced "a result forbidden by invincible objections" and was most "unnatural." Amalgamation contradicted the attraction of like for like.[14] The only proper way to honor the egalitarian principles of 1776 and to halt racial discord was to remove free blacks from American shores. This would eliminate the basic factor inhibiting Americans from treating each other as equals. "*This* is not the black man's country," a Baltimore colonizationist proclaimed. A Negro could only be free and happy in Africa, "his native soil, where he may flourish and be respected."[15] The free Negro "has no home, no position, and no future" in white America, Sarah Hale echoed. This "stranger within her gates" should be removed to Africa to avoid discord in the Promised Land and to allow Americans to live under complete egalitarianism, freedom, and democracy.[16]

The racial-discord argument for colonization obscured more than it clarified. The Southern slaveholders, Old School Federalists, and conservative Protestant clergymen who made up the Colonization Society leadership and much of the membership craved hierarchy, order, and rooted stability in social relationships. They could not have been sincerely committed to an egalitarian society among whites any more than to a biracial order of equals. Even if we assume that certain colonizationists held a vague, half-

[13] Joseph R. Underwood, the Kentucky colonizationist, made his remark in his *Address Delivered to the Colonization Society of Kentucky, at Frankfort, January 15, 1835* (Frankfort, 1835), p. 9. John Latrobe is quoted in George Wilson Pierson, *Tocqueville and Beaumont in America* (New York: Oxford University Press, 1938), p. 516. Charles L. Mosby is quoted in the *African Repository*, VII, No. 8 (October 1831), 230–31.

[14] *National Intelligencer* (Washington, D.C.), December 24, 1816; *African Repository*, X, No. 9 (November 1834), 262–63, 274; XV, No. 2 (February 1839), 62; Alexander, *History of Colonization*, p. 17.

[15] *Twentieth Annual Report of the American Society for Colonizing the Free People of Colour of the United States* (Washington, D.C., 1837), p. 46.

[16] This theme is persistently reiterated in Hale's novel *Liberia; or, Mr. Peyton's Experiments* (reprint. Upper Saddle River, N.J.: The Gregg Press, 1968). See particularly p. iv.

hearted commitment to the purportedly egalitarian principles of 1776, they were often unclear as to the precise group whose degradation violated egalitarianism—free Negroes, slaves, or both. If free Negroes were removed, would not the most blatant of all violations of egalitarianism—slavery—perpetuate the conflict between Revolutionary ideals and nineteenth-century social realities? If all blacks (free and slave) were removed, would influential and prosperous slaveholders like Henry Clay and Bushrod Washington remain colonizationists? Might the very attempt to repatriate all blacks cause tremendous discord in American society? The vaguely stated proposition that black repatriation would remove a source of social conflict and preserve the egalitarianism of the New Nation seemed, therefore, to hide a whole range of problems at the roots of the colonization impulse. Like so much else in the ideological baggage of the early American patriot, this flimsy contention obscured, if it did not repress, more fundamental feelings and longings.

A second argument conspicuous within the colonizationist smoke screen derived from the benevolent reform impulse that pervaded the New Nation in the years after the War of 1812. The Colonization Society was only one of several Christian reform organizations that originated between 1815 and 1828. Many A.C.S. members also belonged to groups like the American Bible Society, the Home Missionary Society, the American Temperance Society, the American Society for the Prevention of Licentiousness and Vice, and the American Education Society. These organizations urged the spread of Christian precepts within the nation and throughout the world in the struggle against paganism. Many colonizationists were therefore attracted to missionary activity. Seeking to extend the boundaries of Christianity, they frequently argued that repatriation of American Negroes to Africa achieved this end. The deported blacks would carry American Christianity to the heathen "Dark Continent." They would free Africa "from savage sway, and [have] her soil made ready for the seeds of knowledge and piety." Through African colonization "light and peace are to pervade a pagan continent." Calvin Colton claimed that the Colonization Society would "spread civilization, sound morals, and true religion throughout the continent of Africa." L. Ives Hoadly envisioned "the introduction of Christianity to an important quarter of our world" where the Devil yet reigned. Other colonizationists reiterated that "an immense continent, now covered with darkness, and full of the habitations of cruelty," would be uplifted and Christianized by blacks from the Promised Land.[17]

The argument for Christian uplift was shabby and contrived. If blacks were subverting America, how could they carry American Christianity to Africa? Repressed and degraded in the Promised Land, blacks somehow imbibed the excellent qualities of Christian America and would transmit them to Africa. In the fall of 1817 the pioneer Ohio abolitionist Charles Osborn noted the illogic of this proposition: "Those who have traveled through the Southern states, and observed the ignorance and vice with which Slavery has enveloped the Children of Africa can hardly be persuaded that they are now fit instruments for propagating the gospel [in Africa]." William Watkins, a leading black Baltimorean, agreed with Osborn. How was it possible, he asked, for the "most vicious" group in the New Nation to improve Africa?[18] The question was never answered. A possible retort—that even the worst elements in America could improve a savage continent—was never invoked. Instead, colonizationists noted how their venture would "overspread the seacoast from Zaire to Gambia, a soil of unexampled tropical fertility, with happy communities of colored freemen, carrying to their countrymen the arts and civilization

[17] *African Repository*, VII, No. 1 (March 1831), 14; Calvin Colton, *Colonization and Abolition Contrasted* (Philadelphia: Herman Hooker, 1839), p. 1; L. Ives Hoadly, *An Address, Delivered at the Union Celebration of Independence, at Sutton, Mass., July 5, 1824* (Worcester, Mass., 1824), p. 15. For similar remarks by other colonizationists, see, e.g., *Tenth Report of the Vermont Colonization Society, to the Annual Meeting, at Montpelier, October 14, 1829* (Montpelier: E. P. Walton & Co., 1829), p. 3; *Colonization Herald* (Philadelphia), II, No. 48 (March 18, 1837), 190; *African Repository*, VII, No. 5 (July 1831), 131–32; VII, No. 7 (September 1831), 218; XI, No. 2 (February 1835), 41.

[18] Ruth Anna Ketring, *Charles Osborn in the Anti-Slavery Movement* (Columbus: Ohio State Archaeological and Historical Society, 1937), p. 39. William Watkins is quoted in Wendell Phillips Garrison and Francis Jackson Garrison, *William Lloyd Garrison, 1805–1879* (reprint. New York: Arno Press, Inc., 1969), I, 148, n. 1.

that they have learned from ours."[19] The Colonization Society settlement in Liberia was somehow becoming "a beautiful monument, erected on a dark and distant shore, to the honor of American benevolence," R. R. Gurley insisted. "We are the guardians of a nation in the bud,—a miniature of this Republic,—a colored America on the shores of Africa," another enthusiast contended. The "proud flag of our Country" was being "unfurled on the shores of Africa."[20] But colonization would do more than extend American influence over a benighted region. Some outspoken antislavery supporters of the A.C.S. argued that the "uplift" of Africa made up for the cruel slave trade that had wrongly carried Africa's sons to the white nation; it compensated as well for the degrading treatment blacks had received in America. The A.C.S. project atoned for whatever wrongs white Americans had inflicted upon blacks; it expunged the misdeeds of centuries.[21]

By invoking the illogical premise that America's downtrodden could become Africa's redeemers, certain colonizationists were possibly attempting to salve white racial guilts. Like other major pro-colonization arguments, the notion of African uplift was no more than a thinly veiled smoke screen for deeper feelings and serious problems.

Black opposition was one of the more serious problems. A sizable number of free Negro resolutions, remonstrances, and speeches were appended to William Lloyd Garrison's famous 1832 pamphlet attacking the A.C.S.—*Thoughts on African Colonization*. According to these documents, free Negroes vehemently opposed the Colonization Society and the concept of African repatriation. This was an accurate characterization of Afro-American thought during the first two decades of the Colonization

[19] *African Repository*, III, No. 12 (February 1828), 375. Interestingly, this statement assumed that American-born blacks and African blacks were "countrymen." Race, not place of birth, determined nationality.

[20] *African Repository*, III, No. 11 (January 1828), 325; IX, No. 2 (April 1833), 47, 56; *Proceedings of the Second Annual Meeting of the New Jersey Colonization Society. Held at Princeton, July 10, 1826* (Princeton, 1826), p. 15; William Fuller to R. R. Gurley, November 26, 1827, Papers of the American Colonization Society, Library of Congress.

[21] *National Intelligencer* (Washington, D.C.), December 24, 1816; *African Repository*, IX, No. 2 (April 1833), 59; George Janvier to Richard Smith, September 24, 1827, and James Steifford to R. R. Gurley, July 13, 1833, both in the Papers of the American Colonization Society, Library of Congress.

Society's existence. Save for John B. Russwurm and a few others, black leaders, North and South, opposed the Society. With the exception of the recently manumitted, all segments of the American black community concurred with Article IV of David Walker's *Appeal* (1829)—that the Society stood for both racial discrimination and slavery.[22]

Colonization Society agents quickly discovered black opposition, and it troubled them. Approached by A.C.S. agents, very few Negroes were willing to consider African repatriation. Reactions ranged from reluctance to blatant opposition. "I am sorry to say, there is a general aversion among them to going to Africa, they seem to prefer Philadelphia," a Pennsylvania agent reported. A Society official from Richmond noted that "the free Negroes of this part of the country are emigrating to the state of Ohio—why they will not go to Liberia I do not know." Many other colonizationists in the field submitted equally disheartening reports.[23] M. L. Fullerton, an agent from Hagerstown, Maryland, described an interview with a Negro. He wanted the man to become a printer in the Colonization Society's Liberian settlement. The Negro balked, contending that America was his country and that he should not be asked to depart for Africa. Fullerton was outraged.

---

[22] Charles M. Wiltse (ed.), *David Walker's Appeal, in Four Articles* (New York: Hill & Wang, 1965), pp. 45–78; Litwack, *North of Slavery*, pp. 24–25, 28; Louis R. Mehlinger, "The Attitude of the Free Negro toward African Colonization," *Journal of Negro History*, I, No. 3 (June 1916), 276–301; Eli Seifman, "The United Colonization Societies of New York and Pennsylvania and the Establishment of the African Colony of Bassa Cove," *Pennsylvania History*, XXXV, No. 1 (January 1968), 25–26. Rosen, *Phylon*, XXXIII, No. 2 (Second Quarter 1972), 179. In *Neither Black Nor White: Slavery and Race Relations in Brazil and the United States* (New York: The Macmillan Company, 1971), pp. 60–61, Carl N. Degler contends that American blacks were much less interested in African repatriation than Brazilian blacks because the slave trade was cut off in the United States at the beginning of the nineteenth century but persisted in Brazil until 1851. Memories of Africa and viable contacts with that continent were, therefore, much stronger for Brazilian blacks.

[23] Caleb White to R. R. Gurley, April 14, 1830, Papers of the American Colonization Society, Library of Congress, is the Pennsylvania agent's report. For the report of the Richmond official, see B. Brand to R. R. Gurley, August 20, 1827, Papers of the American Colonization Society, Library of Congress. For similar reports by colonizationists in the field, see, e.g., Nathan Mendenhall to Richard Smith, December 8, 1829; George S. Edwards to R. R. Gurley, March 13, 1830; D. Meade to R. R. Gurley, April 8, 1830—all in the Papers of the American Colonization Society, Library of Congress.

He could not understand how any Negro could refuse to cooperate with the Society in its humane efforts to solve the race problem and to civilize the black fatherland.[24]

Leading colonizationists recognized that a crisis of credibility was at hand. If the overwhelming number of blacks agreed with David Walker and rejected African repatriation, this damaged Colonization Society pretensions of Christian benevolence. In the milieu of religious proselytizing that characterized the years after the War of 1812, it was necessary to maintain impeccable credentials in the Lord's benevolent crusade. Something was wrong if the afflicted did not flock to God's agents in the field. More basically, Negro resistance called into question whether the A.C.S. would ever have blacks to colonize—whether it would ever be able to do what it professed. Therefore, the continued viability of the organization demanded that arguments be concocted to explain away black opposition.

Colonization leaders hastily concocted two contentions: (1) Negroes did not really oppose colonization. They had simply been propagandized by "calumny and falsehood." With the proper facts, their "unnatural and artificial" opposition to the Society would immediately vanish. (2) Society agents had not properly approached the stubborn Negro mentality: "The more you urge them, the more they won't go [to Africa]. We must hold up emigration as a favor & privilege granted to them—for they will not do it to oblige us." From these two contentions, it followed that black opposition to colonization was easy to remedy. Society agents could give blacks proper information, and they could refer to life in the Liberian colony as a distinct privilege.[25] Thus, widespread and fundamental black opposition to African repatriation was characterized as transitory and easy to remedy. Once again,

[24] M. L. Fullerton to R. R. Gurley, September 6, 1830, Papers of the American Colonization Society, Library of Congress.

[25] Although these two arguments were frequently developed in Colonization Society publications, they were articulated most clearly in the *African Repository*, XIII, No. 1 (January 1837), 29; XVI, No. 23 (December 1, 1840), 353; David I. Burr to R. R. Gurley, November 5, 1833, Papers of the American Colonization Society, Library of Congress; James F. Hopkins (ed.), *The Papers of Henry Clay* (Lexington: University of Kentucky Press, 1961), II, 421–22.

colonizationists were adding to an argumentative smoke screen that obscured deeper goals and frustrations.

III

Strategic necessity probably required A.C.S. spokesmen to foster misleading arguments. Although all elements in their multi-interest constituency were sincerely dedicated to the standard patriotic dogmas of the period, unity broke down over specific racial policies. It had to in an organization of adamant antislavery reformers and Southern planters; the former saw colonization of free Negroes as a way to extinguish the slave system while the latter perceived colonization as a means of fortifying slavery. Between these two opposite poles, other colonizationists espoused a whole range of specific racial postures. And yet, beneath the diverse postures, most colonizationists shared certain fundamental racial longings. These common longings merged with their visceral patriotism and their nostalgic view of an ordered, securely rooted eighteenth-century social existence. It kept men who differed sharply on racial specifics working together in the same group.

The interest of nineteenth-century Americans in the Indian and his future in the Promised Land caused certain of these deeper and common longings to surface. Between 1820 and 1844—the most active years of the Colonization Society—one hundred thousand American Indians were removed from their homes and transported west of the Mississippi. Most white Americans either justified or acquiesced in the removal. Some, like Monroe's Secretary of War, John C. Calhoun, and Thomas L. McKenney of the Bureau of Indian Affairs, did so largely on philanthropic grounds. They saw Indian life being "eroded" by the physical assaults, liquor, and gambling that were part of white frontier culture. To save the tribes from moral decay and physical extinction—to buy time so that they could master the "proper" ways of established white society and then assimilate—tribesmen had to be persuaded to voluntarily move westward beyond the reaches of the frontiersman's rifle. There was no adequate federal military force or bureaucratic structure to protect the Indians on their native lands.[26] By the late 1820's and early 1830's, however, President Andrew Jackson was formulating a federal policy that explicitly sanctioned violent frontiersmen greedy for Indian lands. Federal military power would stand behind the aggressions of white frontiersmen and the states'-rights politicians who sought to expropriate traditional Indian territories. The red man was therefore left with two choices—to migrate beyond the Mississippi or to face annihilation.[27]

Calhoun's and McKenney's thinking differed significantly from Jackson's, and a missionary trying to "uplift" a tribe had to be distinguished from a frontiersman who hoped to extinguish it. Nonetheless, most interested parties in the removal debate agreed on two particulars: (1) the desirability of mass Indian migration beyond the Mississippi and (2) the futility if not the error in Indian efforts to retain a distinctive cultural identity in a white man's country. Calhoun and McKenney would remove Indians so that they could eventually master "proper" white ways; the Indian-hating frontiersman would destroy red Americans because they were different and because they held valuable lands. Missionaries generally sided with Calhoun and McKenney, while Jackson lined up behind the frontiersmen.[28]

By the very logic of their racial posture, one would expect most African colonizationists to have favored Indian removal—if not the forceful Jacksonian type, then the milder Calhoun-McKenney variety. If, as Colonization Society leaders and the *African Reposi-*

26 Francis Paul Prucha, *American Indian Policy in the Formative Years: The Indian Trade and Intercourse Acts, 1790–1834* (Cambridge: Harvard University Press, 1962), pp. 213, 225; Bernard W. Sheehan, *Seeds of Extinction: Jeffersonian Philanthropy and the American Indian* (Chapel Hill: University of North Carolina Press, 1973), pp. 250, 278; Arthur DeRosier, Jr., *The Removal of the Choctaw Indians* (New York: Harper Torchbooks, 1972), pp. 41–42; Allen Guttmann (ed.), *States' Rights and Indian Removal* (Boston: D. C. Heath & Company, 1965), pp. 32–35; Philip Borden, "Found Cumbering the Soil: Manifest Destiny and the Indian in the Nineteenth Century," in *The Great Fear*, edited by Gary B. Nash and Richard Weiss (New York: Holt, Rinehart & Winston, 1970), p. 82.

27 DeRosier, Jr., *Choctaw Indians*, pp. 100, 165; Prucha, *American Indian Policy*, pp. 224, 247.

28 This point is developed in Klaus J. Hansen's outstanding essay "The Millennium, the West, and Race in the Antebellum American Mind," *Western Historical Quarterly*, III, No. 4 (October 1972), 373–90.

tory constantly reiterated, America was the white man's country, it followed that lesser races had to be totally repatriated or their numbers drastically reduced—red as well as black. There were some A.C.S. activists who did, indeed, think along these lines. "We are unable to draw the distinction between removing the Indians and removing free negroes," a group of Virginia colonizationists maintained. Active in the Indiana Auxiliary of the A.C.S., Baptist missionary Isaac McCoy came to perceive Indians as fundamentally similar to blacks. Neither could assimilate into white America; both had to be removed. In 1842 a colonizationist majority on the House Commerce Committee concurred; the same rationale justified removal of Indians to Western territorial districts where there were no whites and sending Negroes to African resettlement areas. From time to time, other colonizationists articulated similar positions; red and black must forever be separated from white.[29]

However, these were not typical Colonization Society reactions. Professor Francis Paul Prucha, one of the most knowledgeable students of Indian removal, places most African colonizationists of the 1820's and 1830's alongside temperance reformers and opponents of the Sunday mails. They differed from Jackson and even from Calhoun and McKenney by defending the Indian's right to remain on his native soil and to continue to live within a quasi-independent Indian nation.[30] Leading Colonization Society members like Henry Clay and Daniel Webster were adamant opponents of removal. Indian nations, particularly the Cherokee Nation, were

[29] *Report of Mr. Kennedy of Maryland, from the Committee on Commerce of the House of Representatives of the United States, on the Memorial of the Friends of African Colonization, Assembled in Convention in the City of Washington, May, 1842* (Washington, D.C., 1843), p. 475, quotes the Virginia colonizationists. William Miles, " 'Enamoured with Colonization': Isaac McCoy's Plan of Indian Reform," *Kansas Historical Quarterly*, XXXVIII, No. 3 (Autumn 1972), 268–86, outlines McCoy's position. *Report of Mr. Kennedy*, p. 6, notes the House Commerce Committee agreement. For similar positions by other colonizationists, see Charles I. Foster, "The Colonization of Free Negroes in Liberia, 1816–1835," *Journal of Negro History*, XXXVIII, No. 1 (January 1953), 41, 47; Rayford W. Logan, "Some New Interpretations of the Colonization Movement," *Phylon*, IV, No. 4 (Fourth Quarter, 1943), 334.

[30] Prucha, *American Indian Policy*, p. 243.

entirely justified in retaining their traditional territory.[31] Between 1826 and 1834 James Gillespie Birney was probably the most influential African colonizationist in the Southwest. He was also legal counsel for the Cherokees in northern Alabama and Georgia in their effort to resist pressures for removal.[32] Less distinguished A.C.S. activists usually shared the views of Clay, Webster, and Birney. Holding up the ideal of the white man's country, most believed that Negroes (or at least free Negroes) subverted that ideal whereas Indians did not. Like Clay, Webster, and Birney, most were also keenly aware that the "stream of white population flows too steadily towards the shores of the Pacific, to be arrested in its progress." Red and white contacts were inevitable in the West just as they had been in the East. Therefore, removal of the tribes beyond the Mississippi would not head off interracial contacts. But since removal was taking place despite their protestations, most colonizationists adamantly opposed exterminating the Indians as whites moved westward. Most also opposed removing the Indians to Mexico, to Canada, or to some other more distant location. Whites would soon follow the removed Indian tribes beyond the Mississippi and a viable red-white biracial society could exist there as it might have existed in the Eastern portions of the nation. Yet blacks were not to be allowed into this new Western society. They had to be colonized in Africa—not beyond the Mississippi. Lacking the sturdy fiber of the red man, they could perish at the hands of the Western Indians. There was also the danger that Negro migrants might join with Indians to form a nonwhite coalition that would threaten the survival of the Promised Land.[33]

[31] Ulrich B. Phillips, "Georgia and States Rights," American Historical Association, *Annual Report*, 1901, II, 66–86; Claude Moore Fuess, *Daniel Webster* (Boston: Little, Brown and Company, 1930), I, 333–34.

[32] Betty Fladeland, *James Gillespie Birney: Slaveholder to Abolitionist* (Ithaca: Cornell University Press, 1955), pp. 35–37; Dwight L. Dumond (ed.), *Letters of James Gillespie Birney, 1831–1857* (New York: D. Appleton-Century Company, 1938), I, 3–4. In time, Birney realized that frontiersmen would occupy the Cherokee Nation regardless of the success or failure of his court fights. Therefore, while opposing Jackson's policy of forceful removal, he gradually moved toward the Calhoun-McKenney position of persuading Cherokees to voluntarily move West in their own interests.

[33] This general thought process regarding Indian removal and the Negro is evidenced in a great number and variety of colonizationist reports, speeches,

Therefore, although most colonizationists were opposed to Indian removal, they recognized that a red-and-white society beyond the Mississippi was inevitable and entirely acceptable. But a society of red, black, and white rubbing elbows was out of the question. A biracial society was no threat to white nationhood so long as there were no Negroes (or at least no free Negroes) in the racial groupings. Clearly, colonizationists were perceiving white nationhood negatively—by the absence of blacks, rather than the presence of whites. They were defining national identity by singling out a deviant group (blacks) and characterizing America as the absence of blackness. More than anything else, this is what the distinction between red and black revealed.

But why did colonizationists single out the Negro and not the Indian as the antithesis of white nationhood? The intellectual heritage of the late eighteenth century may have influenced their thinking. Those were years when the Abbé Raynal, Lord Kames, Comte de Buffon, Corneille de Pauw, and other European theorists had maintained that because America's natural terrain was barren and unsuitable for civilization, New World Indians were a degraded and lowly species. Americans like Thomas Jefferson, Charles Thompson, and numerous *Columbian* contributors had struggled to affirm the New World terrain by refuting these charges—by characterizing the only indigenous American as a brave and skilled hunter-warrior. Defense of the Indian and of the Promised Land went hand in hand. Thus, it was unthinkable to propose colonizing the Indian abroad, for that could give credence to European charges. Moreover, Enlightenment figures like Jefferson, Benjamin Rush, and Samuel Stanhope Smith had persistently noted that the Indian was fundamentally similar to the Caucasian; what differences there were between red and white were temporary and artificial products of the environment. Assimilation of the

---

and essays. See, e.g., *Report of Mr. Kennedy*, pp. 170–71, 952; *First Annual Report of the American Society for Colonizing the Free People of Colour of the United States* (Washington, D.C., 1818), pp. 16–17; *Twenty-first Annual Report of the American Society . . .* (Washington, D.C., 1838), p. 28; *Proceedings of the First Annual Meeting of the New Jersey Colonization Society. Held at Princeton. July 11, 1825* (Princeton, 1825), p. 14; *African Repository*, XIV, No. 5 (May 1838), 143; Alexander, *History of Colonization*, p. 84.

red man into white society was, therefore, predictable and desirable. However, blacks seemed to be more than a mere "variety" of the white race. As Jefferson noted: "I believe the Indian, then, to be in body and mind, equal to the white man. I have supposed the black man, in his present state, might not be so." Indeed, "the blacks, whether originally a distinct race or made distinct by time and circumstances, are [probably] inferior to the whites in the endowments both of body and mind." Therefore, assimilation between white and black was potentially hazardous.[34]

Active in the decades after the War of 1812, African colonizationists did not have to rebut the charges of Raynal, Kames, and Buffon. The European assault on the New World terrain had subsided. But Indian expulsion might have brought on new attacks; Europeans might have construed this as proof that American soil could not produce a viable species. More important, most colonizationists seem to have retained the sharp Jeffersonian distinction between red and black. As blacks were probably distinct from and inferior to whites, they must not assimilate into the white man's country. But because Indians were no more than a "variety" of the white race, they could be equated with Americanism much more easily than Negroes. Given the underlying similarity of red and white, the two races could mix freely together in the American West.

Thus, although Americans at large were repudiating Jeffersonian perceptions of the Indian by the 1820's and 1830's, were often justifying forceful Indian removal, and were characterizing the race as properly doomed to extinction as white civilization captured the West, most colonizationists stood out as important exceptions.[35] It is possible that many of them did not cling to eroding Jeffersonian perceptions with full conviction. Late-nine-

[34] Daniel Boorstin, *The Lost World of Thomas Jefferson* (New York: Henry Holt and Company, 1948), pp. 84, 85, 93–94; Reginald Horsman, "American Indian Policy and the Origins of Manifest Destiny," in *The Indian in American History*, edited by Francis Paul Prucha (New York: Holt, Rinehart & Winston, 1971), pp. 22–23. See also Sheehan, *Seeds of Extinction*, pp. 36–37.

[35] For discussions of the drift from Jeffersonian views of the Indian, see Horsman, "American Indian Policy," pp. 20–28; William G. McLoughlin, "Red, White, and Black in the Antebellum South," *Baptist History and Heritage* (April 1972), p. 70.

teenth-century Californians had little regard for the Negro but were willing to characterize him as a decent and proper national resident in comparison with the dangerous "heathen Chinee." Certain colonizationists may also have been elevating one undesirable out group (Indians) simply to strengthen their case against the other (blacks). Indeed, there were African colonizationists who defended a red-white biracial society but assumed that it would ultimately become a white society—that "inferior" Indian civilization was doomed to extinction.[36] But with even the most sinister interpretation of the colonizationist's opposition to Indian removal and defense of a red-white racial order, it is obvious that most A.C.S. activists differed from other early-nineteenth-century Americans in their expressed racial ideology. Articulating Jeffersonian ideas on the Noble Savage that were becoming obsolete, colonizationists were dissenting intellectually from the views of their countrymen. From the standpoint of red-white relations, they were voicing a more tolerant racial posture than most of their contemporaries. Their posture was even more tolerant than that of John Calhoun and Thomas McKenney, for the latter had maintained that the Indian must eventually cultivate the white man's ways. Dedicated to white nationhood, most colonizationists seemed more concerned with removing blackness than assuring untainted whiteness or full Indian assimilation. Moreover, unlike Calhoun and McKenney, they were part of an American minority that saw no sense in Indian removal—voluntary or compulsory.

But if most colonizationists had little in common with their contemporaries on the matter of Indian policy, they were also distinguishable from Jefferson and other Enlightenment defenders of the Noble Savage in one important respect. They agreed with Jefferson that blacks had unusually "ardent" sexual appetites—that they were more sexual than Indians. But they went on to draw a much stronger contrast between black and red sexual proclivities than Jefferson ever had. Compared to the lustful Negro, the red man was almost asexual. Henry Clay, the most influential member of the A.C.S., articulated this view most clearly. As whites moved

---

[36] See, e.g., "Amalgamation of the Races," *The Colonizationist and Journal of Freedom* (Boston) (June 1833), pp. 73–74; *Twentieth Annual Report of the A.C.S.*, p. 46.

West, Clay acknowledged, they would be making frequent contacts with Indian tribes. However, "there is no danger to whites, or to their purity, from the power or from the vices of the Indians. The case is widely different with those who form the immediate object of this address [Negroes]." Since blacks were sexually promiscuous, particularly free blacks, they posed a distinct threat to white racial purity and had to be removed to Africa. Because Indians did not have such ardent sexual appetites, they could remain.[37] Many if not most colonizationists shared Clay's view of the differing sexual propensities of red and black despite frequent reports of Indians kidnapping white women and marrying them. Unlike the Negro, the Indian was no amalgamationist: "The spirit of an Indian warrior would have revolted at the thought of mingling the pure blood of the children of the soil with that of the pale-faced intruders. It was nature that taught him to reject union, but he thought and called it pride."[38] Colonizationists insisted that because Indian society would not amalgamate, it would not obstruct or "pollute" white society as the superior race moved West and monopolized the region's natural resources. Unlike Negroes, Indians would not force themselves upon white civilization; they recognized the proper role of a lesser race.[39] The A.C.S. program of African repatriation would therefore remove the threat of black sexual assault that red society did not present. Colonization may also have been intended (subconsciously) to remove certain white cravings to be "assaulted"—the temptation of certain whites to fornicate with blacks but not with Indians. Sexual cravings for blacks, but not for Indians, may explain why colonizationists seemed oblivious to reports of Indians running off with white women. The Noble Savage was not a sexual creature; he had no interest in white women.

The Negro clearly tapped an element deep within the colonizationist's libidinal recesses that the Indian did not draw to the

---

[37] Quoted in *Report of Mr. Kennedy*, pp. 938–39. Also quoted in Alexander, *History of Colonization*, p. 305.

[38] *Colonizationist and Journal of Freedom* (June 1833), pp. 73–74.

[39] See, e.g., *Twentieth Annual Report of the A.C.S.*, p. 46; *Report of Mr. Kennedy*, p. 211. Interestingly, Alexis de Tocqueville made this same contention in *Democracy in America* (New York: J. & H. G. Langley, 1841), I, 363–66.

surface—a fear of, along with a fascination for, interracial sexual congress. Unlike white-red relations, white-black contacts could result in amalgamation and the undermining of white civilization. This sexual distinction was not new in the early American experience. Since the first settlements in British North America, most whites disliked red-white fornication; but few regarded it with horror. There was some reluctance to characterize it as amalgamation. However, colonial Americans persistently feared and fretted over intercourse between white and black.[40] Virginians of Jefferson's generation sometimes voiced pride in having Indian blood. Patrick Henry proposed subsidies and tax relief for any whites who married Indians. But marriage or congress between white and black always remained the taboo of taboos—the symbol of amalgamation.[41]

The rigid distinction that colonizationists, like whites before them, had drawn between red and black in most areas of life, particularly in the bedchamber, may be explained by sociologist Harmannus Hoetink's concept of the somatic-norm image. According to Hoetink, a group prefers and is most willing to coexist with those who appear physically most like itself. Therefore, American whites have naturally perceived a greater "somatic distance" between themselves and blacks than between themselves and Indians. Visually, the Negro has contrasted much more markedly with the white man's self-image than the Indian.[42] If Hoetink is correct, the Indian was much more compatible with the colonizationist's vision of a white man's country than the black man could ever be. Like Thomas Jefferson, one of the earliest articulate proponents of black repatriation, colonizationists may

[40] This is very thoroughly documented in Jordan, *White over Black,* especially pp. 90–91, 162–63, 477–79.
[41] Robert McColley, *Slavery and Jeffersonian Virginia* (Urbana: University of Illinois Press, 1964), p. 138; Horsman, "American Indian Policy," pp. 22–23.
[42] H. Hoetink, *The Two Variants in Caribbean Race Relations: A Contribution to the Sociology of Segmented Societies* (New York: Oxford University Press, 1967). The concept of the somatic-norm image is discussed on pp. 120–60, while pp. 157–58 deal specifically with the contrast between perceptions of blacks and Indians. A current research project at the University of Calgary on late-nineteenth-century Western Canada seems to be validating Hoetink's somatic-norm thesis. Indians were welcomed into Canadian society; blacks were seen as dangerous and had to be kept at a distance.

have perceived property-owning Indians as swarthy white men but propertyless Negroes as a distinctly separate and alien group. After all, did not the tan-colored Cherokee of Georgia honor Locke's and Blackstone's emphasis upon private property? Did they not dress like whites, own their farms individually, hold black slaves, participate in Protestant denominations, and model their government structure after the Federal Constitution? And were not the Choctaw of Mississippi also quite similar to whites in their political practices and their efficient agricultural methods? Certainly, both Cherokee and Choctaw were more like the superior race than dirty, impoverished Negroes. They belonged in the white man's country.[43]

Whether one accepts or rejects Hoetink's concept of the somatic-norm image, it is apparent that most African colonizationists perceived the Negro, unlike the Indian, as non-white and therefore unfit for the white nation. Willing to embrace a red-white racial order, they argued and wanted desperately to believe that the Negro was fundamentally different from the Caucasian. Most slaveholding colonizationists would regulate the race through the peculiar institution. Most other colonizationists wanted Negroes entirely removed from America, free or slave. Why, though, did most supporters of the A.C.S. want to believe that the Negro was so different from the Caucasian that he had to be expelled or at least enslaved—that the Negro, unlike the Indian, was antithetical to white nationhood? What underlying factors in their psychological make-up caused this diverse group of patriots to perceive the Negro as a grave threat to the white man's country while they were almost oblivious to color in the case of the Indian? To answer these questions is to probe for the most fundamental source of the colonizationist impulse in early-nineteenth-century America.

IV

Because most colonizationists differed from their contemporaries in opposing Indian removal and in perceiving that a red-and-white

[43] Jordan, *White over Black*, pp. 477–79; McLoughlin, *Baptist History and Heritage* (April 1972), p. 71; Borden, "Cumbering the Soil," p. 84; DeRosier, Jr., *Choctaw Indians*, pp. 9–10.

society was compatible with white nationhood, one does not uncover the inner core of the colonizationist impulse by focusing
entirely on color. This is the most important point that comparison
of A.C.S. attitudes toward Negroes and Indians leaves us with. In
the minds of most colonizationists—antislavery reformers as well
as slaveholders—color had to be related to deeper problems. For
most A.C.S. activists, the Negro's complexion, unlike the Indian's,
was the outer sign of inner impurity. In addition to his sexual
excesses, the Negro was a sick "black element," the "deadliest
blight," "a vile excrescence," a "blotch," a "mildew," "polluting,"
and a "foul stain" upon the nation.[44] Blacks were dangerously
"contaminated." They "extend their vices to all around them,"
particularly as cholera carriers. This "polluting process" would
inevitably spread, "infect" whites, and undermine the nation.[45] As
the "vile, filthy stain" deepened—as sexually ardent American
Negroes increased their numbers—the burden the white nation
was required to carry worsened. White Americans were forced
"to keep in their midst an uncultivated, degraded and inferior
race." Malignant black hordes filled "the bosom of the country"
and "impregnated" its vital organs.[46] To rid the country of this
contamination that clogged its vital parts, there was one remedy;
the impure blotch had to be expelled. Colonizationist after coloni-

[44] *African Repository*, II, No. 11 (January 1827), 343; VII, No. 7 (Septem-
ber 1831), 211; VII, No. 8 (October 1831), 230; Logan, *Phylon*, IV, No. 4
(Fourth Quarter 1943), 328; George W. Benedict, *An Oration Delivered at
Burlington, Vt. on the Fourth of July, 1826. Being the Fiftieth Anniversary of
American Independence* (Burlington, 1826), p. 22; Mary B. Blackford,
"Public Letter," 1829, Papers of the American Colonization Society, Library
of Congress; *The Liberator*, February 4, 1832; Louis Ruchames (ed.), *Racial
Thought in America* (Amherst: University of Massachusetts Press, 1969), I,
395.
[45] *African Repository*, IX, No. 1 (March 1833), 3, 10; Henry Clay, *Speech
of the Hon. Henry Clay, before the American Colonization Society, in the
Hall of the House of Representatives, January 20, 1827* (Washington, D.C.,
1827), p. 12; Hoadly, *An Address*, p. 10; *Tenth Annual Report of American
Society for Colonizing the Free People of Colour of the United States*
(Washington, D.C., 1827), p. 21; Charles E. Rosenberg, *The Cholera Years:
The United States in 1832, 1849, and 1866* (Chicago: University of Chicago
Press, 1962), pp. 59–61; Richmond *Enquirer*, October 2, 1832.
[46] Eugene H. Berwanger, *The Frontier Against Slavery: Western Anti-
Negro Prejudice and the Slavery Extension Controversy* (Urbana: Uni-
versity of Illinois Press, 1967), p. 53; "The Colonization Society," *North
American Review*, XLII (January 1824), 62; *African Repository*, VII, No. 4
(June 1831), 97.

zationist—Old School Federalists, Southern slaveholders, evangelical clergymen, and representatives of other groups—spoke of
"cutting off a morbid excrescence," "throwing off the suffocating
and infectious load," "discharg[ing] the free blacks upon the
shores of Africa," "drain[ing] them off," and cutting loose the
"load which presses it [America] down to the earth."[47] Through
vigorous exertion, America would "be cleared" of blacks. They
would be expelled into Colonization Society "Receptacles" in
Liberia—six-month conditioning tenements where they would be
cleansed and "seasoned" to the ways of the African continent.
Thus, the country would be "relieved from its heaviest curse." It
would experience the "relief" and "satisfaction" that comes of a
thorough "clearing" and "cleansing" within. America would feel
the lightness, the purity, and the renewed potential of a true Promised Land.[48]

The colonizationist's underlying quest for purity overlapped, to
an extent, with the widespread medical assumption that human
disease could be cured by draining and thereby depressing the
body—by bloodletting, sweating, laxatives, and purgatives. An
organized program to induce bodily emissions cleansed the patient
of disease and other ills, just as organized Negro removal to Africa
cleansed the New Nation.[49] But the colonizationist's purity crusade corresponded even more closely with the human defecation
process. In America the Negro was a dark "blight" and a "stain"

[47] See, e.g., *National Intelligencer*, December 24, 1816; *African Repository*,
IX, No. 6 (August 1833), 172; XIV, No. 5 (May 1838), 142; *Ninth Annual
Report of the American Society for Colonizing the Free People of Colour of
the United States* (Washington, D.C., 1826), p. 13; *Sixteenth Annual Report
. . .* (Washington, D.C., 1833), p. x.
[48] See, e.g., *Seventeenth Annual Report of the American Society for
Colonizing the Free People of Colour of the United States* (Washington,
D.C., 1834), p. xviii; *African Repository*, I, No. 1 (March 1825), 2; III, No. 1
(March 1827), 6; IV, No. 10 (December 1828), 303; VI, No. 12 (February
1831), 361; Gerrit Smith to R. R. Gurley, October 10, 1827, and William
Pope to R. R. Gurley, December 2, 1827, Papers of the American Colonization Society, Library of Congress; Early Lee Fox, *The American Colonization Society, 1817–1840* (Baltimore: The Johns Hopkins Press, 1919), p. 32. If,
as colonizationists maintained, American blacks were essentially Africans, one
wonders why they had to be "seasoned" in Liberian "Receptacles" before
taking up life in Africa. None commented on this apparent contradiction.
[49] This "fever" theory of disease is discussed quite comprehensively in
Henry Burnell Shafer, *The American Medical Profession, 1783–1850* (reprint.
New York: AMS Press, Inc., 1968), pp. 96–102.

that "polluted" if he remained, much as retained excrement endangered the human body. Negro expulsion granted the same "relief" and "clearing" of the national body that defecation allowed to the human body. Even the Liberian "Receptacle" bore a striking resemblance to the privy. Psychiatrist Joel Kovel characterizes this entire excremental analogy as basic to white racist psychology, while historian Winthrop D. Jordan finds it particularly important in understanding early-nineteenth-century American racial thought.[50] Colonizationists seemed to be struggling to gain the sense of control, pleasure, and relief through their racial venture that young children experience playing with their feces.

But the defecation analogy falls short in one important particular. Talk as they did of the need to remove American blacks to Africa, colonizationists never came close to achieving their goal. The 1822–32 period was the Colonization Society's most active decade—a time when it raised revenues of $112,842 to meet expenses of $106,458. However, during these years the Society succeeded in transporting only 1,857 blacks to Africa. This did almost nothing to offset a rapidly increasing domestic black population. In the half century between 1816 and 1867, the A.C.S. emancipated and repatriated 6,000 slaves. During this interval, the average annual increase in the American slave population was 50,000. If their aim was to remove the black "blotch" from the white nation, colonizationists were conspicuous failures.[51] The Society's leading spokesman, Henry Clay, was busy augmenting his stock of slaves. So were other leading Southern colonizationists. Bushrod Washington, the first president of the A.C.S., had partici-

[50] Joel Kovel, *White Racism: A Psychohistory* (New York: Vintage Books, 1971), pp. 84, 89–90; Jordan, *White over Black*, p. 567. See also Earl E. Thorpe, *The Old South: A Psychohistory* (Durham, N.C.: E. Endrus Thorpe, 1972), p. 107.
[51] Walter M. Merrill, *Against Wind and Tide: A Biography of Wm. Lloyd Garrison* (Cambridge: Harvard University Press, 1963), p. 61; John L. Thomas, *The Liberator: William Lloyd Garrison* (Boston: Little, Brown and Company, 1963), p. 96; Rosen, *Phylon*, XXXIII, No. 2 (Spring Quarter 1972), 179; Merton L. Dillon, "The Failure of the American Abolitionists," *Journal of Southern History*, XXV, No. 2 (May 1959), 165; Jack E. Eblen, "Growth of the Black Population in *ante bellum* America, 1820–1860," *Population Studies*, XXVI, No. 2 (July 1972), 273–89; Keith E. Melder, "The Beginnings of the Women's Rights Movement in the United States, 1800–1840" (Ph.D. dissertation, Yale University, 1963), p. 129.

pated in the domestic slave trade. Charles Carroll, the second president, owned two thousand slaves and never freed or repatriated any. James Madison, the Society's third president, left a hundred slaves to his heirs. Clay and Charles Mercer both favored extending slavery into new federal territory—a policy which encouraged domestic slave breeding.[52] A New York Colonization Society spokesman openly acknowledged to R. R. Gurley that although he favored the idea of repatriating the nation's Negroes, Americans still "must have the blacks for our servants. We cannot consent to sending them [the Negro servant class] out of the country." "I am ready to confess that *I entertain no hopes* of seeing the number of our coloured population sensibly reduced," the prominent New Jersey colonizationist Lucius Q. Elmer acknowledged. Because sufficient federal funding was not forthcoming, precious few blacks would ever be sent to Africa. From Indiana, Isaac McCoy made the same admission: "We have no hope that the society & our benevolent government will ever be able to carry back to Africa all our negroes." Nonetheless, A.C.S. efforts must continue to be supported. James Madison conceded that a significant number of blacks might never be sent to Africa. However, "a partial success will have its value and an entire failure will leave behind a consciousness of the laudable intentions with which relief from the greatest of our calamities was attempted in the only mode presenting a chance of effecting it." Writing in 1824, Thomas Jefferson reaffirmed his support of African colonization but added that the project was economically impractical. Thus, talk as they might of the need to "expel" the "stain" of Negro "pollution" into Liberian "Receptacles," many influential colonizationists had no hope of success, while others sought to increase their Negro holdings.[53]

[52] Glyndon G. Van Deusen, *The Life of Henry Clay* (Boston: Little, Brown and Company, 1937), p. 137; Jordan, *White over Black*, p. 566; Dwight L. Dumond, *Antislavery: The Crusade for Freedom in America* (New York: W. W. Norton & Company, 1966), p. 130; Jane H. Pease and William H. Pease, *Bound with Them in Chains: A Biographical History of the Antislavery Movement* (Westport, Conn.: Greenwood Press, 1972), p. 101.

[53] H. Sessions to R. R. Gurley, June 17, 1825, Papers of the American Colonization Society, Library of Congress, represents the report of the New York Colonization Society spokesman. Lucius Elmer is quoted in *Proceedings*

One can only speculate why a patriotic organization supported by public opinion, by countless leading officials in national and local government, and by major cultural figures like Sarah Hale and Noah Webster, was so remarkably ineffective in its quest for national purification. Perhaps the rhetoric, not the reality, was what mattered. Perhaps planters like Henry Clay could not live without their blacks, while non-slaveholders like Lucius Elmer were willing to crusade for colonization because they knew it would never materialize. Winthrop D. Jordan's *White over Black* (1968), the definitive study of seventeenth- and eighteenth-century American racial attitudes, demonstrates that visions of filthy, excrement-like blacks existed since the first British settlements in the New World and were traceable to Elizabethan England. Simultaneously, however, Jordan demonstrates that whites in the New World were unwilling to part with blacks. Early Americans *needed* "vile" blacks to give them a sense that they were not "vile" themselves, that they were not losing their cultivated, civilized, perfumed values in the unregulated, unscented wilds of the new continent.[54] The Colonization Society was a movement for national purity; as such, it implied the continuation of colonial American racial attitudes during the early nineteenth century—the abhorrence of "vile" excrement-like blacks on the one hand and the unwillingness to part with those blacks on the other. For assurances of white purity, the excrement-like Negro may have been required as a point of contrast.

In 1840 the editors of the Society's official organ, the *African Repository*, charged that Americans should feel for the underprivileged with *"bowels of compassion."*[55] This phrase may have pointed to the innermost racial feelings of a large and diverse array

of the First Annual Meeting of the New Jersey Colonization Society, p. 16 (emphasis added). McCoy is quoted in Miles, *Kansas Historical Quarterly*, XXXVIII, No. 3 (Autumn 1972), 279. James Madison to Thomas R. Dew, February 23, 1833, in Gaillard Hunt (ed.), *The Writings of James Madison* (New York: G. P. Putnam's Sons, 1910), IX, 500. William Cohen, "Thomas Jefferson and the Problem of Slavery," *Journal of American History*, LVI, No. 3 (December 1969), 523–24, notes Jefferson's 1824 statement.

[54] Jordan clearly states the basic lines of his argument in *White over Black*, pp. 110, 134.

[55] *African Repository*, XVI, No. 17 (September 1, 1840), 259 (emphasis added).

of colonizationists. The concept of expelling "underprivileged" black "bowels" with benevolent "compassion" may have satisfied both the long-standing white American compulsion to remove a contagious black population from the white nation, and the economic and psychological advantages of keeping a servile black labor force within that nation. One's "bowels" had to be expelled. Yet, there was time to reflect upon those "bowels" with "compassion" prior to expulsion—a great deal of time. The important thing was the benevolent thought, not the coarse facts of removal. This ideological framework may explain how Henry Clay could look forward to the day when "but few vestiges of the black race will remain among our posterity" while busily accumulating slaves on his Ashland plantation and even staying with his "impure" bondsmen during the dangerous 1832 cholera epidemic.[56] The same framework may explain how a non-slaveholder like Lucius Elmer could favor massive colonization of American blacks while admitting that meaningful repatriation would never be effected. It may even help to explain the racial thinking of Madison and Jefferson— men who advocated African colonization while recognizing that it would probably fail. What mattered was the benevolent thought of expelling the impure black "stain" from the white man's country—not the actual expulsion. Good words and proper thoughts may have been more important than financial contributions and implementing actions in the colonizationist's purity crusade. After all, concrete success would have terminated both the expulsive process and the benevolent thought. It might also have cost slaveholding colonizationists a great deal of money and Northern colonizationists a cheap labor supply. Like alchemists of the Middle Ages, a variety of colonizationists may have seen links between feces and economic wealth; feces might be turned into gold and black labor into profits.

"These two races [black and white] are attracted to each other without intermingling," Alexis de Tocqueville noted in *Democracy in America*, "and they are alike entirely unable to separate or to combine."[57] Tocqueville based his observation upon frequent

[56] Ruchames (ed.), *Racial Thought*, I, 396; Rosenberg, *Cholera Years*, p. 61.

[57] Tocqueville, *Democracy in America*, I, 386.

interviews with a variety of colonizationists and seemed to capture the inner core of the colonizationist impulse. Beneath a number of deceptive and misleading arguments, and beneath their distinction of red from black, colonizationists generally perceived Negroes as impure, diseased, and sexually dangerous. But they were notoriously ineffective in "cleansing" the nation of impurity—in repatriating a significant number of blacks. They were struggling to retain enthusiasm for a purity crusade that would keep white civilization free of black contamination. But had the crusade ever been effective—had the nation ever been "cleansed" of a significant number of blacks—the concept of purification would have lost much of its attraction. Hence, blacks remained in the Promised Land in ever-increasing numbers though vilified for impurities and kept at a distance or enslaved.

With their strange cast of mind, most colonizationists seemed to be at once integrationists and segregationists. Like Henry Clay, they could have warm and sustained contacts with a black servant class and constantly augment their slaveholdings yet recommend an organized procedure "to drain them [blacks] off."[58] Like Clay, colonizationists could also proclaim abhorrence of slavery and plead for its demise while defending slave breeding, the domestic slave trade, the recovery of fugitive slaves, and the stability of a slave society.[59] There is little wonder that men like Clay and Gurley made the Colonization Society into a powerful patriotic organization—a multi-interest constituency of slaveholders, abolitionists, and negrophobes of every variety. The benevolent concept of a purity crusade for the Promised Land seems to have held these diverse elements together, obscuring specific issues of interracial contact and emancipation.

V

We have seen how a diverse assortment of colonizationists, as they proposed a white man's country through Negro resettlement,

[58] Van Deusen, *Life of Clay*, pp. 136–37; Rosenberg, *Cholera Years*, p. 61; Hopkins (ed.), *Papers of Clay*, II, 263–64; *African Repository*, XII, No. 10 (October 1836), 297; XIII, No. 1 (January 1837), 38.

[59] Van Deusen, *Life of Clay*, pp. 136–38, 311, 361; *First Annual Report of the A.C.S.*, pp. 16–17; Fox, *Colonization Society*, p. 29.

shared visions of a nation without a blemish. A pure nation was a flawless nation; by expelling the most "unwholesome" and "polluting" element in the society, the Republic was perfected. In their quest for national perfection, colonizationists were ideological bedfellows with *Columbian* contributors like David Ramsay and Noah Webster and shared their hopes for "the Rising Glory of America." Webster was, in fact, a strong supporter of the A.C.S. The colonizationist's pure and perfect nation also resembled visions of a nation forged by a pure and flawless Founding Father. Indeed, both the colonizationist and the Washington eulogist looked nostalgically to an idyllic late-eighteenth-century social order. It may have been more than coincidence that at a July Fourth ceremony in 1848 marking the erection of the Washington Monument, the annual report of the American Colonization Society was inserted beneath the 24,500-pound marble cornerstone.[60] The A.C.S. vision of pure, hence perfect, nationhood through black expulsion was also linked to the cult of True American Womanhood. Both pliable women and "noxious" blacks were rungs upon the white man's ladder of perfection. By restricting women's lives so that they could be no more than malleable, putty-like creatures and by characterizing blacks as feces, the white male was subordinating both women and blacks to his own need to climb and achieve. Because women and Negroes were below him and could be manipulated to facilitate his needs, both he and his country were rising—the white man and the New Nation were heading toward perfection. Whatever their problems, white men of the Promised Land were several steps above women and Negroes.

Yet colonization thought represented more than a carry-over of perfectionist aspirations into race relations. We have repeatedly noted the strong nostalgic yearnings of the men of the A.C.S. to restore an ordered and securely anchored America of 1776 where diverse peoples and institutions were hierarchically and effectively regulated. To restore the supposed conditions of the late eighteenth century was to achieve a society where the citizen enjoyed a sense of place and rooted stability. Since blacks caused "pollu-

---

[60] "George Washington's Monument," *American Heritage*, XX, No. 1 (December 1968), 70.

tion," "stain," and social dislocation in the New Nation, their removal would restore the anchored stability of 1776. By excluding "the children of Africa," America would once again be *"the white man's country"* and would provide the citizen with a *"homestead"*—a place where he could feel secure and rooted— George Washington Parke Custis declared.[61] Other colonizationists frequently echoed this theme—that the white man's country would confer a secure homestead. Blacks within its borders (or at least free blacks) were disorienting intruders and should go where they belonged. When they were gone—when America consisted of "one homogeneous people" (or at least an overwhelming number of white freedmen along with some black bondsmen)—it would be the country of and for white men, a nation that they could call their homeland and where they could feel at ease. Free of Negroes—the prime forces of social chaos— America would give white men a sense of place, rootedness, and contentment.[62] Through these sorts of words and phrases, colonizationists hoped to find a new anchor on life—a very vague and highly personalized feeling of living in a rooted homeland—much as doctrinaire patriots before them had hoped for.

The colonizationist crusade for national purity incorporated, therefore, two very basic aspects of patriotic thought in the New Nation—perfectionism and a search for rootedness. But the colonizationist as racial patriot also made a unique ideological contribution. Though his concept of national purification overlapped with perfectionism and with the quest for rootedness, the concept carried a special implication. By expelling a troublesome element, the Promised Land could cleanse itself of all its ills. Through expulsion of "noxious" elements, the country's problems might be remedied; the great potential of the Promised Land might be restored. Early-seventeenth-century New England Puritans had imagined themselves erecting a "City Upon a Hill"; citizens of the world were watching to see if they, like the ancient Israelites, could build a godly community on earth. By expelling "noxious"

---

[61] Quoted in Logan, *Phylon*, IV, No. 4 (Fourth Quarter 1943), 330.
[62] See, e.g., *African Repository*, IV, No. 3 (May 1828), 76; IX, No. 2 (April 1833); XIII, No. 1 (January 1837), 33; *Tenth Annual Report of the A.C.S.*, p. 16.

elements, colonizationists hoped to gain this same vision of fresh, breathtaking opportunity as the Old World watched. They could rid the United States of the one element that was setting American against American and threatening to "contaminate" the country. They could give the New Nation a fresh start; they could help their countrymen to regain the supposed purity and freshness of opportunity of the American Revolutionary generation so that Zion could be built in the New World.

Thinking along these lines—reflecting more than acting— patriots like Noah Webster, Ralph Randolph Gurley, Henry Clay, and Robert Finley supported African colonization. The psychology beneath their ideology was crucial. They were clinging to a built-in defense—an apparent safety valve—against national failure. When their patriotic spirit might languish—when their aspirations for national perfection seemed to undermine their need for rootedness—they could deploy sentences and paragraphs that counterpointed their perfectionist aspirations alongside their desires for anchored stability. Through the spoken and written word, they could draw together incompatibles just as Washington eulogists had done. But this sort of intellectual gymnastics could not bring long-range peace of mind. There was also the possibility of attributing their ills to the failures of patriotic womanhood—the insufficient pliancy of the female appendage. But this scapegoat feature inherent in the notion of True American Womanhood could never remedy the uprooting essence of perfectionist strivings. It gave patriots a culprit but not a solution. By identifying the nation's ills and patriots' personal anxieties with "pernicious," "noxious" blacks and by programming systematic black expulsion, they could resort to a third seeming solution in addition to counterpointing and casting blame upon the female appendage. Therefore, organized colonization represented another potential source of relief from the frustrations inherent in the crusade for the Promised Land.[63]

[63] In *The Pursuit of Loneliness: American Culture at the Breaking Point* (Boston: Beacon Press, 1970), p. 15, Philip E. Slater characterizes the notion of black expulsion as part of the "Toilet Assumption" of American culture and maintains that it has survived to the present. It is fundamentally "the notion that unwanted matter, unwanted difficulties, unwanted complexities and obstacles will disappear if they are removed from our immediate field of vision. . . . Our approach to social problems is to decrease their visibility; out of sight, out of mind."

But though this colonizationist crusade for national purification was distinguishable from counterpointing and from the cult of True American Womanhood, it resembled them in one essential. All three restricted spread-eagle patriots' lives and made it difficult for them to experience many of life's diversities. By trying to emulate a flawless and anchored Founding Father who never existed, they were diverted from the rich and varied possibilities within daily reality—experiential possibilities in which perfecting and stabilizing qualities rarely balanced one another. By insisting that patriotic women were retiring, tractable, and served male needs, they were simultaneously limiting women's experiential possibilities and their own. If female patriots were to strive to become soft and malleable to male demands, it almost followed that male patriots were properly hard and inflexible. Men did not have to be sensitive to other people's feelings and needs, particularly if the others were of the "serving" sex. Thus, the cult of True American Womanhood not only inhibited men's softer, more yielding propensities, but stood to retard their gregarious instincts. Like the counterpointed Founding Father and True Womanhood, the colonizationist ideal of black expulsion significantly reduced human experience. It set limits on viable interracial relationships where white and black cultural forces could enrich each other, it diverted attention from racial oppressions within America, and it encouraged white propensities to fear "filth" and "stain." All three seeming safety valves were, then, abstractions which discouraged patriots from dealing with the complex and diverse realities of daily existence. All three offered simplistic and artificial order patterns to cope with a New Nation that was in constant flux.

CHAPTER 7

THE IDEOLOGICAL LEGACY
OF COLONIZATION

In December of 1833 Ralph Randolph Gurley wrote an apprehensive letter to James Gillespie Birney: "If the Colonization
Society could attract and hold to it the great community of the
wise and good from all parts of the Country, if its resources could
be increased tenfold and the scheme which it promotes could be
advanced with vastly more power and rapidity, we might hope to
save the country, from the most terrible convulsion that has ever
threatened it." More colonizationists North and South were
needed, better funding was essential, and greater A.C.S. agitation
was required if blacks were ever to be removed to Africa in sufficient numbers to save the New Nation.[1] By January of 1838
Gurley had become pessimistic. His benevolent and patriotic society faced difficulties from membership decline, inadequate funding, and a variety of other factors. The crisis was of such
magnitude that the A.C.S. "operations must be exceedingly irregular and inefficient, if not, in a short time, altogether suspended."[2]

The unwillingness of the Federal Government to appropriate
funds and the departure of wealthy supporters from the A.C.S.
caused the financial crisis. The *laissez-faire* ideology behind Presi-

[1] Dwight L. Dumond (ed.), *Letters of James Gillespie Birney* (New York:
D. Appleton-Century Company, 1938), I, 110–11.
[2] *African Repository*, XIV, No. 1 (January 1838), 27.

dent Andrew Jackson's rejection of internal improvements and destruction of the Bank of the United States mitigated against Colonization Society efforts to acquire federal funding. In a voluntaristic Jacksonian society aspiring to narrow the scope of national action, it was unlikely that the American Colonization Society or any association could have received massive federal funding despite the urgency of its appeal.[3] The decline in private contributions and support is more difficult to assess. There was the recurrent charge that the Society's Board of Managers was a group of bunglers who mismanaged funds.[4] But new managers could easily have been selected. Thus, there must have been more fundamental reasons for the increasing disillusionment with the A.C.S. during the 1830's.

William Lloyd Garrison's 1832 publication, *Thoughts on African Colonization*, was a scathing indictment of the Society for its alleged proslavery commitment and turned many influential Northern reformers away from the organization. Within nine months of publication, 2,750 copies of the pamphlet had been sold. This was an unprecedented volume by antislavery standards and telling proof of the impact of recent changes in printing technology.[5] Garrison charged that the Colonization Society was lulling Americans, making them think that gradual emancipation was taking place while the Southern slave system continued unimpeded. His

[3] George M. Fredrickson, *The Black Image in the White Mind: The Debate on Afro-American Character and Destiny, 1817–1914* (New York: Harper & Row, 1971), pp. 25–26, provides an excellent discussion of this point.

[4] See, e.g., Eli Seifman, "The United Colonization Societies of New York and Pennsylvania and the Establishment of the African Colony of Bassa Cove," *Pennsylvania History*, XXXV, No. 1 (January 1968), 34; Elliot Cresson to R. R. Gurley, April 12, 1831, Papers of the American Colonization Society, Library of Congress.

[5] Early in the Jacksonian period, the mechanization of the printing process and the mass production of print made it possible for relatively obscure authors with scant resources to put their thoughts into books and pamphlets at greatly reduced costs. Cheap postal rates allowed their materials to circulate widely throughout the country. For useful discussions of this printing revolution, see, e.g., James L. Crouthamel, "The Newspaper Revolution in New York, 1830–1860," *New York History*, XLV (April 1964), 91–113; Leonard L. Richards, *"Gentlemen of Property and Standing": Anti-Abolition Mobs in Jacksonian America* (New York: Oxford University Press, 1970), pp. 71–73; Helen Waite Papashvily, *All the Happy Endings* (New York: Harper & Brothers, 1956), pp. 36–37.

argument caused defections from the A.C.S. by important Northern antislavery men like Beriah Green, Elizur Wright, Jr., and Charles B. Storrs. Although the pioneer Ohio abolitionist Charles Osborn had made the same argument fifteen years earlier, Garrison's pamphlet contributed much more substantially to an abolitionist alternative to colonization.[6] *Thoughts on African Colonization* was followed by a decade of editorials against the A.C.S. in Garrison's *Liberator*. Persuaded by these editorials, several Northern antislavery activists refused to fund or to participate in Colonization Society activities. By 1839 Francis Jackson and Garrison jointly reported that while the A.C.S. had once flourished in the North "like a green-bay tree, having secured the approbation of both Church and State," its "popularity has given place to abhorrence . . . it lies prostrate, helpless, bankrupt."[7]

To head off Northern defections, many A.C.S. leaders emphasized that they were not proslavery and had no stake in perpetuating the peculiar institution. Their words confirmed recurrent suspicions among a number of Southern planters that the Society was an abolitionist group in disguise, more intent on emancipating slaves than on removing free Negroes. Opposition came earliest (in the mid-1820's) and most intensely from South Carolina, the one slaveholding region where the Colonization Society had not been able to build viable state and local organizations. Carolinians nervously drafted legislative resolutions, editorials, and polemical essays defending the slave system against the "duplicity" of colonization agents. By the early 1830's, it was impossible to discuss the potential merits of the colonization ideal in South Carolina without risking mob violence.[8] Opposition to the Colonization Society as

[6] Ruth Anna Ketring, *Charles Osborn and the Antislavery Movement* (Columbus: Ohio State Archaeological and Historical Society, 1937), pp. 39–40; John L. Thomas, *The Liberator: William Lloyd Garrison* (Boston: Little, Brown and Company, 1963), p. 154; Louis Filler, *The Crusade Against Slavery, 1830–1860* (New York: Harper & Brothers, 1960), p. 61.

[7] Louis Ruchames (ed.), *The Letters of William Lloyd Garrison* (Cambridge, Mass.: The Belknap Press, 1971), II, 489.

[8] For data on South Carolina opposition to the Colonization Society from the mid-1820's on, see William W. Freehling, *Prelude to Civil War: The Nullification Controversy in South Carolina, 1816–1836* (New York: Harper Torchbooks, 1968) pp. 123–25, 197; Herman V. Ames (ed.), *State Documents on Federal Relations: The States and the United States* (Philadelphia: University of Pennsylvania, 1906), p. 207; Frederick Bancroft, "The Early Anti-

an abolitionist front soon followed in Georgia, Mississippi, Kentucky, North Carolina, and Virginia. Of all Southern states, only Maryland remained firmly committed to A.C.S. activities.[9]

Attacked in the North as proslavery and in the South as abolitionist, the Colonization Society lost influence and power during the middle and late 1830's. The hope of uniting antislavery Northern reformers and proslavery Southern planters by restoring the promise of 1776 and the ideal of white nationhood seemed to be coming to naught. With revenues and membership declining in both sections, the A.C.S. disbanded its Board of Managers in 1838 and relinquished autonomy to state auxiliaries. For a time, some of these auxiliaries continued to exist (most often in the border states). The national organization persisted until 1964. Yet the effective days of the A.C.S. were over.[10] Members departed for newly formed abolitionist societies or to defend the slave system. But despite this organizational disintegration, certain ideas and ideals lived on. As colonizationists dispersed among contending camps in the intensifying debate over slavery, they carried with them certain ideological assumptions that they derived from the Colonization Society's patriotic crusade for white nationhood. This ideological carry-over—the colonization legacy—is a ne-

---

slavery Movement and African Colonization," in Jacob E. Cooke, *Frederick Bancroft, Historian* (Norman: University of Oklahoma Press, 1957), pp. 174–77; Robert James Turnbull, *The Crisis: or, Essays on the Usurpations of the Federal Government* (Charleston, 1827), 37–38, 89, 124, 133; "Colonization Society," *Southern Review*, I, No. 1 (February 1828), 219–34; Charleston *Mercury*, July 3, 1830, as quoted in the Richmond *Enquirer*, July 20, 1830; James M. McPherson, "Slavery and Race," *Perspectives in American History*, III (1969), 465.

9 Ames (ed.), *State Documents*, p. 211; *Pennsylvania Archives*, 4th Ser. (Harrisburg: The State of Pennsylvania, 1900), V, 556, 643–44; *African Repository*, VII, No. 5 (July 1831), 144; Charles S. Sydnor, *Slavery in Mississippi* (New York: D. Appleton-Century Company, 1933), pp. 205, 217; James Nourse to R. R. Gurley, December 29, 1827, and William H. Craven to Richard Smith, September 2, 1829, Papers of the American Colonization Society, Library of Congress; J. Winston Coleman, Jr., "Henry Clay, Kentucky and Liberia," *Register of the Kentucky Historical Society*, XLV (October 1947), 313.

10 P. J. Staudenraus, *The African Colonization Movement, 1816–1865* (New York: Columbia University Press, 1961), p. 237; Bruce Rosen, "Abolition and Colonization, the Years of Conflict: 1829–1834," *Phylon*, XXXIII, No. 2 (Second Quarter 1972), 192.

glected but fundamental dimension to patriotic thought in the New Nation.

II

Students of antebellum American abolitionism have made little of the movement's colonizationist antecedents. However, almost every important proponent of immediate emancipation without repatriation during the 1830's had supported the A.C.S. a few years earlier. In 1829 Elizabeth Chandler urged American women to raise funds for the Society's Liberian colony; it was a "cause of humanity and justice." Four years later she continued to characterize African colonization as a benevolent cause but felt that it was more important to emancipate blacks and to improve the quality of Negro life within the New Nation.[11] A New Haven printer and engraver in the late 1820's, Simeon S. Jocelyn, was also a Colonization Society fund raiser who supported missionary uplift for the "Dark Continent." A few years later, as the new white pastor of a black Congregational Church in New Haven, he argued for immediate abolition. Like Chandler, however, Jocelyn continued to cling to the colonization ideal while urging immediate improvements for blacks within America.[12] The wealthy New York philanthropist Arthur Tappan underwent a similar metamorphosis. Supporting the Colonization Society until 1833, he renounced it for immediate abolition. The founders of the A.C.S. had conceived of an ideal and benevolent solution to racial turmoil, Tappan explained, but subsequent leaders had sinfully transported liquor to the Society's Liberian colony and were helping to perpetuate slavery.[13] Gerrit Smith was another notable example. In 1827 he announced support for the Colonization Society "to relieve our country of its black population" and "to raise Africa

[11] *Genius of Universal Emancipation*, IV, No. 11, New Ser. (November 20, 1829), 84; III, No. 8, 3rd Ser. (June 1833), 128.
[12] Simeon S. Jocelyn to R. R. Gurley, February 20, October 5, 1829, Papers of the American Colonization Society, Library of Congress; Staudenraus, *African Colonization Movement*, p. 127.
[13] Seifman, *Pennsylvania History*, XXXV, No. 1 (January 1968), 31; Staudenraus, *African Colonization Movement*, p. 212; *African Repository*, IX, No. 3 (May 1833), 65–66; Arthur Tappan to R. R. Gurley, n.d., Papers of the American Colonization Society, Library of Congress.

from death to life." Eight years later, he joined the American Anti-Slavery Society because the A.C.S. was not sufficiently antislavery and had not been diligent in "building up its [Liberian] colony."[14] The cases of men like Edward Beecher and Theodore Dwight Weld were similar. Both had lauded the colonization ideal early in their careers. They did not repudiate this idealization when they subsequently renounced the A.C.S. and embraced immediate abolition.[15] Their carefully qualified departure from the Colonization Society indicates that the colonization legacy was crucial to the abolitionist intellectual perspective. To understand why so many important antebellum abolitionists refused to repudiate the colonization ideal and therefore white nationhood, it is profitable to consider three of the leading architects of abolitionist ideology in the early Jacksonian period.

Historian Herman Von Holst characterized Benjamin Lundy as "the immediate precursor, and in a certain sense the founder of [nineteenth-century] abolitionism."[16] Born to Quaker parents in Sussex County, New Jersey, in 1789, Lundy moved at nineteen to Wheeling, West Virginia, where he "first saw the slaves in chains, forced along like brutes to the southern markets for human flesh and blood." The sight of black bondsmen committed him to antislavery agitation at a time when very few other white Americans found cause to crusade against human bondage. In 1815 Lundy organized an antislavery association in St. Clairsville, Ohio, moved on to repeat the effort at Mount Pleasant, and then traveled to other locations. He was constantly on the road and rarely in one place for any extended period. By 1827 he had organized one hundred and thirty antislavery organizations (mostly in the upper South) and published the most influential abolitionist periodical of

---

[14] Gerrit Smith to R. R. Gurley, October 10, 1827, Papers of the American Colonization Society, Library of Congress; Staudenraus, *African Colonization Movement*, p. 128; *African Repository*, IV, No. 9 (November 1828), 272; XII, No. 1 (January 1836), 36–37; *The Philanthropist* (New Richmond, Ohio), April 1, 1836; Ruchames (ed.), *Letters of Garrison*, II, 47.

[15] Ruchames (ed.), *Letters of Garrison*, II, 355; Betty Fladeland, *James Gillespie Birney: Slaveholder to Abolitionist* (Ithaca: Cornell University Press, 1955), p. 53. Benjamin P. Thomas, *Theodore Weld: Crusader for Freedom* (New Brunswick: Rutgers University Press, 1950), pp. 33–36.

[16] Quoted in Fred Landon (ed.), *The Diary of Benjamin Lundy Written during his journey through Upper Canada January, 1832* (Ontario Historical Society, 1922), p. 2.

the period—the *Genius of Universal Emancipation*. A roaming editor whose newspaper shifted locations almost as often as he moved, Lundy had become the most significant figure in the pre-Garrisonian phase of antislavery agitation. But there had been a cost. Lundy ended up with no sense of geographic rootedness. Like David Ramsay, there was no city or town or crossroad that he could call home.[17]

A deeply committed patriot, Benjamin Lundy was certain that racial turmoil was the major obstacle to the realization of "the Rising Glory of America." But unlike many members of the Colonization Society, he viewed slavery, not blacks *per se*, as the basic problem. By abolishing slavery, the unfinished work of the Revolution would be completed; the last blemish on the New Nation would be removed.[18] In 1823 Lundy noted emancipation in the British colonies and pleaded with Americans to keep pace with the mother country: *"Arouse ye, My Countrymen!—Awake from your slumbers! Our Republic is losing its glory, and our Patriots their Laurels, for Monarchists are outstripping us in the grand, the benevolent, and the holy work of Abolishing personal Slavery!!!"*[19] As long as slavery survived, the potential of the Promised Land to set a lasting example for mankind could not be realized. The *"monarchists* of Europe are in advance of the high professing *'republicans'* of this country, in their *practical* advocacy of the principle of general liberty, or, at least, the 'equal' rights of man."[20]

Time and again Lundy distinguished himself from African colonizationists of the 1820's and early 1830's by stressing emancipation, not black removal: "This must be done, sooner or later, whether he [the Negro] remains where he is, or removes to a

[17] For data on Lundy's career to 1827, see Benjamin Lundy, *The Life, Travels and Opinions of Benjamin Lundy* (Philadelphia: William D. Parrish, 1847), pp. 16–24; Landon (ed.), *Diary of Lundy*, p. 1; *Genius of Universal Emancipation*, III, No. 1, 3rd Ser. (November 1832), 8; John Lofton, "Enslavement of the Southern Mind: 1775–1825," *Journal of Negro History*, XLIII, No. 2 (April 1958), 135.

[18] Merton L. Dillon, *Benjamin Lundy and the Struggle for Negro Freedom* (Urbana: University of Illinois Press, 1966), p. 61.

[19] *Genius of Universal Emancipation*, III, No. 15 (July 1823), 177–78 (emphasis Lundy's).

[20] *Genius of Universal Emancipation*, III, No. 4, 3rd Ser. (February 1833), 55 (emphasis Lundy's).

distant land." This was not to say that the A.C.S. was an evil organization or that African colonization was detrimental: "I would not wish it to be thought that I am opposed to the *ostensible* views of the American Colonization Society." On the contrary, "I have ever approved the motives by which the founders of it professed to be actuated, and have until lately cherished the hope that much good would result from its establishment."[21] Indeed, Lundy allowed the A.C.S. to advertise in his *Genius of Universal Emancipation*. The ideal of Negro removal and the Christianizing of the "Dark Continent" were patriotic goals; they promoted white nationhood. The problem was that removal of Negroes to Africa would not assure universal emancipation in the Promised Land. Too few slaves would be freed and colonized abroad to destroy the peculiar institution. The cost of moving an American Negro to Africa was too great for extensive manumission with repatriation. Therefore, although African colonization was a meritorious and useful "auxiliary" to "universal emancipation," it would not destroy slavery.[22]

During the 1820's, Lundy became suspicious of the intentions of certain members of the Colonization Society. He began to wonder about their motives as well as their approach. Were they really out to "meliorate the condition of blacks in our country" by sending them to Christianize the "ignorant and barbarous natives of the African continent"? He feared that certain African colonizationists were simply racist negrophobes; others like Henry Clay and Charles Mercer worked halfheartedly for repatriation in order to perpetuate slavery. With serious misgivings, Lundy continued to cooperate with the A.C.S. until 1837. Indeed, it was not until the end of his career that he dared to condemn the Colonization Society as a foe of universal emancipation.[23]

---

[21] *Genius of Universal Emancipation*, I, No. 4 (October 1821), 50–52; III, No. 1, 3rd Ser. (November 1832), 1.

[22] Lundy, *Life, Travels and Opinions*, pp. 220, 233; *Genius of Universal Emancipation*, I, No. 7 (January 1822), 109; III, No. 11 (March 1824), 132; XI (December 1830), 130; II, No. 9, 3rd Ser. (February 1832), 143; III, No. 2, 3rd Ser. (December 1832), 20.

[23] *Genius of Universal Emancipation*, I, No. 4 (October 1821), 51; Fred Landon, "Benjamin Lundy in Illinois," *Journal of the Illinois State Historical Society*, XXXIII, No. 1 (March 1940), 62; Lundy, *Life, Travels and Opinions*, pp. 191–92; Dillon, *Lundy*, pp. 27–28; Jane H. Pease and William H.

Benjamin Lundy's racial ideology differed significantly, then, from most African colonizationists'; emancipation, not Negro removal, was his highest priority. Black repatriation to Africa might promote emancipation, but the incompetence and insincerity of African colonizationists necessitated other measures. Interestingly, these other measures also involved Negro repatriation—to Haiti, Upper Canada, and the Mexican provinces of Texas. These three "American hemisphere" locations were closer to the United States and therefore less costly. Larger numbers of blacks could be removed, their rights and liberties could be protected through the New Nation's influence within the "American hemisphere," and they could rise above the degrading positions that they occupied in the United States. Finally, the success of Lundy's three repatriation programs would prove the benevolence and egalitarianism of American civilization. By removing blacks from one section of the "American hemisphere" to other sections, the peculiar institution would be destroyed and anti-Negro discrimination eliminated. The egalitarian vision of the Revolutionary generation would be vindicated.[24]

Convinced that "American hemisphere" repatriation was the most practical solution to black bondage in the New Nation, Lundy devoted his life to these ventures. He traveled to Haiti, Upper Canada, and Texas, negotiated with governments there, publicized continental ventures, and tried desperately if unsuccessfully to implement them. He was a more active colonizationist than most leaders of the Colonization Society. Yet he persistently noted that universal emancipation, not Negro colonization, had to be the ultimate goal: "I could not give the toss of a copper for a system of philanthropy that extends no further than this [Negro removal]." Nonetheless, unlike leading abolitionists of the 1830's, 1840's, and 1850's, Lundy could not conceive of immediate emanci-

Pease, *Bound with Them in Chains: A Biographical History of the Antislavery Movement* (Westport, Conn.: Greenwood Press, 1972), p. 101.

[24] *Genius of Universal Emancipation*, I, No. 8 (February 1822), 119; III, No. 14 (June 1824), 177; IV, No. 1 (October 1824), 4; IV, No. 4 (January 1825), 54; IV, No. 6 (March 1825), 36; II, No. 8, 3rd Ser. (January 1832), 128; III, No. 1, 3rd Ser. (November 1832), 7; XIII (May 1833), 97; Landon (ed.), *Diary of Lundy*, pp. 22–23; Landon, *Journal of the Illinois State Historical Society*, XXXIII, No. 1 (March 1940), 58.

pation without repatriation and could not envision Negroes living happily in the Promised Land. He was firmly committed to white nationhood as a patriotic ideal. While remarking that "it is not impolitic to set the slaves free among us when they are prepared to enjoy their freedom" and while suggesting that successful repatriations might ease white fears and encourage "general emancipation at home" within a biracial society, Lundy never systematically pursued emancipation's logic. He never stressed manumission, egalitarianism, and biracialism as the interrelated goals of racial reform. Unless "a large portion of our colored population can be removed from those districts where they are most numerous, it will be impossible to do away with the [slave] system." This was Lundy's basic message. America's growing black population formed an "immense mass of ignitible materials" that would not "remain in a quiescent state" for long. Blacks had to be removed and their numbers reduced or "our cities will be laid in ashes, and our plains strewed with mangled corpses." Racial conflict would destroy the country.[25]

Lundy therefore stressed emancipation through "American hemisphere" colonization. But like Clay, Gurley, and most other leaders of the A.C.S., he felt that Negro removal from the New Nation could help to restore America's "Rising Glory." Although he wanted the colonized area to become more than a mere dumping ground for American "refuse," the psychology sustaining Lundy's ideology was strikingly similar to that of leading African colonizationists. He, too, was at least partially driven by the hope of removing discord from the Promised Land and restoring order by benevolently expelling the black element within. He, too, viewed black removal as a useful measure in the crusade for a stable, orderly, and perfect Promised Land.[26]

Whereas Benjamin Lundy was the leading American abolitionist of the 1820's, William Lloyd Garrison became a central figure in

[25] Dillon, *Lundy*, p. 90; Lundy, *Life, Travels and Opinions*, pp. 190–91; *Genius of Universal Emancipation*, I, No. 7 (January 1822), 109; IV, No. 2 (November 1824), 17, 21–22; III, No. 1, 3rd Ser. (November 1832), 7; III, No. 8, 3rd Ser. (June 1833), 119.
[26] Pease and Pease, *Bound with Them in Chains*, pp. 90–114, includes an excellent study of Lundy's racial ideas. The authors conclude that he perceived colonization ventures as his principal philanthropic and patriotic contribution.

the abolitionist movement through most of the 1830's. An obscure New England journalist, Garrison was only remotely concerned with slavery until the early spring of 1828; temperance and observance of the Sabbath seemed more important than emancipation. On March 17, 1828, Garrison heard Lundy lecture in Boston. He was impressed with the way the pioneer abolitionist cited incidents and statistics to demonstrate the cruelty and immorality of black bondage. Garrison met privately with Lundy that evening and pledged "to concentrate my life to the extirpation of that barbarous subject [slavery]." In the months that followed, Lundy persuaded Garrison to become co-editor of his *Genius of Universal Emancipation.* The partnership lasted ten weeks, ending when Garrison was jailed for libeling a Newburyport merchant as a slave dealer. Freed in June of 1831, Garrison founded *The Liberator* and launched his own campaign for immediate emancipation.[27]

Influenced by his close association with Lundy, young Garrison accepted his mentor's formula for universal emancipation. Planters would be encouraged to manumit their slaves if they knew that those slaves would all be transported to "American hemisphere" colonization sites—that there would be no "troublesome" free Negroes around. He assisted Lundy in his "American hemisphere" projects (especially the Haiti project) and continued to advocate these repatriation efforts after he had founded *The Liberator.* "American hemisphere" colonization (especially in Haiti) involved shorter distances and therefore was less costly than the Colonization Society's Liberian settlement, Garrison noted. Hence, more blacks could be removed to hemisphere locations than could ever be transported to Liberia; planters could be assured that all of their manumitted bondsmen would be removed. Therefore, unlike

---

[27] The essential facts of the early Garrison-Lundy relationship are noted in E. A. Snodgrass, "Benjamin Lundy: A Sketch of His Life and of His Relations with His Disciple and Associate, William Lloyd Garrison," *Northern Monthly Magazine,* II, No. 5 (March 1868), 510, 514-15; William Lloyd Garrison, *Helen Eliza Garrison: A Memorial* (Cambridge, 1876), p. 6; Thomas, *The Liberator,* pp. 74-78; *The Liberator* (Boston), December 1, 1832, February 22, 1834; Walter M. Merrill (ed.), *The Letters of William Lloyd Garrison* (Cambridge, Mass.: The Belknap Press, 1971), I, 75; Landon (ed.), *Diary of Lundy,* p. 3; Bennington (Vt.) *Journal of the Times,* December 12, 1828.

African colonization, hemisphere repatriation could genuinely "relieve the country" of both blacks and slavery.[28] But Garrison did not repudiate the Colonization Society during these years. He praised Richmond women for contributing funds to the A.C.S. and urged New England ladies to follow their patriotic example. He lauded Henry Clay as a great and patriotic statesman "because he is a friend to the cause of emancipation, and an efficient advocate of the American Colonization Society." Garrison also noted his pleasure with the rapid growth of the A.C.S. In 1829 he accepted a Society invitation to deliver the annual July Fourth fund-raising speech at Park Street Church in Boston and used the occasion to explain why he was willing to cooperate with the A.C.S. Colonization efforts were quite useful in eroding slavery and effecting emancipation, he explained, whether blacks were removed to Africa, Haiti, or Upper Canada. The A.C.S. was helping to reduce the black population of the United States. Therefore, there should be Colonization Society auxiliaries "in every State, county, and town."[29]

Although young Garrison remained a staunch supporter of colonization and black removal, by late 1829 and early 1830 he began to express reservations about A.C.S. intentions. He lived in Baltimore at the time and the arguments of local black leaders aroused his suspicions. The Colonization Society would never be able to remove very many blacks. To claim, as African colonizationists were wont to do, that the Society would solve the race problem was sheer "delusion" perpetuated by "those who ought to

---

[28] Wendell Phillips Garrison and Francis Jackson Garrison, *William Lloyd Garrison, 1805-1879* (reprint. New York: Arno Press, Inc., 1969), I, 143, 147; *Genius of Universal Emancipation*, IV, No. 1, New Ser. (September 2, 1829), 5-6; IV, No. 14, New Ser. (December 11, 1829), 105; IV, No. 26, New Ser. (March 5, 1830), 201; *The Liberator*, June 25, July 2, 1831; Dillon, *Lundy*, p. 167.

[29] Bennington (Vt.) *Journal of the Times*, December 12, 1828, January 2, 1829; *Genius of Universal Emancipation*, IV, No. 6, New Ser. (October 16, 1829), 42; Thomas, *The Liberator*, p. 92; Merrill (ed.), *Letters of Garrison*, I, 86, n. 2. It is noteworthy that in 1830 Garrison considered purchasing Walter Colton's *American Spectator and Washington City Chronicle*. This newspaper was an organ of a Colonization Society subsidiary, the African Education Society (see Staudenraus, *African Colonization Movement*, pp. 193-94).

act better." Moreover, Society members seemed strangely reluctant to condemn slavery outright. Were they actually conspiring with the slaveocracy?[30] By the spring of 1831 Garrison felt that his suspicions had been confirmed. He was sure that the A.C.S. was becoming a tool of devious proslavery men who were trying to convince the public that a few sporadic African migrations meant the end of the slave system. In reality, Society leaders knew that slavery was stronger than ever. Thus, the A.C.S. created a smoke screen to obscure Southern proslavery interests. Moreover, the Society sanctioned prejudice and discriminatory practices against blacks as the inevitable consequence of a biracial society. This was "a Libel upon the Declaration of Independence."[31]

These charges marked the beginning of Garrison's crusade against the Colonization Society. In public lectures throughout the Eastern states, in *The Liberator*, in his pamphlet *Thoughts on African Colonization*, and in private letters, he emphasized the importance of destroying the A.C.S. Between 1831 and 1834 he characterized the Colonization Society, not the slaveocracy, as the major obstacle to universal emancipation. "I am more and more convinced, that the permanency of the bloody system [slavery] depends upon the stability of the Colonization Society," he proclaimed. "The union between them is perfect—the overthrow of one must be the destruction of the other." If the A.C.S. fell, public opinion would be won over to immediate abolition, the denigration of black Americans would cease, and the nation's "Rising Glory"

[30] *Genius of Universal Emancipation*, IV, No. 1, New Ser. (September 2, 1829), 5; IV, New Ser. (February 12, 1830), 179; IV, New Ser. (March 5, 1830), 202; John L. Thomas (ed.), *Slavery Attacked: The Abolitionist Crusade* (Englewood Cliffs, N.J.: Prentice-Hall, Inc., 1965), p. 9; Samuel J. May, *Some Recollections of Our Antislavery Conflict* (Boston: Fields, Osgood & Company, 1869), pp. 18–19; David K. Sullivan, "William Lloyd Garrison in Baltimore, 1829–1830," *Maryland Historical Magazine*, LXVIII, No. 1 (Spring 1973), 65.

[31] *The Liberator*, April 23, 1831; Merrill (ed.), *Letters of Garrison*, I, 122–24; *Genius of Universal Emancipation*, II, No. 6, 3rd Ser. (October 1831), 93; William Lloyd Garrison, *Thoughts on African Colonization* (reprint. New York: Arno Press, Inc., 1968), Part I, pp. 12–14; Seifman, *Pennsylvania History*, XXXV, No. 1 (January 1968), 26. See also Louis Hartz, *The Liberal Tradition in America: An Interpretation of American Political Thought Since the Revolution* (New York: Harcourt, Brace & World, Inc., 1955), p. 155.

would be realized.[32] Armed with these arguments, Garrison went to England, where he persuaded Wilberforce, Buxton, Zachary Macaulay, Daniel O'Connell, and other leading British abolitionists to attack the A.C.S. for obstructing emancipation.[33] By March of 1834 he sensed that the Colonization Society was disintegrating and he hoped that universal emancipation was at hand. "Having now effectively crippled the Colonization Society, and measurably overthrown that wall of partition which has so long protected the slaveholders and slavery from the shafts of truth and the blows of justice, there is a fair prospect that the chains of every bondsman will soon fall to the earth, and every captive be set free."[34]

During his fierce war against the Colonization Society, Garrison demonstrated a sincere and fundamental commitment to general emancipation. But he did not repudiate colonization. Between 1831 and 1834 he continued to support "American hemisphere" repatriation projects. They were "benevolent" projects and would probably succeed. Lundy's colony in Haiti was a particularly solid enterprise; black migrants to the area "met such a reception as never yet given to any sojourners in any country since the departure of Israel into Egypt."[35] Garrison even announced that he could support organized African colonization as "well meaning" if

[32] Merrill (ed.), *Letters of Garrison*, I, 194, 427, 441; William Lloyd Garrison, *The Maryland Scheme of Expatriation Examined* (Boston: Garrison & Knapp, 1834), pp. 14–15; Garrison, *Thoughts on Colonization*, especially Part I, pp. 124, 146.

[33] Cooke, *Frederick Bancroft*, p. 180. It was not difficult to persuade British abolitionists to condemn the ambiguous A.C.S. approach to emancipation. Slaves were freed in Great Britain in 1772 and the imperial slave trade was abolished thirty-five years later. After 1808 most proslavery interests were therefore confined to the British colonies (Liverpool slave traders were almost put out of business). This significantly reduced anti-abolition sentiment in England. Moreover, in 1833 Parliament formally abolished slavery throughout the British Empire. To the victorious British abolitionists, A.C.S. ambiguity on emancipation appeared all the more unsatisfactory from this date on.

[34] "Letters of William Lloyd Garrison to John B. Vashon," *Journal of Negro History*, XII, No. 1 (January 1927), 38.

[35] Garrison, *Thoughts on Colonization*, Part II, p. 5. Garrison's endorsements between 1831 and 1834 of other "American hemisphere" colonization projects are printed in *The Liberator*, January 15, June 25, July 2, 1831; May 26, 1832; Merrill (ed.), *Letters of Garrison*, I, 261–62. See also Dillon, *Lundy*, pp. 147–48.

only "the American Colonization Society [were] bending its energies directly to the immediate abolition of slavery" instead of sustaining it.[36] After the disillusioning realization of the "true nature" of the A.C.S., Garrison's enthusiasm for black repatriation never reached the peak of 1828–30. At times, he questioned the entire colonization ideal. But questioning was usually followed by qualified endorsements of both the concept of Negro removal and specific "American hemisphere" repatriation projects.[37]

Like Lundy, Garrison was therefore markedly influenced by the colonizationist ideological legacy. Unlike most African colonizationists, however, both men conceived of universal emancipation as a higher good than black repatriation. Both emancipation and repatriation were desirable, but if the latter did not facilitate the former, it had to be disowned. This was why the two abolition spokesmen eventually repudiated the A.C.S. while remaining loyal to the colonization ideal. To be sure, neither man ruled out the possibility of a biracial America. Garrison persistently crusaded against segregation and other anti-Negro discriminations *within* the New Nation. His actions benefited blacks in the United States far more than the actions of most African colonizationists, and this was of extreme importance.[38] At the same time, he shared Lundy's fears of a racial war and slave rebellions if the Southern slave system was not rapidly destroyed. There was no time to wait until prejudices abated and a peaceful biracial society was facilitated. The Republic might not last that long: "Blood will flow like water—the blood of guilty men, and of innocent women and children. Then will be heard lamentations and weeping such as will blot out the remembrance of the horrors of St. Domingo. The terrible judgment of an incensed God will contemplate the catastrophe of republican America."[39] Effective "American hemi-

---

[36] Garrison, *Thoughts on Colonization*, Part I, pp. 20–21, 24–25; *The Liberator*, February 12, 1831.

[37] See, e.g., *The Liberator*, January 15, 22, 1831; Garrison, *Thoughts on Colonization*, Part II, p. 5.

[38] See, e.g., Garrison, *Maryland Scheme of Expatriation*, p. 19; Merrill (ed.), *Letters of Garrison*, I, 458–59; Thomas, *The Liberator*, p. 147; Leon F. Litwack, "The Abolitionist Dilemma: The Antislavery Movement and the Northern Negro," *New England Quarterly*, XXXIV, No. 1 (March 1961), 52.

[39] Robert B. Abzug, "The Influence of Garrisonian Abolitionists' Fear of

sphere" colonization was necessary to ward off this nightmare and to avoid a racial bloodbath worse than the Nat Turner insurrection. But the Negro threatened national order and stability not simply because slavery had made him rebellious. To Garrison, the race had a certain "noxious" or "impure" quality: "The black color of the body, the wooly hair, the thick lips, and other peculiarities of the African, forms so striking a contrast to the Caucasian race, that they may be distinguished at a glance. . . . They are branded by the hand of nature with a perpetual mark of disgrace."[40] This points to another, less vocalized reason Garrison continued to plead for colonization while repudiating the A.C.S. and combating racial discrimination within the United States. "My bowels, my bowels! I am pained at my heart," Garrison declared. He called for emancipatory repatriation to remove slavery from the nation's capital—"to cleanse that worse than Augean stable, the District of Columbia, from its foul impurities." This would be a start in "cleansing" and "purifying" the entire nation.[41] Committed to equal rights for blacks *within* the Promised Land, Garrison was simultaneously attracted to the concept of colonization as a remedy—a way to remove a "noxious" element that was "polluting" American society and making it an unstable and unfit homeland.

Clearly, the publisher of *The Liberator* clung to variant if not contradictory racial ideas during the first half-dozen years of his antislavery career. He believed in universal emancipation at all costs. But beyond that goal, much was confused and shifting

---

Slave Violence on the Antislavery Argument, 1829–1840," *Journal of Negro History*, LV, No. 1 (January 1970), 15–28; Wendell Phillips Garrison, *W. L. Garrison*, I, 135. In *The Liberator*, January 8, 1831, Garrison cautioned American slaves against resorting to violence:

> Not by the sword shall your deliverance be;
> Not by the shedding of your masters' blood,
> Not by rebellion—or foul treachery,
> Unspringing suddenly, like swelling flood;
> Revenge and rapine ne'er did bring forth good.

[40] *The Liberator*, January 22, 1831, as quoted in Nathaniel Weyl and William Marina, *American Statesmen on Slavery and the Negro* (New Rochelle, N.Y.: Arlington House, 1971), p. 158.
[41] Wendell Phillips Garrison, *W. L. Garrison*, I, 137; Garrison, *Thoughts on Colonization*, Part I, p. 141.

within his racial perspective. Blacks were entitled to equal treatment within the United States, for it was their home too. Yet it would be wise to colonize many of them abroad, hopefully in Haiti, Texas, or Upper Canada, in order to avoid a domestic bloodbath. Although African colonization was financially impractical, it was a useful vehicle for eradicating racial ills so long as A.C.S. leaders were committed to emancipation. Between 1828 and 1834 these confused racial thoughts persisted in Garrison's mind. But amidst the confusion, the colonization panacea always seemed to come into play; there was always the possibility of resolving national ills by removing a potential source of disorder and "impurity." Try though he might, young Garrison could not quite break from the conceptual framework of those Colonization Society leaders whom he came to abhor. Like Lundy, he could not quite repudiate their patriotic ideals of white nationhood and a securely anchored homeland.

By the late 1830's James Gillespie Birney seriously rivaled Garrison in abolitionist leadership circles. Exerting enormous influence within the American Anti-Slavery Society by 1837, Birney strongly objected to Garrison's growing disavowal of the political process in the crusade against slavery. Splitting with Garrison and his followers over the value of antislavery politics, Birney helped to organize the Liberty party and became its Presidential candidate.[42] Old and weary by the late 1830's, Lundy sided with Birney; political action was more effective than Garrisonian "moral suasion" in compelling planters to liberate bondsmen. Although Lundy had never met Birney, he considered Birney's abolition posture ideal: "Thy public course meets with my decided and unqualified approbation. Thy plan of proceeding accords more strictly with my own views, than those of any of our editorial contemporaries."[43]

[42] *A Letter on the Political Obligations of Abolitionists, by James G. Birney: with a Reply by William Lloyd Garrison* (Boston, 1839), p. 10; Ruchames (ed.), *Letters of Garrison*, II, 553.

[43] Dillon, *Lundy*, pp. 245–50; Dumond (ed.), *Letters of Birney*, I, 312–15. We have no record of Birney's commentary on Lundy. However, there is an undated manuscript in Birney's handwriting (James G. Birney Papers, Library of Congress) consisting of extensive notes taken from the *Genius of Universal Emancipation*. A substantial proportion of these notes concern Lundy's Haiti colonization scheme.

A latecomer to the abolitionist crusade, Birney was connected by birth and marriage to leading slaveholding families in Kentucky. During the 1820's he became one of the most prosperous planter-attorneys in Madison County, Alabama. Part of his wealth derived from an inheritance of nearly $12,000—all in slaves. The "malignant influence that I saw slavery exerting upon my children, determined me to visit Illinois with the purpose of removing thither," he later acknowledged.[44] Uncomfortable as a slaveholder, Birney accidentally came across a copy of the *African Repository* in 1826; he was impressed with the concept of African colonization as a humane and efficacious way of eliminating slavery. Consequently, he began to solicit funds for the A.C.S. and helped to found a Madison County auxiliary. His reputation as an effective local organizer spread rapidly and in the early summer of 1832 R. R. Gurley offered him a salaried position as the Southwestern agent of the Colonization Society. Urged on by Theodore Dwight Weld, he accepted the position.[45]

Working full time for the Colonization Society for the next two years, Birney fully believed in the potential of colonization. He watched the *Ajax,* a ship filled with American blacks, depart for Liberia, and was overwhelmed with joy: "Sir, Sir," he wrote to Gurley, "if it be weakness to sympathize with the miserable made happy—to rejoice, even to tears, at the contemplation of my country's true glory—to feel an overmastering expansion of the heart at this practical exhibition of benevolence so like God's, then I am most weak indeed."[46] In transporting American blacks to their fatherland to enjoy full liberties, the founders of the A.C.S. "were actuated by motives of patriotism as well as philanthropy." They were benevolent yet practical reformers and were restoring humanism to the Promised Land. But Birney felt that African colonization was more than a philanthropic enterprise. Like other leaders of the Colonization Society, he was fearful of a growing

44 Dumond (ed.), *Letters of Birney,* I, 149.
45 Birney's early attraction to the A.C.S. and his acceptance of an agent position within that organization is noted in Fladeland, *Birney,* pp. 38, 42, 51–54; Dumond (ed.), *Letters of Birney,* I, 5–6, 9, 20–23; Staudenraus, *African Colonization Movement,* pp. 146–47.
46 James G. Birney to R. R. Gurley, April 13, 1833, Papers of the American Colonization Society, Library of Congress. Also quoted in Dumond (ed.), *Letters of Birney,* I, 72.

domestic black population and was particularly disturbed by "noxious" free Negroes. Blacks were a "degraded people," "evil," and a "suffocating and infectious load." Their numbers were increasing phenomenally, particularly in the Southern states, and they threatened "to displace, and drive off the whites." It "may be, that in our lives it [the South] will be given up to them." But blacks would also spread their "contagion" northward from Virginia and Kentucky beyond "the beautiful Ohio." There was only one way to "relieve us of the black population": immediate and extensive African colonization. Emancipation should be accompanied by compulsory repatriation. Leaders of the Colonization Society must "call upon their whole country, to rouse up, and, by one magnanimous effort, throw off the suffocating and infectious load 'as easily as the lion shakes the dew-drop from his mane.' "[47] While Birney demanded expulsion of the "infectious load," he followed the pattern of Henry Clay, Bushrod Washington, and other leading Southern colonizationists; he seemed to require physical proximity to his slaves. To be sure, he told R. R. Gurley that he intended "to remove to Illinois that I might rid myself and my posterity of the curse of slavery." And unlike Clay or Washington, Birney eventually gave his slaves legal freedom. But he urged the manumitted to continue to serve his family as wage laborers and fervently hoped that they would.[48] Thus, although Birney legally manumitted his slaves, his behavior corresponded to Clay's and Washington's. He, too, demanded immediate expulsion of "infectious" Negroes but was reluctant to fully implement his ideas. Propounding white nationhood, he found it difficult to part with his bondsmen.

In the fall of 1833 Birney told Gurley that he was moving from Alabama to Danville, Kentucky; he was resigning as an A.C.S. agent but would remain loyal to the colonization cause.[49] Soon after his arrival in Danville, Birney was elected vice-president of

[47] *African Repository*, IX, No. 6 (August 1833), 172; IX, No. 10 (December 1833), 312; *Ohio Observer* (Hudson), April 3, 1834; Dumond (ed.), *Letters of Birney*, I, 88–90, 97; Fladeland, *Birney*, pp. 73–74; James G. Birney to R. R. Gurley, September 24, 1833, Papers of the American Colonization Society, Library of Congress.

[48] Dumond (ed.), *Letters of Birney*, I, 51–52; Fladeland, *Birney*, p. 82.

[49] James G. Birney to R. R. Gurley, September 24, 1833, Papers of the American Colonization Society, Library of Congress.

the Kentucky Colonization Society, but his zeal for the colonization ideal was dissipating. Theodore Weld, the friend who had
urged Birney to accept an A.C.S. agency, now tried to convince
him to renounce African colonization. Weld persuaded Arthur
and Lewis Tappan to pledge an annual salary of $1,500 if Birney
would become an agent for the abolitionist American Anti-Slavery
Society.[50] Birney accepted this offer and wrote a formal letter of
resignation from the Colonization Society in June of 1834. He
noted that the initial purpose of the A.C.S.—colonizing American
blacks in Africa—was a philanthropic and practical remedy to the
race problem. Planters would manumit their bondsmen if they
knew that these blacks would be repatriated—that they would not
add to the troublesome domestic free Negro population. Thus,
colonization would both remove blacks and undermine slavery.
The problem was that most members of the A.C.S. felt that
"slavery never *is*—but always *to be* removed." They were not
committed to its concrete eradication. Moreover, they sanctioned
discriminations against blacks within the United States. Finally,
they were not diligent at doing what they professed—at removing
blacks to Africa. For these reasons, Birney was leaving the colonization movement for the cause of immediate abolition.[51]

Birney's thoughts and actions obviously paralleled those of
Lundy and Garrison. He had repudiated the Colonization Society
while retaining qualified allegiance to the colonization ideal of
white nationhood. During his active years in the abolition movement, he continued to attack the A.C.S. for failure "to lay hold of
men's consciences" so that men would emancipate their slaves, and
for failure to transport an ample number of blacks to Africa.[52] All
the while, Birney persisted in viewing African repatriation as both
a useful emancipatory tool and a desirable end in itself. Negro
removal from the Promised Land to Christianize the "Dark Conti-

[50] Staudenraus, *African Colonization Movement*, pp. 229-30; Dumond
(ed.), *Letters of Birney*, xii-xiii; Fladeland, *Birney*, pp. 81-82.

[51] James G. Birney, *Letters on Colonization, Addressed to the Rev.
Thornton J. Mills, Corresponding Secretary of the Kentucky Colonization
Society* (New York, 1834), especially pp. 7, 10-12, 16-19, 28, 43-45.

[52] See, e.g., James G. Birney to Gerrit Smith, November 14, 1834,
November 11, 1835, James G. Birney Papers, Library of Congress; *The
Liberator*, October 4, 1834; *African Repository*, XVI, No. 20 (October 15,
1840), 315; Dumond (ed.), *Letters of Birney*, I, 147-48, 150.

nent" would benefit both Africa and America. Yet slavery would end only if Americans departed from the ineffective A.C.S. approach—if they sanctioned immediate, unconditional emancipation. Once black bondsmen were manumitted, they "would naturally look to the land of their forefathers." Emancipated benevolently and without compulsion to migrate, they would "naturally" seek out their "fatherland."[53] At times during the 1840's Birney's distaste for the A.C.S. weakened his devotion to the colonization ideal of white nationhood. In an 1845 letter, for example, he seemed totally resigned to blacks "forever remaining amongst [us] and making part of the social structure" of the New Nation.[54] But by the early 1850's Birney was reconciled with his earlier abolitionist views. Once again he opposed the A.C.S. but recommended Liberia as the "best *retreat*" blacks could find, and repatriation as the ideal remedy for America's depressing racial ills. Once again, he firmly committed himself to white nationhood.[55]

Like Lundy and Garrison, Birney had been able to assume leadership in the abolitionist movement while retaining qualified allegiance to the colonization ideal. Committed to universal emancipation, he was also willing to solve problems by removing a "noxious," troublesome element from the Promised Land. But Birney may have felt greater urgency in solving the race problem than either Lundy or Garrison. A slaveholding Southerner by birth and marriage, he came to prefer the ideals of the "free" North to the "Unchristian" South, particularly after October of 1835, when he was forced to leave Kentucky or face anti-abolitionist violence. Yet Birney always retained the hope of renewing old friendships in the slave states and even cultivating a better understanding with his proslavery wife. If the race problem could have been remedied by ending slavery and colonizing free blacks, antagonisms between the sections would have ceased. Then Birney

[53] James G. Birney to Gerrit Smith, December 30, 1834, January 31, 1835, James G. Birney Papers, Library of Congress; William Birney, *James G. Birney and His Times* (reprint. New York: Bergman Publishers, 1969), pp. 153–54; *African Repository*, XI, No. 4 (April 1835), 105, 107.

[54] Dumond (ed.), *Birney Letters*, II, 945–46.

[55] James G. Birney, *Examination of the Decision of the Supreme Court of the United States, in the Case of Strader, Gorman and Armstrong vs. Christopher Graham* (Cincinnati: Truman & Spofford, 1852), especially p. iii; Fladeland, *Birney*, p. 281.

might have been able to renew personal contacts with the Southern planter class and to have mended his severed Southern roots. For Birney, the colonizationist goal of purifying and thus perfecting the nation went hand in hand with the hope of restoring his own geographic roots.[56]

Clearly, three leading architects of nineteenth-century American abolitionism retained qualified colonizationist goals while they devised abolitionist tactics. Lundy, Garrison, and Birney each related to the Colonization Society in his own peculiar way and the three were distinguishable from other abolitionists in this particular. But by ultimately disowning the A.C.S. while retaining some devotion to the ideal of pure white nationhood, they typified a propensity evident in abolitionist thought from the 1820's to the 1840's. Restore national harmony by abolishing slavery and encouraging Negro migration beyond United States borders: this vision united the three and was shared by Gerrit Smith, Samuel J. May, Arthur Tappan, Simeon Jocelyn, Elizabeth Chandler, Edward Beecher, Theodore Weld, and other advocates of immediate emancipation. To be sure, these abolitionists were often theoretically inconsistent, erratic, and confused proponents of Negro repatriation. Moreover, they were much more concerned with the well-being of those blacks who would always remain within the Promised Land than colonizationists like Henry Clay and R. R. Gurley. Indeed, they distinguished themselves from white Americans generally in struggling to advance the civil rights and opportunities of American Negroes amidst widespread hostility. Nonetheless, they demonstrated that the colonizationist ideal of pure white nationhood survived the Colonization Society's demise, if only as a theoretical construct. The ideal was shared by a number of humanistic reformers who were genuinely concerned with aiding Negroes within American borders. Harriet Beecher Stowe's advocacy of black repatriation in the closing pages of *Uncle Tom's Cabin* is the most telling proof of the strength of the concept of white nationhood in antebellum reform thought.[57]

[56] Gordon E. Finnie, "The Antislavery Movement in the Upper South before 1840," *Journal of Southern History*, XXXV, No. 3 (August 1969), 335; Dumond (ed.), *Letters of Birney*, I, 149, 296, 334, 485, 567, 571.

[57] Harriet Beecher Stowe, *Uncle Tom's Cabin or, Life Among the Lowly* (Boston: Houghton Mifflin Company, 1895), pp. 510–515.

III

In the years that followed the War of 1812, Southern slave-holders within the Colonization Society had also expressed their patriotic commitment to national purity and perfection through white nationhood. However, unlike antislavery elements within the A.C.S., they insisted that white nationhood and slavery were compatible—that the controls of the slave system assured white hegemony in the Promised Land. Therefore, as a patriotic organization, the Society was obligated to strengthen slavery by removing subversive free Negroes—by eliminating those blacks who made bondsmen dissatisfied with their lot. John Randolph made all of this quite explicit at the organizational meeting of the A.C.S. in 1816. Henry Clay concurred and pointed out that removal of free blacks would "render the slaves more docile, manageable, and useful." Bushrod Washington, the first president of the A.C.S., also felt that white nationhood, promoted by the repatriation of free Negroes, was totally compatible with slavery. During the active years of the Colonization Society, a great many other Southern colonizationists defended African repatriation as a way of affirming slavery.[58] "As far as I could learn," Harriet Martineau observed, "no leading [Southern] member of the Colonization Society has freed any of his slaves." None felt that by repatriating free Negroes, they were obligated to abolish slavery; colonization had nothing to do with abolition.[59] Thus, as a Northern and

[58] *National Intelligencer*, December 24, 1816, quotes Randolph. Clay is quoted in Glyndon G. Van Deusen, *The Life of Henry Clay* (Boston: Little, Brown and Company, 1937), p. 313. Winthrop D. Jordan, *White over Black: American Attitudes Toward the Negro, 1550–1812* (Chapel Hill: University of North Carolina Press, 1968), p. 566, notes Bushrod Washington. For similar Southern colonizationist claims that repatriation affirmed slavery, see, e.g., *African Repository*, III, No. 7 (September 1827), 196–97, 202; "Reflections on the Census of 1840," *Southern Literary Messenger*, IX, No. 6 (June 1843), 351–52; Penelope Campbell, *Maryland in Africa: The Maryland State Colonization Society, 1831–1857* (Urbana: University of Illinois Press, 1971), p. 178; *Second Annual Report of the American Society for Colonizing the Free People of Color* (Washington, D.C., 1819), p. 9.

[59] Harriet Martineau, *Society in America* (London: Saunders and Otley, 1837), II, 111.

mildly antislavery influence became more conspicuous within the A.C.S. high command in the late 1820's and early 1830's, the displeasure of Southern planters with the Society was predictable. For them, colonization lost its legitimacy when it ceased to shore up slavery.

Early in 1825 Senator Rufus King of New York proposed using federal revenues from public land sales to fund the emancipation and colonization of slaves. Opposition by Southern congressmen was vehement.[60] From that date on, the colonization ideal began to be overshadowed below Mason-Dixon by an increasingly energetic defense of slavery. This new concern with defending the positive merits of slavery and the concomitant suspicion of plans to repatriate "noxious" blacks was strongest in South Carolina, the one state where an effective colonization movement had never taken root. Always suspicious that the A.C.S. was not simply out to remove free Negroes—that colonizationists secretly aspired to abolish slavery—the state's low-county planter elite became exceedingly distressed during the 1820's and early 1830's over accumulating threats to the peculiar institution. In addition to A.C.S. activities, they fretted over slave insurrection and sabotage, incompetent overseers, the susceptibility of bondsmen to malaria, and declining profits.[61] With these apprehensions, low-county planters denounced colonization and proclaimed the *positive good* of the slave system several years before the first issue of *The Liberator* was published. To draw other Southerners away from the A.C.S. and more solidly behind a slave order, articulate South Carolinians like William Smith, Edwin Holland, Thomas Cooper, and eventually John C. Calhoun contended that the region's labor system was in jeopardy. Underscoring slavery's humanism, patriotism, and economic efficiency, they maintained that the South simply could not survive if its right to a servile black labor force was negated.[62]

60 Staudenraus, *African Colonization Movement*, p. 172.

61 For an excellent discussion of this sense of crisis among South Carolina's low-county planters during the 1820's and early 1830's, see Freehling, *Prelude to Civil War*, pp. 49–86.

62 The need to convince guilt-ridden, "doubtful" Southerners to line up behind slavery is noted in Freehling, *Prelude to Civil War*, pp. 76–82; McPherson, *Perspectives in American History*, III (1969), 462, 465. For South Carolina articulations of the positive-good argument, see, e.g., Peter F. Detweiler, "Congressional Debate on Slavery and the Declaration of In-

Theoretical defenses of the positive benefits of slavery spread from South Carolina to other regions of the South before Garrison began his crusade for immediate abolition.[63] Committed to black bondage from the start, slaveholding colonizationists were easily won over to South Carolina's positive-good defense of slavery and to contempt for the A.C.S. once they were convinced that colonization jeopardized the slave system.

In their efforts to draw Southerners away from the Colonization Society, positive-good theorists exaggerated their commitment to a biracial social order. Attacking the colonization goal of Negro removal as antithetical to slavery, they characterized the relationship of white masters and black bondsmen as nearly utopian. Although most slaveholders accepted the colonizationist premise that "noxious" or defiant blacks had to be kept at a distance— although they restricted them to field-hand status away from the "main house," segregated them in urban centers, and sold them at the auction block—the positive-good argument de-emphasized these realities. To discredit the A.C.S. goal of black removal, Alexander Sims noted "the ardent sympathy with which they [all slaves] enter into the scenes and vicissitudes of the master's life and family; how they sorrow in adversity, and mingle the joyous laugh, and [are] happy, in the glad scenes of the household." Because Southern Negroes (as bondsmen) were all "peaceful and industrious, and always to be seen at their honest employments," Robert Turnbull charged that planters "have no interest whatever in the views of the Colonization Society." Since there were no "noxious" bondsmen, there was no cause to break up the pleasant

---

dependence, 1818–1821," *American Historical Review*, LXIII, No. 3 (April 1958), 605–06; Edwin C. Holland, *A Refutation of the Calumnies Circulated Against the Southern & Western States* . . . (Charleston, 1822); Dumas Malone, *The Public Life of Thomas Cooper, 1783–1839* (New Haven: Yale University Press, 1926), pp. 288–89; Fredrickson, *Black Image*, p. 47; W. G. Bean, "Anti-Jeffersonianism in the Ante-Bellum South," *North Carolina Historical Review*, XII, No. 2 (April 1935), 103.

[63] William B. Hesseltine demonstrates this phenomenon in his exciting article "Some New Aspects of the Pro-Slavery Argument," *Journal of Negro History*, XXI, No. 1 (January 1936), 1–14. Kenneth M. Stampp lends support to Hesseltine in his "An Analysis of T. R. Dew's Review of the Debates in the Virginia Legislature," *Journal of Negro History*, XXVII, No. 4 (October 1942), 382, and his "The Fate of the Southern Antislavery Movement," *Journal of Negro History*, XXVIII, No. 1 (January 1943), 10–22.

and highly patriotic interracial relationship of the peculiar institution through repatriation. Florida planter Zaphaniah Kingsley concurred. The slave was so productive and pleasant to be with that he was like a member of his master's family; it would be unpatriotic to cast him out. Numerous other positive-good theorists voiced similar sentiments; they stressed the multiple benefits of interactions between kind white masters and docile, diligent slaves. Beverly Tucker characterized white-black relationships in the slave South as "stronger than they would be under like circumstances between individuals of the white race." William Gilmore Simms even defended interracial fornication under the slave system for "the production of a fine specimen of physical manhood, and of a better mental organization, in the mulatto." In building a case against the A.C.S., the positive-good theorist would not even concede that race mixing in the white nation justified the removal of "sexually dangerous" Negroes.[64]

Positive-good theory was thus increasingly popular below Mason-Dixon during the 1820's and 1830's and seemed to strike at the heart of colonization ideology. It was a theory designed to deny the presence of "noxious" or "polluting" blacks and therefore could not concede the need to remove them. Any justification of Negro removal under any circumstances seemed to run counter to this new emphasis on proslavery biracialism. Yet there was a subtle conceptual overlap between the new defense of slavery and the older colonizationist posture. Leaders of the A.C.S. had defended Negro repatriation as an alternative to a biracial, semi-egalitarian society. Black and white could not live together or the Promised Land would be contaminated and decline. "Polluting," assertive, defiant free Negroes had to be removed at once. Some Southern colonizationists were less anxious to repatriate slaves. Many saw no need at all; there was more safety in a non-egalitarian, hierarchical racial relationship. Positive-good theorists ideal-

[64] Alexander D. Sims, *A View of Slavery, Moral and Political* (Charleston, 1834), pp. 25–26; Robert J. Turnbull, *The Crisis: or, Essays on the Usurpations of the Federal Government* (Charleston, 1827), pp. 134–35; Zaphaniah Kingsley, *A Treatise on the Patriarchal or Co-operative System of Society* . . . (reprint. Freeport, N.Y.: Books for Libraries Press, 1970), pp. 8, 16; Beverly Tucker, "Slavery," *Southern Literary Messenger*, II, No. 5 (April 1836), 338; William Gilmore Simms, "Miss Martineau on Slavery," *Southern Literary Messenger*, III, No. 11 (November 1837), 647.

ized a hierarchical racial relationship with kind masters directing contented slaves. Without racial hierarchy there was no slave order and therefore no reason for retaining a black population. Since the "noxious" free Negroes that colonizationists sought to expel did not fit into the hierarchical structure of a slave order, the new defense of slavery was not theoretically incompatible with the old Southern advocacy of colonization. Adherents of both positions were fundamentally committed to a well-ordered and stabilized society. Therefore, the transition that was occurring within Southern racial thought during the early Jacksonian decades was one of emphasis. The benefits of racial hierarchy were stressed; the value of removing "noxious" free Negroes was de-emphasized.

The basis for this new emphasis in Southern racial thought was the ability of South Carolina planters to convince others of the region that their hierarchical racial order was in jeopardy—that the A.C.S. was not out to shore up slavery by removing free Negroes but was intent on removing their bondsmen as well. The proper response, Carolinian positive-good theorists argued, was to reject colonization outright and to line up behind a distinctly biracial slave system. For Southern regional unity, some were even willing to enslave free Negroes; that would surely undermine A.C.S. operations. However, the most influential South Carolina theorists—men like Edwin Holland, James Hammond, and John Calhoun—did not go that far. They simply maintained that the hierarchy of slavery precluded or minimized "polluting" Negro behavior, it assured maximum agricultural profits, and it guaranteed that the talented would have the time and the cultivation to rule wisely.[65] Other leading Carolinians, particularly Thomas Cooper, Stephen D. Miller, Robert Y. Hayne, William Harper, and George McDuffie, drew upon spread-eagle patriotism and outlined the national benefits of Southern slavery. The discipline of

---

[65] See, e.g., Holland, *Refutation of the Calumnies*, p. 45; James H. Hammond, *Selections from the Letters and Speeches of the Hon. James H. Hammond, of South Carolina* (New York: John F. Trow & Co., 1866), pp. 44–45; James Henry Hammond, *Remarks of Mr. Hammond, of South Carolina, on the Question of Receiving Petitions for the Abolition of Slavery in the District of Columbia* . . . (Washington, D.C., 1836), p. 11; and the basic racial argument within John C. Calhoun's *A Disquisition on Government, and a Discourse on the Constitution of the United States* (Charleston: Press of Walker and James, 1851).

the slave system prevented "polluting" racial mixture and thus preserved the white man's country. Because of slavery, a vast quantity of raw materials could be produced, and this was the source of national prosperity and greatness. With slaves performing domestic labors, Southern whites were freed to join the nation's military forces, assuring victory against foreign foes. Finally, because the slave system was predicated upon a black laboring class, it guaranteed genuine freedom from menial chores for white men. Freedom and white skin became synonymous. Therefore, more than any other institution, slavery would promote "the Rising Glory of America."[66]

By the early 1830's these South Carolina positive-good arguments, particularly the patriotic arguments, had become commonplace in the lower South. They were even beginning to gain a foothold in the Old Dominion, a base for Colonization Society operations.[67] Virginia proved to be a veritable storm center where colonizationists and a few hardy abolitionists contended against positive-good theorists. On January 11, 1832, the state House of Delegates commenced a two-week debate on the future of the Virginia Negro. In the aftermath of the Nat Turner slave revolt, a number of legislators were prepared to repatriate all blacks, slaves as well as freemen. Unlike Carolinians, they were convinced that all Negroes were "noxious" and had to be expelled. With their stronghold in the western part of the state, these legislators pointed to a decline in the fortunes of the Old Dominion since the illustrious Revolutionary generation. Free Negroes and slaves were on

[66] William Harper, *Memoir on Slavery, Read before the Society for the Advancement of Learning, of South Carolina, as Its Annual Meeting at Columbia, 1837* (Charleston: James S. Burges, 1838), pp. 49–50, 58; Thomas Cooper, *Two Essays* (Columbia, S.C., 1826), p. 46; Theodore D. Jervey, *Robert Y. Hayne and His Times* (New York: The Macmillan Company, 1909), p. 370; *Colonizationist and Journal of Freedom* (January 1834), p. 285; Albert Bushnell Hart (ed.), *Sourcebook of American History* (New York: The Macmillan Company, 1899), pp. 247–48; William Jay, *Miscellaneous Writings on Slavery* (reprint. New York: Negro Universities Press, 1968), p. 85; Hammond, *Remarks of Mr. Hammond*, p. 18.

[67] See, e.g., Kingsley, *Treatise*, pp. 5, 11; W. J. Hobby, *Remarks upon Slavery; Occasioned by Attempts Made to Circulate Improper Publications in the Southern States* (Augusta, Ga., 1835), p. 30; A. P. Upshur, "Domestic Slavery, as it exists in our Southern States, considered with reference to its influence upon free government," *Southern Literary Messenger*, V, No. 10 (October 1839), 678–79, 687.

the increase; a "black cloud" was "rising and swelling" the Virginia countryside, degrading the value of energetic white labor, fornicating madly, "polluting" the land, and constituting an "enemy within" that had performed "domestic butchery."[68] Moreover, the very presence of a large, degraded, defiant black population contradicted the egalitarian principles of 1776; it perverted the ideals upon which the Promised Land was founded. By gradually removing blacks, slave and free, thereby whitening the complexion of the Old Dominion, Virginians would somehow regain a sense of place and rootedness. Black repatriation would "give to every white man in the state, that certain assurance that this is his country."[69]

Urging the removal of the "foul black stain" in these broad terms, several legislators then backtracked and differentiated between slaves and free Negroes. They noted that once troublesome free Negroes were repatriated, slaves would be more docile and valuable; the slaveholder could rest secure "that his slave is his own property."[70] Against these diverse colonizationists, a large bloc of legislators concentrated on defending slavery. Despite the recent Turner revolt, their faith in a slave order seemed undampened. Like those who favored repatriating all blacks, they acknowledged that a breakdown in the system would require massive colonization. But they did not see the Turner revolt as a major breakdown; slavery remained a viable mode of racial control for most blacks. It was sanctioned by the Revolutionary generation, it elevated white society, and it provided the necessary social order "to preserve the forms of a Republican Government." There was more wisdom rallying behind slavery than contemplating colonization, for the latter could lead to general emancipation.[71]

---

[68] Richmond *Enquirer*, January 21, February 14, 1832; Joseph Clarke Robert, *The Road from Monticello: A Study of the Virginia Slavery Debate of 1832* (Durham: Duke University Press, 1941), pp. 62–63, 92; *African Repository*, IX, No. 1 (March 1833), 10; Beverly B. Munford, *Virginia's Attitude toward Slavery and Secession* (London: Longmans, Green and Co., 1909), p. 131.

[69] Richmond *Enquirer*, January 19, 28; February 4, 16, 1832; Robert, *Road from Monticello*, pp. 80, 92.

[70] See, e.g., Robert, *Road from Monticello*, pp. 80–81.

[71] Richmond *Enquirer*, January 21, 26, 31, February 11, 1832; Robert, *Road from Monticello*, pp. 72–73.

Throughout the debate in the Virginia House of Delegates, overlaps between colonization and positive-good theory were detectable. There had to be overlaps, for even the most committed Virginia slaveholders regularly transferred defiant house servants to remote field labor and auctioned off their most "noxious" bondsmen. There was overwhelming agreement that if the slave system could not regularly avert "noxious," "polluting" behavior among most bondsmen, colonization procedures would become mandatory. Roughly sixty delegates felt that slavery was performing well enough and that plans to gradually emancipate and colonize all Virginia blacks were unnecessary. Another sixty favored the emancipation-colonization formula. Twelve legislators held the balance of power; they fretted over the evils of slavery and saw the desirability of removing "noxious" blacks like Nat Turner but ultimately voted against emancipation-repatriation legislation. Thus, the attempt to repulse the mounting positive-good crusade was defeated in the Old Dominion. Because the Colonization Society had joined forces with legislators favoring emancipation and repatriation, it suffered a serious setback. But it is well to note that the victorious proslavery majority in the House of Delegates shared a degree of pro-colonization sentiment—the feeling that if slavery could not ward off "noxious" Negro behavior, large-scale colonization would become imperative. The minority vote was also ideologically mixed; there were a number who voted for emancipation-colonization legislation with the thought that they would be strengthening the slave order by eliminating the "subversive" free Negro population. By a subsequent vote of 79 to 41, the House agreed to fund the removal of formerly manumitted blacks who consented to their own deportation. Although the Virginia Senate killed this bill on an 18-to-14 roll call, House passage indicated that colonization sentiment was far from dead in the Old Dominion. In voting against emancipation-repatriation legislation, most House members had not repudiated the concept of Negro removal.[72]

---

[72] The final vote in the Virginia House of Delegates on the emancipation-colonization bill is discussed intelligently in Daniel J. Boorstin, *The Americans: The National Experience* (New York: Vintage Books, 1967), pp. 186–87. See also Rosen, *Phylon,* XXXIII, No. 2 (Second Quarter 1972), 180.

Although the Colonization Society had been repudiated in South Carolina, and although the specific emancipation-repatriation legislation that it had endorsed was rejected in a close vote in the Virginia House of Delegates, the colonization ideal remained quite viable in Southern racial thought. A.C.S. auxiliaries and agents continued to be active in the Old Dominion and elsewhere in the upper South. And as the Virginia House debate demonstrated, neither Southern colonizationists nor proponents of slavery without repatriation could brook "noxious" black behavior; both assumed that if a hierarchical racial system could not head off the danger of Negro "pollution," repatriation of all blacks remained the only means to preserve pure white nationhood.

In the years that immediately followed the Virginia debate, positive-good theory commanded an increasing following in the Old Dominion. In part, this was because the slave trade between the upper South and the Southwest seemed to be increasing. There was widespread belief that many of Virginia's bondsmen could be sold to the expanding cotton plantations in Mississippi and Alabama. A number of Virginians quickly came to the position that this domestic slave trade was preferable to colonization. It could reduce the ratio of blacks to whites in the state without undermining slavery and it provided a procedure for removing those blacks who happened to be troublesome. More important, the domestic slave trade gave Virginians hopes for substantial profits, whereas manumission with colonization represented an enormous expense.[73]

Whereas many Virginians had sided with John Randolph, John Marshall, and James Madison in the aftermath of the War of 1812 and had supported the A.C.S., the positive-good argument of Thomas R. Dew came into vogue in the mid-1830's. The Old Dominion's most articulate proponent of black bondage in the

Carl N. Degler, *The Other South: Southern Dissenters in the Nineteenth Century* (New York: Harper & Row, 1974), pp. 23–24, notes the House-approved bill to colonize manumitted blacks.

[73] For discussions of the effect of the slave trade upon Virginia colonization thought, see Robert, *Road from Monticello*, pp. 51–52, and Clement Eaton, *The Mind of the Old South* (rev. ed. Baton Rouge: Louisiana State University Press, 1967), p. 18. Robert William Fogel and Stanley L. Engerman, *Time on the Cross: The Economics of American Negro Slavery* (Boston: Little, Brown and Company, 1974), pp. 47–52, minimizes the extent of actual interregional slave trading.

aftermath of the Virginia debate, Dew drew upon the arguments of Thomas Cooper, Edwin Holland, Stephen Miller, and other South Carolina theoreticians of the 1820's. Mastering these sources, the learned William and Mary professor charged that hierarchy was essential for black and white to live within the same society: "One must rule the other, or exterminating wars must be waged." With benevolent Southern planters ruling black slaves, the "lower race" was contented and productive. The Negro's "savage ferocity" was tamed and his "wandering habits eradicated."[74] Moreover, Dew noted that Southern slavery benefited white society. A black laboring class promoted relative equality among whites: "The true spirit of genuine republicanism may exist here." Slave labor also freed whites to cultivate the arts and sciences. White women benefited more than all others, for they were freed from the burdens of domestic economy.[75] Finally, Dew dismissed the idea of African colonization as an impractical and visionary alternative to slavery. There would have to be very high taxes for revenues to repatriate even the annual increase in blacks. Since slaves constituted one-third of the wealth of Virginia, colonizationists would impoverish the state by repatriating them. But Dew added that African colonizationists could never remove the black population even if they rose to power. As the number of Negroes declined through early colonization ventures, the laws of supply and demand would stimulate slave breeding and restore the black population to what it had been.[76]

Although Dew was adamant and persuasive in stating the case against African colonization, his positive-good argument did not

[74] Thomas R. Dew, "Review of the debate in the Virginia Legislature, 1831–32," in *The Pro-Slavery Argument; As Maintained by . . . Chancellor Harper, Governor Hammond, Dr. Simms, and Professor Dew* (reprint. New York: Negro Universities Press, 1968), pp. 333, 410, 457, 482.

[75] Thomas R. Dew, "An Address, on the Influence of the Federative Republican System of Government upon Literature and the Development of Character," *Southern Literary Messenger*, II, No. 4 (March 1836), 277–79; Dew, in *The Pro-Slavery Argument*, pp. 338–39; Stampp, *Journal of Negro History*, XXVII, No. 4 (October 1942), 385–87; Rollin G. Osterweis, *Romanticism and Nationalism in the Old South* (New Haven: Yale University Press, 1949), p. 90.

[76] Thomas R. Dew, *Review of the Debate in the Virginia Legislature of 1831 and 1832* (Richmond, 1832), pp. 48, 69; Stampp, *Journal of Negro History*, XXVII, No. 4 (October 1942), 386–87.

undermine the patriotic colonization ideal of white nationhood. He dismissed colonization at a time when substantial profits from slavery seemed assured with the argument that colonization was "impractical and visionary"—not that it was "erroneous." Because Southern slavery afforded an orderly and (at the time) a potentially profitable biracial relationship, there was no need to repatriate blacks. However, Dew acknowledged that if the slave system ever ceased to provide these benefits—if irrevocable disorder and persistent economic losses ensued—he would embrace the colonization ideal of white nationhood. By arguing against repatriation on the "practical" grounds of current economic realities and by refusing to use universalized arguments against the colonization ideal, Dew suggested what the early South Carolina positive-good theorists and the Virginia debate made quite clear. The conceptual gulf between positive-good theory and Southern colonization thought was never very great. Southern leaders of the A.C.S. like Henry Clay and Bushrod Washington had no great objections to slavery, and positive-good theorists like Thomas R. Dew and Thomas Cooper had no grudging words against the ideal of a purified white man's country free of racial discord. In this sense, positive-good theory and the colonization ideal were complementary concepts. The one became more popular when the profits of the slave system promised to run high; the other was more attractive when profits declined.

IV

The theoretical responses of both Northern abolitionists and Southern slaveholders to the disintegrating American Colonization Society demonstrated that the colonizationist vision of pure white nationhood did not die. Committed to universal emancipation, abolitionist leaders like Benjamin Lundy, William Lloyd Garrison, and James Gillespie Birney clung to the notion that by colonizing blacks they might ameliorate racial ills, stabilize national life, and promote "the Rising Glory of America." Devoted to the slave order, the dozen "swing" legislators in the Virginia House of Delegates and even positive-good theorists like Thomas Cooper and Thomas R. Dew held the colonization option in reserve in the event that slave-system controls broke down and profits ebbed. For even the most adamant champion of black bondage, repatriation was preferable to an egalitarian biracial order.

This is not to say that Lundy, Garrison, and Birney were similar to the "swing" legislators, Cooper, or Dew. A fundamental and humanistic commitment to universal emancipation and civil rights cannot even remotely be equated to the defense of Negro slavery; the former generally helped American blacks while the latter did not. What the common attraction of abolitionists and slaveholders to the colonization ideal signified was not the similarity of their racial approaches; rather, it pointed to the durability of the colonizationist ideological legacy.

Given the frustrations inherent in any crusade against slavery— the nation's strongest racial institution—abolitionists experienced chronic failures and irresolvable impasses. Men like Garrison and Birney were sometimes tempted, in moments of desperation, to break impasses and resolve the race problem by borrowing a concept from their days in the A.C.S.—Negro removal. Southern proslavery men sometimes shared this impulse amidst the frustrations of the Nat Turner revolt, the irregular profits of slave labor, and feelings of guilt over the ethics of human bondage. Overwhelmed at times by anxiety, some felt the impulse to do away with racial ills by repatriating blacks—at least "troublesome" free Negroes, as Southern auxiliaries of the A.C.S. had long advocated. The periodic attractions of the concept of Negro removal allowed a pious New England reformer like Garrison, who was deeply committed to Negro rights, to participate for a time in an organization headed by slaveholders like Bushrod Washington and Henry Clay. But if the appeal of the concept of Negro removal did not keep them in the same organization for long, the concept survived the collapse of the A.C.S. When other racial "reforms" seemed to fail—emancipation crusades as well as efforts to fortify slavery—blacks could always be removed from American shores. At least men like Garrison, Clay, and even Dew needed to assume that massive black repatriation was a potential remedy that could be held in reserve. The problem, of course, was that it was no remedy at all. Like other apparent panaceas in the crusade for the Promised Land, black repatriation was an unworkable abstraction that drew Americans away from confronting and resolving the many and varied problems of a multiracial society. Like the other seeming cure-alls, it tended to anesthetize them to daily realities. It promoted a vision of white nationhood that was as unreal as the visions of a flawless Founding Father and a pliant True American Woman. To be sure, the abstract world that many and varied sorts of patriots were forging promoted a sense of purpose and mastery over life's affairs. But it was a false sense, and it often blinded them to life's rich complexities, ambiguities, and experiential diversities.

PART Four

THE FUTURE OF
THE PROMISED LAND

The principle of patriotism stands in need of the reinforcement of prejudice, *and it is well known that our strongest prejudices in favor of our country are formed in the first one and twenty years of our lives.*
—BENJAMIN RUSH, 1786

I would give our people a strongly marked national character; I would make ourselves truly a peculiar *people—peculiar as well for our moral as our political greatness; I would teach our children to feel proud of the points in which we differ from other people.*
—JAMES HUMPHREY WILDER, 1832

Never, since the creation, were the youth of any age or country so imperiously called upon to exert themselves, as those whom I now address. Never before were there so many important interests at stake. Never were such immence results depending upon a generation of men, as upon that which is now approaching the stage of action. These rising millions are destined, according to all human probability, to form by far the greatest nation that ever constituted an entire community of freemen, since the world began.
—WILLIAM A. ALCOTT, 1833

From the founding of the *Columbian Magazine* to the ascendance of positive-good proslavery thought in the Old Dominion, patriots of diverse orientations pleaded for "the Rising Glory of America"—the success of the American experiment in nation building. The persistence of the plea from the 1780's through the 1830's indicated a general awareness that flawless nationhood had not materialized. An aging Noah Webster was certain that it never would—that the Jacksonian nation was experiencing "retrogression." Others, like Sarah Hale and R. R. Gurley, occasionally shared Webster's gloom. And yet the characterization of a New Nation moving toward "Rising Glory" continued to dominate patriotic writing and oratory.

In the late 1780's and early 1790's contributors to the *Columbian Magazine* had pleaded for "the Rising Glory of America" from relatively simple motives. The cultural renaissance that they had hoped would accompany national political independence had not eventuated. Worse yet, they realized that their efforts to bring about a cultural renaissance were failing. Repudiated by past and present, they turned to the future.

By the 1830's, however, the patriotic cry for "Rising Glory" was sustained by an interrelated network of goals and cure-alls that had developed over several decades. "Rising Glory" required patriots to strive for personal and national flawlessness, and this provoked or intensified an inner sense of rootless discontent. Refusing to understand that perfectionist strivings and rooted stability were inherently contradictory, diverse patriots restored to what they saw as safety valves or cure-alls—attempts at escape that held out the hope of reconciling the unreconcilable. But these panaceas intensified their problems. Holding up a flawless and rooted Founding Father, True American Womanhood, and black expulsion as cure-alls, patriots were using simplistic abstractions which tended to draw them even further away from the complex and varied features of daily reality. Because their so-called remedies encouraged patriots to view the people about them as abstractions, viable interpersonal relationships became increasingly difficult to sustain. This was especially true of relationships between men and women and between whites and blacks—relationships that were marred by deceptive "little games" and, sometimes, by overt conflicts. Thus, presumed cure-alls engendered tensions and conflicts of their own which were bound to make patriots feel even more uprooted and insecure in their daily lives. This, in turn, helped to perpetuate their search for flawless nationhood—a "Rising Glory of America" where interpersonal relationships would be satisfying. Clearly, the devout patriot was caught within a vicious cycle. The tragedy was that he did not know it.

By the early Jacksonian period, a number of patriots had come to believe that if they themselves could not seem to bring on "the Rising Glory of America" and to live satisfying, well-rooted lives, they could at least raise a future generation that would be capable of achieving these ends. American children had to be taught to be virtuous and effective patriots. The family—the traditional source of education for most of the nation's youth—seemed to be losing influence and power. Indeed, it had not reared Americans who had proven capable of promoting "Rising Glory." Massive and efficient educational systems—common schools and institutions for advanced training—could assure a future citizenry that would cure all ills, reconcile perfectionism with rootedness, and bring on a contented and flawless Promised Land. Patriots had discovered another way to solve the unsolvable—or so it seemed.

CHAPTER 8

PATRIOTIC EDUCATION
IN THE
AGE OF JACKSON

The concept of mass schooling was largely a product of the early Jacksonian period. The immediate post-Revolutionary wave of cultural nationalism that had produced the *Columbian Magazine*, David Ramsay's histories, and Noah Webster's "American language" had not affected the education of most American children. Few received even the most rudimentary formal schooling. Indeed, many children grew up without the ability to read the *Columbian*, Ramsay, or Webster, and therefore unable to learn "precious" patriotic lessons. Even in New England—the one section Ramsay had looked to as the center of American literacy and cultivation—most young people escaped the schoolroom. Education was thought to be primarily a private responsibility involving families and occasionally churches. The problem was that these traditional agencies had been negligent.

The old Calvinist notion of infant depravity—the assumption that the young child was intrinsically limited by a heritage of sin—contributed to this negligence. But Calvinist determinism gradually receded in the early decades of the nineteenth century. Correspondingly, patriots began to emphasize redemption of the Promised Land through proper schooling for the masses of the nation's youth.[1] George Washington had stressed the importance

[1] Bernard Wishy, *The Child and the Republic: The Dawn of Modern American Child Nurture* (Philadelphia: University of Pennsylvania Press,

of schooling to better educate "the future guardians of the liberties of the country" in both his January 1790 message to Congress and his Farewell Address. Thomas Jefferson, Benjamin Rush, and Noah Webster had made much the same plea. Unlike monarchies, which had legitimate powers to coerce citizens to behave, republics required formal education and schooling to make virtuous citizens who would perpetuate national institutions and liberties.[2] As the concept of infant damnation receded and the admonitions of the Founding Fathers generation came to be venerated, the importance of formal education in cultivating a virtuous and patriotic future generation received added emphasis. Patriotism and education emerged as complementary concepts. During the War of 1812 flags were elevated over schoolhouses to help children perceive the glory of their nation.[3] Throughout the 1820's and 1830's there was a virtual outpouring of sentiment that a school system was to be judged by its success or failure in inculcating children with emotional love of country. Thomas Fox stated this proposition most clearly: "The mere feeling of attachment [by the child] to the land of our birth is not patriotism. When the love of our native land, so analogous to the instinctive love of the child for its parent, is cultivated and expanded, beneath the care of reason and religion, then, but not till then, it becomes patriotism." Schools were duty-bound to effect this end. The schoolhouse was not to open American children to life's rich and varied potentialities but to make permanent visceral patriots out of all of them.[4] Horace Mann had

1968), pp. 11–23; John R. Howe, *From the Revolution Through the Age of Jackson: Innocence and Empire in the Young Republic* (Englewood Cliffs, N.J.: Prentice-Hall, Inc., 1973), p. 112; Peter Gregg Slater, "Views of Children and Child Rearing during the Early National Period: A Study in the New England Intellect" (Ph.D. dissertation, University of California, Berkeley, 1970), p. 7.

[2] Monica Kiefer, *American Children Through Their Books, 1700–1835* (Philadelphia: University of Pennsylvania Press, 1948), p. 133; Rush Welter, *Popular Education and Democratic Thought in America* (New York: Columbia University Press, 1962), p. 26; David Tyack, "Forming the National Character: Paradox in the Educational Thought of the Revolutionary Generation," *Harvard Educational Review*, XXXVI, No. 1 (Winter 1966), 29–41.

[3] Merle Curti, *The Roots of American Loyalty* (New York: Columbia University Press, 1946), p. 133.

[4] Thomas B. Fox, *An Oration, Delivered at the Request of the Washington Light Infantry Company* (Newburyport, 1832), p. 12. See also James Humphrey Wilder, *An Oration Delivered at the Request of the Young Men*

no difficulty accepting Fox's proposition. By his day, the school-house was commonly conceived of as an institution to inculcate Americanism—to weld a diversity of peoples into a single nation with relatively uniform values. In a simple subsistence-agriculture society, Mann maintained, the family may have been able to educate the young and to inculcate children with patriotic doctrines. But with fathers spending more and more time away from the hearth, with older sons and unmarried daughters dispersing across the continent, and with younger children getting out of hand, the family was no longer an effective agency in the crusade for the Promised Land. It had to be replaced by formal education and common schools.[5]

Patriots of the early Jacksonian period generally agreed with Mann. They acknowledged the need for a systematic approach to formal education and focused on means through which the school-house could inculcate Americanism. There was general accord that teachers had to be competent and dedicated to instilling patriotic fervor in their young charges. Eighteenth-century patriots who stressed formal schooling had often emphasized teacher quality. One reason David Ramsay had been so deeply alienated from late-eighteenth-century South Carolina was that local schoolmasters were "deficient in that knowledge which republicans ought to possess" and could not properly educate the young.[6] A contemporary of Ramsay's, *Delaware Gazette* editor Robert Coram, claimed that poor teachers pervaded the nation: "The [American] teachers are generally foreigners, shamefully deficient in every qualification necessary to convey instruction to youth and not seldom addicted to gross vices." As ignorant foreigners, they could never convey

of Hingham, on the Fourth of July, 1832 (Hingham, 1832), p. 10; Carl N. Degler, *Out of Our Past: The Forces that Shaped Modern America* (New York: Harper Colophon, 1962), p. 159.

[5] Jonathan C. Messerli, "Localism and State Control in Horace Mann's Reform of the Common Schools," *American Quarterly*, XVII, No. 1 (Spring 1965), 111; R. Freeman Butts and Lawrence A. Cremin, *A History of Higher Education in American Culture* (New York: Holt, Rinehart & Winston, 1953), p. 217; Degler, *Out of Our Past*, p. 159; Max Lerner, *Tocqueville and American Civilization* (New York: Harper Colophon, 1969), p. 90.

[6] Robert L. Brunhouse (ed.), "David Ramsay, 1749–1815: Selections from His Writings," *Transactions of the American Philosophical Society*, New Ser., LV, Pt. 4 (1965), 141.

patriotic emotions to the nation's youth.[7] Many nineteenth-century commentators took the same position; the nation's teachers were so inadequate that they were not conveying an unadulterated love of country to the future generation.[8]

By the 1820's and 1830's some patriots tried to upgrade teacher quality through training manuals. In 1829 Samuel R. Hall published his *Lectures on School-Keeping*, a popular pioneer manual in teacher training, to convince the nation's instructors that they must strive harder to inspire patriotism in the young.[9] In the years that followed, others penned strikingly similar manuals. Over time these manuals came to be directed at female teachers, and this reflected an important transition in the classroom. As more and more schools were constructed in the new communities of the West as well as in the settled regions of the East, the demand for teachers increased. Yet the frontier and the factory were draining off male labor, and state revenues to sustain the new schools were scant. A large supply of underpaid teachers was therefore required, and women satisfied this need. Academies, female seminaries, and normal schools were founded to train them, but the number of these institutions was grossly insufficient.[10] To compensate, Samuel Hall, Lydia Sigourney, Catharine Beecher, and others published manuals instructing female teachers in their responsibilities. Above all, the female instructor was duty-bound to inculcate a love of country in the future builders of the Promised Land. As a True American Woman, this was the schoolmarm's duty.[11]

[7] Frederick Rudolph (ed.), *Essays on Education in the Early Republic* (Cambridge, Mass.: The Belknap Press, 1965), p. 136.

[8] Merle Curti, *The Social Ideas of American Educators* (Paterson, N.J.: Pageant Books 1959), offers a good analysis of this sort of commentary, particularly on p. 62. See also Eleanor Wolf Thompson, *Education for Ladies, 1830–1860* (New York: King's Crown Press, 1947), pp. 95–96.

[9] Samuel R. Hall, *Lectures on School-Keeping* (Boston: Richardson, Lord and Holbrook, 1829), especially p. 37.

[10] For analysis of this transition in teachers and schools, see Curti, *Social Ideas*, pp. 172–73; Ruth Miller Elson, *Guardians of Tradition: American Schoolbooks of the Nineteenth Century* (Lincoln: University of Nebraska Press, 1964), p. 8; Kiefer, *American Children*, p. 137; Wishy, *The Child*, pp. 72–73; Keith E. Melder, "Woman's High Calling: The Teaching Profession in America, 1830–1860," *American Studies*, XIII (Fall 1972), 22–23.

[11] See, e.g., Samuel R. Hall, *Lectures to Female Teachers on School-Keeping* (Boston: Richardson, Lord and Holbrook, 1832); Lydia H. Si-

Neither Hall, Sigourney, Beecher, nor others who wrote early teacher manuals detailed the precise ways in which an instructor was to inculcate avid love of country. But they and other doctrinaire patriots stressed the overriding importance of schoolbooks. Somehow, the teacher was to transplant the patriotic doctrines of the solid American schoolbook into the hearts and souls of the young. Perhaps because the Jacksonian revolution in printing technology made it easier and cheaper to produce a required number of acceptable schoolbooks than an adequate supply of proficient teachers, it came to be assumed that a good schoolbook compensated for a bad teacher. Through this logic, the teacher became a transmission belt, carrying vital volumes of Americanism from the printer's room to the classroom. The teacher's potential for intellectual development could hardly have been more limited.[12]

Perceived as crucial in breeding future Americans, the New Nation's schoolbooks often resembled George Washington eulogies and even Colonization Society rhetoric in their nostalgic and dogmatic patriotic tone. Many schoolbooks reproduced Daniel Webster's famous statement: "Let our object be, *our country, our whole country, and nothing but our country.*"[13] Schoolbook authors like Noah Webster, John Pierpont, Jedidiah Morse, and Charles Goodrich collected similar quotations and added documents like the Declaration of Independence and the Federal Constitution. Succeeding generations would never uphold America's unique institutions and traditions unless they were learned and admired. Brief essays which characterized Americans as God's chosen people supplemented documents. The intervention of Divine Providence accounted for American victory over mighty Britain in the Revolution and the War of 1812; divine intervention explained the moral superiority of American institutions over a

---

gourney, *Letters to Young Ladies* (New York: Harper & Brothers, 1837); Catharine E. Beecher, *The Duty of American Women to Their Country* (New York: Harper & Brothers, 1845).

[12] Elson, *Guardians of Tradition,* the definitive study of nineteenth-century American schoolbooks, comments on these and other points. See particularly pp. 101–85, 282, 339–42. See also Curti, *Social Ideas,* p. 62, and Wishy, *The Child,* p. 73.

[13] Elson, *Guardians of Tradition,* p. 282.

decadent Old World.[14] Above all, schoolbook writers cited George Washington to prove to the young that the New Nation was the Promised Land. They characterized the Founding Father precisely as Washington eulogists had—at once the embodiment of national perfection and the source of national rootedness. Students became solid patriotic citizens by meticulously following his impeccable example.[15]

Nineteenth-century patriots therefore came to perceive education in general and schoolbooks in particular as basic to the future of the young Republic. In her exhaustive study of hundreds of nineteenth-century schoolbooks, historian Ruth Miller Elson has found only one obscure 1832 reader that departed from the pattern of spread-eagle patriotism. Indeed, schoolbooks were remarkably uniform in theme and emphasis.[16] Although Benjamin Rush, Noah Webster, and a few others of the Revolutionary generation had stressed the need for heavy doses of patriotism in the educational curriculum, many more were making this plea during the Age of Jackson. One reason seems obvious—the growth of educational institutions in numbers and importance. New educational institutions were constantly being founded during the first half of the nineteenth century. Normal schools, academies, and female seminaries were established to supply the growing demand for teachers. Free school systems were instituted in Massachusetts, Delaware,

[14] For typical examples of these themes in the schoolbooks of the New Nation, see Ignatius Thomson, *The Patriot's Monitor for New Hampshire* (Randolph, Vt., 1810); Jedidiah Morse, *The American Geography* (reprint. New York: Arno Press, Inc., 1970); Charles A. Goodrich, *Lives of the Signers of the Declaration of Independence* (New York: William Reed & Co., 1829); William A. Alcott, *The Young Man's Guide* (Boston: T. R. Marvin, 1844), particularly p. 32; Curti, *Social Ideas*, p. 54; Curti, *Roots of American Loyalty*, p. 127; Elson, *Guardians of Tradition*, p. 120.

[15] See, e.g., Ignatius Thomson, *Patriot's Monitor*, p. 70; Samuel George Arnold, *The Life of George Washington, First President of the United States* (New York: Carlton & Lanahan, 1840); *The Early Life of Washington; Designed for the Instruction and Amusement of the Young. By a Friend of His Youth* (Providence: Knowles, Vose and Company, 1838); Samuel G. Goodrich, *The Life of George Washington* (Philadelphia: Desilver, Thomas & Co., 1837); Anna C. Reed, *The Life of George Washington* (Philadelphia: American Sunday School Union, 1832); Charles W. Upham, *The Life of Washington* . . . (Boston: Marsh, Capen, Lyon, and Webb, 1840); Ruth Miller Elson, "American Schoolbooks and 'Culture' in the Nineteenth Century," *Mississippi Valley Historical Review*, XLVI, No. 3 (December 1959), 418.

[16] Elson, *Guardians of Tradition*, p. 2.

Pennsylvania, Vermont, Indiana, Ohio, and Iowa. The increased quantity of teachers and schools made it possible for American children to devote a larger segment of their lives to the class-room—from an average of four months and two days in 1800 to ten months and eight days in 1840 and to twenty-two months and ten days in 1850.[17] Along with basic schooling, "booster colleges" arose—academically shabby institutions of higher education to give local communities a claim to eminence and tradition, particularly in the rapidly developing and comparatively traditionless West. Even in South Carolina, where David Ramsay had complained of minimal respect for the schoolhouse, Thomas Cooper transformed the College of South Carolina into a competent and well-financed institution that educated some of the most influential men of the Old South.[18]

Amidst the disintegration of viable institutions of social cohesion that Alexis de Tocqueville characterized so vividly in *Democracy in America,* school systems stood out as important exceptions. As social classes, preordained authorities, established churches, historic families, and long-standing communities weakened in the face of an intensely self-centered Jacksonian competitive mobility, more and more patriots turned to the developing school systems as agencies of social organization, discipline, and interpersonal co-hesion. By exalting an American tradition of ordered liberty and devotion to national community within their schoolbooks, and by requiring teachers to implant this message in the hearts of their students, patriots sought to ward off anarchic potentialities of their time. Disciplined and orderly devotion to the Promised Land became youth's ticket to a mature and successful life as kinship groups dispersed throughout the continent and the power of complementary institutions began to wane. In a nation in tumult, an unpatriotic, undisciplined, or heterogeneous and diversified future generation was out of the question. Along with penitentiaries, reformatories, and insane asylums, which were also under-

---

[17] Elson, *Guardians of Tradition,* pp. 5–8.
[18] Daniel J. Boorstin, *The Americans: The National Experience* (New York: Vintage Books, 1967), pp. 152–61, comments on the "booster colleges." Daniel Walker Hollis, *South Carolina College* (Columbia: University of South Carolina Press, 1951), pp. 82, 95, 104–05, 266–69, notes Cooper's presidency of the school and stresses his decided states'-rights emphasis.

going significant growth during the first half of the century, the schoolhouse was becoming a necessary corrective to the mobile, self-seeking, unregulated life. It would help to stabilize and anchor the American's existence and to create uniformity and order in national life.[19]

Patriotic education was therefore coming to be perceived as an antidote to the seemingly anarchic quality of Jacksonian society. If it limited the child's potential for wide-ranging experiences and for confrontation with diverse ideologies, this could not be helped. The anarchic potentialities of the time made it necessary to inculcate youth in solid patriotic dogmas. It is therefore ironic that proponents of the patriotic schoolhouse could not see that by giving even rudimentary and dogmatic education to the masses, they were promoting new modes of thought and behavior that could eventually cause further instability. Once a person mastered the linear logic necessary to read, he could never be counted on to behave as his illiterate parents and grandparents had behaved. The traditional pattern of social interactions was bound to change.[20]

Perceiving the need for schools throughout the nation to arrest the trend of the times, patriots were most anxious over the specific schools, teachers, and books in their own local communities. More than in any other arena, their own local communities were places where their voices could be heard and their ideas implemented. For a better grasp of the crusade for the schoolhouse in Jacksonian America, the community case study becomes imperative. Since both the patriotic impulse and educational efforts were most intensive above Mason-Dixon, the experiences of two sharply contrasting Northern communities are particularly revealing—Canterbury, Connecticut, in the older, settled Northeast and Oberlin, Ohio, in the newer, rugged Northwest.

[19] For cogent analyses along these broad lines, see Curti, *Social Ideas*, p. 60, and Timothy L. Smith, "Protestant Schooling and American Nationality, 1800–1850," *Journal of American History*, LIII, No. 4 (March 1967), 679–95. See also William R. Taylor, *Cavalier and Yankee: The Old South and American National Character* (New York: Harper Torchbooks, 1969), pp. 146–47; Michael B. Katz, *The Irony of Early School Reform: Educational Innovation in Mid-Nineteenth Century Massachusetts* (Cambridge, 1968), pp. 163–211.

[20] Edward Shorter brilliantly develops this point in "Illegitimacy, Sexual Revolution, and Social Change in Modern Europe," in *The American Family in Socio-Historical Perspective*, edited by Michael Gordon (New York: St. Martin's Press, 1973), particularly on p. 307.

Andrew T. Judson, an ambitious Jacksonian Democratic politician, was the dominant voice in the older Eastern community, while Charles Grandison Finney, the apolitical New School revivalist, set the guidelines in the experimental new community. Both communities looked to education to shape the future. For Canterburians the schoolhouse was to perpetuate the well-rooted stability and enlarge upon the economic potentialities of a materially prosperous past. For Oberlinites, on the other hand, education could structure the West's first godly community—Zion in the wilderness—and could eventually bring on the millennium. It could perfect the nation and, ultimately, the world. But though Canterburians emphasized rooted stability and prosperity while Oberlinites stressed millennial perfection, influential figures in both communities were primarily concerned with the well-being of the white male residents. Both wanted a community where neither women nor Negroes obstructed the goals of white men. Therefore, the leadership of both communities testified to the strength and viability of the concept of white male nationhood.[21]

II

The history of the small eastern Connecticut town of Canterbury began with migrations from other parts of that colony at the end of the seventeenth century. By a 1703 enactment, the Connecticut General Assembly formally recognized the site as a dis-

[21] Although spread-eagle patriotism in the early nineteenth century was primarily a Northern phenomenon, the study of a specific Southern school would be desirable. It would also be useful to consider a public school in a large Northern urban center. But there are no secondary works concerning the impact of patriotism upon either type of school situation during the early Jacksonian period. (See, e.g., Joe Park, *The Rise of American Education: An Annotated Bibliography* [Evanston, Ill.: Northwestern University Press, 1965.]) This is probably because primary source material on the influence of patriotism upon specific Southern and urban Northern schools is very thin before the late 1840's. Rather than attempt to squeeze insights out of the meager data for either type of school, I have elected to focus on the comparatively rich and varied data available for Canterbury and Oberlin. The data conveniently fall within the chronological limits of this book. Moreover, they indicate ways in which patriotic concerns were linked with the racial and sexual concerns that we have discussed earlier. Thus, one of the principal advantages of focusing upon Canterbury and Oberlin is that it draws together many crucial ingredients within the early American patriotic crusade.

tinct legal entity. Over the next hundred and twenty-five years, Canterbury became one of the most prosperous communities in New England. A fertile gravelly loam soil, lush natural meadows, and the bordering Quinebaug River all promoted easy farming and large harvests. Trade flourished and new merchants set up shop. Agricultural and commercial prosperity plus the development of three cotton factories induced wealthy men throughout the Northeast to settle on outlying farms or to purchase homes within the town itself. By the early nineteenth century, the most prosperous Canterburians began to construct large, substantial houses with classical pilasters and architraves, delicate lighting fixtures, and triple-arched Palladian windows. They were also diligent patrons of the town's religious institutions—one Baptist and two Congregational churches—and participated in the Canterbury temperance society, perhaps the largest in eastern Connecticut.[22]

Despite economic prosperity and moral diligence, Canterbury's leading citizens were troubled during the early 1830's. Church membership was decreasing, unpredictable new migrants were settling in their community, respect for constituted authority was declining, and, most significant of all, the younger generation seemed more and more disobedient. Early in 1831 a group of the town's leading citizens called on Prudence Crandall, a young, attractive, and very competent superintendent of a young ladies' school in nearby Plainfield, and urged her to relocate the school in Canterbury. Such an institution, run by a woman who was supposed to be an effective disciplinarian and a firm patriot, might make their daughters more obedient. Moreover, it might add refinement, patriotism, cohesion, and a renewed sense of female propriety to the town. Although other measures were also required to arrest the disorderly trend of the times, a competent girls' school was a move in the right direction. Leading Canter-

---

[22] The best survey of the origins and early history of Canterbury continues to be John Warner Barber's *Connecticut Historical Collections Containing a General Collection of Interesting Facts, Traditions, Biographical Sketches, etc. Relating to the History and Antiquities of Every Town in Connecticut with Geographical Descriptions* (New Haven: Durrie & Peck, 1836), pp. 420–23. See also Alfred Thurston Child, Jr., "Prudence Crandall and the Canterbury Experiment," *Bulletin of Friends Historical Association*, XXII, No. 1 (Spring Number, 1933), 37–38.

burians offered Crandall a financial advance and a large building on the village green to house her school, and the schoolmistress came to instruct the town's white maidenhood.[23]

Until early March of 1833, Canterburians voiced no displeasure with their new school; their hopes for order, patriotism, and refined young womanhood remained high. That month they received a shock. Rumor spread that Crandall intended to allow a black girl to become a student—an unprecedented act in their Colonization Society stronghold. Delegation after delegation of townsfolk tried to dissuade her; they threatened to withdraw their daughters if the school was racially "contaminated." Crandall responded quickly. She converted her institution into a boarding school for black girls, sent white students home, and openly proclaimed her intentions to a furious community: "The object, and the sole object of this school is to instruct the ignorant—and fit and prepare teachers for the people of color, that they may be elevated, and their intellectual and moral wants supplied."[24] This turned even more Canterburians against her. Townsmen complained to the Connecticut Legislature, pressed lawsuits, and refused to sell Crandall goods and services. They charged that the school would draw blacks with demoralizing and unpredictable habits and ideas into their community. More specifically, the first black girls who enrolled would attract others, drawing masses of blacks into lovely Canterbury until the town was dangerously darkened. Canterburians therefore concluded that Crandall had to be a secret agent for the emerging amalgamationist-oriented abolitionist movement. With black hordes schooled in egalitarian amalgamationist doctrine by Crandall and her Garrisonian cohorts, the superior race would be subverted. Racial mixture originating at the schoolhouse would spread chaos through eastern Connecticut; in time it would infect the bloodstream of the entire nation. The great "nation of free white Americans" would be destroyed.

[23] Barber, *Connecticut Historical Collections*, p. 421; Child, Jr., *Bulletin of Friends Historical Association*, XXII, No. 1 (Spring Number, 1933), 39; Edmund Fuller, *Prudence Crandall: An Incident of Racism in Nineteenth-Century Connecticut* (Middletown, Conn.: Wesleyan University Press, 1971), 12–13.
[24] Quoted in *The Liberator*, May 25, 1833.

Therefore, the existence of the Promised Land was contingent on nullifying Crandall's educational experiment. National obligation and community spirit required purity in the schoolroom.[25]

This argument was vocalized almost everywhere in Canterbury—at town meetings, in church gatherings, and in private conversation. The argument originated with Andrew T. Judson, the most powerful man in the vicinity and one of the prime movers in the original effort to establish a girls' school in town. Nearly fifty years old at the time of the Crandall episode, Judson was an ambitious if unethical Jacksonian Democrat. After a publicized dispute with the Connecticut Comptroller in 1819 because he "neglected" to pay his taxes for six years "for want of an adequate method of keeping accounts," he served briefly in the state legislature and was active in local Democratic party affairs. A town selectman and the dominant voice in the local auxiliary of the American Colonization Society by the early 1830's, Judson sought a cause that might project his name into state and national prominence.[26] When Crandall established a "nigger school," Judson saw his chance. He recalled that abolitionists had attempted to found a school for black boys in New Haven a few years earlier. A coalition of colonizationists and New Haven city officials had closed

[25] Petition to the General Assembly of the State of Connecticut from the Citizens of Canterbury, April 9, 1833; Petition of the Town of Canterbury to the Connecticut General Assembly, May, 1833 (both in the Connecticut State Archives); *A Statement of Facts, Respecting the School for Colored Females, in Canterbury, Ct., Together with a Report of the Late Trial of Miss Prudence Crandall* (Brooklyn, Conn.: Advertiser Press, 1833), p. 9; Fuller, *Crandall*, pp. 27, 32–33; *Colonizationist and Journal of Freedom*, May 1833, pp. 59–60; Bernard C. Steiner, *History of Slavery in Connecticut* (Baltimore: The Johns Hopkins Press, 1893), pp. 47–48; *The Liberator*, April 6, 1833, February 15, 1834; William Jay, *Miscellaneous Writings on Slavery* (reprint. New York: Negro Universities Press, 1968), p. 36; Ralph Foster Weld, *Slavery in Connecticut* (New Haven: Yale University Press, 1935), p. 23; Ellen D. Larned, *History of Windham County, Connecticut* (Worcester, Mass.: Ellen D. Larned, 1880), II, 501.

[26] Andrew Judson, *A Letter to James Thomas, Esq. Comptroller* (New London, 1819), reveals Judson's taxation squabble. Other biographical information is supplied in Louis Ruchames (ed.), *The Letters of William Lloyd Garrison* (Cambridge, Mass.: The Belknap Press, 1971), II, 73; Leonard L. Richards, *"Gentlemen of Property and Standing": Anti-Abolitionist Mobs in Jacksonian America* (New York: Oxford University Press, 1970), p. 38; Wendell Phillips Garrison and Francis Jackson Garrison, *William Lloyd Garrison, 1805–1879* (reprint. New York: Arno Press, Inc., 1969), I, 322, n. 2. Despite these citations, known details on Judson's life remain scarce.

down the school, and the leaders of that coalition became prominent almost overnight. By leading a similar and equally successful crusade against the Crandall school, Judson calculated, he might become the next governor of Connecticut. At the same time, he might ward off a serious financial threat. Living adjacent to the school on the village green, he sensed that the proximity to "nigger girls" would "cut the value of [his] real estate."[27] But Judson was motivated by more than political and economic considerations. He seemed to genuinely believe that "a school for nigger girls" in the neighborhood was unbearable. The girls were not inherently dangerous, he cautioned. But Crandall and the Garrisonians were determined to teach them abolitionist-amalgamationist doctrine— not the imperatives of sound Americanism. Moreover, book learning would arouse any Negro's desire to mix with whites; the black girls would inevitably seek out the white men of New England, cohabit, and intermarry before a cheering Garrisonian audience.[28] Tempted and threatened in this way, white men in the vicinity would be endangered. Should they give in to lustful passions— should they fornicate with and marry black seductresses—Canterbury and eventually the nation was doomed to disorganizing confusion and anarchy. This must never happen, Judson warned. "America is ours—it belongs to a race of white men who first redeemed the wilderness." The American Revolutionaries were white men who "were oppressed by taxes by the king—they assembled in Convention, and at the peril of their lives declared this *white nation* free and independent. It was a nation of *white men*, who formed and have administered our government." Since the Constitutional Convention, America had remained "the white man's country, and the white man is an American citizen." If white men fornicated with black students and married them, then their children would be born impure and "the white man's country" would be doomed. This was why blacks had to be removed to Africa, where they could not be forced into the American educational system: "They belong to Africa. Let them be sent back

[27] Quoted in Samuel J. May, *Some Recollections of Our Antislavery Conflict* (Boston: Fields, Osgood & Co., 1869), pp. 45–47.
[28] May, *Recollections*, p. 45; *Connecticut Journal* (New Haven), July 30, 1833; Norwich *Courier*, March 27, 1833; Russel B. Nye, *Fettered Freedom* (Lansing: Michigan State University Press, 1963), p. 106.

there." With blacks removed, white men's passions would not be tempted. The "white nation" would not be subverted, and schools could be used to stabilize, not destroy, community existence.[29]

Like authors of the first teachers' manuals and many other early-nineteenth-century educational theorists, Judson assumed that the schoolhouse could help bring on "the Rising Glory of America" as an agency promoting national order and stability. The Crandall school was subversive of the white man's institutions because it fostered amalgamation and it had to be opposed at all costs. At the beginning of the Canterbury school crisis, Judson tried to convey these feelings to his friend Samuel J. May, Crandall's principal proponent.[30] He expected to win May over to his position, for the young Harvard-educated Unitarian minister from nearby Brooklyn, Connecticut, had championed African colonization. Four years before the school crisis, May had pledged the first and only Unitarian pulpit in the state to the cause of black repatriation and had founded the A.C.S. auxiliary that Judson dominated.[31] But May had also been an early convert to William Lloyd Garrison and the doctrine of immediate abolition, and had been one of Garrison's first and most dependable financial supporters. He had also joined the New England Anti-Slavery Society and was a founder of the American Anti-Slavery Society. As with Garrison and several other leading abolitionists, May's commitment to immediate emancipation did not eliminate his allegiance to the colonization ideal. Through the hottest days of the Crandall controversy, he remained active in Colonization Society affairs and criticized Garrison for being "too severe" with the organization.

[29] *Report of Arguments of Counsel, in the Case of Prudence Crandall, Plff. in Error, vs. State of Connecticut, before the Supreme Court of Errors, at their Session at Brooklyn, July Term, 1834* (Boston: Garrison & Knapp, 1834), pp. 18, 22; *Andrew T. Judson's Remarks to the Jury, on the Trial of the Case, State v. P. Crandall. Superior Court, Oct. Term, 1833. Windham County, Ct.* (Hartford, n.d.), p. 21; *Report of the Trial of Miss Prudence Crandall Before the County Court for Windham County, August Term, 1833. On an Information Charging Her with Teaching Colored Persons not Inhabitants of This State* (Brooklyn, Conn.: Unionist Press, 1833), p. 6; May, *Recollections*, pp. 47–48; Fuller, *Crandall*, pp. 30–31.

[30] May, *Recollections*, pp. 46–48.

[31] P. J. Staudenraus, *The African Colonization Movement, 1816–1865* (New York: Columbia University Press, 1961), p. 127; Samuel J. May to James C. Dunn, July 5, 1829, Papers of the American Colonization Society, Library of Congress.

Even after leaving the A.C.S., he vigorously defended the concept of ameliorating race relations and improving national life by deporting blacks to Africa.[32]

Realizing that May retained allegiance to the colonization ideal, Judson tried to turn him against the Crandall school. Blacks should be removed to Africa, Judson explained. They should not be educated in amalgamationist doctrine by Crandall and her cohorts or they would pollute the Promised Land. But May persisted as a friend of the Crandall school. He did not disagree with Judson over the theoretical importance of lightening America by sending blacks to Africa. Rather, he felt that the Colonization Society would never have the funds "to transport any considerable portion of the blacks to Africa. . . . While, therefore, we must cherish the colony [of the A.C.S.] at Liberia, we must not forget that we have a much greater work to do at home. We are to provide for the welfare and continued improvement of more than two millions of the descendants of Africa, who will ever be a part of our population."[33]

Here was the rub. Judson and his Canterbury following were so involved in trying to remove the black threat to the white man's country that they construed efforts to educate American blacks as counterproductive. American schools for blacks wasted financial resources—money that was desperately needed to send blacks to Africa. Moreover, because educated blacks became amalgamationists, efforts to teach them contradicted the purpose of formal education—order, discipline, and reverence for the white man's country amidst increasingly chaotic conditions. May's perspective differed from Judson's in several essentials. He was more pessimistic than Judson as to the potential of the A.C.S. Sensing that

---

[32] Louis Ruchames (ed.), *The Abolitionists: A Collection of Their Writings* (New York: G. P. Putnam's Sons, 1963), pp. 17–18; Walter M. Merrill, *Against Wind and Tide: A Biography of William Lloyd Garrison* (Cambridge: Harvard University Press, 1963), pp. 41–43; Samuel J. May, *A Discourse on Slavery in the United States, Delivered in Brooklyn, July 3, 1831* (Boston, 1832); *The Abolitionist*, I, No. 8 (August 1833), 113; *African Repository*, XI, No. 9 (September 1835), 279; Jane H. Pease and William H. Pease, *Bound with Them in Chains: A Biographical History of the Antislavery Movement* (Westport, Conn.: Greenwood Press, 1972), pp. 284–85; Jane H. Pease and William H. Pease, "Samuel J. May: Civil Libertarian," *Cornell Library Journal*, No. 3 (Autumn 1967), p. 7.

[33] May, *Discourse on Slavery*, pp. 26–28.

there could never be a pure white man's country—that blacks could never be completely or even substantially repatriated—May insisted upon educating the Negro majority that would remain on American shores. Agreeing with Judson that schools should facilitate social stability and patriotism while recognizing that blacks were permanent fixtures on the national landscape, he felt that by bringing members of the race into the schoolhouse, they could become more orderly and loyal citizens. At the very least, education could cultivate blacks and make them more pleasant to live with—it could "cure" the disorderly idiosyncrasies of the race. Moreover, May contended that no successful colony could ever be established in Africa "until an improved class of colored people shall be raised in our country. They must be educated here that they may be prepared for Africa." Through the discipline and "moral uplift" that the schoolroom could inculcate, the black minority that was repatriated would be prepared to evangelize and civilize the "Dark Continent." Without institutions of "moral uplift" like the Crandall school, degenerate blacks would therefore continue to be a source of disorder in America and those who were repatriated would merely add to Africa's problems.[34]

Although May was obviously more concerned with the Negro's well-being than Judson and supported Negro education while Judson opposed it, the primary antagonists in the Canterbury crisis agreed on two ideological points. Both men preferred to remove all blacks from the white nation despite sharp differences over the practicality of doing so. Both also shared the assumption of many contemporary educational theorists that schools should promote order, discipline, and "the Rising Glory of America." Therefore, although May's defense of the Crandall school helped to widen black opportunities while Judson's opposition harmed blacks, there was a disturbing ideological similarity between the two opponents. If massive colonization had seemed practical, May, like Judson,

[34] Samuel J. May, *The Right of Colored People to Education, Vindicated* (Brooklyn, Conn.: Advertiser Press, 1833), especially p. 23; *The Abolitionist*, I, No. 8 (August 1833), 113. It is important to note that May departed somewhat from the A.C.S. argument on "African uplift." American blacks, *per se*, would not improve Africa. They had to be educated in America if they were to be of any use to Africa.

might have been left defending an all-white school system for its order-rendering patriotic benefits. This was a danger inherent in the colonizationist ideological legacy.

Canterbury's school crisis of 1833–34 therefore featured a debate over racial and educational ideology between Andrew Judson and Samuel May in which both men shared important ideological assumptions. It also featured a three-cornered controversy on the relationship between sex and education in which Prudence Crandall challenged her abolitionist defenders as well as the Judson-led opposition. The young teacher evoked images of Woll-stonecraft-like strength and daring that upset most men involved in the controversy irrespective of their feelings about race. Two Connecticut abolitionists who tried to assist Crandall through most of the controversy had mixed emotions about her; they had never seen a woman with such strength and determination.[35] When Esquire Frost, spokesman for a Canterbury citizens' committee, warned Crandall that intermarriage would come of her venture, he was shocked by her reply: *"Moses had a black wife."*[36] When another group of Canterbury men charged that Crandall violated a pledge by conducting her black girls to white women's pews in the town church, she replied that the girls would continue to sit in those pews—that she would never honor wrong pledges.[37] Contrary to the retiring, supportive True American Womanhood, Crandall seemed unpredictable. Her father once threatened to sell the land beneath the school that she legally owned. If "you will sell the property," she charged, "I will give no title and you must abide the consequences." The old man backed down.[38] During the

[35] *The Abolitionist*, I, No. 4 (April 1833), 63; S. J. May, "Miss Prudence Crandall," in Lydia M. Child (ed.), *The Oasis* (Boston: Benjamin C. Bacon, 1834), 189–90.

[36] Quoted in Larned, *Windham County*, II, 492; Fuller, *Crandall*, p. 15 (emphasis added).

[37] Quoted in Edward S. Abdy, *Journal of a Residence and Tour in the United States of North America from April, 1833 to October, 1834* (London: John Murray, 1835), I, 200–03.

[38] William Lloyd Garrison (ed.), *Fruits of Colonization: The Canterbury Persecution, Containing Important Documents Relative to Miss Crandall's School in Canterbury* (Boston[?], 1833[?]), pp. 5–6; Steiner, *Slavery in Connecticut*, p. 49; Child, Jr., *Bulletin of the Friends Historical Association*, XXII, No. 1 (Spring Number, 1933), 43.

hottest days of the Canterbury crisis, Crandall even flouted the Quaker ban on marriage outside of the Society of Friends.[39] She was not the pliant schoolmarm Canterburians had counted on to follow their wishes and to promote orderly, patriotic ways among the younger generation. To white men on both sides of the school controversy, Crandall's strong, confident, independent qualities were cause for alarm; the dreaded Wollstonecraft tradition seemed to be reviving.

Despite these apprehensions, Andrew Judson and his followers persistently described Crandall as a puppet whose strings were manipulated by male Garrisonians. Judson charged that she was "the mere nominal defendant" in the controversy and was totally controlled by the Garrisonians.[40] Other male opponents repeated the charge and noted that the young woman did not have the capacity to run a school, much less conduct a campaign in its defense. Male Garrisonians had to be secretly directing her; a woman could not have initiated such a bold experiment in amalgamationist education.[41]

Given the widespread alarm over Crandall's bold words and deeds, we cannot accept this charge at face value. Judson and his followers probably belittled her role to assuage their own doubts, for they had characterized her as defiant, irresponsible, and unwomanly. While charging that Crandall was a puppet, Judson attacked her for establishing a Negro school *on her own* without consulting the town fathers and for refusing to negotiate with them. The consequence of her belligerence, he warned, was widespread disorder throughout the community.[42] Like their leader, other male opponents of the Crandall school were of two minds, accusing her of being "easily led" while chastising her for stubbornness, "reckless disregard of the rights and feelings of her

[39] Thomas E. Drake, *Quakers and Slavery in America* (New Haven: Yale University Press, 1950), p. 138. By joining the Packerville Baptist Church in July 1831, Crandall technically broke with the Quakers. She met her husband at this church.

[40] *Andrew T. Judson's Remarks . . . Superior Court, Oct. Term, 1833*, p. 22; Norwich *Courier*, March 27, 1833; *Connecticut Journal*, July 30, 1833.

[41] Norwich *Republican*, n.d., as quoted in *The Liberator*, April 6, 1833; *Connecticut Journal*, August 27, 1833; New York *Commercial Advertiser*, July 16, 1833; Larned, *Windham County*, II, 501.

[42] Norwich *Courier*, March 27, 1833; *Connecticut Journal*, July 30, 1833.

neighbors," and "obstinate adherence to her plan."[43] These conflicting characterizations may have represented attempts by frightened men to persuade themselves that the young schoolmistress
was "easily led" despite strong evidence to the contrary. After all,
if it became too apparent that Crandall was in command, then the
new Canterbury school was doubly dangerous to order and stability. On top of a miscegenation threat, the opposition would have
to confront a crisis of perverted white womanhood—a revival of
the dangerous Wollstonecraft tradition. Even if Samuel May had
accurately noted that the black girls in the school were disciplined
and cultivated—even if they would not seek out white males—
uncontrolled white womanhood posed the same danger to racial
purity, order, and community stability. Even if Crandall's black
girls were not tempting white men, a white woman on the loose, a
wild schoolmistress, could entice black males and perhaps do
worse. The schoolhouse could exert a subversive influence upon
the white man's country. Whether she taught black girls or white,
a defiant, uncontrollable white woman at the head of a school
negated the order-rendering, nation-sustaining effects that were
required of an educational institution. For this reason, Judson and
his followers had much less to worry about if they could convince
themselves that Crandall was a mere puppet, entirely directed "by
the combined efforts and energies of Buffum, Tappan, Garrison
and May."[44]

Although abolitionists like Arnold Buffum, Arthur Tappan, and
Samuel May tried to dominate the Crandall defense effort, they
were always repulsed. No evidence indicates that any male abolitionists ever made a significant policy decision without Crandall's
full consent. They were agitated by this fact. Their desires to take
command also irritated Crandall, for she was forced to confront
her defenders as well as her Judson-led opponents, running a
boarding school all the while.[45]

---

[43] *Windham County Advertiser*, n.d., as quoted in *The Liberator*, July 20,
1833; New York *Commercial Advertiser*, July 16, 1833; Edwin W. Small and
Miriam R. Small, "Prudence Crandall, Champion of Negro Education," *New
England Quarterly*, XVII, No. 4 (December 1944), 522.
[44] Quoted in Larned, *Windham County*, II, 501.
[45] Prudence Crandall to William Lloyd Garrison, March 19, 1833, George
W. Benson to Samuel J. May, March 10, 16, 1833—all in the Prudence

Crandall's relationship with the most influential of her abolitionist defenders, William Lloyd Garrison, turned out to be the key to the survival or demise of her school. This relationship may have been the most important factor in accounting for the course of the entire Canterbury crisis. In March of 1833 Garrison declared absolute support for the Crandall school: "If possible, Miss C. must be sustained at all hazards. If we suffer the school to be put down in Canterbury, other places will partake of the panic, and also prevent its introduction in their vicinity." If Judson and his following won out in eastern Connecticut, other community leaders would be encouraged to bar Negroes from the classroom. In the long run, the state of Negro education would suffer irreparably.[46] Active in Crandall's behalf through the next year, Garrison had nothing but praise for the way she fought for an educational system that was consistent with the ideals of the Declaration of Independence. "She is a wonderful woman," Garrison wrote, "as undaunted as if she had the whole world on her side." In a letter to Samuel May, he described her as "the noble, christian heroine." "O, the persecuted, the dauntless, the heroic Prudence Crandall," Garrison noted to his fiancée, Helen Benson. In *The Liberator* he characterized her as a daring educator, "effulgent, fresh, and lovely to the sight."[47]

However, Garrison became upset when he learned, during the early spring of 1834, that Crandall planned to marry an unknown Baptist minister from Ithaca, New York, Calvin Philleo. He advised Crandall against the marriage, as he later advised Angelina Grimké against marrying Theodore Weld. With no basis in fact, he charged that Philleo was probably "a worthless person" and he dropped other innuendos.[48] Crandall retorted that she was deter-

---

Crandall Collection, Boston Public Library; Larned, *Windham County*, II, 492; *The Liberator*, May 25, 1833; April 19, 1834.

[46] Quoted in W. P. Garrison and F. J. Garrison, *W. L. Garrison*, I, 320.

[47] William Lloyd Garrison to Isaac Knapp, April 11, 1833, William Lloyd Garrison Papers, Boston Public Library; Garrison to Samuel J. May, February 18, 1834, in Walter M. Merrill (ed.), *The Letters of William Lloyd Garrison* (Cambridge, Mass.: The Belknap Press, 1971), I, 286; Garrison to Helen E. Benson, February 18, 1834, in Merrill (ed.), *Letters of Garrison*, I, 284. Fuller, *Crandall*, pp. 109–10, quotes Garrison's tribute to Crandall in *The Liberator*.

[48] Merrill (ed.), *Letters of Garrison*, I, 315, 360, 399; Ruchames (ed.), *Letters of Garrison*, II, 163.

mined to marry Philleo. At this point, Garrison called on his abolitionist followers to abandon the Canterbury school. "Prudence tells me he [Philleo] is for continuing her school in Canterbury, and increasing the number of scholars, if possible, to one hundred," he noted. "In my opinion, however, she had better take advantage of her marriage and move off with flying colors." Her usefulness to education and abolition causes had ended. "I think if Prudence marries him, she will act wisely in giving up her school," Garrison exclaimed on another occasion.[49] Once he accidentally met Crandall and Philleo in Boston. He was cool toward the recently wed couple, displayed no interest in their Canterbury struggle, and became irritated because he could see that "the hymeneal yoke has been put on" and "the maiden has been transformed into a wife." This was so disturbing that he "could not congratulate them upon their union."[50] He did not explain why a woman who had been conducting a spirited fight for black education as a schoolmistress could not do so married, particularly when her husband intended to assist her. Garrison also failed to explain why a basic educational and civil-rights battle had ceased to be worth winning when, only a year earlier, he had pledged his resources to that battle because of its enormous long-range significance. A married woman would be ineffective in civil-rights efforts, particularly when her name was Prudence Crandall Philleo. At least Helen Benson, Garrison's fiancée, construed this as his position on the Crandall matter. Committed to the position that a married woman should remain by the hearth, Benson agreed with Garrison.[51]

However, Garrison abandoned the Canterbury school for more than the conviction that a married woman was ineffective in civil-rights battles. He was also distressed by the fact that, unlike many abolitionists, Crandall refused to obey him. She would not let him

[handwritten margin note: corrupted by sexual experience]

[49] Merrill (ed.), *Letters of Garrison*, I, 361, 365; John L. Thomas, *The Liberator: William Lloyd Garrison* (Boston: Little, Brown and Company, 1963), p. 193.

[50] Merrill (ed.), *Letters of Garrison*, I, 398–99.

[51] Helen E. Benson to William Lloyd Garrison, June 16, 1834, Garrison-Benson Letters, Houghton Library, Harvard University. See also another letter from Benson to Garrison, May 22, 1834, in this same collection: "She [Crandall] really makes me blush, I feel as if I did not think of the poor slaves half enough; when I see her."

tell her how to run her school and she went ahead with her marriage.

We must also bear in mind that Garrison repudiated Crandall and her school while he was engaged to Helen Benson. During the eight-month period of the engagement, Garrison's attitude toward women seemed odd. Once, for example, he anonymously inserted "A Wife Wanted" advertisement in *The Liberator:* "Information would be thankfully received of any young, respectable, and intelligent Colored Woman, . . . who would be willing to endure the insults and reproaches that would be heaped upon her for being the partner of a white man. . . ."[52] Helen Benson sharply reprimanded Garrison for this supposed prank. It also dismayed Crandall. She already had to confront the charge that her school was a front for Garrisonian intermarriage, and Garrison's advertisement strengthened the case against her. Even more striking, Garrison had desired an intimate personal relationship with Crandall while he was engaged to Benson. Along with displays of affection for his retiring domestic fiancée, he sought to cultivate viable personal ties with the strong and daring Canterbury schoolmistress. At times he seemed to conceive of Benson and Crandall as virtually one person. He would kiss Crandall and ask her to pass the kiss on to Benson. He would arrange for Crandall to have her portrait painted so that he could have an engraved copy for himself and could send another to Benson. He would even write love sonnets for *The Liberator* and claim that they were descriptive of Benson while acknowledging that many would think they were tributes to Crandall.[53] This suggests that Garrison needed both the soft, dependent Benson and the strong, self-willed Crandall. The two seemed to balance each other, producing, in sum, the ideal woman. Rapport with one but not with the other may have seemed incomplete—a frustrating sort of partial satisfaction.[54]

[52] *The Liberator*, June 28, 1834. Garrison defended his advertisement against criticism in a letter to Samuel May dated July 23, 1834 (Merrill [ed.], *Letters of Garrison*, I, 381–82). In this letter, he went on to ask May to marry him to Benson on September 4.

[53] Merrill (ed.), *Letters of Garrison*, I, 312, 317, 322–25, 336–37.

[54] This point is suggested most strongly in Garrison's 1876 memorial to Benson, which included a great many loving memories of the Crandall of the Canterbury crisis (*Helen Eliza Garrison: A Memorial* [Cambridge, 1876]).

Thus, when Crandall shattered his sexual fantasies by marrying Philleo, Garrison was reacting against more than her disobedience. He was also rebelling at the loss of a crucial female relationship. If Crandall could throw his personal life into disarray by marrying Philleo, the woman could not expect his support for her Canterbury venture. Cast into confusion, Garrison may have felt the need to break entirely from a married Crandall in order to somehow regain his bearings and face his own unenticing wedding bells.

This is not a definitive explanation of the complex Garrison-Benson-Crandall triangle. But there can be no doubt that Garrison abandoned the Canterbury school because personal and sexual factors undermined abolitionist strategy considerations.

The conduct of a strong, independent-minded schoolmistress seems to have had a more disruptive impact upon Garrison than it had upon Judson and his followers. On September 9, 1834, Crandall was forced to close her school because the propaganda and overt violence of the Judson camp were accelerating while funding and publicity from Garrisonians were being phased out.[55] Garrison, however, did not completely forsake Negro education. Like Samuel May, he retained mild allegiance to the colonization ideal through 1834 but realized that most blacks would remain in America and that they had to be educated. Without the ordering, refining, loyalty-instilling qualities of the classroom, Garrison, like May, felt apprehensive about the conduct of blacks in the New Nation. But while Garrison remained deeply committed to the stabilizing, justice-rendering, patriotic necessity and desirability of Negro education, certain disordering sexual features of his personality caused him to contradict his commitment and withdraw his support from the Crandall school.

Garrison had little in common with Andrew Judson. Yet both men assumed that a schoolhouse could bring order and stability to Canterbury and to the nation, and then both men went on in their own ways and for their own reasons to undermine the Crandall school. In resisting what he saw as Crandall's attempt to pervert

[55] For pertinent data on the closing of the Crandall school, see *The Liberator*, September 13, 20, 1834; May, *Recollections*, p. 71; Larned, *Windham County*, II, 501; Fuller, *Crandall*, pp. 93–95.

the proper function of a school and the essence of female propriety, Judson provoked more disorder and havoc in Canterbury than the community had ever experienced. In withdrawing from a battle for Negro education that he had strongly championed a year earlier and was far from lost, Garrison wrought comparable confusion in abolitionist circles, particularly among Crandall's local proponents. Therefore, the Canterbury educational crisis of 1833–34 pointed to a self-defeating quality in the quest for a school system that would restore order, stability and uniformity, inculcate national loyalty, and thus assure "the Rising Glory of America." Frightened, disordered, uprooted men could not be counted upon to promote stabilizing, cohesive institutions whether those institutions were schools, churches, political parties, or even banks.

Where the existence of a domestic black population could cause Judson, May, and even Garrison to cling to the fantasy of repatriation and where the presence of a strong, independent woman could cause Judson and Garrison to lose perspective as to the consequences of their conduct, there was little chance for stabilizing institutions much less for an orderly future generation. As Canterbury's children watched their fathers break schoolhouse windows in the name of a patriotic school system, and as they learned that the nation's leading abolitionist was abandoning a black school that he wanted "sustained at all hazards," life must have seemed disoriented. What was happening to the community from which they were to acquire a sense of calm, rooted stability? And what was happening to the country which, according to their schoolbooks, they were obligated to serve and to perfect?

III

While eastern Connecticut was in tumult over the Crandall school, men in northern Ohio were establishing an institute for higher education in the woods of the Connecticut Western Reserve twelve miles south of Lake Erie. Thoroughly isolated in a swampy, heavily forested area, the Oberlin Collegiate Institute was a tiny rural colony. At first it could not be approached by carriage road. The school opened for instruction in December of 1833 and was chartered the following February. The leading figure in the community for decades to come, Charles Grandison Finney, arrived in 1835 and was taken aback by the primitive settlement: "It had no permanent buildings, and was composed of a little colony in the woods; and just beginning to put up their own houses, and clear away the immense forest, and make a place for a college."[56]

The wilderness terrain was not all that distinguished Oberlin from the older, more prosperous, established Canterbury community of the early 1830's. Whereas Canterbury's leading citizens had called upon Crandall to found a school that would restore order and re-establish older ways in a community that appeared to be increasingly unstable, the Oberlin settlement stood, from the start, for a repudiation of older ways. It represented an extension of those religious fires that Finney had ignited in the burned-over district of western New York and elsewhere in the Northeast during the 1820's and 1830's.

During this interval, Finney and his followers had conducted a systematic attack upon the extreme determinist Calvinist doctrines of election, original sin, and infant damnation. Acknowledging a natural tendency in men toward evil and degeneracy, Finneyites charged that the traditional Calvinist stress upon human sin and damnation had fostered a deplorable passivity in mankind. Feeling degraded and impotent before an all-powerful God, churchgoers sensed that they were powerless to change their own fate. If a man was predestined to be saved, traditional Calvinism held, he would be saved "in God's own good time"; meanwhile it was worse than useless for a sinner to exert himself. Finney took issue with this theological posture:

> Sinners ought to be made to feel that they have something to do, and that is to repent; that it is something which no other

[56] Charles G. Finney, *The Memoirs of Rev. Charles G. Finney* (New York: A. S. Barnes & Company, 1876), p. 342. For other data on Oberlin's physical setting and legal status during this early period, see the *Ohio Observer* (Hudson), November 13, 1834; J. H. Fairchild, *Oberlin: Its Origin, Progress and Results* (Oberlin: Shankland and Harmon, 1860), pp. 4–5, 9; Robert S. Fletcher, "The Government of Oberlin Colony," *Mississippi Valley Historical Review*, XX, No. 2 (September 1933), 190.

being can do for them, neither God nor man, and something which they can do and do now. Religion is something to do, not something to wait for.[57]

Using colloquial, emotion-filled words, praying for individuals by name, and calling upon a "holy band" of personal assistants to help him rouse an audience, Finney charged that moral depravity was a voluntary attitude of the human mind and could therefore be changed by voluntary human effort. Since man was responsible for his own sins, he could accomplish his own regeneration; the sinner could repent of his ill ways and experience a "second birth." Once man determined to follow Biblical truths and pursue God's law, he would experience conversion and feel Christ's salvation. The moment that man was converted to God's way and experienced salvation was the moment Christian life began. He became duty-bound to spend the balance of his days sustaining his conversion through strenuous Christian benevolence and persistent warfare against the institutional sins of society. When Americans at large brought this struggle to sustain conversion into their everyday affairs—when they tried to keep themselves and their communities under "the sweet perfect subjection to the will of Christ"—society would reach a state of "Christian perfection," "sanctification," or, more simply, "Holiness." But how was national Holiness to be accomplished? For Finneyites, the Holy Spirit resided within the preacher. Through emotional revivalist tactics (Finney's "new measures"), the preacher could convince the sinful masses to learn the truths of the Bible and follow the path to Holiness. A certain measure of excitement generated by the preacher and his "holy band" could penetrate immoral souls and convince them of the danger of personal damnation if they did not change. Revivalism became the path to national Holiness.[58]

[57] William G. McLoughlin (ed.), *Lectures on Revivals of Religion by Charles Grandison Finney* (Cambridge, Mass.: The Belknap Press, 1960), pp. xxviii–xxix.

[58] Robert Samuel Fletcher, *A History of Oberlin College: From Its Foundation Through the Civil War* (Oberlin: Oberlin College, 1943), I, 16, 89–90, 223; Gilbert Hobbs Barnes, *The Antislavery Impulse, 1830–1844* (New York: Harcourt, Brace & World, Inc., 1964), pp. 9–12; Asa Mahan, *Scripture Doctrine of Christian Perfection; with other Kindred Subjects, Illustrated and Confirmed in a Series of Discourses designed to Throw Light on the Way of Holiness* (Boston: D. S. King, 1840), pp. 8–9, 13, 41, 162; Thomas,

Charles Finney and his followers believed that their success in western New York proved the efficacy of persistent and wide-spread revivals. Many sinners had repented of their evil ways, strived to conform to God's law, and sought to retain their con-versions through Christian benevolence. But the Lord needed a great new task force—a vast supply of evangelists dedicated to Finneyite theology and revivalist methodology—to extend His sway beyond New York's burned-over district into the sinful valley of the Mississippi. This valley was the key to America's "Rising Glory"—the testing ground for any crusade for national Holiness. Finneyites acknowledged that Jean Frédéric Oberlin had sacrificed his worldly career to carry the Lord's ways to a barren and neglected part of Alsace. An institute founded in his name could train ministers to carry the Lord's ways into the barren, ungodly valley of the West, and hasten the day when Christian perfection would come to the New Nation. From America it would spread to "cheer our benighted world" and ultimately bring on the mil-lennium.[59]

Several young men from Ohio, western New York, and New England were impressed by the doctrines of Finneyites and wanted to join the evangelical invasion of the valley of the Missis-sippi. They were lawyers, farmers, teachers, students, and even businessmen. Abandoning their work, they saw the new Oberlin Collegiate Institute as an attractive training ground. The prospect of four years in a traditional theological seminary was far worse. The standard Northeastern colleges and seminaries were costly and seemed deficient in piety and morality. By taking the theological course at Oberlin, they could pay for their expenses through the Institute's manual-labor program, have more exposure to Gospel Truths, and graduate to join the Lord's ministry in almost half the usual time.[60] Thus, Oberlin offered hope for young men (espe-

---

The Liberator, pp. 228–29; Charles C. Cole, Jr. *The Social Ideas of Northern Evangelists, 1826–1860* (New York: Columbia University Press, 1954), pp. 61–68.

[59] Fletcher, *Oberlin College*, I, 119, 205, 210; James H. Fairchild, *Oberlin: The Colony and the College. 1833–1883* (Oberlin: E. J. Goodrich, 1883), pp. 18–19; *Ohio Observer*, April 9, 1835; *Oberlin Evangelist*, June 22, 1842; McLoughlin (ed.), *Lectures on Revivals*, pp. xli–xlii.

[60] Fletcher, *Oberlin College*, I, 34–35.

cially those with deficient finances) who were impressed by the
Finneyites and who wanted ministerial careers. At the same time, it
provided a means of training a large supply of men in Finney's
"new measures" without the traditional Calvinist emphasis of older
Eastern seminaries. If the school succeeded, the "savory influence
of the Gospel" was certain to cleanse the West of "moral putrefac-
tion" and ultimately save the nation and the world.

In 1841 Finney directed Oberlin's faculty and students: "We are
to regard all moral beings as our neighbors, in whatever world
they may exist." The Lord recognized no national boundaries.[61]
This was consistent with the concept of universalized humanity
that permeated Finneyite theology. *All* peoples could bring on
their own regeneration; *all* could live the strenuous life of Christian benevolence. Salvation was not monopolized by the Elect of
any society or nation. Finney seemed to be departing from a tenet
propounded by Andrew Judson's Canterbury following, and contradicting a basic assumption of early American patriotic thought.
For patriots like Judson, Noah Webster, Sarah Hale, and R. R.
Gurley, Americans were God's chosen people and lived within the
Promised Land. Finney and his Oberlin following seemed to
contradict this vision by characterizing America as a sinful nation.
They chastised their country's self-seeking materialistic ways and
noted how "liberty-loving America" repressed its black population
and deprived its women of basic rights. In view of these ills,
Oberlinites concluded, the nation's sacred July Fourth celebration
was a "cruel mockery" and hardly worth observing.[62]

Despite these unorthodox ideas, Finney and his Oberlin following never departed from the most fundamental premises of patriotic thought in the New Nation. Although they de-emphasized the
concept of an Elect—a specially chosen people—they were primarily concerned with bringing the ways of the Lord to the

---

[61] *Oberlin Evangelist*, March 3, 1841.

[62] See, e.g., Fletcher, *Oberlin College*, I, 232, 249; Clayton Sumner Ells-
worth, "Oberlin and the Anti-Slavery Movement up to the Civil War"
(Ph.D. dissertation, Cornell University, 1930), p. 33; Frances Juliette Hos-
ford, *Father Shipherd's Magna Carta: A Century of Coeducation in Oberlin
College* (Boston: Marshall Jones Company, 1937), p. 66; *Oberlin Evangelist*,
February 13, November 6, 1839; February 3, June 9, October 27, 1841.

American heartland. During the Jacksonian decades, they never formulated systematic plans to spread Finney's "new measures" to foreign parts; only Americans were offered any chance at Holiness. And despite their scathing indictments of the nation for its self-seeking sins, early Oberlinites shared a deep faith in "the Rising Glory of America." The principles of the Declaration of Independence and the Federal Constitution were sound and compatible with "the great principles of the law of God." Obedience to these national principles could help to bring about conversion and a life devoted to Christ.[63] Moreover, the Lord approved of the democratic institutions that derived from American principles. Therefore, the New Nation provided the most fertile soil for the birth of Finney's Christian millennium. Like most other Oberlinites, Finney was certain that the entire American population would be converted to Holiness and that this would start the millennium of God's Kingdom on Earth.[64]

The task at hand was to implement the nation's principles and to stimulate its democratic institutions; the millennium would inevitably follow. Oberlinites were frequently optimistic. When a Connecticut federal court and the United States Supreme Court issued decrees antagonistic to slavery, for example, the *Oberlin Evangelist* characterized the American judiciary as a prime agency for salvation: "In that branch of the government lies our safety." When the Whigs rejected the slaveholding Colonization Society leader Henry Clay for their 1840 Presidential nomination, the *Evangelist* perceived Holiness emerging, a "practiced recognition of the principles of the Declaration of Independence," and great hope for the future of the Promised Land.[65] And when President

[63] *Oberlin Evangelist*, July 17, 1839; May 20, July 29, 1840; August 17, 1842; Fletcher, *Oberlin College*, I, 250.

[64] William G. McLoughlin, Jr., *Modern Revivalism: Charles Grandison Finney to Billy Graham* (New York: The Ronald Press Company, 1959), pp. 105–06; McLoughlin (ed.), *Lectures on Revivals*, pp. xli–xlii; Gilbert H. Barnes and Dwight L. Dumond (eds.), *Letters of Theodore Weld, Angelina Grimké Weld, and Sarah Grimké* (New York: D. Appleton-Century Company, 1934), I, 318–19.

[65] The *Oberlin Evangelist*, April 28, 1841, commented on the court decrees. The *Evangelist* for January 1, 1840, remarked on the Whig rejection of Henry Clay.

William Henry Harrison's death was followed by a national fast, Oberlinites found confirmation of their belief that the nation was committed to the Lord. If a country could repent for its sins, salvation was close at hand. On other occasions, Oberlinites persistently referred to "our national honor," "this great people," and America's "high standing in the moral world."[66]

If Oberlinites were not as singularly patriotic as Noah Webster, Sarah Hale, and Andrew Judson—if they seemed mildly concerned with other peoples of "the World"—they were firmly committed to "the Rising Glory of America." Much of their rhetoric had a universal tone and this must not be discounted. They joined Finney to stress that all peoples could seek out Christ and accomplish conversion. Moreover, the Finneyite premise that a converting experience had to be sustained by a life of benevolence made Oberlinites more reform-minded than most patriots. Finney's criticism of American materialism and bigotry made them more tolerant and less self-seeking. But along with their commitment to Finney's universalist tone and to Finney's abhorrence of the dominant ways of American culture, Oberlinites were staunchly patriotic. They believed in the Holiness of the nation's founding principles and democratic institutions, and they were certain that America would lead the world into the Christian millennium. More explicitly, Oberlinites were torn between a theological commitment to the peoples of "the World" and a patriotic commitment to Americans as the chosen people.

Despite the patriotic leanings of Oberlinites, many devout patriots perceived the school as a subversive experiment. Critics pointed out that as a coeducational institution Oberlin gave women a false notion of their proper station in life—that the school turned females away from the imperatives of True American Womanhood. Oberlin's first publicity circular contributed to this impression. Solid female education alongside male students was listed as one of the school's primary purposes: "the elevation of female character, by bringing within the reach of the misjudged and neglected sex, all the instructive privileges which hitherto have

[66] The *Oberlin Evangelist*, May 26, 1841, notes Oberlinite reaction to the national fast. For examples of spread-eagle rhetoric at early Oberlin, see, e.g., *Oberlin Evangelist*, April 10, September 25, 1839; April 28, 1841.

unreasonably distinguished the leading sex from theirs."[67] At long last women were to get the same training as men—or so it seemed.

During Oberlin's first decade, 37 percent of the students were females. They were among the first in the nation to share classrooms with the "leading sex." In 1841 the Institute conferred the first three arts degrees that American women had ever received. College education for women on this scale was compatible with an earlier innovation of Finney's in western New York. As a basic part of the "new measures," Finney and his followers had encouraged women to pray alongside men in religious services.[68] In the revival meeting, both sexes were urged to come together to subject their hearts and wills to the inner promptings of the Holy Spirit. They were urged to continue this coeducational allegiance to the Spirit in *all* areas of life. The collegiate training ground was not excluded.

Therefore, the coeducation experiment at Oberlin seemed to stand for a consistent Finneyite break from the ideal of True American Womanhood; all were equal before the Lord. The sexual goals of Mary Wollstonecraft and Charles Brockden Brown seemed to be realized. But if coeducation at Oberlin departed from the pervasive notion of patriotic woman's place, the difference was not substantial. As in the nation at large, governance at Oberlin rested in male hands. Between 1833 and 1836 all matters of importance were resolved by the adult male Oberlinites in open mass meeting. In 1837 a seven-member Board of Directors assumed this function. Elected by a vote of the colony's adult males, directorships were restricted to adult males. No women belonged to the Oberlin faculty. The slight governing power wives of faculty and trustees exercised was restricted to the Ladies' Board of Managers of the school's Female Department. The principal of the Female Department was explicitly excluded from the faculty and the

[67] Quoted in Robert S. Fletcher and Ernest H. Wilkins, "The Beginning of College Education for Women and of Coeducation on the College Level," *Bulletin of Oberlin College*, New Ser. 343 (March 20, 1937), p. 3.

[68] The sexually innovative nature of the Oberlin experiment is noted in Fletcher, *Oberlin College*, I, 376; Fairchild, *Oberlin: Colony and College*, p. 176; Arthur W. Calhoun, *A Social History of the American Family* (Cleveland: Arthur H. Clark Company, 1918), II, 113. Cole, Jr., *Social Ideas of Northern Evangelists*, p. 61, comments on the specific Finneyite innovation of the sexes praying together.

Board of Directors. Moreover, women were not permitted to speak at any public or semipublic gathering—not even at their own commencements. Behind this ban lay a broad condemnation of female participation in any public affairs. During the first four years of instruction, no women were admitted into the regular course in the Collegiate Department. Until this ban was removed, none could matriculate. And though the primary purpose of the Oberlin Institute was to train ministers, women were refused admission as regular students in the Theological Department. The female student's role was more domestic than academic or theological. She was assigned to cook, clean, wash, and mend for the entire college community and to wait on tables at the commons. This was part of the special "Ladies' Course" in "domestic economy." Reducing maintenance costs at the revenue-starved college, coeducation along these lines had strong economic advantages.[69]

However, Oberlinites were mainly committed to coeducation from non-economic considerations. Men like President Asa Mahan and John Jay Shipherd were determined to train ministers in Finney's "new measures" so that they could carry the "savory influence of the Gospel" into the Mississippi Valley. For the Oberlinite minister to perform properly, the minimal education requirements of the Baptist and Methodist clergy would not do; systematic training was required to master the "new measures" in the heart as well as in the mind. The Roman Catholic model of permanent celibacy was also ruled out for the Oberlinite minister-in-training. Finney noted how his own wife had stabilized his life and he stressed how she helped him to ward off sin: "An unmarried minister is a peculiar temptation to the other sex."[70] Some-

---

[69] Fletcher, *Mississippi Valley Historical Review*, XX, No. 2 (September 1933), 185; Hosford, *Father Shipherd*, pp. 25–27; Fletcher, *Oberlin College*, I, 269, 290, 292–93; II, 612, 636–40; Keith E. Melder, "The Beginnings of the Women's Rights Movement in the United States, 1800–1840" (Ph.D. dissertation, Yale University, 1963), p. 116; Alice Stone Blackwell, *Lucy Stone: Pioneer of Woman's Rights* (Norwood, Mass.: Alice Stone Blackwell Committee, 1930), p. 57; Fletcher and Wilkins, *Bulletin of Oberlin College*, New Ser. 343 (March 20, 1937), pp. 3–6; Fletcher, "Oberlin and Co-Education," *Ohio State Archaeological and Historical Quarterly*, XLVII, No. 1 (January 1938), 2–3.

[70] *Oberlin Evangelist*, January 5, 1848; Ronald W. Hogeland, "'The Female Appendage': Feminine Life-Styles in America, 1820–1860," *Civil War History*, XVII, No. 2 (June 1971), 111; Robert S. Fletcher, "The Pastoral

how the Institute had to give its young ministers-in-training an education under the celibate conditions required for thorough mental, moral, and religious training and then quickly find these young men suitable, devoted wives in the short interval between graduation and assignment to a specific pastorate. By introducing coeducation, prohibiting marriage before graduation, and training female students in "domestic economy," Oberlin administrators sought to promote all of the future minister's needs. A young woman who knew how to maintain a household and who had been schooled to revere the "new measures" pastorate would become available to the Oberlin theology graduate immediately after commencement but just before he was assigned to a congregation. Woman's role at early Oberlin could hardly have been more malleable. It seemed explicitly designed to serve male needs.[71] Alumnus Lucy Stone noted that she had felt like a "female appendage" during her Oberlin years.[72]

The president of Oberlin, Asa Mahan, wrote the most extensive justification of the coeducation experiment. By bringing the sexes together, he explained, "all disposition to mischief and disorder among the students" was precluded. Students regularly saw each other in their proper social roles—the women cooking, cleaning, and praying, the men studying and imbibing the spirit of the Lord. There was "unconsciously to all concerned, as it is in families and in the community generally, an all-constraining incentive to diligence in study, purity of thought and conversation, and general propriety of behavior everywhere." The pure, mature, accepted roles of the adult community became part and parcel of the student's life, Mahan concluded. Oberlin women learned that their chief duty was to serve the needs of God's agents-in-training while

---

Theology of Charles G. Finney," *Proceedings of the Ohio Presbyterian Historical Society*, III (June 1941), 30.

[71] The most cogent and well-documented discussion of these sexual aims at early Oberlin is found in Ronald W. Hogeland, "Co-Education of the Sexes at Oberlin College: A Study of Social Ideas in Mid-Nineteenth Century America," *Journal of Social History*, VI, No. 2 (Winter 1972–73), 160–76. See also Fletcher, *Oberlin College*, I, 291. Judging from the long list of wedding announcements that appeared in the *Oberlin Evangelist* after every commencement, the college was effective in regulating the timing of most marriages.

[72] *Woman's Journal*, XVII (May 1, 1886), 140.

male students learned to honor this display of female propriety.[73] Most of the Oberlin faculty agreed with Mahan. In March of 1836 they resolved that the school's coeducation experiment was "correcting the irregularities, frivolities & follies common to youth." Students of both sexes were learning the roles that God had assigned to them. If the experiment was abolished, "unparalleled and most disgusting licentiousness" would result. Therefore, the order of the Oberlin community demanded its continuance.[74]

The rationale for enrolling women at Oberlin was thus quite compatible with the primary aim of the Institute—training a Finneyite ministry to extend the Lord's sway over the sinful West. While they were in training, Christ's young agents would learn how to behave before the other sex. And when they left Oberlin for their pastorates, they would depart with pious young wives schooled in the domestic arts and pledged to support their husbands in propagating the "new measures." The Finneyite experiment in coeducation was also compatible with the patriotic assumption that the True American Woman was duty-bound to become pliable and meet the specific needs of her husband. Finally, the coeducation venture seemed to sustain the patriotic doctrine that the schoolhouse could produce stability, uniformity, and cohesion to counter the increasing chaos and dislocation of early Jacksonian society. Immoral student intrigues and other disruptive propensities of youth were curbed; pervasive sexual and social roles that were basic to community stability were perpetuated.

Thus the basis for Oberlinite conceptions of woman's place and America's national role overlapped. Like distinctions among nations, sexual distinctions contradicted the Finneyite de-emphasis of the Calvinist Elect. Because all people could bring about and sustain their own conversions, all were equal before the Lord. As it

---

[73] Asa Mahan, *Autobiography Intellectual, Moral, and Spiritual* (London: T. Woolmer, 1882), pp. 266–70.

[74] Quoted in Fletcher, *Oberlin College*, I, 377. See also Fletcher, "The First Coeds," *American Scholar*, VII, No. 1 (Winter 1938), 80. It is noteworthy that this rationale for coeducation persisted for years. On June 7, 1854, for example, an article in the *Oberlin Evangelist* justified male and female students on the same campus: "We take it the golden mean lies in so shaping the association of young gentlemen with young ladies as to make its general tone elevated and pure; the topics of conversation solid, not vapid; more sensible than sentimental."

was immoral to castigate foreign peoples, it was wrong to deprive women of formal education. But for all of their allegiance to Finneyite theology, Finney and other leading Oberlinites had a second commitment. The ways of the Lord had to be served, but the ways of the New Nation had to be obeyed as well. All people were equal in the sense that all could find Holiness, but Americans were the chosen people and American women were duty-bound to serve men.[75]

To some extent, Finney's Oberlin resembled Judson's Canterbury. Leaders in both communities subscribed to basic patriotic tenets, particularly the ideal of True American Womanhood. From a racial perspective, however, early Oberlin seemed fundamentally different from Judson's Canterbury. Finney's Institute admitted black students and permitted them to be educated alongside whites. Even Prudence Crandall had stopped short of racial integration; she had transformed her school from an all-white institution to a refuge for black girls. In a Jacksonian North plagued by nightmares of amalgamation and captivated by visions of the schoolhouse as the key to the future, integrated education was abhorrent. All-white schools were needed as stabilizing institutions. All-black schools were undesirable but tolerable when removed from white population centers. However, the racially and sexually integrated school stood to promote a disastrous national future—an American populace that was neither white nor black.[76]

At first Oberlinites had mixed feelings regarding the admission of Negro students. John Jay Shipherd, a founder of the Institute, represented a minority faction on campus in 1834 when he campaigned to terminate Oberlin's white-only policy. Although Shipherd charged that Negro admissions did not mean intermarriage or

[75] In an important paper delivered at the 1972 Annual Meeting of the American Historical Association, "Evangelical Protestantism and Its Influence on Women in North America, 1790–1860," Jill K. Conway presented a strong case for the very conservative ideological, social, and sexual impact of the general evangelical Protestant movement for Christian Perfection that had sparked the founding of Oberlin and had promoted other social developments.

[76] Leon F. Litwack, *North of Slavery: The Negro in the Free States 1790–1860* (Chicago: Phoenix Books, 1965), pp. 113–52. Litwack provides a very comprehensive discussion of Northern racial attitudes and their impact upon the schoolhouse during the antebellum decades.

even social contact between the races, most of Oberlin's trustees were unwilling to depart from the admissions policy of "similar institutions of our land." Late in December of 1834 a questionnaire was circulated to determine student opinion; most students who responded opposed Negro admissions. The prevailing opinion was that "the place would be at once overwhelmed with colored students, and the mischiefs that would follow were frightful in the extreme." "Why not have a black Institution, Dyed in the wool— and let Oberlin be?" a financial agent for the Institute queried.[77] But in the next several weeks special considerations shifted the balance on the admissions question to the Shipherd minority. At the end of 1834 many of Oberlin's old debts remained unpaid, no funds were available for new buildings or equipment, the teaching staff was much too small, and the school had no president. Only a year after instruction began, the Institute was on the verge of collapse. Noting the school's financial ills, Shipherd proved to be resourceful in his campaign for the admission of blacks. The trustees of Cincinnati's Lane Theological Seminary had clamped down on abolitionist students by outlawing public discussion of slavery. Lane's student "rebels" were supported by a minority trustee, Asa Mahan, and by a dissident faculty member, John Morgan. Shipherd urged the group to come to Oberlin, the "rebels" as students, Morgan as professor, and Mahan as president. The group was receptive. However, they stipulated that Oberlin's trustees had to guarantee the "rebels" freedom to campaign against slavery and they insisted that the Oberlin campus be open to blacks. After meeting with this group, Shipherd approached Charles Finney and offered him a position at the Institute. Then he turned to the Oberlin trustees and made them a proposal. If they dropped the color line as the Lane "rebels" demanded and Finney wished, the great Minister for the Lord would join the Oberlin community as professor of theology, Mahan would come as president, Morgan and the "rebels" would come as well, and wealthy New York abolitionist Arthur Tappan would promise

[77] Trustee and student opinion on Negro admissions is noted in Ellsworth, "Oberlin and Anti-Slavery," pp. 17–18; Fletcher, *Oberlin College*, I, 170–71; J. H. Fairchild, "A Sketch of the Anti-Slavery History of Oberlin," *Oberlin Evangelist*, XVIII, Whole No. 457 (July 16, 1856), 114. Fletcher, *Oberlin College*, II, 523, quotes the Oberlin financial agent.

significant new funding. With money, a president, and particularly the chance to draw Finney, the Oberlin trustees opened the school's doors to black students by a five-to-four vote. Head trustee John Keep cast the deciding vote, explaining that Finney would never "congregate such a mass of negroes at Oberlin as to darken the whole atmosphere." Shortly after the vote, the son of another trustee saw a Negro walking into town. He ran home alarmed: "They're coming, father—they're coming!"[78]

The closeness of the trustees' vote, despite the attractiveness of the Shipherd offer, pointed to the racist sentiment in the early Oberlin community. To keep the Institute white, four of nine trustees were willing to rebuff Charles Finney in a school pledged to the spread of Finneyite theology. They were even willing to have Oberlin destroyed for lack of funding rather than let blacks into the Holy Community. But John Keep's apprehensions that Oberlin might be "dangerously darkened" were dispelled. Very few blacks sought to enter the school after the color line was lifted. In the 1840's and 1850's Negro enrollments increased, but they were never more than 4 or 5 percent of the entire student body. Blacks seemed as suspicious of Oberlin as many Oberlinites were suspicious of blacks.[79]

Dedication to the colonization ideal may account for much of the resistance to black admissions. Although evidence regarding racial attitudes is thin for the first years of classes, it indicates that the overwhelming number of students and faculty initially supported the Colonization Society and its plan to repatriate blacks in Africa. But their support for the A.C.S. was short-lived. By the

---

[78] Fletcher, *Oberlin College*, I, 167, 175–78; Charles G. Finney to George Whipple and Henry B. Stanton, January 18, 1835; John Keep to Charles G. Finney, March 10, 1835; Charles G. Finney to Board of Trustees of the Oberlin Collegiate Institute, June 30, 1835—all in the Charles G. Finney Papers, Oberlin College; Finney, *Memoirs*, pp. 333–34; Fairchild, *Oberlin: Colony and College*, pp. 55, 255; Fairchild, *Oberlin: Origin, Progress, Results*, pp. 21, 24; Barnes, *Antislavery Impulse*, pp. 75–76.

[79] Frank U. Quillin, *The Color Line in Ohio: A History of Race Prejudice in a Typical Northern State* (reprint. New York: Negro Universities Press, 1969), p. 47; Fairchild, *Oberlin: Colony and College*, p. 111; Litwack, *North of Slavery*, pp. 140–41; Geoffrey Blodgett, "John Mercer Langston and the Case of Edmonia Lewis: Oberlin, 1862," *Journal of Negro History*, LIII, No. 3 (July 1968), 202; Benjamin Quarles, *Black Abolitionists* (New York: Oxford University Press, 1969), p. 114.

late 1830's and early 1840's the organization had fallen into general disrepute because it had not repatriated enough blacks. Disenchanted with the A.C.S. because of its inefficiencies but not its goals, Oberlinites strongly supported James Birney's political-action faction of the abolitionist movement and wanted Birney to join the faculty. But while they repudiated the Colonization Society, many Oberlinites retained a faith that Negro repatriation could remedy domestic racial tensions. In this sense, they resembled most significant abolitionists—Birney included. As they became increasingly attracted to the abolitionist crusade, many never shed the colonization ideal of a white nation free of racial ills.[80]

Although the ideological legacy of colonization probably accounts for some of the opposition to black admissions and may help to explain why the number of black students remained small, the role of Charles Finney was even more central to the racial milieu of early Oberlin. In large measure, the sentiment against black admissions on the Board of Trustees and within the student body was reversed because Finney refused to join the faculty if the color line persisted. The egalitarian thrust of his "new measures" prompted his insistence upon black educational opportunity. All of God's creatures could repent of their sins, give up the self-seeking ways of the world, and discover Holiness. In this sense, the slave was the equal of the master and blacks were the equal of whites. Finney also argued that the spirit of benevolence required Christ's flock to labor to abolish slavery and to promote civil rights. But though he had been induced by the logic of his own theology to press against Oberlin's ban on black students and to allow the Institute to become a major stop on the underground railroad, his theological commitment also accounted for the limited nature of Oberlin's racial experiment. Perceiving the accelerating violence of anti-abolitionist mobs during the middle 1830's, the divisive conflicts among antislavery forces, and even the racial debate within the Oberlin community, Finney lost some of his ardor for social reform. Men's hearts had to be purged of sin through massive revivalism before antislavery or any reform cause

[80] Fletcher, *Oberlin College*, I, 194; II, 705; Ellsworth, "Oberlin and Anti-Slavery," p. 11; Fairchild, *Oberlin: Colony and College*, p. 110; *Oberlin Evangelist*, February 16, 1842; September 13, 1843; July 16, 1856.

could succeed. With this frame of mind, Finney cracked down on the Lane "rebels," the most militant civil-rights force on campus. In 1836 he conferred with the group. They were wasting their time at Oberlin if they planned to become full-time abolitionists after graduation, he explained. Widespread revivals, not abrasive abolitionist campaigns, were the way to promote Holiness and national salvation. Therefore, they must train to join the Lord's evangelical ministry or move on.[81] Finney also criticized the "rebels" and other abolitionists for linking racial amalgamation to antislavery agitation. "You err in supposing that the principles of Abolition and Amalgamation are identical," he told Arthur Tappan. "A man may certainly from *constitutional taste* feel unwilling to mar[r]y a colored woman or have a daughter mar[r]y a colored man and yet be a devoted friend of the colored people." Abolitionists should realize that racial mixture was wrong and that no "wicked prejudice" was involved in racial segregation. This was Finney's justification for instituting segregated seating during his pastorate at the Chatham Street Chapel in New York, for trying to keep Negroes off the platform at antislavery rallies, and for seeking to segregate student seating at Oberlin. The most influential man in the Oberlin community was a long-standing proponent of separation of the races to avoid conflict and racial "contamination."[82]

Thus, Finney's "new measures" committed him to broadened black educational opportunities and abhorrence of slavery. But this same theological allegiance turned him against the Lane "rebels" and other abolitionists, and for segregation. On the deepest level, Finney seemed to be torn between a theologically based commitment to racial equality and a visceral repugnance of interracial association. As he was the dominant figure at Oberlin, his own

[81] McLoughlin, *Modern Revivalism*, pp. 101, 107–12; Gilbert H. Barnes and Dwight L. Dumond (eds.), *Letters of Theodore Dwight Weld, Angelina Grimké Weld and Sarah Grimké, 1822–1844* (New York, London: D. Appleton-Century Company, 1934), I, 317, 318, 327–28; Fletcher, *Oberlin College*, I, 179–80, 252.

[82] Charles G. Finney to Arthur Tappan, April 30, 1836; C. Stuart to Charles G. Finney, August 19, 1836—both in the Charles G. Finney Papers, Oberlin College; McLoughlin, *Modern Revivalism*, p. 110; Leon F. Litwack, "The Abolitionist Dilemma: The Antislavery Movement and the Northern Negro," *New England Quarterly*, XXXIV, No. 1 (March 1961), 55; McLoughlin (ed.), *Lectures on Revivals*, p. xliv.

ambivalence must have contributed to the racial inconsistencies of the community. On the one hand, Oberlin was one of the first integrated colleges in the nation. On the other hand, there was only token integration, Oberlinites refused to consider Negroes for faculty positions, the trustees debated removing black students from the school's boardinghouse, and a white student wrote reassuringly to her parents that "we don't have to kiss the Niggars nor to speak to them."[83]

The way leading Oberlinites dealt with racial issues resembled the way they responded to coeducation and to the nation's destiny. Allegiance to the "new measures" caused Oberlinites to espouse unorthodox postures—concern for people regardless of their nationality, gender, or race. They condemned the self-seeking materialism of the New Nation and became one of the first college communities to admit women and blacks. At the same time, the campus was receptive to basic tenets of early American patriotic thought, particularly the notion of True American Womanhood and the colonization ideal. Finney's Oberlin differed sharply from Judson's Canterbury, but not in every important essential.

IV

Broad comparisons between these two communities as they tackled the dilemmas of the schoolhouse in the Age of Jackson are revealing. The quest for rootedness—for a vague, amorphous, and highly subjective sense of anchored stability—was more conspicuous in Judson's Canterbury. Canterburians had initially sought a girl's school to restore a sense of order and place in their community—to anchor their homeland. Although their quest for rootedness was less conspicuous, Oberlinites were also intent upon fortifying community bonds and stabilizing village life. They organized their settlement around the Oberlin Covenant, and it required all inhabitants to pledge "a perfect community of interest

---

[83] Fletcher, *Oberlin College*, II, 527, discusses the issue of Negro faculty appointments. The *Ohio Observer*, April 9, 1835, notes details regarding trustee plans to remove blacks from the boardinghouse. For evidence of racial paternalism at Oberlin, see the *Oberlin Evangelist*, February 13, 1839; August 17, 1842. Litwack, *North of Slavery*, p. 140, quotes the coed's letter to her parents.

as though we held a community of property" and to subordinate personal interests to the order, stability, and well-being of the Holy Settlement.[84] Strivings for "Rising Glory" were obviously more intense at Oberlin, with its Finneyite commitment to Christian perfection (Holiness). Persistent, disinterested, benevolent Christian striving sustained personal Holiness; it would culminate in national salvation and ultimately in a universal millennium. Perfectionist strivings in Judson's Canterbury were more secular and less overt. Whereas Oberlinites struggled to create a flawless society of the future, Judson and his supporters followed the pattern of many Washington eulogists and national Colonization Society activists by looking to the past. When they urged Prudence Crandall to come to Canterbury, they held a shared if vague and nostalgic vision of a perfect social order—an organized, friendly, predictable, and wholesome *pre-Jacksonian* community. In time Judson and his followers nearly came to perceive the Crandall school as a barrier, the removal of which would restore their idyllic old order.[85]

Thus, the two basic and fundamentally incompatible elements in early American patriotism—the quest for perfection and the need for a sense of rooted stability—were evident in both Canterbury and Oberlin. Strivings for perfection had to diminish the stable ground of daily existence; stable, rooted existence hindered perfectionist strivings. A gain in one sphere was a loss in the other. Like several *Columbian* contributors, Washington eulogists, proponents of True Womanhood, and A.C.S. activists, leading Canterburians and Oberlinites failed to comprehend this basic fact.

Most of the seeming safety valves or cure-alls that other patriots had employed to ease or remove the conflict between perfectionist striving and rootedness (to resolve the unresolvable) were also invoked in the two communities. Canterburians perceived True American Womanhood as a panacea. They contended that their problems would be solved if Prudence Crandall stopped her belligerence and deferred to their demands as pliable patriotic

[84] Fletcher, *Oberlin College*, I, 110–11.
[85] This vision of recapturing a simple, orderly, and stable Old Republic community corresponded strikingly with the vision Marvin Meyers attributes to Jacksonians generally in his sensitive study *The Jacksonian Persuasion: Politics and Belief* (Stanford: Stanford University Press, 1957).

womanhood must. Oberlinites infused the concept of True Womanhood into the everyday operations of their Institute; female students cooked and cleaned for their diplomas and they married newly trained Finneyite ministers after graduation. Residents of both communities also perceived Negro repatriation as a cure-all. Judson and his Canterbury following firmly supported the A.C.S. and the notion that America is "the white man's country, and the white man is an American citizen." Opposing Judson, abolitionists like May and Garrison never quite departed from this colonization ideal of Negro removal. Nor did the Finneyites at Oberlin. The initial popularity of the A.C.S. on campus, the controversy over Negro admissions, and Finney's own segregationist inclinations all pointed toward the survival of the colonizationist ideological legacy. Like the reliance upon True Womanhood, commitments to the colonizationist racial approach fostered controversies in both Canterbury and Oberlin. Instead of solving problems and restoring order, the panaceas of True Womanhood and Negro removal limited the roles of women and Negroes, and even heightened tensions between white men. Indeed, feelings of instability intensified in both communities.

Canterburians and Oberlinites saw relief in another apparent safety valve—one that had not come into wide use before the early Jacksonian decades and the rise of mass education. Leaders in both communities clung to the hope that a properly organized schoolhouse could cure all ills, restore order to disintegrating community life, and assure a flawless "Rising Glory of America." But such a schoolhouse was no more than an empty abstraction and efforts to impose it upon Canterbury and Oberlin provoked both conflicts and insecurities. Judson's followers, like Finney's, held rigid and uncompromising opinions of what the schoolhouse was to achieve, and almost everything in conflict with their goals was subject to attack. Consequently, possibilities for diversified and wide-ranging educational experiences were curtailed in both communities.

Thus, most of the essential ingredients in the patriotic crusade for the Promised Land surfaced in Canterbury and in Oberlin, although in different degrees and under different conditions. The abstraction of interpersonal relationships, the intensification of tensions and conflicts, and the enlargement of feelings of instability in two very different communities were the result. This is not to say that perfectionism and the need for rootedness, plus the apparent remedies of female malleability, black repatriation, and the order-rendering schoolhouse, always merged together. To the contrary, they were usually disconnected. Since the founding of the *Columbian Magazine,* many patriots had felt the uprooting consequences of their perfectionist strivings. However, most had focused upon only one apparent panacea at a time to cure the incurable.

But the Canterbury and Oberlin examples indicated that the early Jacksonian schoolhouse—the road to the future—could draw together most of the diverse and disconnected ingredients in the patriotic crusade for the Promised Land. In a Jacksonian America where social classes, established churches, traditional family structures, and other long-standing institutions of authority were weakening before an intensifying competitive mobility, patriots were more apprehensive about the future than ever before. Would the future bring a firmer sense of place—a rooted order? What would be the roles of blacks and women? Would a pure white man's country emerge? Would the Promised Land be perfected? These and other questions were raised in Canterbury and in Oberlin. And all questions centered on the role of the schoolhouse, one of the few new institutions of social control to develop in an increasingly voluntaristic, *laissez-faire* Jacksonian nation where patriots seemed to crave order, control, and suppression of diversity more than ever before.

The fact that the same basic questions could be raised in two very different communities—Judson's prosperous, well-established Eastern town and Finney's financially pinched Holy Settlement in the Western wilds—demonstrated the pervasiveness of patriotic thought in the New Nation. Basic elements of an early American patriotic crusade were detectable in a town that deployed narrowly nationalistic slogans to justify the expulsion of black female students and the humiliation of an independent white schoolmistress. The same elements surfaced in a community that opened itself to black and female students, and dedicated itself to the salvation of all peoples of "the World." Developing over the prior forty years, several ingredients of early American patriotic thought seemed to converge during the 1830's in the context of the schoolhouse and under the unifying concept of white male nationhood. The converging was possible because the essential ingredients in patriotic thought—"the Rising Glory of America," the flawless Founding Father, True American Womanhood, black removal, and the patriotic schoolhouse—all made intellectual abstractions out of interpersonal relations, promoted uniformity, and discouraged experimentation with life's rich diversities. The essential elements in the patriotic crusade for the Promised Land could come together under the most repressive of all abstractions—white male nationhood—because all elements shared fundamental qualities. All promoted depersonalization and uniformity over concrete, personalized, and diversified human relationships.

By the late 1830's and early 1840's, men like John L. O'Sullivan, Moses Yale Beach, and James K. Polk came into prominence by blatantly proclaiming that the Promised Land was the white male nation. According to these influential Manifest Destiny expansionists, it was the duty of strong, aggressive white male Americans to regulate the lesser and often effeminate dark-skinned peoples of the world. They drew upon a devoutly patriotic ideological tradition that had been evident since the day the *Columbian Magazine* commenced publication in 1786. The tradition had been embellished by Washington eulogists, True Womanhood theorists, and proponents of the colonization ideal. By the time of the Canterbury controversy and the founding of Oberlin College, the elements within this ideological tradition seemed to be merging. The ideas of patriotic crusaders from David Ramsay to Andrew Judson seemed to be unifying under the proclamation that the Promised Land was "the white man's country, and the white man is an American citizen." O'Sullivan, Beach, and Polk simply incorporated this slogan and the assumptions upon which it was based. They called it Manifest Destiny, and they used it to justify territorial acquisitions through negotiation, intimidation, and military intervention.

But as spread-eagle patriots of the 1840's added Texas, much of the Oregon Country, and the Mexican cession to the Promised Land with the hope of effecting "the Rising Glory of America," one wonders whether they were doing more than synthesizing old ideas. One wonders whether they were deploying still another apparent panacea to resolve the unresolvable—perfection and rootedness. There is cause to suspect that the call for territorial expansion during the 1840's—Manifest Destiny—was invoked for some of the same underlying reasons for which patriotic panaceas had always been invoked. After all, the history of spread-eagle patriotic thought in the New Nation had been marked by recourse to one new cure-all or safety valve after another. It was a history characterized by a groping toward new slogans and tactics, each of which promised an American paradise and left patriots more discontented and uprooted than before. But they never seemed to learn from their mistakes. From the founding of the *Columbian Magazine* to the education controversies at Canterbury and Oberlin, patriots usually found it easier to grasp for new cure-alls than to examine the condition which required cure-alls. It is unlikely that this practice ceased in the 1840's or that O'Sullivan, Beach, and Polk differed, in this respect, from Ramsay, Webster, Weems, Gurley, Judson, or Finney. The search for "Rising Glory" may have represented an endless crusade.

APPENDICES

A NOTE ON TOCQUEVILLE'S "TYRANNY OF THE MAJORITY"

There was no vigorous, effective, or even noticeable tradition of dissent against spread-eagle patriotism in the New Nation. Not a single critic of *le patriotisme irritable* appeared in the pages of the *Columbian Magazine*, the country's first important literary journal. Over three hundred and forty separate eulogies on the death of George Washington were written and/or delivered between December 14, 1799, and February 22, 1800. None were even mildly critical of the Founding Father or his country. Commentary on patriotic woman's place in the New Nation revealed the same phenomenon—persistent patriotic harangues and pleas for True American Womanhood, but no signs of ideological dissidence. Thousands of dogmatically patriotic schoolbooks were produced to meet the demands of the nation's booming school system. But only one text, an obscure 1832 reader, was critical of the Promised Land. No conspicuous or rigorous opposition to patriotic assumptions was evident in Canterbury or in Oberlin, among African colonizationists or among the staunchest opponents of the colonization ideal.

This is not to deny important instances of dissent. Noah Webster, one of the most enthusiastic patriots in the New Nation, became totally disenchanted with the Promised Land in his last years. Between 1797 and 1801 Charles Brockden Brown fundamentally departed from the spread-eagle mentality as he discovered a world of randomness and contingency that most Americans never consciously perceived. Although Mercy Warren exalted the Promised Land in her *History* and in her plays, she refused to characterize George Washington as the impeccable Founding Father and she covertly defied the ideal of True American Womanhood. Moving from Philadelphia's restrictive Quaker reform circles to an active physical life on the Michigan frontier, Elizabeth Chandler also departed from True Womanhood. She found Lenawee County a haven for sexual dissidence. Living in boardinghouses and shedding family responsibilities, even Sarah Hale might be characterized as a dissenter. The large number of blacks who opposed the American Colonization Society—the nation's major patriotic organization—were defying the spread-eagle mentality. Even A.C.S. activists dissented in one particular. Most clung to the Jeffersonian view that the Indian was a "variety" of the white race and was therefore assimilable, and most opposed Indian removal at a time when pressures for both removal and Indian extermination were pervasive. Private correspondence and guarded commentary also reveals that major national leaders—men like Benjamin Rush, Thomas Jefferson, John Adams, and John Quincy Adams—sometimes voiced intense displeasure with patriotic ideas and ideals.[1] Less powerful men like Elisha Bates, Henry C. Wright, and Henry David Thoreau were more direct and explicit in their opposition. Compared to the vast array of patriotic articulations and activities, however, instances of dissent were rare. Moreover, they were not very consequential. Usually they represented no more than the secret whispers of the powerful and the random chantings of the weak.

Why was there so little rigorous, overt, and consequential dissent against the crusade for the Promised Land? Historians have not addressed themselves to the question in any systematic way. Fortunately, the brilliant young author of *Democracy in America* focused upon the topic. Visiting the New Nation from the spring of 1831 until late the following winter, Alexis de Tocqueville was taken aback by the patriotic fervor of Jared Sparks, Josiah Quincy, Daniel Webster, Edward Everett, and others with whom he conversed: "It is impossible to conceive of a more garrulous patriotism; it wearies even those who are disposed to respect it." Americans "love their country just as they love themselves, and they transfer the habits of their private vanity to their vanity as a nation." Therefore, the Frenchman concluded, Americans "appear impatient of the smallest censure and insatiable of praise." They would not brook any criticism of the Promised Land.[2]

Wherever he traveled and whomever he met, Tocqueville experienced

[1] See, e.g., John A. Schutz and Douglass Adair (eds.), *The Spur of Fame: Dialogue of John Adams and Benjamin Rush, 1805-1813* (San Marino, Calif.: The Huntington Library, 1966), pp. 30, 108; Lester J. Cappon (ed.), *The Adams-Jefferson Letters* (Chapel Hill: University of North Carolina Press, 1959), II, 453, 516; Perry Miller, *The Life of the Mind in America: From the Revolution to the Civil War* (New York: Harcourt, Brace & World, Inc., 1965), p. 282; Francis J. Grund, *Aristocracy in America: From the Sketch-Book of a German Nobleman* (reprint. New York: Harper Torchbooks, 1959), pp. 93-94.
[2] Alexis de Tocqueville, *Democracy in America* (New York: J. & H. G. Langley, 1841), II, 238-40.

le patriotisme irritable. He perceived it as part of a larger pattern—a widespread attitudinal uniformity throughout the New Nation: "I know of no country in which there is so little true independence of mind and freedom of discussion as in America." "When I survey this countless multitude of beings, shaped in each other's likeness, amidst whom nothing rises and nothing falls, the sight of such universal uniformity saddens and chills me," the French aristocrat remarked.[3] "A stranger does, indeed, sometimes meet with Americans who dissent," Tocqueville acknowledged, "but no one is there to hear these things beside yourself, and you, to whom these secret reflections are confided, are a stranger and a bird of passage."[4] Almost the entire second volume of *Democracy in America* represented an extended footnote on the uniformly mediocre attitudes, ideals, arts, literature, and mores of the New Nation—the staid, conventional fruits of an intensely conformist society. "The aspect of American society is animated, because men and things are always changing," Tocqueville concluded, "but it is monotonous, because all changes are alike."[5]

St. Thomas Aquinas, Jacques Bénigne Bossuet, Edmund Burke, and other European theorists had romanticized a sense of structured differences among peoples as the cement of Old World civilization and culture. Tocqueville charged that structured differences were on the wane in Western civilization and that the New Nation was a case in point. Americans were not drawn together by the vision that they were different and unequal parts of a corporate whole. What made for national cohesion was their sense of being similar and equal participants in a relatively uniform way of existence. The feeling of equality in a monotonously uniform social structure undermined the rich ideological and cultural diversities of the Old World. In place of enriching diversity, *le patriotisme irritable* emerged as doctrinal justification for egalitarian uniformity and cultural drabness. Considered to be part of the cement that held the nation together, devout patriotism generally went unchallenged.

Tocqueville commented at length on the way egalitarianism discouraged dissent. "In periods of aristocracy," he noted, "every man is always bound so closely to many of his fellow-citizens, that he cannot be assailed without their coming to his assistance. In ages of equality every man naturally stands alone; he has no hereditary friends whose co-operation he may demand—no class upon whose sympathies he may rely; he is easily got rid of, and he is trampled on with impunity."[6] In

[3] Tocqueville, *Democracy*, I, 285; II, 353.
[4] Tocqueville, *Democracy*, I, 289.
[5] Tocqueville, *Democracy*, II, 242.
[6] Tocqueville, *Democracy*, II, 345.

America, the protections afforded by European class obligations, church, guild, or local ruling elites—protections which had been viable in Europe before the French Revolution—were all missing. Americans were isolated and lonely people of roughly comparable wealth; each desperately sought out a bit more wealth and status than his neighbor. Always very competitive with those about them, Americans could trust nobody; they stood alone against the egalitarian conformity pressures symbolized by *le patriotisme irritable*. But they were not distressed with their isolation. Because material self-seeking was their central pursuit, most Americans were not troubled by the absence of traditional European safeguards for ideological unorthodoxy. Isolated and unprotected in their exercise of ideological dissent, most were so captivated by the materialist quest that they had neither time nor energy to formulate and articulate unconventional new thoughts. Doctrinaire patriotism therefore went unchallenged as the cement of egalitarian national existence for Americans too busy making money to analyze, much less criticize, its essential tenets.[7]

But what about the exceptional few who had somehow transcended the quest for wealth and status and who harbored unique thoughts? If the quest for material aggrandizement did not suppress all vigorous dissent, a second and more fundamental force would. Tocqueville called this force the "tyranny of the majority"—a broad-based moral-social consensus that pervaded the society. Decades earlier James Madison had voiced fears of tyranny by the majority—total domination by electoral majorities over political institutions. But Tocqueville's concept of the "tyranny of the majority" was more vague, nebulous, and far-reaching. Certain broad social-moral ideas and ideals pervaded the nation; they were endemic to American democratic culture. Deriving from mass culture, these ideas and ideals took on a force of their own and became binding upon the general populace. Rooted in their own commonplace beliefs, many Americans could not see that majority ideas and ideals had become binding upon themselves and upon all others. They could neither see that they were the authors of their own conformity pressures nor perceive the extreme limits upon their own capacities to dissent.[8]

Conscious of the insensitivity of Americans to the "tyranny of the majority," Tocqueville comprehended the meaning of incidents that many Americans would not even acknowledge. He discovered how mob action had silenced an anti-war newspaper in Baltimore during the

[7] This theme is reiterated persistently throughout *Democracy in America*, particularly in Vol. I (Ch. 15) and Vol. II (Chs. 6 and 7).

[8] Tocqueville, *Democracy*, I, 276, 284, 287. Morton J. Horwitz, "Tocqueville and the Tyranny of the Majority," *Review of Politics*, XXVIII, No. 3 (July 1966), 301–03, provides an excellent discussion of this point.

War of 1812, and he understood why Pennsylvanians would not allow enfranchised Negroes to vote. The anti-war editor and the voting Negro violated principles of majority consensus—principles with a moralistic extralegal standing. But accepted ideas and ideals of the community at large were usually imposed without force or overt coercion or even much fuss:

> In America, the majority raises very formidable barriers to the liberty of opinion: within these barriers an author may write whatever he pleases, but he will repent it if he ever steps beyond them. Not that he is exposed to the terrors of an *auto-da-fé*, but he is tormented by the slights and persecutions of daily obloquy. His political career is closed for ever, since he has offended the only authority which is able to promote his success. Every sort of compensation, even that of celebrity, is refused to him. Before he published his opinions, he imagined that he held them in common with many others; but no sooner has he declared them openly, than he is loudly censured by his overbearing opponents, while those who think, without having the courage to speak, like him abandon him in silence. He yields at length, oppressed by the daily efforts he has been making, and he subsides into silence as if he was tormented by remorse for having spoken the truth.[9]

Though occasional mob action and regular, if covert, intimidation pressures, opinions outside of a broadly orthodox consensus were cast into disrepute. Dissenters or potential dissenters were silenced.

Tocqueville maintained that this "tyranny of the majority" opposed dissidence of all sorts. But it was most intolerant of critics of the Promised Land. Even mild chastisement of the New Nation was unacceptable; "everything must be made the subject of encomium. No writer, whatever be his eminence, can escape from the tribute of adulation to his fellow-citizens. The majority lives in perpetual exercise of self-applause; and there are certain truths which the Americans can only learn from strangers or from experience." Praise of the Promised Land was always in demand; criticism was intolerable.[10] Thus, Tocqueville concluded that the "tyranny of the majority" was the underlying factor that allowed *le patriotisme irritable* to go unchallenged. To be sure, the Frenchman detected several factors mitigating this "tyranny"—freedom of association, liberty of the press, the strength of the legal profession, an independent judiciary, the absence of a strong central government, and "enlightened deference" to formal rights. Yet an invidious extralegal "tyranny of the majority" would continue to thrive and to exert increasing conformity pressures, Tocqueville maintained,

[9] Tocqueville, *Democracy*, I, 285.
[10] Tocqueville, *Democracy*, I, 286.

and "I do think that they are insurmountable."[11] He concluded *Democracy in America* on this note, ruling out the possibility of a meaningful challenge to doctrinaire patriotism.

Tocqueville's analysis of widespread conformity to *le patriotisme irritable* remains the only systematic explanation for the dearth of sustained, effective dissent in the New Nation. The explanation has significant shortcomings. Like most other contentions in *Democracy in America*, it was vague and abstract; it did not derive from a specific body of reliable data but was rooted in impressionistic assumptions and logical deductions. Such critics as Cushing Strout, Morton J. Horwitz, Irving M. Zeitlin, and George Wilson Pierson fault Tocqueville on other counts. They note that he commenced his study of America troubled by crumbling French aristocratic and monarchical traditions. This caused Tocqueville to overemphasize facets of American life that seemed to differ from traditional French society. A sharp contrast between the Old World and the New allowed him to preach more persuasively to his French countrymen on the changing shape of Western civilization. More specifically, critics stress that Tocqueville placed too much emphasis upon the alleged democratic tradition of the New England town meeting and the formalities of universal manhood suffrage, and that he de-emphasized the enormous power of New World economic and political elites. "With his [Tocqueville's] fears of the mob, and his concern for the atom individual," Pierson notes, "he did not enough allow for the ingenuity of the designing few, the potential indifference of the many."[12] Drawing upon Pierson, historian Edward Pessen has conducted an extensive investigation of the major cities of the Northeast during the second quarter of the nineteenth century and has found extreme inequality of wealth. Because individual wealth differentials were increasing, this could not have been the "Era of the Common Man." Jackson Turner Main concurs. He notes that whereas 10 percent of the American population held slightly more than half the national wealth during the Revolutionary period, by the middle of the nineteenth century 10 percent held 70 percent of the wealth.[13] Other

---

[11] Tocqueville, *Democracy*, II, 351.

[12] George Wilson Pierson, *Tocqueville in America* (Garden City, N.Y.: Doubleday-Anchor, 1959), p. 468. See also Cushing Strout, "Tocqueville's Duality: Describing America and Thinking of Europe," *American Quarterly*, XXI, No. 1 (Spring 1969), 87–99; Horwitz, *Review of Politics*, XXVIII, No. 3 (July 1966), 293–307; Irving M. Zeitlin, *Liberty, Equality, and Revolution in Alexis de Tocqueville* (Boston: Little, Brown and Company, 1971), pp. 57–62.

[13] Edward Pessen, "The Egalitarian Myth and the American Social Reality: Wealth, Mobility, and Equality in the 'Era of the Common Man,'" *American Historical Review*, LXXVI, No. 4 (October 1971), 989–1034; Jackson Turner Main, "Trends in Wealth Concentration before 1860," *Journal of Economic History*, XXXI, No. 2 (June 1971), 445–47.

studies have shown that the increasingly powerful economic elites exercised such a disproportionate influence upon political life that *de facto* democracy could not have existed. Wealthy men controlled both major parties. If there ever had been a democratic New England town meeting tradition, it did not survive into the nineteenth century.[14]

Perhaps because his focus was upon social and cultural conditions, Tocqueville failed to see that a relatively small number of economic and political power brokers lay behind the seeming "tyranny of the majority." But this does not invalidate his perception of such a consensus—of an all-powerful "tyranny of the majority" curbing the potential for meaningful individual dissent. The actualities of power in elitist hands were not necessarily perceived by many people—perhaps not even by the elites themselves. Lee Benson concludes, for example, that by 1834 leading New York Whigs and Democrats had committed themselves to egalitarianism as the basis of political life. Benson insists that the New York example was not unique.[15] Combining scholarly findings on objective power distribution in Jacksonian society with the lack of any sustained dissent against *le patriotisme irritable*, it would seem that Tocqueville came to the right explanation for conformity pressures from faulty data. Either by inaction, by acceding to popular demand, or by agreeing with the public at large, economic-political elites permitted a strong majority consensus behind *le patriotisme irritable* to emerge. Whether elites perceived their enormous power and the potential of their power to thwart or modify this majority consensus is not a controlling factor. What matters is that an irresistible "tyranny of the majority" came into being demanding universal praise of the New Nation. It would be instructive to learn the precise roles various elites played in the structuring of majority pressures. But Tocqueville's claim is not negated; majority pressures could not have been surmounted by a significant number of isolated individuals once the pressures were applied.

Thus, although scholars are justifiably questioning certain aspects of *Democracy in America*, particularly the assumption of egalitarianism and democracy, Tocqueville's explanation of the nearly unchallenged

---

[14] See, e.g., Frank Otto Gatell, "Money and Party in Jacksonian America: A Quantitative Look at New York City's Men of Quality," *Political Science Quarterly*, LXXXII (1967), 235–52; Edward Pessen, *Jacksonian America: Society, Personality, and Politics* (Homewood, Ill.: Dorsey Press, 1969); Alexandra McCoy, "The Political Affiliations of American Economic Elites: Wayne County, Michigan, 1844–1860, as a Test Case" (Ph.D. dissertation, Wayne State University, 1965); Zeitlin, *Tocqueville*, pp. 61–62.

[15] Lee Benson, *The Concept of Jacksonian Democracy: New York as a Test Case* (Princeton: Princeton University Press, 1961), p. 86.

reign of *le patriotisme irritable* remains quite plausible. It is the only plausible explanation that we have. This is no small achievement for a man who penned his thoughts on the New Nation almost one hundred and fifty years ago.

DAVID WALKER'S
APPEAL RECONSIDERED

With rich detail and analysis, Benjamin Quarles's *Black Abolitionists* (1969) has become the definitive study of the antislavery efforts of antebellum free Negroes. From the standpoint of patriotic thought, one chapter ("Duet with John Bull") is quite suggestive. Quarles notes that few black abolitionists were doctrinaire patriots. Rather, he claims that they recognized the disparity between patriotic rhetoric of American freedom and equality and the actualities of slavery and racism. Indeed, black abolitionists were more impressed with Britain than the Promised Land. Risking their lives on the American lecture platform, they were lionized in London, Edinburgh, and Dublin. Whereas America's slave system seemed stronger than ever by the Jacksonian decades, Parliament formally abolished slavery in the British West Indies on August 1, 1834. Black abolitionists perceived this pattern of American reverses and British success. Consequently, they began to celebrate August First instead of July Fourth.[1]

Professor Quarles's appraisal of black abolitionists suggests that Tocqueville's "tyranny of the majority" applied mainly to white Americans. Free Negro antislavery activists did not honor the dogmas of *le patriotisme irritable*. Hated and discriminated against as the New Nation developed, they were not markedly influenced by patriotic conformity pressures.

There is much validity to Quarles's finding. However, one fact must be kept in mind. Even if black abolitionists were not devout patriots,

[1] Benjamin Quarles, *Black Abolitionists* (New York: Oxford University Press, 1969), pp. 116–42.

they stopped short of repudiating the New Nation. Few considered repatriation in any serious or systematic way before 1850. Instead, most maintained that the American Colonization Society was an evil organization and that its proposal for black removal was deplorable: "Truly, this is our home, here let us live and here let us die."[2] John B. Russwurm was an important black abolitionist who dissented from this dominant view. He followed the lead of Paul Cuffé, endorsed repatriation, and embraced the A.C.S. As a result, Russwurm noted "violent persecution" from "the most influential [Afro-American] people" and had to resign the editorship of a black newspaper he had established.[3] It was not until the Fugitive Slave Act of 1850 made it difficult for the Northern states to provide havens from the Southern slave system that a great many black abolitionists began to consider American race relations beyond remedy. Only then did they seriously consider massive black emigration from the Promised Land. Frederick Douglass continued to resist colonization proposals until the eve of the Civil War.[4]

In view of the widespread and long-term black disenchantment with the ways of the New Nation, one wonders why it took an 1850 federal statute to cultivate black abolitionist interest in repatriation. Why did it take so long for the Martin R. Delaneys, Henry Highland Garnets, Alexander Crummells, James Theodore Hollys, and their followers to give up on the New Nation as the Negro's homeland?

David Walker, one of the most significant black abolitionists, sheds considerable light upon this question. His 1829 *Appeal to the Coloured Citizens of the World* was the first systematic and sustained attack on American slavery and racism ever written by an American Negro. It presaged many basic Garrisonian arguments of the 1830's. Like other black abolitionists, Walker concluded that America's oppressive racial practices made the New Nation a universal disgrace. And like others before the 1850 Fugitive Slave Act, Walker rejected emigration from

[2] Quoted in Louis R. Mehlinger, "The Attitude of the Free Negro toward African Colonization," *Journal of Negro History*, I, No. 3 (June 1916), 286. For evidence that this resolution by Middletown, Connecticut, black abolitionists typified black abolitionist thought in the decades before 1850, see, e.g., Quarles, *Black Abolitionists*, pp. 3–4, 7, 8; David K. Sullivan, "William Lloyd Garrison in Baltimore, 1829–1830," *Maryland Historical Magazine*, LXVIII, No. 1 (Spring 1973), 65; Mehlinger, *Journal of Negro History*, I, No. 3 (June 1916), 278, 287.

[3] Quarles, *Black Abolitionists*, p. 7; William M. Brewer, "John B. Russwurm," *Journal of Negro History*, XIII, No. 4 (October 1928), 418–19.

[4] Black abolitionist attitudes after the 1850 Fugitive Slave Act are noted in Quarles, *Black Abolitionists*, pp. 215–18; Howard H. Bell, "Expressions of Negro Militancy in the North, 1840–1860," *Journal of Negro History*, XLV, No. 1 (January 1960), 19; Mehlinger, *Journal of Negro History*, I, No. 3 (June 1916), 295–96. Quarles, *Black Abolitionists*, p. 222, notes Douglass' resistance to colonization.

"our country." Although white Americans treated blacks "more cruel and barbarous than any Heathen nation did any people whom it had subjected" and made American Negroes "the most wretched, degraded and abject set of beings that ever lived since the world began," the New Nation "is as much ours as it is the whites," and repatriation was out of the question.[5] Conscious recognition of a horrendous American racial climate did not turn Walker into an emigrationist eager to leave the New Nation. In this respect, his *Appeal* spoke for most black abolitionists of the time.

Because Walker's *Appeal* typified black abolitionist perceptions of American racial oppression and the repatriation issue, it must be explored with some delicacy. Close, systematic analysis of Walker's language and argumentation is required to discover why he, like black abolitionists generally, could abhor American racial conditions yet flatly dismiss emigration. Perhaps because it was a polemical pamphlet, the *Appeal* has not been the subject of close, sustained inquiry. Contemporaries reacted to it with shock and emotion. Henry Highland Garnet lauded it as "the boldest and most direct appeal in behalf of freedom," Benjamin Lundy called it counterproductive and "inflammatory," and William Lloyd Garrison termed it an intelligent but "most injudicious publication."[6] White Southerners feared and detested Walker and his *Appeal*. Legislatures were convened in Georgia and North Carolina to deal with the "threat." Negroes possessing the pamphlet were jailed. Several Southern states even took measures to curtail black literacy.[7] Historians have generally followed the pattern of contemporaries. They have evaluated Walker's *Appeal* from a Manichaean perspective and have failed to probe for the nuances in Walker's thoughts. Clement Eaton called the *Appeal* "obnoxious" and properly suppressed, J. Saunders Redding characterized it as "scurrilous, ranting, mad," while Alice Dana Adams noted that it was "a most bloodthirsty document." To Herbert Aptheker and Dwight Lowell Dumond, on the other hand, the *Appeal* was a humane attack against oppression and Walker was an intelligent and heroic abolitionist.[8] Although contemporaries and historians recog-

[5] Herbert Aptheker (ed.), *"One Continual Cry": David Walker's Appeal to the Colored Citizens of the World (1829–1830)* (New York: Humanities Press, Inc., 1965), pp. 62, 121.

[6] Aptheker (ed.), *Walker's Appeal*, pp. 1–3; Quarles, *Black Abolitionists*, p. 17; Charles M. Wiltse (ed.), *David Walker's Appeal, in Four Articles* (New York: Hill & Wang, 1965), x–xi; *The Liberator*, January 8, 1831.

[7] Aptheker (ed.), *Walker's Appeal*, pp. 47, 48; Clement Eaton, "A Dangerous Pamphlet in the Old South," *Journal of Southern History*, II, No. 3 (August 1936), 323–34.

[8] Eaton, *Journal of Southern History*, II, No. 3 (August 1936), 333–34; Eaton, *Freedom of Thought in the Old South* (Durham: Duke University Press, 1940), pp. 121, 125; J. Saunders Redding, *They Came in Chains: Ameri-*

nized the importance of Walker's *Appeal*, and although it is representative of black abolitionist thought before the 1850's, it has not been given the close reading that it merits.

The meager evidence concerning Walker's life sheds light on the basic conflict in his *Appeal*—his contempt for American racism but his refusal to consider emigration. Walker was probably born in Wilmington, North Carolina, in 1785. His father was a slave and his mother was a free Negro. According to state law, the legal condition of the child followed that of the mother, making Walker a freeman. He somehow learned to read in North Carolina but was not able to endure "living in this bloody land" of slavery and emigrated to Boston sometime in the 1820's. By 1827 (perhaps earlier) Walker opened a "slop shop" on Brattle Street. He paid bartenders for the clothing that sailors had given up in exchange for drinks, and he resold this clothing at a higher price—often to sober sailors. In 1828 he married a fugitive slave from the South and had one son—Edward Garrison Walker. By this time he had also become a regular abolitionist lecturer and the Boston agent for the New York-based *Freedom's Journal*. A leading figure in Boston's black community, he was a regular member of the local Methodist Church and belonged to the Massachusetts General Colored Association for racial self-help and abolition. Seeking to communicate directly with slaves, he wrote his *Appeal* in September 1829 and planted copies of the pamphlet in the pockets of clothing sold to sailors bound for Southern ports. He hoped that the pamphlets would eventually fall into the hands of slaves.[9]

These are the main facts known about Walker's life to September 1829 and they suggest something of a divided and ill-defined existence. He was free only because of a peculiarity of North Carolina law and therefore had a parental background identical to that of many blacks who remained in bondage. Classified as a free Negro, he married a fugitive slave. A regular churchgoer and a public lecturer, he had some measure of esteem within the Boston black community. But as the owner of a "slop shop," he did not labor at a prestigious calling. Belonging to the Massachusetts General Colored Association and serving as agent for *Freedom's Journal*, he was helping to forge an independent black aboli-

cans from Africa (Philadelphia: J. B. Lippincott Company, 1950), p. 90; Alice Dana Adams, *The Neglected Period of Anti-Slavery in America, 1808–1831* (Boston: Ginn & Company, 1908), p. 94; Aptheker (ed.), *Walker's Appeal*, p. 58; Dwight Lowell Dumond, *Antislavery: The Crusade for Freedom in America* (New York: W. W. Norton & Company, 1966), p. 329.

[9] The known facts of Walker's life up to September 1829 are reported in Wiltse (ed.), *Walker's Appeal*, vii–ix; Aptheker (ed.), *Walker's Appeal*, pp. 41–44; Quarles, *Black Abolitionists*, pp. 16, 22; Eaton, *Journal of Southern History*, II, No. 3 (August 1936), 324; Donald M. Jacobs, "David Walker: Boston Race Leader, 1825–1830," *Essex Institute Historical Collections*, CVII (January 1971), 94–107.

tionist tradition. But he named his only child Edward Garrison Walker. The few available facts on David Walker's life point to a man who seemed to be part free and part slave, part reputable and part reprobate, part independent black abolitionist and part early "Garrisonian."

These bits of biographical data do not prove that David Walker lived in a state of personal and social flux. But the specific language of the *Appeal* strongly re-enforces this characterization; the pamphlet is one of the most ambivalent documents in Afro-American history. Although contemporaries and many historians construed the *Appeal* as vehemently anti-white, for example, this was not quite the case. Walker's views were mixed. "The whites have always been an unjust, jealous, unmerciful, avaricious and bloodthirsty set of beings, always seeking after power and authority," he proclaimed.[10] Americans represented the worst of the white race: "They have, and do continue to punish us for nothing else, but for enriching them and their country." They treated blacks worse "than devils themselves ever treated a set of men, women and children on this earth."[11] Thomas Jefferson was the spokesman for white American oppression and he had to be rebutted. And yet the leader of the racist white nation had penned the Declaration of Independence—the most beautiful and forceful statement for freedom and equality ever written.[12] Therefore, Jefferson was part devil and part saint. So was the white American society he represented: "Some of you are good men; but the will of my God must be done. Those avaricious and ungodly tyrants among you, I am awfully afraid will drag down the vengeance of God upon you." Some white Americans opposed racial oppression and slavery while others did not. Walker characterized English society along these same lines. Some white Englishmen "oppress us *sorely*," particularly in the West Indies. But other Englishmen had done much for "the melioration of our condition." For this reason "the blacks cannot but respect the English as a nation, notwithstanding they have treated us a little cruel." Thus, Walker distinguished among whites in both America and England. He did not stereotype the race. His attitude was one of contempt for the "oppressive race" but many whites were not "oppressors."[13]

In contrast to most nineteenth-century white racial theorists, Walker tended to characterize blacks as the locus of humanism and kindness in a cruel and exploitive world: "I know that the blacks, take them half enlightened and ignorant, are more humane and merciful than the most enlightened and refined European that can be found in all the earth." A

[10] Aptheker (ed.), *Walker's Appeal*, pp. 79–80.
[11] Aptheker (ed.), *Walker's Appeal*, pp. 76, 62.
[12] Aptheker (ed.), *Walker's Appeal*, pp. 72, 77–78, 142–43.
[13] Aptheker (ed.), *Walker's Appeal*, p. 111, characterizes American whites. On p. 106 white Englishmen are characterized.

humane but suffering black folk had given the New Nation its most positive asset: "America is more our country, than it is the whites—we have enriched it with our *blood and tears*."[14] However, not all blacks were humane and meritorious. Some aided slaveholders in recapturing fugitive slaves. Some even tried to repudiate their race by marrying whites. Blacks of this sort deserved to be called "NIGER" [*sic*].[15] Walker was therefore as ambivalent on blacks as he was on whites; the Negro race was humane but did contain its "NIGER" element.

Therefore, the precise words of the *Appeal* do not outline the simplistic clash between oppressed blacks and exploitive whites that contemporaries and historians perceived. Both races had their meritorious and their degenerate elements. Still, Walker repeatedly warned that white American oppression of blacks would have to stop. This was God's wish and command: "God has commenced a course of exposition among the [white] Americans, and the glorious and heavenly work will continue to progress until they learn to do justice." White oppressors had better "listen to the voice of the Holy Ghost" and cease to degrade or enslave blacks or they would offend God.[16] But what if slaveholders and other white Americans persisted in their oppression? Here, too, Walker's cry was neither firm nor clear. He maintained that God would intervene: "God will deliver us from under you." He "will tear up the very face of the earth" if necessary to eliminate white oppression. At the same time, Walker urged blacks to alter their oppressive condition by standing up to those whites who were degrading them: "Let no man of us budge one step, and let slaveholders come to beat us from our country." Standing up to whites might even require blacks to fight: "And wo, wo, will be to you [whites] if we have to obtain our freedom by fighting."[17] Although God's resistance and black resistance would be directed against a common target (oppressive whites), Walker never noted the precise relationship between God and blacks. Blacks who resisted oppression were "under God." But it was unclear whether God could or would overthrow the white oppressors without black resistance—whether black actions were required to call God into action. Blacks should "stand still and see the salvation of God and the miracle which he will work for our delivery from wretchedness under the [white] Christians!!!!"[18] Yet what did Walker mean by "stand still" and would the "miracle" of God eventuate if blacks did not "stand still"? Conveying the appearance of a bold and clear-headed abolitionist, David

14 Aptheker (ed.), *Walker's Appeal*, pp. 88, 131.
15 Aptheker (ed.), *Walker's Appeal*, pp. 71, 86–88.
16 Aptheker (ed.), *Walker's Appeal*, pp. 111, 119–20.
17 Aptheker (ed.), *Walker's Appeal*, pp. 104, 131, 137.
18 Aptheker (ed.), *Walker's Appeal*, p. 121.

Walker was remarkably vague and ambiguous as he delineated the road to freedom.

Walker's entire *Appeal* testified to a loose and ambivalent ideological framework. Some whites were oppressors while others were not; some blacks were humane while others were "NIGERS." God would intervene and bring down oppressors but blacks should "stand still" and perhaps "fight" to effect that end. The conflicts within Walker's racial characterizations may account for the conflict in his proposed remedy for oppression. If not all whites were oppressors and not all blacks were humane, then no clear-cut path to liberation may have been possible. Indeed, "NIGERS" did not deserve to be liberated and there were "good [white] men" who would not bring on God's wrath.

This, in turn, suggests why Walker deplored the barbarism of the "white Christians of America" yet flatly rejected repatriation. The attack on barbaric white oppression represented one side of an ambivalent mental cast. Walker also recognized that some whites were friends and some blacks were enemies. Therefore, there was hope for a biracial coalition to redeem the Promised Land. Repatriation was premature. It was preferable to remain in a country where humane blacks could cooperate with "good" whites than to emigrate and have to forge a nation with "NIGERS." Through a biracial coalition of humane blacks and whites, "there is not a doubt in my mind, but that the whole of the [American] past will be sunk into oblivion, and we yet, under God, will become a united and happy people."[19]

Like many other black abolitionists, Walker also rejected black emigration out of distaste for the American Colonization Society. He suspected that the A.C.S. was a proslavery agency in disguise and devoted one of four sections of his *Appeal* to a blistering attack on the Society as a racist organization. Because the A.C.S. was the only significant organization devoted to "viable" American-African relationships during the 1820's, Walker's acute distaste for its "oppressive" intentions tended to block out serious consideration of an African homeland. Most of the positive (or semi-positive) images of Africa that were presented to Americans during the early Jacksonian period were disseminated by the Colonization Society. Unqualified rejection of the A.C.S. predisposed Walker (and other black abolitionists) to reject those positive images. To be sure, he acknowledged that "learning originated" in Africa "and was carried thence into Greece, where it was improved upon and refined." And he recognized "that mighty African, HANNIBAL" as "one of the greatest generals of antiquity, who defeated and cut off so many thousands of white Romans or murderers." But these were the only positive references to Africa within Walker's *Appeal*,

[19] Aptheker (ed.), *Walker's Appeal*, p. 137.

and both were to the African *past*. It was "a land of pagans and of blood," where "the words of the Lord Jesus" were unknown. Compared to Americans, native Africans lived "in ignorance" and were easily misled.[20] This hardly furnished incentives for emigration from the United States through the offices of the A.C.S. or even through non-racist repatriation organizations.

Like other black abolitionists of the early nineteenth century, David Walker therefore lacked the positive vision of an African homeland that made emigrationists out of men like Martin Delaney, Alexander Crummell, James Holly, and Henry Highland Garnet in the 1850's. Throughout the *Appeal*, he referred to Afro-Americans as "Africans" and whites as "Americans." Given his negative image of Africa and his rejection of the repatriation alternative, Walker was therefore telling blacks that they were better off remaining in the white man's country—that white America was preferable to their "pagan" black African homeland. At one point in his *Appeal*, Walker remarked: "If any of us see fit to go away, go to those who have been for many years, and are now our greatest benefactors—the English." Because England was a progressive, civilized nation, it was preferable to Africa.[21] Yet Walker also recognized racial oppressions among the English. He stressed that he would not emigrate from the United States to any foreign site and firmly recommended that other blacks remain as well. Whereas a negative image of Africa contributed to his dismissal of African repatriation, a more positive image of England could not make a migrant of him.

By characterizing Walker's *Appeal* as a militant plea, commentators have therefore been off the mark. The *Appeal* pointed in a very different direction. Although many white Americans were "oppressive barbarians" and caused blacks to suffer horribly, blacks were better off remaining in the Promised Land and struggling for a biracial coalition of the "better" elements of both races. Given Walker's negative image of Africa and his unwillingness to seriously consider emigration to England, there was no viable alternative. The Afro-American did best by forgetting about his black African homeland and remaining in but not of the white man's country. Until oppressive conditions in the United States were overturned, he therefore had to resign himself to estrangement and rootlessness.

Thus, Walker's *Appeal* does not quite sustain Professor Quarles's appraisal of antebellum black abolitionists as vehement opponents of the crusade for the Promised Land. Like other early-nineteenth-century black abolitionists, Walker debunked the United States for its racial oppressions. And like other black abolitionists, Walker perceived these

[20] Aptheker (ed.), *Walker's Appeal*, pp. 82, 83, 107, 115.
[21] Aptheker (ed.), *Walker's Appeal*, p. 121.

American oppressions as so wretched that even the English came off well by comparison: "The English are the best friends, the coloured people have upon earth."[22] Had he lived to 1834 and witnessed Parliamentary abolition of slavery in the British West Indies, Walker would almost certainly have joined other black abolitionists and traded off July Fourth for August First as the day of national jubilation. But vehement attacks against the Promised Land and praise for the English were balanced by other considerations. Walker had hope for a biracial coalition to overturn American oppressions. Moreover, given the "ignorance" and "paganism" of the African homeland and the dismissal of emigration to England as a viable alternative, the black man simply had no choice but to remain in the New Nation.

Whereas David Walker's *Appeal* cannot be classified along with a Washington eulogy or a July Fourth oration as a patriotic document, the pamphlet did not point to a viable black abolitionist dissenting tradition. Rather, it suggested a tragic dilemma for the early-nineteenth-century black abolitionist. Walker did not see himself as an integral part of the white man's country. Yet he had no strong sense of racial identity or proud vision of a black African heritage to effectively remedy his marginal American existence. He had only two hopes—coalition with humanitarian whites and divine intervention. Given the deepening racism of the Promised Land, North and South, by the middle decades of the nineteenth century, biracial coalitions were often ineffective while divine intervention was at least improbable.

For nine months following publication of the *Appeal*, Walker met with conditions that demonstrated the futility of his two hopes. White abolitionists like Benjamin Lundy and William Lloyd Garrison would have nothing to do with him, while white Southerners characterized him as the devil incarnate. Therefore, there was no chance for a biracial coalition. With rumors of a $1,000 price on his head, divine intervention became his only hope. Faith that God would protect him kept Walker in Boston revising his *Appeal* for reissue while friends urged him to leave the country. He would not depart from the nation that he had characterized as the most oppressive on earth. On June 28, 1830, Walker was found dead near the doorway of his Brattle Street "slop shop."[23] Although his *Appeal* was a confused and ambivalent document, it attacked the Promised Land and therefore ran against the grain of *le patriotisme irritable*. Alexis de Tocqueville might have predicted Walker's fate. The "tyranny of the majority" would not even brook an unclear and impotent challenge to national virtue.

[22] Aptheker (ed.), *Walker's Appeal*, p. 106.
[23] Wiltse (ed.), *Walker's Appeal*, x–xi. Although the circumstances of Walker's death have never been fully ascertained, it was rumored that he was poisoned.

BIBLIOGRAPHICAL
ESSAY

Most of the pertinent sources for this study have been cited in the footnotes. However, because of the very wide range of topics and materials in this book, the relative merit and use of certain sources require comment. Above all, several secondary studies and manuscript collections should be evaluated.

Background

Almost forty years ago Merle Curti issued a call: "Wanted: A History of American Patriotism," *Proceedings of the Middle States Association of History and Social Science Teachers*, XXXVI (1938), 15–24. This was a crucial topic, Curti noted, and should not remain within the exclusive province of polemicists. Eight years later Curti published *The Roots of American Loyalty* (New York, 1946), the first scholarly treatment of American patriotism. The book surveyed patriotic attitudes throughout all of American history and was necessarily thin in many areas. William McCarty (ed.), *Songs, Odes, and other Poems, on National Subjects* (Philadelphia, 1842), typified the sort of materials Curti drew upon to cover the first half of the nineteenth century. Curti also exploited July Fourth orations, and these are very fruitful documents in understanding the doctrinaire patriot mentality. The Rare Book Division of the Library of Congress houses over five hundred printed orations while others were printed within newspapers. Cedric Larson surveyed recurrent themes in "Patriotism in Carmine: 162 Years of July 4th Oratory," *Quarterly Journal of Speech*, XXVI, No. 1 (February 1940), 12–25. Robert Pettus Hay has made extensive and systematic use of the nineteenth-century July Fourth oration in "Freedom's Jubilee: One Hundred Years of the Fourth of July, 1776–1876" (Ph.D. dissertation, University of Kentucky, 1967), and "Providence and the American Past," *Indiana Magazine of History*, LXV, No. 2 (June 1969), 79–101. See also Fletcher M. Green, "Listen to the Eagle Scream: One Hundred Years of the Fourth of July in North Carolina (1776–1876)," *North Carolina Historical Review*, XXXI (July, October 1954), 295–320, 529–49, and L. H. Butterfield, "The Jubilee of Independence: July 4, 1826," *Virginia Magazine of History and Biography*, LXI, No. 2 (April 1953), 119–40.

Other than Curti's book and studies of July Fourth orations, few scholarly works have focused exclusively upon American patriotism. However, there are valuable insights on patriotism within a number of studies of American nationalism. See, particularly, Yehoshua Arieli, *Individualism and Nationalism in American Ideology* (Cambridge, Mass., 1964); Richard W. Van Alstyne, *Genesis of American Nationalism* (Waltham, Mass., 1970); Hans Kohn, *American Nationalism: An Interpretive Essay* (New York, 1961); Martin E. Marty, *Righteous Empire: The Protestant Experience in America* (New York, 1970); and two fine books by Paul C. Nagel, *One Nation Indivisible: The Union in American Thought, 1776–1861* (New York, 1964) and *This Sacred Trust: American Nationality, 1798–1898* (New York, 1971).

In *The Roots of American Loyalty*, Curti focused on the years between the American Revolution and the Mexican War. He characterized this period as the crucial interval in the history of American patriotic thought. Most historians have agreed. For important general studies of the quest for American national identity during these years, see Clinton Rossiter, *The American Quest, 1790–1860: An Emerging Nation in Search of Identity, Unity, and Modernity* (New York, 1971); Fred Somkin, *Unquiet Eagle: Memory and Desire in the Idea of American Freedom* (Ithaca, N.Y., 1967); William Brock, "The Image of England and American Nationalism," *Journal of American Studies*, V, No. 3 (December 1971), 225–45; and Part I of Seymour Martin Lipset, *The First New Nation: The United States in Historical and Comparative Perspective* (New York, 1963). The search for a unique national history and literature during these decades has been covered in a number of studies. Arthur H. Shaffer's *The Politics of History: Writing the History of the American Revolution, 1783–1815* (New York, 1975) is the most sophisticated. See also Benjamin T. Spencer, *The Quest for Nationality: An American Literary Campaign* (Syracuse, 1957); David D. Van Tassel, *Recording America's Past* (Chicago, 1960); and Sidney G. Fisher, "The Legendary and Myth-Making Process in Histories of the American Revolution," *Proceedings of the American Philo-*

sophical Society, LI, No. 204 (April–June 1912), 53–75. Lillian B. Miller, *Patrons and Patriotism: The Encouragement of the Fine Arts in the United States, 1790–1860* (Chicago, 1966), and Neil Harris, *The Artist in American Society: The Formative Years 1790–1860* (New York, 1970), are outstanding studies of the arts, artists, and nationalist fervor.

A number of narrower period studies of the movement to forge a national identity should also be consulted. Edwin G. Burrows and Michael Wallace, "The American Revolution: The Ideology and Psychology of National Liberation," *Perspectives in American History*, VI (1972), 167–306, has been one of the most creative attempts in recent years to coordinate political theory, economic development, and changes in family structure in accounting for America's break with Britain. Gordon S. Wood, *The Creation of the American Republic, 1776–1787* (Chapel Hill, 1969), and John R. Howe, Jr., "Republican Thought and the Political Violence of the 1790s," *American Quarterly*, XIX, No. 2, Pt. 1 (Summer 1967), 147–65, are the finest studies of political thought (particularly republican theory) during the late eighteenth century. Leon Howard's "The Late Eighteenth Century: An Age of Contradictions," *Transitions in American Literary History*, edited by Harry Hayden Clark (Durham, 1953), pp. 51–89, remains the most sensitive appraisal of the literary figures of the period. Sophisticated discussions of patriotism and partisan politics in the early national years abound, but David Hackett Fischer, *The Revolution of American Conservatism: The Federalist Party in the Era of Jeffersonian Democracy* (New York, 1965), and Roger H. Brown, *The Republic in Peril: 1812* (New York, 1964), are particularly good. Jacksonian politics has been covered by an even more extensive literature. From the standpoint of patriotic thought, the most useful studies are Marvin Meyers, *The Jacksonian Persuasion: Politics and Belief* (Stanford, 1957); Lee Benson, *The Concept of Jacksonian Democracy: New York as a Test Case* (Princeton, 1961); and Richard P. McCormick, *The Second American Party System* (Chapel Hill, 1966).

CHAPTER I.

"The Rising Glory of America"

Analysis of the New Nation's first significant literary venture, the *Columbian Magazine*, must begin with that publication itself. It has been microfilmed and may be purchased at a small cost. William J. Free, *The Columbian Magazine and American Literary Nationalism* (The Hague, 1968) has been the only detailed study of the publication and has focused on literary criticism. Free may be supplemented by a useful discussion of the *Columbian* in Frank Luther Mott, *A History of American*

Magazines, 1741–1850 (Cambridge, Mass., 1939). What little data we have on the *Columbian*'s publishers and the financial affairs of the publication derive from "The Belknap Papers," *Collections of the Massachusetts Historical Society*, Series 5 (Vols. II, III) and Series 6 (Vol. IV).

Thanks to Robert L. Brunhouse, research on the leading *Columbian* contributor, David Ramsay, is an easy task. Brunhouse has gathered together all intellectually and biographically significant Ramsay letters along with several of Ramsay's shorter writings in "David Ramsay, 1749–1815: Selections from His Writings," *Transactions of the American Philosophical Society*, New Ser., LV, Pt. 4 (1965). Brunhouse's article "David Ramsay's Publication Problems, 1784–1808," *Papers of the Bibliographical Society of America*, XXXIX (First Quarter 1945), 51–67, has noted a persistent and central theme in the Ramsay correspondence. Robert Y. Hayne was friendly with Ramsay and has given valuable insights on the man's personal qualities in "Biographical Memoir of David Ramsay, M.D.," *Analectic Magazine*, VI (September 1815), 204–24. Josephine Fitts' Master's essay, "David Ramsay: South Carolina Patriot, Physician, and Historian" (Columbia University, 1936), has also cited certain useful personal data. The best appraisals of Ramsay's history and ideas are Page Smith, "David Ramsay and the Causes of the American Revolution," *William and Mary Quarterly*, 3rd Ser., XVII, No. 1 (January 1960), 51–77, and a chapter in William Raymond Smith, *History as Argument: Three Patriot Historians of the American Revolution* (The Hague, 1966).

As Emily Ellsworth Ford Skeel's *A Bibliography of the Writings of Noah Webster* (New York, 1971) has demonstrated, the second major *Columbian* contributor probably wrote more than any other figure in the New Nation. The extensive Noah Webster Papers at the New York Public Library are indispensable, although Webster letters may be found in several other libraries in the Eastern states. Skeel's *Notes on the Life of Noah Webster* (New York, 1912) contains some of the most informative letters plus a number of entries from Webster diaries. However, the most comprehensive printed collection of Webster correspondence is Harry R. Warfel (ed.), *Letters of Noah Webster* (New York, 1953). The man's publications were even more voluminous than Ramsay's. Homer D. Babbidge, Jr., has collected representative patriotic expressions from a great variety of these publications and has included them in *On Being American: Selected Writings, 1783–1828* (New York, 1967). Webster's periodical, *The American Magazine*, and his newspapers, *The American Minerva* (New York) and *The Herald* (New York), should also be consulted. Harry R. Warfel's *Noah Webster: Schoolmaster to America* (New York, 1936) remains the most complete biography, although Ervin C. Shoemaker, *Noah Webster: Pioneer of Learning* (New York, 1936), is a respectable study of his published writings Shoemaker emphasized Webster's shallowness in linguistics, as did Kemp Malone, "A Linguistic Patriot," *American Speech*, I, No. 1 (October 1925), 26–31, and Charlton Laird, "Etymology, Anglo-Saxon, and Noah Webster," *American Speech*, XXI, No. 1 (February 1946), 3–15.

CHAPTER 2.

The Flawless American

There is no end to research on the development of the Washington myth. Eulogies delivered between December 14, 1799, and February 22, 1800, are the most voluminous and useful sources. Margaret B. Stillwell noted those which were printed and the particular libraries holding them in her "Checklist of Eulogies and Funeral Orations on the Death of George Washington, December, 1799–February, 1800," *Bulletin of the New York Public Library*, XX, No. 5 (May 1916), 403–41. William Spohn Baker noted most early-nineteenth-century published sketches of Washington in his *Bibliotheca Washingtoniana: A Descriptive List of the Biographies and Biographical Sketches of George Washington* (Philadelphia, 1889), and these should also be consulted. Baker has published some of them in *Early Sketches of George Washington* (Philadelphia, 1893) and in *Character Portraits of Washington as Delineated by Historians, Orators and Divines* (Philadelphia, 1887). For information on the major Washington myth maker, see Emily Ellsworth Ford Skeel (ed.), *Mason Locke Weems: His Works and Ways* (New York, 1929), and Marcus Cunliffe's excellent introduction to Weems's *Life of Washington* (Cambridge, Mass., 1962).

There have been a number of scholarly studies of the Washington myth. William Alfred Bryan's *George Washington in American Literature, 1775–1865* (New York, 1952) has been the most comprehensive (if unimaginative) treatment. Marcus Cunliffe, *George Washington: Man and Monument* (New York, 1958), is also useful. For shorter but insightful appraisals, see the appropriate chapters in Daniel Boorstin, *The Americans: The National Experience* (New York, 1965); Dixon Wecter, *The Hero in America: A Chronicle of Hero-Worship* (New York, 1941); Marshall W. Fishwick, *American Heroes: Myth and Reality* (Washington, D.C., 1954); and Bernard Mayo, *Myths and Men: Patrick Henry, George Washington, Thomas Jefferson* (Athens, Ga., 1959). See also Robert P. Hay, "George Washington: American Moses," *American Quarterly*, XXI, No. 4 (Winter 1969), 780–91, and Charles Warren, "How Politics Intruded into the Washington Centenary of 1832," *Proceedings of the Massachusetts Historical Society*, LXV (October 1932), 37–62. Although Michael Kammen did not treat counterpointing within the Washington myth, his *People of Paradox: An Inquiry Concerning the Origins of American Civilization* (New York, 1972) brilliantly characterized counterpointing (biformity) as the central dynamic within early American culture. It is therefore mandatory reading for all students of the Washington myth.

CHAPTER 3.

Dissidence

It is unfortunate that few of Charles Brockden Brown's unpublished writings have survived. The Brown Papers at the Historical Society of Pennsylvania consist of a few letters, a handwritten draft of *Alcuin*, and three Common Place Books covering the years between 1783 and 1808 (consisting largely of hand copies of newspaper articles). David Lee Clark (ed.), "Unpublished Letters of Charles Brockden Brown and W. W. Wilkins," *Studies in English*, XXVII, No. 1 (June 1948), 74–107, covers the years between 1787 and 1793, when Brown decided to abandon law and take up literature. William Dunlap's two-volume *The Life of Charles Brockden Brown* (Philadelphia, 1815) remains the most useful source for Brown materials. Dunlap included several Brown letters, unfinished manuscripts, and a variety of materials that are unavailable elsewhere. In addition, Dunlap conveyed the impressions of a close personal friend and these more than compensate for his occasional factual inaccuracies. Dunlap's *Memoirs of Charles Brockden Brown, the American Novelist* (London, 1822) is an English abridgment of the 1815 Philadelphia edition.

Appraisals of Brown have centered on his novels and his magazine writings. There are two competent and comprehensive biographies—Harry R. Warfel, *Charles Brockden Brown: American Gothic Novelist* (Gainesville, 1949), and David Lee Clark, *Charles Brockden Brown: Pioneer Voice of America* (Durham, 1952). However, Warner B. Berthoff has been the most probing analyst of Brown's ideas. Berthoff's best works are "The Literary Career of Charles Brockden Brown" (Ph.D. dissertation, Harvard University, 1954); "Charles Brockden Brown's Historical 'Sketches': A Consideration," *American Literature*, XXVIII, No. 2 (May 1956), 147–54; and "Adventures of a Young Man: An Approach to Charles Brockden Brown," *American Quarterly*, IX, No. 4 (Winter 1957), 421–34. For specific analysis of Brown's sexual ideas, see David Lee Clark, "Brockden Brown and the Rights of Women," *University of Texas Bulletin No. 2213* (April 1, 1922), pp. 5–48, and Raymond Andrew Miller, Jr., "Representative Tragic Heroines in the Work of Brown, Hawthorne, Howells, James and Dreiser" (Ph.D. dissertation,

University of Wisconsin, 1957). Jane Townsend Flanders, "Charles Brockden Brown and William Godwin: Parallels and Divergences" (Ph.D. dissertation, University of Wisconsin, 1965), argued persuasively that Brown belonged to the Anglo-American radical intellectual community of the 1790's and that his novels can only be explained with this in mind. Deborah Bingham's perceptive Master's essay, "The Literary and Philosophical Evolution of Charles Brockden Brown" (Bowling Green State University, 1973), and Charles C. Cole, Jr.'s "Brockden Brown and the Jefferson Administration," *Pennsylvania Magazine of History and Biography*, LXXII, No. 3 (July 1948), 253–63, represent the only systematic attempts to analyze Brown's drift toward conservative nationalism. Finally, bits and pieces of useful data may be garnered from Donald A. Ringe, *Charles Brockden Brown* (New York, 1966); Martin S. Vilas, *Charles Brockden Brown: A Study of Early American Fiction* (Burlington, Vt., 1904); Lulu Rumsey Wiley, *The Sources and Influence of the Novels of Charles Brockden Brown* (New York, 1950); and Annie Russel Marble, *Heralds of American Literature* (Chicago, 1907), Ch. 7.

CHAPTER 4.

True American Womanhood

Hasty, undeveloped references to True American Womanhood appeared in a large variety of late-eighteenth- and early-ninteenth-century materials. The concept was probably articulated most fully by James Fenimore Cooper in *Notions of the Americans* (Philadelphia, 1828) and *The American Democrat* (Cooperstown, 1838), and by Thomas R. Dew, "Dissertation on the Characteristic Differences between the Sexes and on the Position and Influence of Women in Society," *Southern Literary Messenger*, I (May 1835), 493–512; I (July 1835), 621–32; I (August 1835), 672–91. Toasts to True American Womanhood were traditional at most July Fourth celebrations. The Richmond *Enquirer* is therefore invaluable, for it printed toasts given at July Fourth celebrations throughout the nation. Several foreign travelers also took note of the notion of True American Womanhood. See, particularly, Kenneth and Anna M. Roberts (eds.), *Moreau de St. Méry's American Journal* [*1793–1798*] (Garden City, N.Y., 1947); Frances Trollope, *Domestic Manners of the Americans* (1832) (reprint. New York, 1949); Harriet Martineau, *Society in America* (London, 1837); and Francis J. Grund, *Aristocracy in America* (1837) (reprint. New York, 1959).

Chapter 4 is a corrective to Barbara Welter's "The Cult of True Womanhood: 1820–1860," *American Quarterly*, XVIII, No. 2, Pt. 1 (Summer 1966), 151–74. A number of other studies have sensitively considered changes in sexual ideas and institutions between the Revolution and the middle decades of the nineteenth century. See, particularly, Janet Wilson James, "Changing Ideas about Women in the United States, 1776–1825" (Ph.D. dissertation, Harvard University, 1954); Keith E. Melder, "The Beginnings of the Women's Rights Movement in the United States, 1800–1840" (Ph.D. dissertation, Yale University, 1963); Gerda Lerner, "The Lady and the Mill Girl: Changes in the Status of Women in the Age of Jackson," *Midcontinent American Studies Journal*, X, No. 1 (Spring 1969), 5–15; Ronald W. Hogeland, " 'The Female Appendage': Feminine Life-Styles in America, 1820–1860," *Civil War History*, XVII, No. 2 (June 1971), 101–14; G. J. Barker-Benfield, "The Horrors of the Half Known Life: Aspects of the Exploitation of Women by Men" (Ph.D. dissertation, U.C.L.A., 1968); and Stephen Willner Nissenbaum, "Careful Love: Sylvester Graham and the Emergence of Victorian Sexual Theory in America, 1830–1840" (Ph.D. dissertation, University of Wisconsin, 1968). Less analytic studies should also be consulted for relevant data, particularly Augusta Genevieve Violette, "Economic Feminism in American Literature prior to 1848," *The Maine Bulletin*, XXVII, No. 7 (February 1925), 7–114; Eleanor Wolf Thompson, *Education for Ladies, 1830–1860: Ideas on Education in Magazines for Women* (New York, 1947); and Anne L. Kuhn, *The Mother's Role in Childhood Education: New England Concepts, 1830–1860* (New Haven, 1947). Edward Raymond Turner, "Women's Suffrage in New Jersey: 1790–1807," *Smith College Studies in History*, I, No. 4 (July 1916), 165–87, remains the most comprehensive study of the New Jersey controversy over voting women. Aileen S. Kraditor, *Means and Ends in American Abolitionism: Garrison and His Critics on Strategy and Tactics, 1834–1850* (New York, 1969); Gerda Lerner, *The Grimké Sisters from South Carolina: Rebels against Slavery* (Boston, 1967); and Keith E. Melder, "Forerunners of Freedom: The Grimké Sisters in Massachusetts, 1837–38," *Essex Institute Historical Collections*, CIII, No. 3 (July 1967), contain a great deal of information on the debate over female abolitionism.

A number of theorists have maintained that a society idolizing soft, retiring women and hard, aggressive men is a society that represses part of the human potential; all human beings are part "hard" and part "soft." See, especially, Gregory Zilboorg, "Masculine and Feminine: Some Biological and Cultural Aspects," *Psychiatry*, VII, No. 3 (August 1944), 257–96; Theodore Roszak, "The Hard and the Soft: The Force of Feminism in Modern Times," in *Masculine/Feminine*, edited by Betty and Theodore Roszak (New York, 1969); Lawrence J. Friedman, "Art Versus Violence," *Arts in Society*, VIII, No. 1 (1971), 325–31.

CHAPTER 5.

"A Little Game"

Much of the material on late-eighteenth- and early-nineteenth-century sexual ideology cited for Chapter 4 is pertinent background in understanding the thoughts of women of the period. The most useful general studies have been Elizabeth Anthony Dexter's classic *Career Women of America, 1776–1840* (Francetown, N.H., 1950); Page Smith, *Daughters of the Promised Land: Women in American History* (Boston, 1970); and Carl N. Degler, "Revolution Without Ideology: The Changing Place of Women in America," *Daedalus*, XCIII, Pt. 1 (Winter–Spring, 1964), 653–70. In "Two 'Kindred Spirits': Sorority and Family in New England, 1839–1846," *New England Quarterly*, XXXVI, No. 1 (March 1963), 23–41, William R. Taylor and Christopher Lasch have perceptively noted how early nineteenth-century women increasingly felt the need for sorority—how they were unable to establish viable relationships with men. Taylor and Lasch may have detected the most important development in women's history between the Revolution and the Civil War.

Mercy Warren, one of the strongest women in this period, is not difficult to research. The key to an understanding of the woman is her private letters in the Massachusetts Historical Society. For published Warren correspondence, see *Warren-Adams Letters* (Boston, 1925), and "Correspondence between John Adams and Mercy Warren relating to her 'History of the American Revolution,' July–August, 1807," *Collections of the Massachusetts Historical Society*, 5th Ser., IV (1878), 315–511. Warren has not had the skillful, probing biographer that she deserves. Maud Macdonald Hutcheson's "Mercy Warren: A Study of Her Life and Works" (Ph.D. dissertation, The American University, 1951) has been the most comprehensive biography. Katharine Anthony, *First Lady of the Revolution: The Life of Mercy Otis Warren* (Garden City, N.Y., 1958); Alice Brown, *Mercy Warren* (New York, 1896); and Jean Fritz, *Cast for a Revolution: Some American Friends and Enemies, 1728–1814* (Boston, 1972), have been polemical and partisan studies but contain some useful data. A chapter in William Raymond Smith, *History as Argument: Three Patriot Historians of the American Revolution* (The Hague, 1966), represents the most sophisticated analysis of Warren's *History*.

Materials for Elizabeth Margaret Chandler are more difficult to uncover than they are for Warren. The Chandler Papers, Michigan Historical Collections, University of Michigan, consists of only twenty-seven letters; most focus on her 1830–34 years in Michigan. Merton L.

Dillon has covered these years in "Elizabeth Chandler and the Spread of Antislavery Sentiment to Michigan," *Michigan History*, XXXIX (December 1955), 481–94. For Chandler's earlier antislavery years in Philadelphia, one must consult her essays and editorials in the *Genius of Universal Emancipation*, Benjamin Lundy's anthology *The Poetical Works of Elizabeth Margaret Chandler* (Philadelphia, 1836), and even *Essays, Philanthropic and Moral, by Elizabeth Margaret Chandler: Principally Relating to the Abolition of Slavery in America* (Philadelphia, 1836). Although Chandler was a very important woman, most scholars have ignored her.

However, scholars have not ignored Sarah Hale. William R. Taylor's treatment of her in *Cavalier and Yankee: The Old South and American National Character* (New York, 1961) has been the most sophisticated in print. Karol Gyman, "The 'Woman's Sphere': A Study of the Life and Work of Sarah Josepha Hale" (M.A. thesis, Bowling Green State University, 1973), represents a second skillful analysis of the woman's ideology and psychology. However, the standard Hale biographies leave much to be desired. Ruth E. Finley, *The Lady of Godey's: Sarah Josepha Hale* (Philadelphia, 1931), and Isabelle Webb Entrikin, *Sarah Josepha Hale and Godey's Lady's Book* (Philadelphia, 1946), have both included useful information but have fallen short on analysis. Helen Waite Papashvily's underrated study of the romantic-sentimental novel, *All the Happy Endings* (New York, 1956), placed Hale in the intellectual and cultural tradition of the mid-nineteenth-century "Scribbling Women." Lawrence Martin's "The Genesis of Godey's Lady's Book," *New England Quarterly*, I, No. 1 (January 1928), 47–70, and Glenda Lou Gates Riley, "From Chattel to Challenger: The Changing Image of the American Woman, 1828–1848" (Ph.D. dissertation, Ohio State University, 1967), have treated *Godey's* in detail and have noted how Hale related (economically, professionally, and ideologically) to the magazine. Hale's letters are scattered thinly over a number of collections (the Edward Carey Gardiner Collection at the Historical Society of Pennsylvania being perhaps the most useful). For this reason, her many editorials, poems, essays, and novels constitute the major primary sources.

CHAPTER 6.

The American Colonization Society

Because the American Colonization Society drew support from a variety of interest groups, the student of the colonization movement has no difficulty finding materials. The Papers of the American Colonization Society are on deposit at the Library of Congress and they are voluminous. Above all else, they reveal much about the Society's local agents in the field, their ideas, and their problems. The Board of Managers regularly published the *Annual Report of the American Society for Colonizing the Free People of Colour of the United States*. The reports contain speeches delivered at the Society's annual meeting and reveal much about its internal workings. The Society's official periodical, *The African Repository and Colonial Journal*, was published monthly. Printing essays, letters, and speeches by national and local leaders, it is the major source for colonizationist thought. The *National Intelligencer* (Washington, D.C.) was quite sympathetic with the A.C.S. and also printed a large amount of pertinent information. Publications of local colonization groups like the *Colonization Herald* (Philadelphia) and the *Colonizationist and Journal of Freedom* (Boston) should also be consulted.

Secondary literature on the Colonization Society abounds. P. J. Staudenraus, *The African Colonization Movement, 1816–1865* (New York, 1961), has become the definitive study of the organization and replaces Early Lee Fox, *The American Colonization Society, 1817–1840* (Baltimore, 1919). Like Fox, Staudenraus has concentrated on institutional history at the expense of colonizationist ideology. The best ideological analyses have been the first chapter of George M. Fredrickson, *The Black Image in the White Mind: The Debate on Afro-American Character and Destiny, 1817–1914* (New York, 1971), and Frederick Bancroft, "The Early Antislavery Movement and African Colonization," in Jacob E. Cooke, *Frederick Bancroft, Historian* (Norman, Okla., 1957). See also Philip C. Wander, "Salvation through Separation: The Image of the Negro in the American Colonization Society," *Quarterly Journal of Speech*, LVII, No. 1 (February 1971), 57–67; Rayford W. Logan, "Some New Interpretations of the Colonization Movement," *Phylon*, IV, No. 4 (Fourth Quarter 1943), 328–34; and Brainerd Dyer, "The Persistence of the Idea of Negro Colonization," *Pacific Historical Review*, XII, No. 1 (March 1943), 53–65. Louis R. Mehlinger, "The Attitude of the Free Negro toward African Colonization," *Journal of Negro History*, I, No. 3 (June 1916), 276–301, remains the definitive study of black hostility toward the A.C.S. Bits of pertinent data on the Colonization Society can be drawn from Archibald Alexander, *A History of Colonization on the Western Coast of Africa* (Philadelphia, 1846); Henry Noble Sherwood, "The Formation of the American Colonization Society," *Journal of Negro History*, II, No. 3 (July 1917), 209–28; and Charles I. Foster, "The Colonization of Free Negroes in Liberia, 1816–1835," *Journal of Negro History*, XXXVIII, No. 1 (January 1953), 41–66. The best of several studies of state colonization organizations have been Penelope Campbell, *Maryland in Africa: The Maryland State Colonization Society, 1831–1857* (Urbana, Ill., 1971), and Eli Seifman, "The United Colonization Societies of New York and Pennsylvania and the Establishment of the African Colony of Bassa Cove," *Pennsylvania History*, XXXV, No. 1 (January 1968), 23–44. Unfortunately, there are no systematic studies of colonizationist attitudes toward Indians. However, William Miles's " 'Enamoured with Colonization': Isaac McCoy's Plan of Indian Reform," *Kansas Historical Quarterly*, XXXVIII, No. 3 (Autumn 1972), 268–86, and Klaus J. Hansen's "The Millennium, the West, and Race in the Antebellum American Mind," *Western Historical Quarterly*, III, No. 4 (October 1972), 373–90, are good pioneer essays comparing early-nineteenth-century white attitudes toward blacks and Indians.

CHAPTER 7.

The Ideological Legacy of Colonization

By the early 1830's the American Colonization Society was rapidly losing power and influence. Some members left for abolitionist organizations while others defended slavery. Bruce Rosen, "Abolition and Colonization, the Years of Conflict: 1829–1834," *Phylon*, XXXIII, No. 2 (Second Quarter 1972), 177–92, and the first chapter of George M. Fredrickson, *The Black Image in the White Mind: The Debate on Afro-American Character and Destiny, 1817–1914* (New York, 1971), have been the only systematic studies of the topic. Both focused upon growing abolitionist opposition.

There have been a number of competent general studies of American abolitionism. Both Gilbert H. Barnes, *The Anti-Slavery Impulse, 1830–1844* (New York, 1933), and Dwight L. Dumond, *Antislavery: The Crusade for Freedom in America* (Ann Arbor, 1961), underestimated the Garrisonian impact upon abolitionism but remain invaluable studies. Louis Filler's *The Crusade Against Slavery, 1830–1860* (New York, 1960) has been another valuable and detailed introduction. Martin Duberman (ed.), *The Antislavery Vanguard: New Essays on the Abolitionists* (Princeton, 1965), contains essays reflecting the pro-abolitionist trend of scholarship in the 1960's. Lewis Perry's brilliant study *Radical Abolitionism: Anarchy and the Government of God in Antislavery Thought* (Ithaca, 1973), represents a continuation of this trend. However, Leon F. Litwack, "The Abolitionist Dilemma: The Antislavery Movement and the Northern Negro," *New England Quarterly*, XXXIV, No. 1 (March 1961), 50–73, and William H. Pease and Jane H. Pease, "Antislavery Ambivalence: Immediatism, Expediency, Race," *American Quarterly*, XVII, No. 4 (Winter 1965), 682–95, have offered important correctives by noting covert patterns of racism within abolitionist circles. The Peases' more recent study, *Bound with Them in Chains: A Biographical History of the Antislavery Movement* (Westport, Conn., 1972), has demonstrated how far historians are from understanding the complexities of the movement—how many obscure abolitionists will have to be studied before certain important generalizations can be made.

Of the three leading abolitionists considered in Chapter 7, Benjamin Lundy is the most difficult to research. Because most of his private papers were destroyed, the researcher must focus upon his published writings. Lundy's *Genius of Universal Emancipation* is a crucial source, and so is his autobiographical *The Life, Travels and Opinions of Benjamin Lundy* (Philadelphia, 1847). Merton L. Dillon's comprehensive biography, *Benjamin Lundy and the Struggle for Negro Freedom* (Urbana, Ill., 1966), has noted other pertinent sources the researcher might consult.

If Lundy materials are scant, William Lloyd Garrison materials are not. One would do well to consult the extensive Garrison Collection at the Boston Public Library. However, Walter M. Merrill and Louis Ruchames are editing and publishing Garrison's important letters through the Belknap Press. Judging from the first several volumes, their editing is of excellent quality. Next to his correspondence, *The Liberator* (Boston) is obviously the major source in comprehending Garrison. John L. Thomas, *The Liberator: William Lloyd Garrison* (Boston, 1963), is an exceedingly sensitive study of the man and perhaps the best single book on American abolitionism. Whereas Thomas focused upon Garrison's ideology, Walter M. Merrill was more attentive to personal psychology in his detailed study, *Against Wind and Tide: A Biography of William Lloyd Garrison* (Cambridge, Mass., 1963). Wendell Phillips Garrison and Francis Jackson Garrison, *William Lloyd Garrison, 1805–1879* (New York, 1885), lacks the balance and analysis of Thomas and Merrill but contains a good deal of pertinent information. Finally, Aileen S. Kraditor's *Means and Ends in American Abolitionism: Garrison and His Critics on Strategy and Tactics, 1834–1850* (New York, 1969) has been the most successful of all recent attempts to rehabilitate Garrison's reputation.

James G. Birney has not captured the attention of scholars the way Garrison has. Betty Fladeland's detailed biography *James Gillespie Birney: Slaveholder to Abolitionist* (Ithaca, 1955) remains the only comprehensive, non-polemical study of the man. The Birney Papers at the William L. Clements Library, University of Michigan, are extensive. Most of the important letters have been included in Dwight L. Dumond (ed.), *Letters of James Gillespie Birney* (New York, 1938). While the Birney Collection at the Library of Congress is small, several letters and diaries shed light on his abandonment of the Colonization Society in favor of abolitionism.

Abolitionism was not the only area where colonization ideas and ideals continued to thrive. Colonizationist assumptions were also detectable within Southern proslavery thought. But there have been no systematic studies of the colonization legacy in the antebellum South. A debate between two slaveholding Virginians, *Controversy between Caius Gracchus and Opimius, in Reference to the American Society for Colonizing the Free People of Colour of the United States* (Georgetown, 1827), characterized much of the Southern controversy over the A.C.S. and colonization. Herman V. Ames (ed.), *State Documents on Federal Relations* (Philadelphia, 1906), contains many Southern state legislative resolutions opposing federal aid to the A.C.S.—documents which cry for intensive scholarly analysis.

Playing down the colonization legacy, students of the Old South have focused on the transition from Jeffersonian liberalism to the positive-good proslavery thought of Thomas R. Dew and the closed society for which it stood. Clement Eaton has centered his scholarly activity on this subject; his *Freedom of Thought in the Old South* (Durham, 1940) and *The Mind of the Old South* (rev. ed. Baton Rouge, 1967) are the most fruitful results. Charles S. Sydnor, *The Development of Southern Sectionalism, 1819–1848* (Baton Rouge, 1948), and Guy A. Cardwell, "Jefferson Renounced: Natural Rights in the Old South," *Yale Review*, LVIII, No. 3 (March 1969), 388–407, are also useful general studies of the topic.

Southern opposition to the Colonization Society and dedication to positive-good proslavery premises began and remained most intense in South Carolina. Because Robert Y. Hayne and Thomas Cooper played leading roles in South Carolinian militancy, it is important to consult Theodore D. Jervey, *Robert Y. Hayne and His Times* (New York, 1909), and Dumas Malone, *The Public Life of Thomas Cooper, 1783–1839* (New Haven, 1926). William W. Freehling, *Prelude to Civil War: The Nullification Controversy in South Carolina, 1816–1836* (New York, 1966), has brilliantly characterized increasing sectional fervor and hardening proslavery thought in the Palmetto State.

By the early 1830's Virginia, a colonizationist stronghold, followed the South Carolina lead. Joseph Clarke Robert, *The Road from Monticello: A Study of the Virginia Slavery Debate of 1832* (Durham, 1941), remains the most comprehensive study of developments in the Old Dominion. Portions of Carl N. Degler, *The Other South: Southern Dissenters in the Nineteenth Century* (New York, 1974), are also quite useful. Although Thomas R. Dew took the lead in behalf of the peculiar institution, he lacks a biographer. See Kenneth M. Stampp, "An Analysis of T. R. Dew's Review of the Debates in the Virginia Legislature," *Journal of Negro History*, XXVII, No. 4 (October 1942), 380–87, and Lowell Harrison, "Thomas Roderick Dew: Philosopher of the Old

South," *Virginia Magazine of History and Biography*, LVII, No. 4 (October 1949), 390–404. Because the Richmond *Enquirer* printed the January 1832 debate over slavery and colonization in the Virginia House of Delegates, it is also mandatory reading.

CHAPTER 8.

Patriotic Education in the Age of Jackson

There are two excellent introductions to American educational ideology—Merle Curti, *The Social Ideas of American Educators* (New York, 1935) and Rush Welter, *Popular Education and Democratic Thought* (New York, 1962). Frederick Rudolph (ed.), *Essays on Education in the Early Republic* (Cambridge, Mass., 1965) contains pertinent writings of major post-Revolutionary educational theorists, while David Tyack has sensitively analyzed the patriotic commitment of these writings in "Forming the National Character: Paradox in the Educational Thought of the Revolutionary Generation," *Harvard Educational Review*, XXXVI, No. 1 (Winter 1966), 29–41. Bernard Wishy, *The Child and the Republic: The Dawn of Modern American Child Nurture* (Philadelphia, 1968), and Peter Gregg Slater, "Views of Children and Child Rearing during the Early National Period: A Study in the New England Intellect" (Ph.D. dissertation, University of California, Berkeley, 1970), have both carefully delineated changing concepts of childhood during the early nineteenth century and the sort of childhood education that purportedly contributed to national well-being. Michael B. Katz, *The Irony of Early School Reform: Educational Innovation in Mid-Nineteenth Century Massachusetts* (Cambridge, 1968), represents the most suggestive and far-reaching study of the rise of popular education in Jacksonian America. Keith E. Melder, "Woman's High Calling: The Teaching Profession in America, 1830–1860," *American Studies*, XIII (Fall 1972), 19–32, noted the importance of a female labor pool in meeting demands for cheap teachers during the Jacksonian period. There have been numerous studies of the developing nineteenth-century schoolbook industry and most of them have noted how schoolbooks were filled with patriotic dogma. Ruth Miller Elson, *Guardians of Tradition: American Schoolbooks of the Nineteenth Century* (Lincoln, Nebr., 1964), has been the most comprehensive study. See also Monica Kiefer, *American Children Through Their Books, 1700–1835* (Philadelphia, 1948); Michael V. Belok, "Forming the American Character: Essayists and Schoolbooks," *Social Science*, XLIII, No. 1 (January 1968), 12–21; and J. Merton England, "The Democratic Faith in American Schoolbooks, 1783–1860," *American Quarterly*, XV, No. 2, Pt. 1 (Summer 1963), 191–99.

Of the two Jacksonian educational crises considered in Chapter 8, scholarship on the Prudence Crandall Canterbury crisis has been the most unsatisfactory. Basic resource areas such as the Connecticut State Library have been ignored. Although the Prudence Crandall Collection at the Boston Public Library is small, it should also be consulted. "Abolition Letters Collected by Arthur B. Spingarn," *Journal of Negro History*, XVIII, No. 1 (January 1933), 78–84, contains important Crandall letters written during the Canterbury crisis. A folder of 1834 letters between William Lloyd Garrison and Helen E. Benson at Harvard's Houghton Library are crucial in comprehending why Garrison decided to abandon the Crandall school. Contemporary newspapers such as *The Liberator* (Boston), the *Connecticut Journal* (New Haven), the *Connecticut Courant* (Hartford), and the *Hartford Times* are also instructive. Most scholarship on the Crandall affair has neglected or de-emphasized the basic primary sources while characterizing Crandall's defenders as heroes and her opponents as evil men. Edmund Fuller has been guilty on both counts, although his *Prudence Crandall: An Incident of Racism in Nineteenth-Century Connecticut* (Middletown, Conn., 1971) has been the only book-length study of the affair. The major articles on the affair have not improved upon Fuller: Edwin W. Small and Miriam R. Small, "Prudence Crandall, Champion of Negro Education," *New England Quarterly*, XVII, No. 4 (December 1944), 506–29; Alfred Thurston Child, Jr., "Prudence Crandall and the Canterbury Experiment," *Bulletin of Friends Historical Association*, XXII, No. 1 (Spring Number, 1933), 35–55; C. C. Tisler, "Prudence Crandall, Abolitionist," *Journal of the Illinois State Historical Society*, XXXIII, No. 2 (June 1940), 203–06. Ellen D. Larned, *History of Windham County, Connecticut* (Worcester, 1880), reflects the bias of other historians but contains important background information on Canterbury and Windham County in the 1830's.

Thanks to Robert Samuel Fletcher's definitive two-volume study, *A History of Oberlin College: From Its Foundation Through the Civil War* (Oberlin, 1943), information on the early years at Charles Finney's school in the West is abundant. Fletcher's work was based on manuscript materials in the Oberlin College Library, although virtually every other relevant source was also consulted. Using Fletcher as a guide for pertinent materials, archival work at Oberlin can be accelerated. Finney is the key to an understanding of the early years at the school; therefore, the Finney Papers at Oberlin are mandatory reading. *The Memoirs of Rev. Charles G. Finney* (New York, 1876) is also enlightening. Asa Mahan's *Autobiography, Intellectual, Moral, and Spiritual* (London, 1882) provides insights into another leading Oberlinite. James H. Fairchild had belonged to Oberlin's first freshman class, later joined the Oberlin faculty, and became president in 1883. Three of his publications are particularly informative: "A Sketch of the Anti-Slavery History of Oberlin," *Oberlin Evangelist*, XVIII, Whole No. 457 (July 16, 1856), 113–16; *Oberlin; Its Origin, Progress and Results* (Oberlin, 1860); *Oberlin: The Colony and the College, 1833–1883* (Oberlin, 1883). Although Frances Juliette Hosford's *Father Shipherd's Magna Carta* (Boston, 1937) is not first-rate scholarship, it provides information about another major figure in early Oberlin. College catalogues for the school's first decade shed light on regulations, procedures, and curriculum, while the *Oberlin Evangelist* is an invaluable source on general attitudes and ideologies. The *Ohio Observer* (Hudson) conveys some sense of popular attitudes toward the school among the citizens of northeastern Ohio. Finally, Delazon Smith's *A History of Oberlin, or New Lights of the West* (Cleveland, 1837), a polemical pamphlet by an expelled Oberlin student, requires close scrutiny. Smith's basic charge—that Oberlin was a center of abolition, masturbation, and racial amalgamation—was probably a gross exaggeration, if not entirely false. But the integral race-sex tie-in that Smith perceived at the school requires serious consideration. Ronald W. Hogeland has thoroughly explored sexism in "Coeducation of the Sexes at Oberlin College: A Study of Social Ideas in Mid-Nineteenth Century America," *Journal of Social History*, VI, No. 2 (Winter 1972–73), 160–76. However, there has been no scholarly exploration of the sex-race interplay in one of the first American colleges to admit both women and blacks.

Perfection versus Rootedness

Although patriotic crusades in the New Nation involved sexual, racial, and educational considerations, they more fundamentally involved clashes between perfectionist aspirations and the need for rooted stability. To be sure, early American patriots were not the only people to experience the uprooting consequences of perfectionist strivings. Other crusaders from other nations had as well. However, the clash was so intensive and widespread between the 1780's and the 1830's as to constitute a basic element within early American culture. Yet scholars have either focused upon concepts of perfectionism or on problems of rootlessness and have seldom attempted to trace the interplay between the two.

Martin Foss, *The Idea of Perfection in the Western World* (Princeton, 1946), has chronicled the concept of flawlessness from its Greek and early Christian beginnings. Both Charles L. Sanford, *The Quest for Paradise: Europe and the American Moral Imagination* (Urbana, Ill., 1961), and Ernest Lee Tuveson, *Redeemer Nation: The Idea of America's Millennial Role* (Chicago, 1968), have characterized the quest for perfection as most intensively American and closely bound to the nationalist impulse. John L. Thomas has concurred and has noted that the perfectionist strivings for the Promised Land were most intense during the early nineteenth century ("Romantic Reform in America, 1815–1865," *American Quarterly*, XVII, No. 4 [Winter 1965], 656–81).

At least since Tocqueville's *Democracy in America*, social analysts have regularly studied problems of rootlessness. Indeed, François René de Chateaubríand characterized it as a particularly striking feature of American life after his 1791 trip to the New Nation (*Travels in America* [reprint. Lexington, Ky., 1969]). However, Marvin Meyers, *The Jacksonian Persuasion: Politics and Belief* (Stanford, 1957); William R. Taylor, *Cavalier and Yankee: The Old South and American National Character* (New York, 1961); and David J. Rothman, *The Discovery of the Asylum: Social Order and Disorder in the New Republic* (Boston, 1971), have all brilliantly delineated the early American quest for rooted stability. In large measure, *Inventors of the Promised Land* has been an effort to link their findings with the findings of such scholars as Sanford, Tuveson, and Thomas.

INDEX

A NOTE ABOUT THE AUTHOR

Lawrence J. Friedman is an associate professor of history at Bowling Green State University. A native of Cleveland, Ohio, he was graduated from the University of California, Riverside, in 1962 and received his M.A. and Ph.D. in history from U.C.L.A. He taught at Arizona State University before joining the Bowling Green faculty in 1971. Mr. Friedman is the author of *The White Savage: Racial Fantasies in the Postbellum South* (1970) and has contributed articles to various publications.

A NOTE ON THE TYPE

This book was set on the Linotype in Janson, a recutting made direct from type cast from matrices long thought to have been made by the Dutchman Anton Janson, who was a practicing type founder in Leipzig during the years 1668–1687. However, it has been conclusively demonstrated that these types are actually the work of Nicholas Kis (1650–1702), a Hungarian, who most probably learned his trade from the master Dutch type founder Dirk Voskens. The type is an excellent example of the influential and sturdy Dutch types that prevailed in England up to the time William Caslon developed his own incomparable designs from them.

This book was composed, printed and bound by American Book–Stratford Press, Inc., Saddlebrook, New Jersey. Typography and binding design by Camilla Filancia.

Boston Public Library

Copley Square

General Library

The Date Due Card in the pocket indicates the date on or before which this
book should be returned to the Library.
Please do not remove cards from this
pocket.